Rethinking Ernst Bloch

Historical Materialism Book Series

The Historical Materialism Book Series is a major publishing initiative of the radical left. The capitalist crisis of the twenty-first century has been met by a resurgence of interest in critical Marxist theory. At the same time, the publishing institutions committed to Marxism have contracted markedly since the high point of the 1970s. The Historical Materialism Book Series is dedicated to addressing this situation by making available important works of Marxist theory. The aim of the series is to publish important theoretical contributions as the basis for vigorous intellectual debate and exchange on the left.

The peer-reviewed series publishes original monographs, translated texts, and reprints of classics across the bounds of academic disciplinary agendas and across the divisions of the left. The series is particularly concerned to encourage the internationalization of Marxist debate and aims to translate significant studies from beyond the English-speaking world.

For a full list of titles in the Historical Materialism Book Series available in paperback from Haymarket Books, visit: www.haymarketbooks.org/series_collections/1-historical-materialism.

Rethinking Ernst Bloch

Edited by
Henk de Berg
Cat Moir

Haymarket Books
Chicago, IL

First published in 2023 by Brill Academic Publishers, The Netherlands
© 2023 Koninklijke Brill NV, Leiden, The Netherlands

Published in paperback in 2024 by
Haymarket Books
P.O. Box 180165
Chicago, IL 60618
773-583-7884
www.haymarketbooks.org

ISBN: 979-8-88890-338-4

Distributed to the trade in the US through Consortium Book Sales and Distribution (www.cbsd.com) and internationally through Ingram Publisher Services International (www.ingramcontent.com).

This book was published with the generous support of Lannan Foundation, Wallace Action Fund, and the Marguerite Casey Foundation.

Special discounts are available for bulk purchases by organizations and institutions. Please call 773-583-7884 or email info@haymarketbooks.org for more information.

Cover art and design by David Mabb. Cover art is an adaption developed from *Luibov Popova Untitled Textile Design on William Morris Wallpaper for Historical Materialism*, edition of 100, screen print on wallpaper (2010).

Printed in the United States.

Library of Congress Cataloging-in-Publication data is available.

Contents

Acknowledgements   VII
List of Figures   VIII
Notes on Contributors   IX

1   Ernst Bloch: Life – Work – Reception   1
    Cat Moir

2   Will There Be Nothing Rather Than Something? Ernst Bloch's Overcoming of Gnosticism   38
    Agata Bielik-Robson

3   Art, History and the Language of Death: Bloch's *The Spirit of Utopia* between Hegel and Derrida   71
    Ivan Boldyrev

4   Between Dialectics and Metaphysics: Critical Reflections on Bloch's *Subjekt-Objekt*   84
    Henk de Berg

5   Bloch's Commentary on Marx's 'Theses on Feuerbach' in *The Principle of Hope*   135
    Vincent Geoghegan

6   Natural Law in the Ideas of Bloch, Hegel and Marxism   155
    Holger Glinka

7   The Matter of Bloch's Philosophy of Nature in the Shadow of Idealism   180
    Loren Goldman

8   Ernst Bloch's Utopian Philosophy: From Hegel to Marx and Beyond   206
    Douglas Kellner

9   What Can We Hope For? Reading Ernst Bloch with Antonio Gramsci   222
    Jan Rehmann

10   The Possibility of Envisioning Utopias   252
     Nina Rismal

11   Hegel, Marx, Bloch: On the Margins of the Spirit   268
     Johan Siebers and Sam Dolbear

12   Something's Missing: Bloch's Unfinished Project of Humanity   291
     Peter Thompson

     Index   311

Acknowledgements

We should like to thank our friends and colleagues who commented on parts of the manuscript or helped us in other ways: Ben Lewis, Michael Perraudin and Robert Stern.

Among the scholars we invited to contribute a chapter was Volker Caysa, a great Bloch expert and good friend. Tragically, he died well before our volume could be completed – and much too early – at the age of 60. We dedicate this book to his memory.

List of Figures

11.1 Bloch marginalia I 278
11.2 Bloch marginalia II 279
11.3 Bloch marginalia III 280
11.4 Bloch marginalia IV 281
11.5 Bloch marginalia V 282
11.6 Engels's sketch of Max Stirner 287
11.7 Second sketch of Max Stirner 287

Notes on Contributors

Agata Bielik-Robson
is Professor of Jewish Studies at the University of Nottingham and Professor of Philosophy at the Polish Academy of Sciences. Publishing in Polish, German, French and Russian as well as English, she has written extensively on issues in the philosophy of religion, psychoanalysis and Romanticism. Her books include *The Saving Lie: Harold Bloom and Deconstruction* (2011), *Judaism in Contemporary Thought: Traces and Influence* (co-edited with Adam Lipszyc, 2014), *Philosophical Marranos: Jewish Cryptotheologies of Late Modernity* (2014) and *Another Finitude: Messianic Vitalism and Philosophy* (2019).

Ivan Boldyrev
is Assistant Professor at Radboud University Nijmegen. He is the author of *Ernst Bloch and His Contemporaries* (2014), *Hegel, Institutions and Economics* (with Carsten Herrmann-Pillath, 2014) and *Die Ohnmacht des Spekulativen. Elemente einer Poetik von Hegels Phänomenologie des Geistes* (2021) as well as the editor of *Interpreting Hegel's Phenomenology of Spirit* (with Sebastian Stein, 2021). In addition to German Idealism and critical theory, he also works on the history and philosophy of economics.

Henk de Berg
is Professor of German at the University of Sheffield. He is the author of three monographs, including *Freud's Theory and Its Use in Literary and Cultural Studies* (2003), which was awarded a CHOICE Outstanding Academic Title Award and has been translated into three European languages as well as Chinese, and *Trump and Hitler: A Comparative Study in Lying* (2024). Among his seven edited volumes on literary and cultural theory are *Modern German Thought from Kant to Habermas* (with Duncan Large, 2012) and *Tzvetan Todorov: Thinker and Humanist* (with Karine Zbinden, 2020).

Sam Dolbear
is a Fellow at the ICI Berlin Institute for Culture Inquiry. He completed his PhD at Birkbeck, University of London, in 2018 with a thesis entitled *Names Written in Invisible Ink: Walter Benjamin, Friendship and Historical Generation*. He subsequently became a Visiting Fellow at the Institute of Modern Languages Research, exploring two figures of exile in London: the radio-producer and composer Ernst Schoen (1884–1960) and the sexologist and palmist Charlotte Wolff (1897–1986), about whom he is currently preparing publications. He has

taught and published widely on modern German thought and culture and is a founding member of the audio-radio collective MayDay Radio.

Vincent Geoghegan
is Emeritus Professor of Political Theory at Queen's University Belfast. He is the author of *Reason and Eros: The Social Theory of Herbert Marcuse* (1981), *Utopianism and Marxism* (1987), *Ernst Bloch* (1996) and *Socialism and Religion: Roads to Common Wealth* (2011). He has edited *Political Ideologies: An Introduction* (with Rick Wilford, 1984) and *Political Thought in Ireland Since the Seventeenth Century* (with D. George Boyce and Robert Eccleshall, 1993).

Holger Glinka
is a member of the international research network Natural Law 1625–1850, led by the universities of Halle-Wittenberg and Erfurt, as well as a founding board member of the Harun Farocki Institut in Berlin. From 2001 until 2014, he was based at the Hegel-Archiv in Bochum as an editor of the *Hegel-Studien*. He is the author of *Zur Genese autonomer Moral: Eine Problemgeschichte des Verhältnisses von Naturrecht und Religion in der frühen Neuzeit und der Aufklärung* (second edition, 2012) and *Hegels Naturrechtsaufsatz: Ein interdisziplinärer kooperativer Kommentar* (with Michael Städtler, 2021) as well as the co-editor of *Denker und Polemik* (with Kevin Liggieri and Christoph Manfred Müller, 2013). He is currently preparing an edition of Christian Wolff's 1739–40 lectures on Hugo Grotius's *De iure belli ac pacis*.

Loren Goldman
is Assistant Professor of Political Science at the University of Pennsylvania. He is the author of numerous articles on Immanuel Kant, William James, John Dewey, Ernst Bloch, Richard Rorty and Wendy Brown, as well as the co-translator of Bloch's *Avicenna and the Aristotelian Left* (with Peter Thompson, 2019), which he also introduced and annotated. His most recent publication is *The Principle of Political Hope* (2023).

Douglas Kellner
is George Kneller Chair in the Philosophy of Education at UCLA. His books on contemporary theory include *Critical Theory, Marxism, and Modernity* (1989), *Jean Baudrillard: From Marxism to Postmodernism and Beyond* (1990) and a trilogy of studies on postmodern theory with Steve Best. Works in cultural and media studies include *Media Culture* (1995), *Media Spectacle* (2003) and *Media Spectacle and Insurrection* (2012) as well as *Camera Politica: The Politics and Ideology of Contemporary Hollywood Film* (with Michael Ryan, 1988)

and *Cinema Wars: Hollywood Film and Politics in the Bush/Cheney Era* (2009). Douglas Kellner is also the author of two books on Donald Trump's authoritarian populism, *American Nightmare* (2016) and *American Horror Show* (2017). In addition, he has written a trilogy on the media and the Bush administration: *Grand Theft 2000* (2001), *From 9/11 to Terror War* (2003) and *Media Spectacle and the Crisis of Democracy* (2005). The author of *Herbert Marcuse and the Crisis of Marxism* (1984), Kellner is also the series editor of the *Collected Papers of Herbert Marcuse* (1998–2004).

Cat Moir
is Senior Lecturer in Germanic Studies at the University of Sydney. She previously held lectureships at Cambridge and Durham in the UK. Her main research areas are critical theory and the history of ideas in the German-speaking world. Among her many publications are *Ernst Bloch's Speculative Materialism: Ontology, Epistemology, Politics* (2019) and the co-edited volume *Reform, Revolution and Crisis in Europe: Landmarks in History, Memory and Thought* (with Bronwyn Winter, 2021).

Jan Rehmann
is Visiting Professor for Critical Theories and Social Analysis at Union Theological Seminary in New York and *Privatdozent* at the Freie Universität Berlin. His books include *Deconstructing Postmodern Nietzscheanism: Deleuze and Foucault* (2022), *Max Weber: Modernisation as Passive Revolution: A Gramscian Analysis* (2015), *Theories of Ideology: The Powers of Alienation and Subjection* (2013), *Pedagogy of the Poor* (with Willie Baptist, 2011) and *Die Kirchen im NS-Staat* (1986). He is the co-editor of *Muß ein Christ Sozialist sein? Nachdenken über Helmut Gollwitzer* (with Brigitte Kahl, 1994) as well as *Das Argument* and the *Historisch-Kritisches Wörterbuch des Marxismus*.

Nina Rismal
is the lead of Urban Food Futures, an action-orientated research programme at TMG (Think Tank for Sustainability) in Berlin. She holds a PhD in Political Theory from Cambridge and was previously a postdoctoral fellow at the University of California in Santa Barbara and a researcher at The New Institute in Hamburg. Her book *The Ends of Utopian Thinking* will be published in the Brill/Historical Materialism Book Series in 2023.

Peter Thompson
is the author of *The Crisis of the German Left: The PDS, Stalinism and the Global Economy* (2005), *Karl Marx* (2013) and numerous papers on German politics

and critical theory as well as a variety of articles for *The Guardian*, mostly on Marxism and the Frankfurt School. He is the co-editor of *The Privatization of Hope: Ernst Bloch and the Future of Utopia* (with Slavoj Žižek, 2013) and the co-translator of Bloch's *Avicenna and the Aristotelian Left* (with Loren Goldman, 2019). From 1990 to 2015, he lectured in German politics, history and philosophy at the University of Sheffield. In 2008, he founded the Ernst Bloch Centre, which is currently based at the Institute of Modern Languages Research of the University of London.

CHAPTER 1

Ernst Bloch: Life – Work – Reception

Cat Moir

The present volume of original essays on Ernst Bloch (1885–1977) began its life several years ago as a project that aimed to introduce Bloch – an author who is arguably still less well-known to English-language audiences than his contemporaries Adorno, Benjamin and Lukács – to a readership likely to be more familiar with two major interlocutors, Hegel and Marx. In some respects, the book still bears the traces of this original aim. Several of its contributions situate Bloch's thought explicitly in relation to one or both of these thinkers. This is, one might argue, unavoidable. After all, whatever aspect of Bloch's thought one chooses to focus on, he remains a Hegelian Marxist who transformed both Hegel's and Marx's ideas in light of some of the most pressing political and philosophical questions of his time.

In the intervening years, the book has come to take on a different shape. One of the reasons for this is that Bloch's work has enjoyed more exposure in the interim, including in the English-speaking world. Jack Zipes's *Ernst Bloch: The Pugnacious Philosopher of Hope* (2019) offers the first general introduction to Bloch's thought in English since Vincent Geoghegan's *Ernst Bloch* (1996), and the most comprehensive one since Wayne Hudson's classic *The Marxist Philosophy of Ernst Bloch* (1982).[1] Zipes's book engagingly retells the story of Bloch as the twentieth century's most prominent and challenging thinker of hope and utopia – a 'Marxist who disagreed with most Marxists, an atheist theologian … a man who believed in hope as our "invariant of direction" and yet … lived through the horrors of fascism, war, and Stalinism', as Peter Thompson puts it in his endorsement.

Over the last decade, however, scholars have in various ways begun to complicate this picture, excavating aspects of Bloch's thought that had previously received less attention, situating his work in broader and different contexts from those in which it was usually located, bringing him into conversation with a range of other thinkers, past and present, and applying his ideas to issues of contemporary importance. José Esteban Muñoz's *Cruising Utopia: The Then and There of Queer Futurity* (2009) and Caitríona Ní Dhúill's *Sex in*

---

1 See Geoghegan 1996, Hudson 1982 and Zipes 2019.

Imagined Spaces: Gender and Utopia from More to Bloch (2010), for example, examined utopianism as a mode of thinking and living counter-hegemonic sex and gender identities.[2] As these authors acknowledge, Bloch's personal views on these topics was not always as progressive as one might have wished, yet his concepts of hope and utopia possess significant potential for rethinking the political dynamics of sex and gender.

If Bloch's utopianism had sometimes been criticised as naïve, Ruth Levitas's *The Concept of Utopia* (2010) did much to correct this view.[3] Writing from within the field of utopian studies, where Bloch's thought has been particularly influential, Levitas homes in on Bloch's distinction between abstract utopia – 'compensatory' elements in utopian thinking that do not correspond to possibilities in the real world – and concrete utopia, which is grounded in the actual. As Levitas shows, Bloch's interpretative method centres on discerning moments of concrete utopia in all manner of cultural products as a way of demonstrating what he saw as the ubiquity of a utopian drive in human consciousness. This cultural surplus is at the heart of Benjamin Korstvedt's innovative study *Listening for Utopia in Ernst Bloch's Musical Philosophy* (2010), which reconstructs Bloch's philosophy of music for the first time.[4] For Bloch, music was the utopian art form par excellence; while rooted in the materiality of sound and assuming a form fixed in notation, its interpretation is always unique. In addition to offering Blochian readings of musical works, Korstvedt's study points to Bloch's underpinning metaphysical idea that material reality itself is musical in quality: something is being played out, is playing itself out, in the historical process, with the possibility, though no guarantee, of ultimate harmony.

In the 1960s, the more cosmic dimensions of Bloch's ontology brought him into dialogue with various radical currents in theology, including the liberation theology of Jürgen Moltmann. Though Bloch insisted throughout his life that he was an atheist, he took seriously the heritage of religious thought for Marxism, something which some comrades found scandalous. As Peter Thompson argues in his introduction to the 2009 edition of the English translation of Bloch's *Atheismus im Christentum* [Atheism in Christianity, 1968], the atheist philosopher saw in the Judeo-Christian tradition a kind of will to communism *ante rem*, in the mode of a dialectic of enlightenment in which myth is already enlightened and enlightenment – in this case, Marxism – often reverts

---

2   See Muñoz 2009 and Ní Dhúill 2010.
3   See Levitas 2010. This study was first published in 1990 and thus predates by a decade the renewed English-language engagement with Bloch.
4   See Korstvedt 2010.

to mythology in the obfuscation or disavowal of its own origins.[5] It is precisely Bloch's complex, dialectical understanding of the relation between the religious and the profane that has made his thought fruitful for discussions of post-secularism. Jolyon Agar's *Post-Secularism, Realism, and Utopia: Transcendence and Immanence from Hegel to Bloch* (2013) exemplifies this trend, situating as it does Bloch's 'atheistic metareality' in a philosophical discourse that aims to think transcendence in social rather than theological terms.[6]

In *A Critical Theory of Creativity: Utopia, Aesthetics, Atheism and Design* (2015), Richard Howells explored the ways in which artistic and creative practice can occupy the place evacuated by religion in the modern world.[7] Grounded in a case study of Navajo weaving techniques, Howells's work demonstrates the value of Bloch's ideas in application, not just as an object of analysis. Something similar can be said of Caroline Edwards's *Utopia and the Contemporary British Novel* (2019), which deploys a Blochian conceptual framework as a tool for literary analysis.[8]

Elsewhere, new scholarship on Bloch has put his own philosophy front and centre. Ivan Boldyrev's *Ernst Bloch and His Contemporaries: Locating Utopian Messianism* (2014) examines the entangled perspectives of messianism and utopianism in Bloch's oeuvre by tracing their valency in the intellectual circles in which his philosophy originated; that is to say, by focusing on thinkers such as Georg Lukács, Walter Benjamin and Theodor W. Adorno.[9] Boldyrev's book thus renews and updates in important respects the contextual approach taken by Manfred Riedel in his classic *Tradition und Utopie. Ernst Blochs Philosophie im Licht unserer geschichtlichen Denkerfahrung* (1994).[10] More recently, my own *Ernst Bloch's Speculative Materialism: Ontology, Epistemology, Politics* (2020) reconstructed the speculative materialism Bloch developed in the 1930s, foregrounding his challenge to Soviet philosophy of science and staging a critical confrontation between Bloch and several contemporary speculative materialist and realist thinkers.[11] This work situates Bloch in the *longue durée* of philosophical materialism, in which his Marxism and Marxism *tout court* are just one part of the story, albeit a central one. It is a trend continued by Loren Goldman and Peter Thompson's recent translation of Bloch's *Avicenna und*

---

5   See Bloch 2009; the translation was first published in 1972.
6   See Agar 2013.
7   See Howells 2015.
8   See Edwards 2019.
9   See Boldyrev 2015.
10 See Riedel 1994.
11 See Moir 2020a.

die Aristotelische Linke (Avicenna and the Aristotelian Left), which forms the appendix to the *Gesamtausgabe* edition of Bloch's *Das Materialismusproblem, seine Geschichte und Substanz* [The Problem of Materialism: Its History and Substance, 1972].[12] The publication of *Avicenna* demonstrates the surprising and enduring significance of Islamic thought for Bloch's history of materialism.

Two collections of English-language essays on Bloch published in the last decade deserve special mention, not least because many of the contributions to the present volume build on work begun in these earlier publications. *The Privatization of Hope: Ernst Bloch and the Future of Utopia* (2013), edited by Peter Thompson and Slavoj Žižek, covers a range of issues arising from Bloch's thinking, from systematic engagements with his metaphysics (Frances Daly, Cat Moir, Peter Thompson, Rainer E. Zimmermann) to applications of his ideas in the domains of gender (Caitríona Ní Dhuíll), religion (Roland Boer) and art (Ruth Levitas, David Miller) and to defences of liberal consumerism (Henk de Berg) contra Blochian utopia (Francesca Vidal / Welf Schroeter).[13] Appearing at the height of renewed interest in Bloch studies, this volume documented the state of the field at that time. Something similar can be said of the special issue of *Revue internationale de philosophie* edited by Johan Siebers (2019). Though necessarily smaller in scope, it brought out less well-documented aspects of Bloch's work, including the underground sources of his philosophy of history (in Lucien Pelletier's article, the thinkers Eduard von Hartmann, Emil Lask and Karl Lamprecht replace the canonical dyad of Marx and Hegel), Nietzsche's influence on Bloch (Moir, Pelletier), the place of memory in Bloch's thinking (Vidal) and the defence of fantasy at the heart of his conception of religion (Agata Bielik-Robson).

It goes without saying that this list of contributions to recent Bloch scholarship is not exhaustive, and it only covers work in English. Bloch has also been the focus of much exciting original research in other languages. To single out a few noteworthy examples, the landmark *Bloch-Wörterbuch* in German, edited by Beat Dietschy, Doris Zeilinger and Rainer Zimmermann (2012), remains unsurpassed as a comprehensive reference work, while a special issue of *Das Argument* (2018) demonstrates Bloch's ongoing relevance for contemporary Marxist theory and strategy.[14] In French, the work of Arno Münster and Lucien Pelletier stands out for its originality. Münster is so far one of the only figures to make Bloch's materialism productive for ecological questions (though Loren Goldman's contribution to the present volume also addresses this topic);

---

12   See Bloch 1972a and 2019.
13   See Thompson and Žižek (eds.) 2013.
14   See Dietschy, Zeilinger and Zimmermann (eds.) 2012, and Rehmann et al. (eds.) 2018.

Pelletier has done more than anyone else to reconstruct the significance of neo-Kantianism for Bloch's early thought.[15] In Italian, finally, Mauro Farnesi Camellone's engagement with Bloch vindicates the role of the imagination in politics, and Gerardo Cunico explores the political implications of Bloch's metaphysics by building on his earlier edition of material relating to Bloch's project of a materialist logic, of which *Das Materialismusproblem* and *Experimentum Mundi* (1974) were the only parts to appear in Bloch's lifetime.[16]

It is because of the variety and originality of this recent international Bloch scholarship that the editors of this volume wanted to incorporate more diverse perspectives than the original aim of plotting Bloch's shifting coordinates between Hegel and Marx would have allowed. Thus, instead of a collection of essays focusing on this – undoubtedly perennially interesting, but also relatively narrow – three-way conversation, what we have here is a much richer set of contributions by leading and emerging scholars that reflects the full range of contemporary interest in Bloch's work.

Agata Bielik-Robson's chapter assesses Bloch's thought against the challenge posed by Hans Blumenberg in *Die Legitimität der Neuzeit* [The Legitimacy of the Modern Age, 1966] – the challenge of 'overcoming Gnosticism'.[17] In spite of all its efforts to affirm the existence of material reality – Blumenberg says – modern metaphysics has been unable to free itself from the pull of the Gnostic rejection of being. Bielik-Robson's arguments is twofold: first, that in his late work Bloch attempts to overcome Gnosticism by shifting the register from the metaphysical to the political sphere; second, that this attempt ultimately fails Blumenberg's test, such that the trace of a Gnostic rejection of reality remains.

In his chapter, Ivan Boldyrev reads Bloch's analysis of Egyptian art and culture in *Geist der Utopie* [The Spirit of Utopia, 1918 and – reworked – 1923] as a key to understanding his place between Hegel and Derrida.[18] For Bloch as for Hegel, Egyptian art is life turned to stone, which Bloch contrasts with Gothic art as stone brought to life. However, as Boldyrev points out, Bloch shared with Derrida an understanding of death as immanent and imminent in any attempt to express something, in every aesthetic gesture and in any philosophical proposition. Insofar as the pyramid represents death, then, it comes to stand in Bloch's case for non-identity and in Derrida's case for the unachievability of meaning. Boldyrev's account thus reveals surprising connections between Bloch and Derrida as readers of Hegel.

---

15   See Münster 2011 and 2013, as well as Pelletier (ed.) 2010.
16   See Camellone 2009 as well as Bloch 2000a and Cunico 2020.
17   See Blumenberg 1985.
18   See Bloch 2000b.

Henk de Berg's contribution also focuses on Bloch's Hegel interpretation, weighing up the merits and demerits of *Subjekt-Objekt. Erläuterungen zu Hegel* and then extending this analysis to Bloch's overall philosophy. Bloch's Hegel book is undoubtedly of landmark historical importance, both in terms of Hegel scholarship and of his own intellectual and political fate. Published first in 1951 and then – in a slightly extended edition – in 1962, *Subjekt-Objekt* belongs historically to the twentieth-century Hegel renaissance in European philosophy that encompassed works by Herbert Marcuse (1941), Jean Hyppolite (1946), Alexandre Kojève (1947), Georg Lukács (1948), Theodor W. Adorno (1963) and Lucio Colletti (1969).[19] Of these, Bloch's study is the only one to remain untranslated into English. Yet it offers a unique perspective on Hegel, especially as compared with others in the Marxist tradition. Bloch's explicit claim that Hegel's philosophy had not been superseded by Marxism was scandalous in the GDR context of the 1950s, and *Subjekt-Objekt* was in large measure the reason for his eventual dismissal from his Chair at the University of Leipzig.

Vincent Geoghegan's chapter sets out to elucidate some of the issues at stake in Bloch's relation to Marx in a close reading of Bloch's commentary on the 'Theses on Feuerbach' in *The Principle of Hope*.[20] Geoghegan argues that Marx became progressively more important for Bloch, but that there remained critical differences between the two thinkers. The struggle over Bloch's reception of Marx – which, as the Hegel controversy demonstrates, had major political implications in the East German context – was fuelled by the state orthodoxy that there was a single correct interpretation of Marx's ideas. By highlighting the fact that Bloch brings his own utopian system of thought to bear on Marx's text – a utopianism which includes implicit criticism of Marx on issues such as the interpretation of Feuerbach and the role of philosophy – Geoghegan draws attention to the often porous boundary between analysis and interpretation in the history of ideas, which sheds light on some of the issues surrounding the contestation of Bloch's Marxism.

Holger Glinka's analysis of Bloch's treatment of natural law reveals a further deviation from dogmatic-orthodox Marxism.[21] As Glinka argues, it is neither Marx nor Hegel that Bloch takes as his starting point in this context, even though both figures continue to influence his account of natural law. Rather, it is Johann Gottlieb Fichte's *Der geschlossene Handelsstaat* [The Closed Commercial State, 1800] that Bloch saw as the culmination of classical German

---

19   See Bloch 1962 as well as Adorno 1963, Colletti 1969, Hyppolite 1946, Kojève 1947, Lukács 1957 and Marcuse 1941.
20   See Bloch 1986.
21   See Bloch 1996.

philosophy in the guise of a juridical social utopia, something which is all the more remarkable – Glinka points out – given that Fichte's economic theory exerted hardly any influence on the development of socialist theories in the nineteenth century

If Fichte's impact on socialist thought in the nineteenth century and beyond was relatively small, that of Aristotle was considerable, as Loren Goldman argues in his chapter. Goldman reads both Marx and Bloch as neo-Aristotelian thinkers whose conceptions of matter draw – in Marx's case, more implicitly; in Bloch's case, explicitly – on Aristotle's ideas, albeit applying his logical categories to material human-nature interactions rather than simply taking over his concept of matter. Bloch's 'Left Aristotelianism' is relevant today, Goldman contends, because it offers a way of imposing limits on human activity out of a concern for sustainability. The significance of the neo-Aristotelian reading of Marxist and Blochian materialism for Goldman is thus that it bears on the question of the human-nature relation, which he connects to contemporary debates about the ecological crisis.

In many respects, Douglas Kellner's chapter stays closest to our volume's original aim, plotting Bloch's coordinates in what Martin Jay has called the 'topography of Western Marxism'.[22] Fredric Jameson has claimed that Bloch's Marxism is indebted more to Goethe than to Hegel; and the view that Bloch has nothing in common with Marx has united many otherwise divided Marxists, as Detlef Horster has noted.[23] By contrast, Kellner argues that Bloch's Marxism was undoubtedly part of the broad movement of Western Marxism opposed to the dogmatic orthodoxy of socialist and communist traditions. In particular, Kellner resists interpretations of Bloch that seek to separate out his aesthetics or other aspects of his philosophy from its political dimension. As he points out, and as the studies by Richard Howells and Caroline Edwards have also shown, Bloch's utopian cultural hermeneutics has an ineliminable political dimension.

The political is front and centre in Jan Rehmann's contribution, which is innovative in staging a dialogue between two thinkers whose work is seldom considered together, despite their – as he shows – many similarities; namely, Bloch and the Italian Marxist Antonio Gramsci. Both Bloch and Gramsci develop what Rehmann (following Antonio Labriola) terms a *philosophy of praxis*, a theoretical framework intended above all to help liberate us from the material contradictions of present social alienation. By positioning Bloch as a philosopher of praxis working in the same tradition as Gramsci, Rehmann

---

22   Jay 1984, p. 1.
23   See Jameson 1971, p. 140, and Horster 2005, p. 30.

refutes the criticism – common among Marxists and non-Marxists alike – that Bloch is an idealistic, metaphysical, mystical or irrationalist thinker. Rehmann's Bloch, more successfully than Bielik-Robson's Bloch, has resolutely overcome his early esoteric tendencies to be engaged in a project of practical social and political emancipation. However, Gramsci's ideas are also used here to critique and refine Bloch's position. In particular, Rehmann suggests that a Gramscian analysis of the hegemonic conditions for hope and for hopelessness is required in order to distinguish abstract from concrete utopian possibilities.

The paradoxical task of envisaging utopias is at the heart of Nina Rismal's chapter, which addresses the problem of the historical horizon of utopian thinking. Why does Bloch not see – she asks – as Marx did, that conceptual articulations of the utopian world are almost invariably merely re-articulations of the present one? Rismal aims to answer this question in part by inverting its terms and inquiring why it should be that the contours of an actually possible utopian society cannot be known. Reconstructing the processual dimension of Bloch's utopianism, she arrives at the conclusion that Bloch puts forward a twofold argument: that the content of the specific utopian society that might come into being in the future *cannot* be known in the present, but that the multiplicity of utopian possibilities that present themselves in particular moments *can* be known. The fact that visions of utopia are always circumscribed by the material possibilities of the specific historical context in which they originate is not a limitation from Bloch's point of view, but a necessary feature of their potential efficacy.

Johan Siebers and Sam Dolbear's contribution to this volume is based on a careful reconstruction and interpretation of Bloch's marginalia to his copy of Hegel's *Phänomenologie des Geistes*.[24] Reading Bloch's handmade markings on the page as the trace of his thinking in the later years of his life,[25] Dolbear and Siebers lift out individual words and phrases and bring them into focus through an analysis that is both philological and speculative. The word *hotel*, for instance, jotted down and twice underlined, opens out onto a reflection on the condition of almost permanent exile in which Bloch lived and worked throughout his adult life. By interleaving the marginalia with Hegel's own text,

---

24 See Hegel 1952.
25 As the authors note, there is mention in the marginalia of a seminar Bloch held on the *Phenomenology* in July 1966, but the variety of pen and pencil marks, though all undeniably in Bloch's hand, indicate that he could have written these notes at any time from his earliest days in Tübingen until the early 1970s, when his eyesight became so poor that he no longer made his own notes.

Siebers and Dolbear's chapter becomes a reflection on the practice of writing – on Bloch's philosophical style, but also on the meaning of his work as the material trace of possibilities both realised and unrealised.

Peter Thompson's chapter, finally, returns us to the metaphysical foundations of Bloch's Marxist project. Thompson characterises Bloch's philosophy as a *metaphysics of contingency*, in which chance plays as much of a role as agency in deciding whether the utopian possibilities available in any given moment will be actualised. Reading Bloch through the lens of Žižek's interpretation of Hegel, Thompson argues that reality is the product of contingent developments, and that to the extent that we find ourselves faced with it at a *decisive moment* in time (and the decisive nature of the moment – he stresses – might well be the retroactive result of our own actions subsequent to that moment), it possesses an openness towards the future that enables us to construct both a retrospective narrative and an anticipatory consciousness. Yet this moment inevitably remains dark and distorted, and 'grasping' it requires an oblique look.

This volume thus contributes to a wealth of new work underway today that aims to clarify the historical – intellectual and political – contexts of Bloch's interventions, to reconstruct overlooked aspects of his system and revaluate its better-known features, to assess the relevance of Bloch's ideas for our time and to put them into practice as tools of cultural analysis and political strategy. Since Arno Münster's and Peter Zudeick's biographies of Bloch have not yet found an English equivalent,[26] the second part of this introduction will provide an overview of Bloch's life and work so as to orientate readers who may not be familiar with the contours of his story. A full-length intellectual biography in English remains the most important desideratum in Bloch scholarship.

1   Bloch's Life and Work

Ernst Bloch lived a long life spanning most of a twentieth century that has rightly been called an age of extremes. His personal convictions – which themselves sometimes mirrored the extremities of his era – and accidental affiliations implicated him centrally in the major upheavals, promises and tragedies of his time. His pacifism and anti-authoritarianism were at the centre of a life spent largely in exile from the First World War onwards. His Jewish heritage

---

26   See Münster 2004 and Zudeick 1985.

made him into a target – and eviscerating critic – of National Socialism, as did his Marxism. Early enthusiasm for the Russian Revolution translated into a lifelong commitment to radical politics that took him to places many of his intellectual contemporaries could not or dared not go. Like many of his Frankfurt School colleagues, he sought safety in the United States during the Second World War, and alongside them he diagnosed the ills and potentials of an emerging mass culture. Yet after the war Bloch went to communist East Germany, where he was for a time the country's most prominent intellectual. This did not prevent him from returning to the West in 1961, where he became a leading thinker of the revolutionary student movement and criticised the failures of East German state socialism.

In his own lifetime, as since his death, the currency of Bloch's ideas rose and fell with the concerns of the time. In the interwar years, his ideal of a utopian society inspired a generation of critical thinkers; both Theodor W. Adorno and Walter Benjamin reported being seminally influenced by *The Spirit of Utopia*. During the Third Reich, however, and even after its fall, Bloch's philosophy of hope seemed to many hopelessly out of step with reality. In the early 1960s, Adorno argued that historical reality amply demonstrated that '[h]ope is not a principle'.[27] Yet, in the heady atmosphere of Germany's 1968, Bloch's ideas once again found favour. His correspondence with West German socialist student leader Rudi Dutschke shows the extent to which Bloch's ideas and friendship influenced Dutschke's own thinking and activism.[28]

Bloch himself found biographical questions of little relevance to an understanding of his thought. He did not keep a journal (except for the entries in the *Gedenkbuch für Else Bloch-von Stritzky*),[29] though his correspondence provides an invaluable insight into his personal views, feelings and the course of his life and friendships. He did give many interviews, and a fair number of them also contain information on his biography, his opinions and the contexts in which his thought developed. In some of these interviews, however, Bloch explicitly eschewed attempts to enquire into his personal life. Indeed, in an interview with Wayne Hudson conducted in 1976, Bloch said 'No more biographical questions' in such an angry tone that it almost put an end to the conversation.[30] Bloch believed that the life of a thinker ought to disappear behind the work. On this topic, he liked to cite the famous anecdote about Claude Monet, who was one day approached by a photographer wishing to take his picture: Monet

---

27 Adorno 1993, p. 213.
28 Cf. K. Bloch and Schröter (eds.) 1988.
29 See Bloch 1978, pp. 13–50.
30 See Hudson 1989.

advised the man to photograph the nymphéas in his garden, which he had painted many times, since these were more of a likeness of him than was his own image.[31]

Whatever Bloch himself thought about biography, situating the development of his ideas in the context of his life and times remains significant for his reception. Martin Jay is not alone when he insists that 'Bloch's intellectual and political character seems to have matured at a specific moment in time and remained relatively unchanged for the rest of his life'.[32] A number of other commentators have argued along similar lines. However, it is important not to confuse Bloch's lifelong and often obstinate commitment to Marxism and utopianism with philosophical and political stasis. An intellectual-biographical approach brings to light the ways in which both Bloch's philosophy and his politics did in fact change over time, in response to the shifting historical circumstances in which he found himself. In what follows, I will provide a brief overview of the development of Bloch's ideas against the background of his life and its changing historical context.

2 Origins of Utopia (1885–1918)

Ernst Simon Bloch (1885–1977) was born in Ludwigshafen am Rhein on 8 July 1885, the son of a Jewish railway official, Max Bloch, and his wife, Berta (*née* Feitel). Bloch was fascinated by the history of philosophy from an early age, though his was not a home in which there was a great love of books. This was a source of conflict with his father, whom Bloch only managed to convince of the importance of philosophy by showing him the dedication on Schelling's gravestone made by King Maximillian II. The contrast between Ludwigshafen – a port city and home to the BASF factory – and nearby Mannheim, where Bloch would escape to the palace library to read philosophy, was at the source of his unique conception of uneven and combined development, which he would later term *Ungleichzeitigkeit*, or non-contemporaneity.

From 1905, Bloch studied in Munich and Würzburg, writing his doctoral thesis on Heinrich Rickert's theory of knowledge under Oswald Külpe in 1908. This philosophical formation took place within an academy dominated until the First World War by neo-Kantianism. Bloch's efforts to refute the neo-Kantian Rickert demonstrate his opposition to the movement – the intellectual

---

31 See Weigand 1998, p. 71. For additional biographical sources, see K. Bloch 1981, Markun 1977, B. Schmidt 1982, pp. 1–34, and Weigand (ed.) 2007.
32 Jay 1984, p. 176.

version of the revolt against the father generation that Bloch would later claim was the mood of his age – but they also hint at its lasting influence on him. In the thesis, Bloch argues – against neo-Kantian and positivist approaches – that epistemology can only register successful cognition and critically illuminate its preconditions in retrospect; and he champions the new metaphysical task of understanding 'being' as a process most fully accessible to us in our activity of labour. It was Bloch's engagement with Kant and neo-Kantianism that led him to his 'first and only original thought', the concept of the *not-yet-conscious*, an anticipatory form of consciousness that he identified as a constant in human psychology and cultural history.[33] With the not-yet-conscious, Bloch found the central theme of utopia that would guide his work from now on.

Another important influence during this early period was Nietzsche. Along with many of the Expressionist generation, the young Bloch can be described as representing a form of left-wing Nietzscheanism, which aimed to put Nietzsche's insights into the role of art in re-constructing the world after the total devastation of the First World War to socially just use. In his 1913 essay 'Der Impuls Nietzsches', Bloch wrote of Nietzsche as a thinker of Exodus out of modern culture, heralding a new beginning.[34] Yet Bloch's Nietzsche saw the extraordinary value of fostering the individual life impulse precisely in the fact that it benefits communal life. There was thus for Bloch initially no contradiction between his Nietzscheanism and his emerging Marxism; and in its use of language, if nothing else, his later work continues to bear witness to Nietzsche's early influence even after it was overshadowed by other philosophical concerns.[35]

Bloch's attempts to obtain a university post failed, and he began a life as an independent researcher and writer that would continue until 1949. From 1908 until 1914, he worked as publicist in Berlin and Heidelberg, where he joined the intellectual circles around Georg Simmel and Max Weber. It was in Simmel's orbit that Bloch, in 1910, first encountered Georg Lukács, beginning a friendship that continued to influence both men's thinking even after it soured only a few years later. In July 1913, Bloch married the sculptor Else von Stritzky, who by all accounts must have been an exceptional person: her Christian faith made a great impression on Bloch, and he still spoke of her with deep feeling late into his life. After the outbreak of war, the Blochs moved to Grünwald, near Munich. In the spring of 1917, they emigrated from Germany to Switzerland, where they lived until spring 1919, first in Bern, then in Thun and later in Interlaken.

---

33 Zudeick 1987, p. 37.
34 See Bloch 1964, especially p. 105.
35 On Bloch's relation to Nietzsche, see Baur 2018 and Moir 2019.

Between 1917 and 1919, in his Swiss exile, Bloch wrote journalistic articles – partly under his own name and partly under pseudonyms – in which he took a stand against the war and spoke out on other political issues of the day.[36] Unlike most intellectuals of these years, Bloch, who maintained contacts in Switzerland with other pacifists, such as Hermann Hesse and Hugo Ball, was a staunch opponent of the war, which contributed in no small part to his break with his Berlin teacher Simmel. Inspired by the social economist Emil Lederer, editor of the *Archiv für Sozialwissenschaft und Sozialpolitik*, Bloch also wrote a political piece on Switzerland, entitled 'Über einige politische Programme und Utopien in der Schweiz' (1918), which explores a country spared from war and draws attention to some of the pacifist movements and political programmes to be found there.

Perhaps surprising from the perspective of Bloch's later development are his views at this time of America and the Russian Revolution. When arriving in the German Democratic Republic from the US in 1949, Bloch, by now a staunch, if heterodox, Marxist, spoke scathingly about the country in which he had spent the last eleven years of his life: America was the 'land of Metternich' and a 'rotten world'.[37] But against the backdrop of the First World War, it was Wilsonian American democracy that inspired Bloch, even if he at times expressed criticism of Wilson's peace programme. Moreover, though Bloch greeted the Russian Revolution of November 1917 with enthusiasm, later construing it as the historical event that shaped his whole political orientation, he was at first critical of Lenin the 'red tsar' and the Bolshevik government, particularly of its neutrality vis-à-vis the Central Powers after Brest-Litovsk – a critique that demonstrates the limits, as well as the depth, of his pacifism.

Less explicitly than in his journalistic works, but with similar intensity, Bloch's first book, *Geist der Utopie* [The Spirit of Utopia, written between 1915 and 1917 and published in its first version a year later], is also directed against the First World War. In his afternote to the second version, published in 1923, Bloch calls his debut a 'Storm and Stress book, contra war', and in an interview from the 1970s, he remarks that it was 'against Prussia, against Austria, more gentle in regard to the Entente, somewhat gentler, but sharply polemic against the capitalist, imperialist context'.[38] Yet *The Spirit of Utopia* is much more than a pacifist manifesto; it is a paean to the spirit of Expressionism that made itself felt in art and literature in the early decades of the twentieth century and which would be the subject of heated ideological disputes between Bloch, Lukács,

---

36 See Bloch 1985b.
37 Zudeick 1987, p. 180.
38 Bloch 1985c, p. 347, and Münster (ed.) 1977, p. 162.

Adorno, Benjamin and Brecht in the 1930s.³⁹ Written in a style reminiscent of a religious tract, and indeed conveying a message of salvation to the reader, *The Spirit of Utopia* stands in stark contrast to the journalistic work. To 'build into the blue, and build ourselves into the blue, and there seek the true, the real, where the merely factual disappears' – this was the self-declared aim of *The Spirit of Utopia*, the work in which Bloch found a characteristic voice that carried through his entire oeuvre.⁴⁰

3   Untimely Histories (1919–33)

In 1919, Bloch and his wife returned to Germany, and he continued to work as a publicist until 1933, when he emigrated because of the Nazi threat. During the twenties, he lived mainly in Berlin, where he moved in circles that included Walter Benjamin and Bertolt Brecht (with whom he had two of his most important friendships of those years), Hanns Eisler and Otto Klemperer. He also travelled frequently during this period, with stays in southern France, Paris, Italy and North Africa.

Three events mark this period of Bloch's life and work. First, the untimely death in January 1921 of his wife, who had suffered for several years from a mysterious disease. Bloch was deeply affected by her loss, having cared for her to the end. In 1922, he married the painter Linda Oppenheimer, but it was not a lasting relationship: the couple effectively separated within a year, although they did not officially divorce until 1928. Initially, he did not want to write anything of which Else had not already been a part.⁴¹ Indeed, Bloch's only two major philosophical publications of this period bear the trace of her influence in one way or another. The second, heavily revised edition of *The Spirit of Utopia*, published in 1923, is dedicated to her memory. Among the many changes that this version displays is a noticeably intensified discussion of Marx's ideas. Both in the opening 'Intention' and in the final chapter, which already in the first edition had addressed Marx and socialism, Bloch – inspired in some respects by Lukács – now engaged in more depth with Marx, adding a text dealing with Marxism and anarchism as well as more targeted criticism of what Bloch perceived as Marx's failure to appreciate the heritage of religious utopianism.⁴²

---

39   Cf. Bloch 1985c, p. 347, Münster 1977, p. 162, as well as Leucht 2016, pp. 323–412.
40   Bloch 2000b, p. 3.
41   Bloch 1978, p. 39.
42   On the complicated edition history of *The Spirit of Utopia*, see Boldyrev 2012.

The increasing influence of Marx, as well as Bloch's sense that Marxism needed to engage with the revolutionary heritage of the radical religious traditions, is also on display in *Thomas Münzer als Theologe der Revolution*.[43] Published the year Else died, the book was connected to her interests through its focus on the Christian mysticism of the radical medieval theologian and leader of the Peasant War, Thomas Münzer (ca. 1489–1525). Its publication marks another milestone in Bloch's development, not only because the book was the only major original philosophical work he published during the twenties (in addition to being, together with the Hegel book, one of his only two genuine monographs, with *Subjekt-Objekt* focusing on revolutionary theory and *Thomas Münzer* addressing revolutionary practice), but also because it represents Bloch's first truly historical-materialist work. Though linked through its millenarist theme to *The Spirit of Utopia*, the Münzer book is very different in tone and method: drawing on Münzer's and Luther's contemporary writings, it interprets the ostensibly religious conflicts surrounding the Protestant Reformation in terms of material politics and political ideology.

The book stands in an already established tradition among socialists and others of reading the German Reformation and the Peasant War as precursors to later revolutions.[44] Friedrich Engels was the first to inscribe the Peasant War into the German revolutionary tradition, connecting it to the events of March 1848 in his 1850 book *The Peasant War in Germany*.[45] For Engels, the parallels between the German revolution of 1525 and that of 1848–9 were too striking to be dismissed. As he saw it, in both contexts liberal reformers had betrayed the cause of more revolutionary social change and aligned themselves with the forces of conservatism and reaction. As a result, in 1848 as in 1525, the princes – whether Frederick III or the Prussian Junkers – had ultimately been able to hold on to power at the expense of the interests of the wider populace. On this view, Luther personified the treacherous reformer, the 'protégé of the elector of Saxony' who sacrificed the popular element of the movement and put his weight behind the bourgeois, noble and princely side.[46] According to Engels, Luther's actions set a precedent in German history, establishing a tendency towards conservative compromises with power and against radical change. Equally, Engels interpreted Münzer unambiguously as both a communist and an atheist *ante rem*, whose thwarted efforts to overthrow the corrupt princes and landlords would likewise be replayed in later revolutionary situations.

---

43   See Ernst Bloch 1969a.
44   For more on this tradition, see Moir 2020b and Müller 2007.
45   See Engels 1978.
46   Engels 1978, p. 417.

Engels's interpretation was highly influential among German communists and social democrats seeking to situate themselves within a homegrown revolutionary tradition. In his *Die Vorläufer des neueren Sozialismus* [Forerunners of Modern Socialism, 1895], Karl Kautsky similarly sought to integrate Münzer and the Peasant War into a progressive genealogy of socialist development.[47] Meanwhile, if Engels had earlier explicitly connected 1525 with 1848, Clara Zetkin – in *Revolutionäre Kämpfe und revolutionäre Kämpfer 1919* [Revolutionary Struggles and Revolutionary Fighters of 1919, 1920] – positioned the Peasants' War as a precursor to the German November Revolution, likening Luther to the treacherous social democratic leaders who had betrayed the revolution's aims.[48] During the Weimar years, and against the background of National Socialism, the German Communist Party, to which Zetkin belonged, identified Münzer with anti-fascist figures such as Ernst Thälmann, and Luther with those politicians perceived to have betrayed the 1919 revolution, such as Friedrich Ebert, Gustav Noske and Philipp Scheidemann.

If *The Spirit of Utopia* partly represents Bloch's response to the First World War, *Thomas Münzer* – like Zetkin's book – partly articulates a response to the failed German revolution of 1918. To be sure, Bloch's invocation of the story of Münzer aimed to demonstrate what he would later call the 'invariant of direction' in human history, which reinscribed failures such as Münzer's in a longer story of the march to freedom. In certain respects, however, the book broke with the existing socialist narrative mould. Though it remained broadly faithful to the Engelsian story, Bloch validated Münzer's credentials as a religious mystic to a far greater degree than those on the left previously had. For Engels, Kautsky and Zetkin, the key point when it came to Münzer was to present his religious message as a kind of surplus to his broader social message in a way that would allow him to be seen as a forerunner of modern German communism. While Bloch likewise emphasised the socially radical dimensions of Münzer's message, for him Münzer's real strength was that the peasants' leader did not couch his social criticism in purely economic terms, but also appealed – in a spiritual idiom – to feeling and emotion. It was a line of argument that would become increasingly important for Bloch against the backdrop of the rise of Nazism, which he believed could only be combatted with an equivalent political mobilisation of affect rather than in the arid language of numbers and figures that he heard in the mouths of the German left at the time.

---

47   See Kautsky 1895.
48   See Zetkin 1920.

The emergence of National Socialism during this period marks the third significant event in this period of Bloch's life and intellectual trajectory. Throughout the 1920s, he chronicled the changing political mood in Germany, as reaction and Nazism gradually took hold. Already in the brutal reaction to the newly established workers' council republic in Bavaria in 1919, Bloch saw the seeds of a troubling relation to *Bodenständigkeit* [roughly, 'rootedness'] that would feed into the blood-and-soil rhetoric of the Nazis.[49] The violent suppression of this revolutionary experiment, he said, had changed Bavaria, and Munich in particular, for the worse. Noting that opposition to the workers' council republic had come not only from rural quarters, but also from among the bourgeoisie, he argued that what united these groups was a populist sentiment directed against supposed urban elites and socialists. His early diagnosis of the potential for the rise of National Socialism, first in Bavaria and then in Germany as a whole, was thus highly prescient. Effective opposition to the Nazis, Bloch argued, needed to address the social and cultural problems to which Nazism claimed to be the solution. Anti-fascists therefore sometimes had to use some of the same techniques as their opponents, though that did not mean aping their divisive rhetoric: from the beginning, Bloch denounced Nazi racial ideology as a sham.[50]

Apart from *Thomas Münzer* and the revised version of *The Spirit of Utopia*, Bloch produced no major philosophical work in the twenties. The collection of essays *Durch die Wüste*, which first appeared in 1923, consisted largely of material excerpted from *The Spirit of Utopia* in the revision process, while the essayistic *Traces*, published in 1930, primarily brought together texts that had already appeared during the twenties in publications such as the *Frankfurter Zeitung* and the *Weltbühne*.[51] What exactly was behind this hiatus in Bloch's philosophical production is not clear. His grief played a part, but perhaps the spirit of utopia was also out of joint with the prevailing spirit of new objectivity and creeping fascism.

4 Heimat in Exile (1933–49)

As soon as Hitler came to power, Bloch and his third wife – the Polish architect Karola Piotrkowska, whom he married in 1934 – fled Germany, doubly threatened as Marxist Jews. Thus began fifteen years of exile in Zürich (1933–4),

---

49 Cf. the essay 'Die Bodenständigkeit als Blasphemie' in Bloch 1985a, pp. 74–83.
50 Cf. the essay 'Verband sächsischer Germanen' in Bloch 1985a, pp. 83–6.
51 See Bloch 1964, 1991 and 2006.

Vienna (1934–5), Paris (1935–6), Prague (1936–8) and finally the US (1938–49), where the Blochs spent 11 years between New York and Cambridge, Massachusetts. In exile from Nazi Germany, Bloch took an active part in the anti-fascist struggle of intellectuals abroad, participating in events such as the famous Congress for the Defence of Culture in June 1935 in Paris and continuing to write for the anti-fascist press from afar. Philosophically, these were extremely productive years. He not only published *Heritage of Our Times*, but also produced the material that would form the basis for several major works, including *The Principle of Hope*, *Natural Law and Human Dignity*, *Subjekt-Objekt. Erläuterungen zu Hegel* and *Das Materialismusproblem, seine Geschichte und Substanz*.

During their period of emigration, Bloch's wife was a constant confidante and comrade. Trained at the world-renowned Swiss Federal Institute of Technology (ETH) in Zürich, Karola Bloch was a successful architect whose professional activity often supported the family, particularly during their years in the United States. It was Karola who convinced Bloch to leave Germany the day after the Nazis came to power, joining him in Switzerland a month thereafter.[52] Married in Vienna in 1934, the Blochs had a son, Jan-Robert, in 1937 (Bloch's daughter, Mirjam, was born of a love affair with language teacher Frida Abeles in 1928). From 1935, Karola – who had been a member of the Communist Party since 1931 – also worked as a courier for the party, transporting secret documents in the fight against fascism, undertaking in practice, as she put it, what Bloch pursued in his thinking and writing.

Ironically, Bloch's most important anti-fascist book, *Heritage of Our Times*, published in 1935, might never have seen the light of day had it not been for a member of the National Socialist Party – a certain Elisabeth Waldmann, a young philosophy student with whom Bloch had fallen in love and who agreed to transport the manuscript to him in Basel after he had fled Germany.[53] A collection of essays written over several years, most of which had already been published in the *Frankfurter Zeitung* and elsewhere, *Heritage of Our Times* documents Bloch's experience of the rise of German fascism during the twenties. The essays are centred around one focal point, the treatise 'Non-Contemporaneity and Obligation to Its Dialectic' from 1932, which, similarly to Walter Benjamin's later *Theses on the Concept of History*, breaks with the orthodox Marxist teleological philosophy of history, introducing the idea of a non-linear temporality to explain the success of fascism's atavistic appeal in the context of an apparently modern German culture.[54]

---

52 See K. Bloch 1981.
53 K. Bloch, 1981, p. 31. The book's German title is *Erbschaft dieser Zeit*.
54 See Bloch 1991, pp. 97–148, as well as the earlier version of this text, Bloch 1977. The essay's German title is 'Ungleichzeitigkeit und Pflicht zu ihrer Dialektik'.

The concept of non-contemporaneity – *Ungleichzeitigkeit*, the persistence of historically older or more basic social and socio-psychological structures – was intended to indicate that the cultural superstructure of late capitalism was not simply in harmony with the times; rather, much of it remained out of step not only with the material base, but also with a range of old and perhaps universal collective desires and beliefs. Germany's young democracy – which, particularly after 1929, had not managed to deliver security for the masses – was in competition with the age-old wish for a Führer and for the so-called stability on offer in the idea of a thousand-year Reich. Bloch's essay exposes the progressive roots of such figures, showing that socialists and communists, too, yearn for a strong leader – a tendency Bloch nevertheless resists. In his eyes, Nazism was able to take hold in Germany partly because it successfully tapped into real desires for wholeness, unity, justice, and so on, that persist precisely because they remain historically unfulfilled.

In order to counter the National Socialist mobilisation of the irrational, Bloch insisted – quite in the spirit of a dialectic of enlightenment – that materialist reason must be able to account for the whole of reality, including its complicated and imaginative components. He repeatedly emphasised that non-contemporaneity is not negative per se. That people hope for a saviour, or that they dream of a paradisiacal society in which the good thrive while the bad have to face the consequences of their actions, is not in itself a problem: on the contrary, such wishes can be seen to indicate an unsatisfactory present. The problem for Bloch was that the political left ignored these dreams and saw them as merely reactionary, condemning them to almost the same extent they condemned fascism.

Despite its obvious anti-fascist intent, *Heritage of Our Times* was roundly criticised by some of Bloch's fellow Marxists. In a 1935 review, Lukács identified a contradiction between Bloch's political views and his philosophical approach that recalled the broad lines of their disagreement. Lukács hoped that Bloch's 'honest and brave participation in the fight against fascism will help him to overcome the blatant contradictions present today between his clear political posture against fascism and his philosophical concessions to idealistic and reactionary trends'.[55] Meanwhile, in a critical review in the Moscow-based journal *Internatsionalnaya Literatura*, Hans Günther, editor of the journal's German edition, charged Bloch with exalting the cultural products of late capitalism as containing potential for an ideological fightback. Bloch retorted with scorn, referencing Heinrich Heine's *Der Rabbi von Bacherach*, in which a rabbi

---

55   Cited in Geoghegan 1996, p. 17.

arriving in a non-Jewish city shields his bride's eyes from its supposed iniquities. Marxists, Bloch said, must not close their eyes to their own time and not ignore people's reality – a mistake the fascists did not make.

Heritage of Our Times did receive some favourable reviews, however, counting among its supporters Klaus Mann and Hermann Hesse as well as Günther Anders, who published his review under his birth name, Günther Stern.[56] For Anders, the most important achievement of *Heritage of Our Times* was the break with the myth of progress, a break he detected in the book's underlying philosophy of history. However, unlike Bloch, for whom the hope and optimism that had accompanied the narrative of progress remained intact even after he acknowledged the limitations of historical teleology, Anders – as well as other contemporaries, such as Benjamin, Adorno and Horkheimer – believed that the break with a progressive philosophy of history that the Third Reich demanded had compromised the validity of hope as a political affect. Adorno would later put this pointedly in a critical review of the second edition of Bloch's *Traces*, where he said that, after 1945, hope could not be viewed as a historical principle.[57]

During the period of Bloch's European exile, he intervened in two significant debates that took place against the background of the popular-front policy of the mid-1930s. The first concerned the politics of culture and was centred on the artistic features and political implications of Realism on the one hand and of Modernism in the form of German Expressionism on the other. The contours of this debate, much of which took place in the pages of the Moscow journal *Das Wort*, are well known. It began as a dispute between Klaus Mann and Gottfried Benn, with Mann associating Benn's Expressionist literary style with an obscurantist and irrationalist politics.[58] The self-confessed Nazi supporter Benn replied that Expressionism had formulated a kind of utopia that the Third Reich had merely realised. This reply only added grist to the mill of Alfred Kurella, who, writing under the pseudonym of Bernhard Ziegler and following the Soviet line, explicitly equated Expressionist aesthetics with fascism. The debate culminated in a confrontation between Bloch, who argued that Expressionism could not simply be identified with fascism and who defended the right of the bourgeois avantgarde to stylistic experimentation, and Lukács, who broadly followed Kurella's line and supported the basic thesis of Socialist Realism – not coincidentally also supported by the Nazis, who largely dismissed Modernism as degenerate – that the purpose of art was to depict reality in a way

---

56   For more on the reception of the book, see Pollmann 2020 and Theophil 2019.
57   Adorno 1993, p. 213.
58   Cf. Holtz 2000.

that was accessible to the masses. Here again, Bloch took a heterodox position that brought him into conflict with Marxists who stayed closer to the Soviet line and that allied him with Western Marxists such as Adorno and Benjamin.

The allegiances were inverted in the second debate in which Bloch was involved in this period, which centred on the Moscow trials. The fact that the trials were obviously politically motivated purges led many of Bloch's fellow left-wing émigrés to renounce their support for the Soviet Union. Bloch, however, was worried that the Soviet Union would now be equated with Nazi Germany and hence completely demonised. Thus, in his political writings of the late 1930s, he defended the Soviet Union, drawing attention to the questionable state of information in the West and insisting that the left continue to support the USSR as the only remaining enemy of fascism, particularly against the background of the Western states' various compromises with Hitler. Though he later renounced his support for Stalin, his uncritical stance in the 1930s damaged his relations with many of his peers. In the years following his arrival in the United States, a clear dividing line in the German émigré community separated those who supported the Soviet Union and those who opposed it. Karola Bloch later recalled that during the 1930s Horkheimer openly criticised her husband for being 'too Communist'. Bloch's journalistic writings praising Stalin while the Moscow trials were going on undoubtedly played a part in Horkheimer's refusal to employ Bloch on any regular basis. When later asked why he thought the Frankfurt School had turned down his request for employment, Bloch claimed that they had 'read my Stalin essays, and that was enough'.[59]

Another question of orthodoxy, this time concerning the problem of matter, occupied Bloch while he was still living in Prague (1936–8). During this period, he worked on the large manuscript that would eventually become *Das Materialismusproblem*.[60] In the Soviet context, the related questions of mechanism and the mind – body problem had become a concern of ideological correctness in the wake of the publication of Lenin's *Materialism and Empirio-Criticism* (published in Russian in 1909 and in German translation in 1927): the book's naïve epistemology was canonised in the process of the Bolshevisation of Soviet Marxism. In the late 1920s, the issue was revived in the debate between mechanists and dialecticians, in which Stalin ultimately came down on the side of mechanism, which declared not only the natural world but also history and human behaviour to be subject to the laws of mechanics. Bloch intended to intervene in this debate by reinserting mind (and with it, freedom) into the

---

59   Zudeick 1987, p. 169.
60   For more on the genesis, content and reception of this book, see Moir 2020a.

material world. That *Das Materialismusproblem* remained unpublished until 1972 spared him the scandal the book surely would have caused had it appeared at the time.

Just as he was making his last contributions to these debates on the European left, Bloch, together with Karola and Jan-Robert, was forced to flee the German invasion of Czechoslovakia. He now reached his last country of exile, the United States, where he was to remain until 1949. His isolation in the US is often emphasised, and indeed he did lead a rather solitary existence compared to many of his compatriots, frequenting only a few other émigrés, such as the art historian Joachim Schumacher, the philosopher Arnold Metzger and the national economist Adolf Lowe. Bloch was not completely alone in America, however. In 1944, he played a key role in setting up the publisher Aurora Verlag in New York, which brought revolutionary ideas to the structure of publishing and was arguably the most innovative press in the US until it closed in 1947. To the authorities, Wieland Herzfelde was the founder, owner and the one financially liable for Aurora Verlag, but in practice a collective of authors ran the press, jointly making the decisions of an editor-in-chief. Alongside Bloch and Herzfelde, Bertolt Brecht, Ferdinand Bruckner, Alfred Döblin, Lion Feuchtwanger, Oskar Maria Graf, Heinrich Mann, Berthold Viertel, Ernst Waldinger and F.C. Weiskopf shared editorial responsibility; the press's publications were bookended by Anna Seghers's story collection *Der Ausflug der toten Mädchen* [The Excursion of the Dead Girls] and the anthology *Morgenröte* [Dawn], with an introduction by Heinrich Mann.

Despite such activities, Bloch's relative isolation in the United States seems to have served his productivity well. Here, he was engaged in a period of 'writing in silence', to which important works owe their genesis. His main work, *The Principle of Hope*, was written during these years, while *Subjekt-Objekt*, *Atheism in Christianity* and *Natural Law and Human Dignity* were also drafted.

The Principle of Hope elaborated the central concept of the not-yet-conscious that Bloch had begun to develop in *The Spirit of Utopia*. Now, for the first time, the concept was expounded in explicit, if somewhat polemically simplified, dialogue with Freud, whose doctrine of the unconscious as the merely no-longer-conscious of the (repressed) past Bloch challenged. Consciousness, he argued, is not only backward-looking, but also has an anticipatory dimension that is not purely speculative, being at points in sync with what he called *real objective possibility*. Against what he saw as the central thread of *anamnesis* in the history of Western philosophy – according to which truth is equated with the knowledge only of what has been – Bloch makes a case for the truth of the dreams, wishes and desires that guide our actions against the current of the status quo. Central to *The Principle of Hope* is thus also the question of the relation between freedom and order (*Freiheit und Ordnung* is the title of his 1948 book that contains the sections of *The Principle of Hope* on social utopias). Far from merely advocating unrestrained freedom in an anarchist or libertarian vein, or insisting on the need for order in the process of constructing a different kind of society – as did, for instance, the utopian socialists of the nineteenth century – Bloch is rather more moderate in emphasising the dialectically interrelated nature of these two categories in the social realm. For him, the claim to freedom is not a desire for chaos, but neither must order necessarily be domination. As long as the demand for order takes the form of violence, however, freedom has the right of truth in its favour.

Manfred Riedel has rightly argued that *The Spirit of Utopia* moves in some of the same territory as Heidegger's *Being and Time* (1927) in its positioning of the question of existence in terms of the experience of temporality.[61] As true as that may be, *The Principle of Hope* can undoubtedly be read as turning against an existentialist philosophy that places the human condition historically under a temporality fixated on fear and death. Bloch's concept of anticipatory consciousness is orientated towards another future, one in which human beings can become the co-creators of a world beyond that of mere survival. Underpinning this idea is Bloch's developing theory of matter as itself productive of the realities that condition us, but which we also shape in both our organic being and our cultural activity. As well as being an encyclopaedia of the forms taken by the utopian impulse, Bloch's magnum opus therefore represents an innovation in historical-dialectical materialist philosophy that was both antimechanist and freedom-orientated.

5   New Old World (1949–61)

It was Bloch's unwavering commitment to the socialist project that led him to return in 1949 not to Frankfurt in West Germany – he declined the offer of a Chair there – but to Leipzig in the East. He seemed to have benefited in his appointment from the initially quite liberal cultural policy of the young German Democratic Republic, as described after the fall of the Berlin Wall by Hans Mayer, an old friend of Bloch's, in the book *Der Turm von Babel. Erinnerung an eine Deutsche Demokratische Republik*.[62]

---

61   Riedel 1994, pp. 216–45.
62   See Mayer 1991.

In some respects, Bloch's time in the GDR was a happy one.⁶³ He not only received official honours during his years in Leipzig, but also found friends there, both in his circle of scholars and assistants and among his colleagues, such as the literary historian and critic Hans Mayer, the Romance scholar Werner Krauss and the economist Fritz Behrens; old friends such as Bert Brecht and Hanns Eisler were living in the GDR anyway. Bloch also met Georg Lukács again. Moreover, in 1959 he reached an agreement with the publisher Siegfried Unseld – with whom he subsequently became friends – on the publication of his complete works by Suhrkamp Verlag, thus securing his philosophical legacy.

Bloch's work during his early GDR years demonstrates a certain conformity with the orthodoxy of the time. The essay 'Partisanship in Science and the World' from 1949 indicates his adherence to the Marxist doctrine of partisanship, according to which academic scholarship was obliged to prioritise the history and interests of the oppressed masses above all else.⁶⁴ This was not just a matter of scholarly or political obligation. According to Marxist-Leninist ideology, partisanship in science reflected the objective truth of historical progress whereby the working classes would triumph where they had not already done so. In the essay, Bloch's declaration that Marxism can lay claim to all progressive tendencies around the world sees him toe the party line, as does his argument that genuine partisanship in science is founded on what is most real about the object. At the same time, East German censorship restrictions undoubtedly influenced some of his editorial decisions: the correspondence between Bloch and his editors at the Aufbau Verlag show that he was encouraged to massage more references to Stalin into his manuscripts.⁶⁵

Yet Bloch was never going to be the regime's pet thinker, and his opposition set him on a course that would eventually result in his emigration to the West. In his inaugural address in 1949, he argued strongly for academic freedom and for an openness of educational and research processes, the existence of which were soon to prove illusory in the GDR. Although he was highly appreciated by his students, and although his manuscripts were initially published by Aufbau Verlag in Berlin, he was disgraced just a few years later. The debate that erupted over the publication of his Hegel book in 1951, and later his rejection of Stalinism and his open criticism of the Soviet regime over the handling of the Hungarian uprising in 1956, led to the repression of his students,⁶⁶ the revocation of his publishing rights and ultimately his forced withdrawal from his post.

---

63   For more on Bloch in the GDR, see Amberger 2013.
64   See Bloch 1969b; the essay's German title is 'Parteilichkeit in Wissenschaft und Welt'.
65   See Jahn (ed.) 2006.
66   The story is recounted in Uwe Johnson's novel *Mutmaßungen über Jakob* [Speculations about Jakob, 1959].

Writing on the political implications of reading Hegel in the GDR, Camilla Warnke has argued that the entrenchment of the anti-Hegelian position between 1946 and 1948 reflected the abandonment of hope for an independent German path to socialism.[67] The question of whether Hegel was a progressive thinker or a reactionary one was a proxy, Warnke argues, for the question of whether the new society's philosophy would be allowed to draw on its specific cultural tradition or whether it would be wholly determined by Moscow. In these early years, then, taking a position on Hegel came to signal one's allegiance or otherwise to Soviet orthodoxy and control.

First published in a Spanish translation by the émigré writer and activist Wenceslao Roces (*Sujeto–Objeto. El pensamiento de Hegel*, published in Mexico City by the Fondo de Cultura Economica), Bloch's Hegel book appeared with Aufbau in 1951 and almost immediately provoked the debate that saw its author progressively marginalised. Bloch's insistence on the importance of Marxism's Hegelian legacy, in particular, made him a subversive figure in a context in which Hegelianism was practically a 'swearword'.[68] The central argument in *Subjekt-Objekt* was that speculative reason, which looks beyond the merely empirical to what connects apparently discrete phenomena, was a critical weapon against totalitarianism. For Bloch, Hegelian speculation was the 'positive moment of reason' that demonstrated the ability of human thought to go beyond the merely empirical and thus transgress the status quo.[69] This capacity of thought to go beyond the merely given obviously spelled danger for a regime that, as the reaction to Bloch's Hegel book demonstrated, increasingly sought to curb all attempts at independent thinking. Moreover, Bloch saw the transitivity between concepts and reality asserted by Hegelian metaphysics as evidence of what he called the 'objectively real possibility' of utopia.[70] The implicit suggestion that utopia had not in fact been achieved in the present again undermined the official Soviet narrative, according to which the establishment of Communism represented the de facto realisation of this historic dream.

The backlash was not immediate. Indeed, a positive review of *Subjekt-Objekt* by the philosopher Georg Mende appeared in the journal *Aufbau* in 1952.[71] After Stalin's death in 1953, however, an open debate about Hegelianism could take place. A bitter feud over Hegel's ideological correctness ensued. It largely took

---

67   See Warnke 2000, especially p. 198.
68   Zudeick 1987, p. 180.
69   Bloch 1962, p. 151.
70   Bloch 1986, vol. 1, p. 235.
71   See Meyer (ed.) 2015, p. 24.

place in the pages of the *Deutsche Zeitschrift für Philosophie*, which Bloch coedited with Wolfgang Harich, a fellow dissident thinker and Hegel supporter. Bloch's chief opponent in the discussion was Rugard Otto Gropp, who as Professor of Marxism-Leninism in Leipzig took an orthodox stance, denouncing Hegel as nothing more than a pathbreaker for Marx, as a mere precursor whose decrepit bourgeois philosophy had been irredeemably surpassed. In the still relatively liberal atmosphere in which the *Deutsche Zeitschrift für Philosophie* operated, Bloch and Gropp exchanged their views, but the cordial veneer soon evaporated. In 1955, the journal's liberal line became too risky for some political decision makers, and they imposed a restructure of the editorial staff from above, while also criticising Bloch – as editor – for bringing too many contributions of his own.[72]

After 1955, the relationship between Bloch and the Socialist Unity Party (SED), of which the philosopher was never a member, deteriorated sharply. In that year, Bloch was honoured with two important national prizes – the Fatherland Order of Merit and the National Prize of the GDR – and made a full member of the German Academy of Sciences in Berlin and head of its Philosophy Section. The year of his seventieth birthday also saw the publication of the commemorative volume *Ernst Bloch zum 70. Geburtstag*, edited by none other than Gropp, who opened it with appreciative words of greeting to the anti-fascist. In addition, the SED presented the first volume of The *Principle of Hope* as a gift for newly admitted members, celebrating the very success and visibility that made Bloch a threat that needed to be brought into line.

When Khrushchev's secret speech at the Twentieth Party Congress of the CPSU in February 1956 named the crimes of Stalinism, and when the contents of this speech were subsequently disseminated in the GDR via Western media, there was great horror among convinced but not completely uncritical Communists. Even for Bloch, who in 1937 had still justified the Moscow show trials and had remained silent when East German workers revolted on 17 June 1953, the situation now changed. Already hostile to Walter Ulbricht, he used his prominence to initiate a revolt of critical intellectuals for more freedom and against dogmatism. At the Freedom Conference in March 1956, he criticised the narrowing of Marxism-Leninism. This was the first time that the philosopher caused a political stir in public. He was supported above all by Wolfgang Harich as well as by Leszek Kołakowski, who emphasised Bloch's call for a strengthening of the subjective factor by looking towards a social state 'in which subjective freedom can be expanded to a maximum degree'.[73]

---

72   For more on this, see Heyer 2013.
73   Cited in B. Schmidt 1982, p. 6.

Inspired by Bloch's and Lukács's demands for reform, a group of people, led by Wolfgang Harich and Walter Janka, at Aufbau Verlag conspired to replace Walter Ulbricht and took the first concrete steps towards implementation. The plan was stopped by arrests at the end of 1956. The General Prosecutor of the GDR, Ernst Melsheimer, had prepared an arrest warrant for Bloch, too, but Ulbricht and Central Committee Secretary Kurt Hager were against imprisonment and relied on Bloch's isolation. The result was an anti-Bloch campaign initiated by an article published by Gropp in *Neues Deutschland* on 19 December, and a follow-up article by Ulbricht in the same newspaper on 31 December. Bloch was now deemed a revisionist who did not represent Marxism-Leninism. In January 1957, Bloch publicly responded to an open letter from the SED party leadership of his university. He gave his view of the recent events, distanced himself from those arrested, praised the Soviet Union's invasion of Hungary in 1956 and professed his loyalty to the system, all while rejecting the accusations of revisionism directed against him. In the end, he offered his retirement, which was immediately accepted. In addition, he was banned from entering the university and the library.

At the beginning of April 1957, the SED party leadership organised a conference on Bloch at the Leipzig Philosophy Institute. The aim was to push back against the pernicious influence that Bloch's philosophy was supposed to have had on the students and certain circles of the intelligentsia. Gropp gave one of the main papers. The conference proceedings were published as *Ernst Blochs Revision des Marxismus. Kritische Auseinandersetzungen marxistischer Wissenschaftler mit der Blochschen Philosophie*, a volume intended to replace the study of Bloch's original work in the GDR.[74] Yet there were sometimes other, even panegyric, tones in the proceedings when it comes to the effect and impression of Bloch's thinking: 'The walls of his auditorium were, as it were, lined with bright red, the red of the revolution, of the struggle of the working class'.[75]

Despite his persecution, Bloch – like almost all GDR dissidents – wanted to stay in East Germany, which is where, he was convinced, he could work best as a Marxist. He also repeatedly tried to seek recognition and release from his isolation, as in December 1957, when he appealed unsuccessfully against his expulsion from the *Kulturbund*. He remained in Leipzig but had the opportunity to travel to the West, where he was able to publish and engage in discussions. In 1959, Aufbau Verlag in East Berlin – perhaps imbued by an illicit spirit of

---

74 See Horn (ed.) 1957.
75 Horn (ed.) 1957, p. 164.

competition – brought out the hitherto missing third volume of *The Principle of Hope*, adding *Thomas Münzer als Theologe der Revolution* in 1960. However, this apparent validation of Bloch's work went hand in hand with further strong criticism, this time by Manfred Buhr, who in 1958 and 1960 wrote a number of negative reviews of Bloch's ideas in the *Deutsche Zeitschrift für Philosophie*.

Despite the increasing atmosphere of repression, Bloch and Karola were surprised when, during a lecture tour in West Germany, they heard about the overnight construction of the Berlin Wall on 13 August 1961. The couple decided not to return to the GDR, and the authorities were relieved when they learned of Bloch's departure. Yet even after he had left, Bloch continued to exercise a powerful influence on dissident GDR intellectuals – including Harich, Rudolf Bahro and Robert Havemann – as well as on writers such as Christa Wolf, Volker Braun, Heiner Müller and Irmtraud Morgner.[76] Hence, Erhard Bahr was able to write in 1980: 'The literature of the German Democratic Republic can be subsumed under Bloch's principle of hope, or, in other words, the literature of the GDR is the Literature of Hope'.[77]

For Bloch, however, the hopes he had pinned on the GDR had been disappointed. In the same year that the Berlin Wall went up, he settled in Tübingen, accepting a guest professorship there at the invitation of bookseller Julie Gastl. When he argued in his inaugural lecture that even grounded, educated hope – *docta spes* – can be disappointed by virtue of its very nature as hope, he was clearly thinking of the failures of the East German regime that had led to his emigration. Yet Bloch also made it clear that he renounced neither Marxism nor the hope for a more just and equal socialist society. Even when the hope for 'real humanism' was betrayed, he argued, it was not erased and could continue to guide both our thinking and our political action.[78]

6   Hope Disappointed? (1961–77)

With his arrival in West Germany, Bloch, now 76, began his final period of emigration. Everything he possessed – furniture, library, correspondence and even photographs – remained in Leipzig, but his manuscripts were secretly transported over the border. In Tübingen, Bloch reached the peak of his influence. He attended conferences, had a significant media presence, influenced the revolutionary student movement and received international recognition in the form

---

76   For more on Bloch's influence on GDR figures, see Amberger 2013 and Kirchner 2002.
77   Bahr 1980, p. 11.
78   See Bloch 1998.

of various honours. His work was translated into a great many languages and discussed in secondary literature published from Japan to Latin America. Not least, he managed to put the final touches to the complete edition of his works before he died, aged 92, in his study in Tübingen.

In exile from the GDR, Bloch was promptly expelled from the East Berlin Academy of Sciences, while his reception in the West was decidedly mixed. Walter Jens, who became Bloch's friend in Tübingen, predicted confrontation at a time when Brecht's works were being banned in a backlash against Marxism, which many, Jens explained, simply equated with Stalinism. For Jens, Bloch's arrival would force West Germany's critical intellectuals to rethink some of these assumptions.[79] Others, including Ludwig Marcuse, demanded that Bloch subject himself to self-criticism (which, ironically, he had also been forced to do in the East) and to admit the failures of the Stalinist legacy he had once supported.[80] For his part, Jürgen Habermas criticised Bloch for wilfully engaging in a form of naïve metaphysics that was neither of practical use nor theoretically up to speed.[81] As Habermas's critique of Bloch's speculative materialism demonstrates, many of Bloch's peers in the West contested his Marxist credentials almost as vigorously as his Marxist contemporaries had done in the GDR.

Not all critical engagements with Bloch were so dismissive, however. Alfred Schmidt, who in a Habermasian vein rejected Bloch's doctrine of a possible subject of nature, nevertheless emphasised the importance of Bloch's qualitative understanding of nature as a productive force: 'Although Bloch's speculation on nature ... with its metaphysical and cosmological expansion ... not only goes beyond Marx, but also leads away from him completely', Schmidt argued, 'it at the same time emphasises a moment in Marx's concept of nature that has since then remained virtually unnoticed ... For Marx, the realm of the forces of nature has something of the Renaissance-like "poetic-sensual splendour"'.[82] Adorno, who elsewhere accused Bloch of undialectical ontologising, also saw that Bloch, through this ontologising, emphasised the subjective factor and in so doing prioritised freedom over the compulsion of nature and law: 'Bloch's *coup de main* renders him capable of an intellectual modus operandi that does not otherwise tend to thrive in the climate of the dialectic, whether idealist or materialist: nothing that exists is idolized for its necessity; speculation attacks necessity itself as an image of myth'.[83]

---

79 Cf. B. Schmidt 1982, p. 28.
80 Cf. his newspaper article 'Bewunderung und Abscheu' in *Stuttgarter Zeitung* of 12 March 1960 (L. Marcuse 1979).
81 Cf. Habermas 1969.
82 A. Schmidt, p. 161; translation modified.
83 Adorno 1993, p. 206.

For many Christian theologians, Bloch's work served as the starting point for a dialogue with philosophy. Catholics like Johann Baptist Metz and Protestants like Jürgen Moltmann saw in Bloch's philosophy a possibility to free religion from its tendency towards the merely private-moral dimension, infusing it with new philosophical meaning and social relevance.[84] Both *The Principle of Hope* and *Atheism in Christianity* sparked a spirited debate in the West German theological community, although – as Bloch's student Hans Heinz Holz noted – it was rather ironic that the atheist Bloch's work found such a lively reception among Christians.[85]

Even more surprisingly, the connection between Christianity and socialism formed a bridge between Bloch and the revolutionary student movement. Bloch's support for the West German student-led extra-parliamentary opposition is apparent from his speech of October 1967, when he was awarded the Peace Prize of the German Book Trade in Frankfurt. Just four months earlier, on the evening of 2 June 1967, German-literature student Benno Ohnesorg had been murdered by a plainclothes police officer during a protest in West Berlin against the Shah of Iran's state visit to Germany. The police had attended the demonstration with the intention of arresting its organisers. When street fighting ensued, a shot was fired from the gun of police detective Karl-Heinz Kurras, striking Ohnesorg fatally in the back of the head. His death radicalised the student movement and the extra-parliamentary opposition, who were grappling with the results of the silent reintegration of fascists into post-war German society and what they saw as the persistence of fascist values. Kurras's acquittal on 21 November 1967 fuelled this perception, though in 2009 he was discovered to have been a committed socialist acting in the service of the Stasi. Nevertheless, Ohnesorg's death continued the generation of student protests against what was seen as the residual authoritarianism of the German state and the repression of criticism and dissent. In his Peace-Prize acceptance speech, Bloch expressed agreement with the idea that fascist traces remained in German society, and he unambiguously supported leftists who were subject to brutal police violence.

Bloch became a leading intellectual influence on the West German student left in these years, taking an active role in many of its events.[86] Yet his initial impression on the revolutionary students was not uniformly positive. Rudi Dutschke, the student movement's main spokesperson, at first viewed Bloch

---

84 Cf. B. Schmidt, p. 30.
85 Ibid.
86 For more on the intellectual influences on the West German student movement, see Kraushaar 1998.

as a Stalinist. It was only in February 1968 that Dutschke began to change his mind, after the pair discussed the revolutionary potential of Christianity at a conference in Bad Boll. When Bloch published *Atheism in Christianity* at the end of that year, he sent a copy with a personal dedication to Dutschke and his wife, Gretchen, a German-American student of theology. By that time, an assassination attempt on Dutschke of 11 April 1968 had already driven the charismatic student leader out of the country, and a nine-year correspondence began, during which the Blochs supported the Dutschkes financially, remaining something of a lifeline to the homeland their young comrades had been forced to leave behind.[87]

Bloch's growing influence on the international student movement undoubtedly contributed to the impact that his ideas had worldwide in the last years of his life, with translations in America, Italy, Japan, Spain, Yugoslavia and France, as well as a growing secondary literature in all these countries. Official honours were not lacking either. Before the Peace Prize in 1967, Bloch was awarded the Culture Prize of the German Trade Union Confederation in 1964, and he subsequently won the Sigmund Freud Prize for academic prose in 1975. Siegfried Unseld published an anniversary publication – *Ernst Bloch zu ehren* – in 1965, which brought together essays on Bloch's work by widely known theologians, philosophers, sociologists and art theorists. A further Festschrift was published on the occasion of his ninetieth birthday in 1975. That same year, he was given an honorary doctorate from the University of Tübingen, where he had taught for so many years; he had already received the same accolade from the Sorbonne in 1965 and from the University of Zagreb in 1969.

In his later years, Bloch was intellectually and politically close to Gajo Petrović and the circle around Yugoslavia's philosophical journal, *Praxis*. He repeatedly spoke at their summer conferences in Korcula, where he also met Herbert Marcuse. Here, as in the context of the student movement, Bloch renewed his connection with active politics, exemplified theoretically in his great work of political philosophy, *Natural Law and Human Dignity*, in which he argued that the pursuit of a social utopia must be mediated with the demand of natural law for human dignity and an upright gait. It was this idea that guided Bloch's political activism during these years, in which he protested against the German emergency laws of 1966, took part in the events of May 1968, protested against the occupation of Czechoslovakia by the Soviet Union in the same year, and

---

87   In 1979, Rudi Dutschke succumbed to the brain injuries he had sustained in the assassination attempt.

later criticised the war in Vietnam. Throughout, Bloch insisted that, because of the origins of all democracies in the idea of natural law, remnants of old demands for justice and equality were still being formulated, such that a real and radical democratic movement could be broadened in the sense of a popular front.

Alongside his political activities, Bloch completed the final editions of his works. *The Principle of Hope* and *Natural Right and Human Dignity* appeared in 1961; *Heritage of Our Times* and *Subjekt-Objekt. Erläuterungen zu Hegel* in 1962; the third edition of *The Spirit of Utopia* in 1964; the *Literary Essays* in 1965; *Atheism in Christianity* in 1968; *Traces, Thomas Münzer als Theologe der Revolution* and *Philosophische Aufsätze* in 1969; and *Politische Messungen* and an expanded version of the *Tübinger Einleitung in die Philosophie* (which had originally appeared in 1963/64 in a two-volume paperback edition) in 1970. In 1972, *Das Materialismusproblem, seine Geschichte und Substanz* was published, and finally *Experimentum Mundi* in 1975, in which Bloch realised his early intention of a systemic work.[88] This was followed by a selection from the Leipzig lectures, *Zwischenwelten in der Philosophiegeschichte*. After completing this lecture work, Bloch went through what was still in the manuscript cabinet, composing what now makes up the seventeenth volume of his complete edition, *Tendenz – Latenz – Utopie*. When he died on 4 August 1977, this volume had just been sent to print. One can thus justifiably say of Bloch, as one has of Plato, that he died writing.

Bloch's impact continued after his death. In 1978, the Sozialistisches Büro organised the first Ernst-Bloch-Tage, which pursued a theme inspired by Bloch contra Habermas – the possibility of a socialist politics rooted in Bloch's philosophy of nature. A year later, the Ernst Bloch Archive was founded in Bloch's birth city of Ludwigshafen, which in 1984 endowed the first Ernst Bloch Prize, honouring outstanding intellectual achievements guided by a spirit of social justice. Learned societies dedicated to Bloch's work were founded in 1985 (Ernst Bloch Assoziation) and 1986 (Ernst Bloch Gesellschaft), and in 1989 Bloch was posthumously rehabilitated in the GDR. Further publications followed. In 1985, Bloch's complete Leipzig lectures were published by his former students there, and his political writings of the First World War period were collected in the volume *Kampf, nicht Krieg*. Letters between Bloch and Karola, between the Blochs and Bloch's former academic assistant Jürgen Teller and his wife

---

88 This period also saw the publication of the volume *Vom Hazard zur Katastrophe* – a new edition of Bloch's political writings of the 1930s – which revised some of his earlier Stalinist positions (Bloch 1972).

Johanna, between the Blochs and the Dutschkes, and between Bloch and Aufbau Verlag, as well as new editions of his doctoral thesis and collections of his writings on materialism from the 1930s – these are just some primary materials that have appeared in the last decades.

Assessing Bloch's legacy today is not an easy task. Is he of purely historical philosophical interest in a world in which optimism, even of the will, is in short supply, or is his thought of continuing relevance for the concrete political struggles of our time? Faced with this question, many commentators appeal to Bloch's apparently perennial non-contemporaneity, perhaps in the hope that what was never in fashion (and fashion is as powerful a driver of the market of ideas as it is of other markets) can never be out of it. We hope that the contributions to this volume demonstrate Bloch's significance as a unique figure in the history of philosophy and of Marxism, and that they exemplify the relevance of his ideas for thinking through and acting in the political struggles for social justice in which we always find ourselves, even as their contours shift historically.

Bibliography

Adorno, Theodor W. 1963, *Drei Studien zu Hegel*, Frankfurt am Main: Suhrkamp.

Adorno, Theodor W. 1993 [1960], 'Ernst Bloch's *Spuren*: On the Revised Edition of 1959', in *Notes to Literature*, Volume 1, translated by Shierry Weber Nicholson, New York: Columbia University Press.

Agar, Jolyon 2013, *Post-Secularism, Realism, and Utopia: Transcendence and Immanence from Hegel to Bloch*, London and New York: Routledge.

Amberger, Alexander 2013, 'Ernst Bloch in der DDR: Hoffnung – Utopie – Marxismus', *Deutsche Zeitschrift für Philosophie*, 61, 4: 561–76.

Bahr, Erhard 1980, 'The Literature of Hope: Ernst Bloch's Philosophy and Its Impact on the Literature of the German Democratic Republic', in *Fiction and Drama in Eastern and Southeastern Europe*, edited by Henrik Birnbaum and Thomas Eekmann, Columbus, Ohio: Slavica.

Baur, Ursula Beata 2018, *Ernst Blochs utopischer Nietzsche: Von der Tragödien- zur Marxismustheorie*, MA thesis Washington University.

Bloch, Ernst 1962 [1951], *Subjekt-Objekt. Erläuterungen zu Hegel*, extended edition, Frankfurt am Main: Suhrkamp.

Bloch, Ernst 1964, 'Der Impuls Nietzsches', in *Durch die Wüste. Frühe kritische Aufsätze*, Frankfurt am Main: Suhrkamp.

Bloch, Ernst 1969a, *Thomas Münzer als Theologe der Revolution*, Frankfurt am Main: Suhrkamp.

Bloch, Ernst 1969b [1949], 'Parteilichkeit in Wissenschaft und Welt', in *Philosophische Aufsätze*, Frankfurt am Main: Suhrkamp.

Bloch, Ernst 1972a, Das Materialismusproblem, seine Geschichte und Substanz, Frankfurt am Main: Suhrkamp.

Bloch, Ernst 1972b, *Vom Hazard zur Katastrophe*, Frankfurt am Main: Suhrkamp.

Bloch, Ernst 1977, 'Nonsynchronism and the Obligation to Its Dialectics', translated by Mark Ritter, *New German Critique*, 11: 22–3.

Bloch, Ernst 1978, *Tendenz – Latenz – Utopie*, Frankfurt am Main: Suhrkamp.

Bloch, Ernst 1985a, *Politische Messungen, Pestzeit, Vormärz*, Frankfurt am Main: Suhrkamp.

Bloch, Ernst 1985b, *Kampf, nicht Krieg. Politische Schriften 1917–1919*, Frankfurt am Main: Suhrkamp.

Bloch, Ernst 1985c [1923], *Geist der Utopie. Bearbeitete Neuauflage der zweiten Fassung von 1923*, Frankfurt am Main: Suhrkamp.

Bloch, Ernst 1986 [1954–9], *The Principle of Hope*, 3 Volumes, translated by Neville Plaice, Stephen Plaice and Paul Knight, Cambridge, Mass.: MIT Press.

Bloch, Ernst 1991 [1935; 2nd, enlarged ed. 1962], *Heritage of Our Times*, translated by Neville Plaice and Stephen Plaice, Oxford: Polity Press.

Bloch, Ernst 1996 [1961], *Natural Law and Human Dignity*, translated by Dennis J. Schmidt, Cambridge, Mass. and London: MIT Press.

Bloch, Ernst 1998 [1961], 'Can Hope Be Disappointed?' in *Literary Essays*, translated by Andrew Joron, Stanford: Stanford University Press.

Bloch, Ernst 2000a, *Logos der Materie. Eine Logik im Werden. Aus dem Nachlass 1923–1949*, Frankfurt am Main: Suhrkamp.

Bloch, Ernst 2000b, *The Spirit of Utopia*, translated by Anthony Nassar, Stanford: Stanford University Press.

Bloch, Ernst 2006 [1930], *Traces*, translated by Anthony Nassar, Stanford: Stanford University Press.

Bloch, Ernst 2009 [1968], *Atheism in Christianity: The Religion of the Exodus and the Kingdom*, translated by J.T. Swann, London and New York: Verso.

Bloch, Ernst 2010 [1908], *Études critiques sur Rickert et le problème de la théorie moderne de la connaissance*, translated by Lucien Pelletier, Paris: Éditions de la Maison des Sciences de l'Homme and Presses de l'Université Laval.

Bloch, Ernst 2019 [1952], *Avicenna and the Aristotelian Left*, translated by Loren Goldman and Peter Thompson, New York: Columbia University Press.

Bloch, Karola 1981, *Aus meinem Leben*, Pfullingen: Neske.

Bloch, Karola and Welf Schröter (eds.) 1988, *Lieber Genosse Bloch ... Briefe Rudi Dutschkes an Karola und Ernst Bloch*, Mössingen: Talheimer Verlag.

Blumenberg, Hans 1985, *The Legitimacy of the Modern Age*, translated by Robert M. Wallace, Cambridge, Mass.: MIT Press.

Boldyrev, Ivan 2012, 'Geist der Utopie, der sich erst bildet: Vorläufige Beobachtungen zur Korrektur des Blochschen Frühwerks', in *Bloch-Jahrbuch*, 2012: 32–54.

Boldyrev, Ivan 2015, *Ernst Bloch and His Contemporaries: Locating Utopian Messianism*, London and New York: Bloomsbury.

Camellone, Mauro Farnesi 2009, *La politica e l'immagine: Saggio su Ernst Bloch*, Macerata: Quodlibet.

Colletti, Lucio 1969, *Il marxismo e Hegel*, Bari: Laterza.

Cunico, Gerardo 2020, *Ernst Bloch. Ritorno al future. Spirito utopico e logica processuale*, Sesto San Giovanni: Mimesis Edizioni.

Dietschy, Beat, Doris Zeilinger and Rainer E. Zimmermann (eds.) 2012, *Bloch-Wörterbuch. Leitbegriffe der Philosophie Ernst Blochs*, Berlin and Boston: de Gruyter.

Edwards, Caroline 2019, *Utopia and the Contemporary British Novel*, Cambridge: Cambridge University Press.

Engels, Friedrich 1978 [1850], *The Peasant War in Germany*, in *Marx-Engels Collected Works*, Volume 10, London: Lawrence and Wishart.

Geoghegan, Vincent 1996, *Ernst Bloch*, London and New York: Routledge.

Habermas, Jürgen 1969/70, 'Ernst Bloch – a Marxist Romantic', in *Salmagundi* 10–1: 311–25.

Hegel, Georg Wilhelm Friedrich 1952 [1807], *Phänomenologie des Geistes*, Hamburg: Meiner.

Heyer, Andreas 2013, 'Zur inhaltlichen Ausrichtung der *Deutschen Zeitschrift für Philosophie* im Zeichen des "Neuen Kurses" der SED', *Deutsche Zeitschrift für Philosophie*, 61, 4: 551–4.

Holtz, Günter 2000, 'Expressionismuskritik als antifaschistische Publizistik? Die Debatte in der Zeitschrift *Das Wort*', *Monatshefte*, 92, 2: 164–83.

Horn, Johannes Heinz (ed.) 1957, *Ernst Blochs Revision des Marxismus. Kritische Auseinandersetzungen marxistischer Wissenschaftler mit der Blochschen Philosophie*, Berlin: DVW.

Horster, Detlef 2005, *Ernst Bloch zur Einführung*, Wiesbaden: Panorama.

Howells, Richard 2015, *A Critical Theory of Creativity: Utopia, Aesthetics, Atheism and Design*, London: Palgrave Macmillan.

Hudson, Wayne 1982, *The Marxist Philosophy of Ernst Bloch*, New York: St. Martin's Press.

Hudson, Wayne 1989, 'Two Interviews with Ernst Bloch', *Bloch-Almanach*, 9: 116–21.

Hyppolite, Jean 1946, *Genèse et structure de la "Phénoménologie de l'esprit" de Hegel*, Paris: Aubier.

Jahn, Jürgen (ed.) 2006, *'Ich möchte das Meine unter Fach und Dach bringen'. Ernst Blochs Geschäftskorrespondenz mit dem Aufbau-Verlag Berlin 1946–1961. Eine Dokumentation*, Wiesbaden: Harrassowitz.

Jameson, Fredric 1971, *Marxism and Form: Twentieth-Century Dialectical Theories of Literature*, Princeton, NJ: Princeton University Press.

Jay, Martin 1984, *Marxism and Totality: The Adventures of a Concept from Lukács to Habermas*, Berkeley: University of California Press.

Kautsky, Karl 1895, *Die Vorläufer des neueren Sozialismus*, Volume 1, Stuttgart: Dietz.

Kirchner, Verena 2002, *Im Bann der Utopie. Ernst Blochs Hoffnungsphilosophie in der DDR-Literatur*, Heidelberg: Winter.

Kojève, Alexandre 1947, *Introduction à la lecture de Hegel*, Paris: Gallimard.

Korstvedt, Benjamin 2010, *Listening for Utopia in Ernst Bloch's Musical Philosophy*, Cambridge: Cambridge University Press.

Kraushaar, Wolfgang 1998, *Frankfurter Schule und Studentenbewegung. Von der Flaschenpost zum Molotowcocktail 1946–1991*, Hamburg: Rogner & Bernhard bei Zweitausendeins.

Leucht, Robert 2016, *Dynamiken politischer Imagination. Die deutschsprachige Utopie von Stifter bis Döblin in ihren internationalen Kontexten, 1848–1930*, Berlin and Boston: de Gruyter.

Levitas, Ruth 2010 [1990], *The Concept of Utopia*, Frankfurt am Main: Peter Lang.

Lukács, Georg 1975 [1948], *The Young Hegel: Studies in the Relations between Dialectics and Economics*, translated by Rodney Livingstone, London: Merlin Press.

Marcuse, Herbert 1941, *Reason and Revolution: Hegel and the Rise of Social Theory*, Oxford: Oxford University Press.

Marcuse, Ludwig 1979 [1960], 'Bewunderung und Abscheu', in *Essays, Porträts, Polemiken*, Zürich: Diogenes, 285–95.

Markun, Sylvia 1977, *Ernst Bloch*, Reinbek bei Hamburg: Rowohlt.

Mayer, Hans 1991, Der Turm von Babel. Erinnerung an eine Deutsche Demokratische Republik, Frankfurt am Main: Suhrkamp.

Meyer, Andreas (ed.) 2015, *Wolfgang Harich an der ideologischen Front. Hegel zwischen Feuerbach und Marx. Schriften aus dem Nachlass Wolfgang Harichs*, Volume 5, Marburg: Tectum.

Moir, Cat 2019, 'The Birth of Materialism out of the Spirit of Expressionism: Nietzsche and Bloch's Philosophy of Language', *Revue internationale de philosophie*, 289, 3: 303–32.

Moir, Cat 2020a, Ernst Bloch's Speculative Materialism: Ontology, Epistemology, Politics, Leiden: Brill.

Moir, Cat 2020b, 'Panorama 1989: The Political Aesthetics of the Early Bourgeois Revolution in Germany' in *Reform, Revolution and Crisis in Europe: Landmarks in History, Memory and Thought*, edited by Bronwyn Winter and Cat Moir, London and New York: Routledge.

Müller, Laurenz 2007, 'Revolutionary Moment: Interpreting the Peasants' War in the Third Reich and in the German Democratic Republic', *Central European History*, 40, 2: 193–218.

Muñoz, José Esteban 2009, *Cruising Utopia: The Then and There of Queer Futurity*, New York: NYU Press.

Münster, Arno (ed.) 1977, *Tagträume vom aufrechten Gang. Sechs Interviews mit Ernst Bloch*, Frankfurt am Main: Suhrkamp.
Münster, Arno 2004, *Ernst Bloch. Eine politische Biographie*, Berlin and Vienna: Philo.
Münster, Arno 2011, *Principe Espérance ou Principe Responsabilité*, Paris: Le Bord de l'Eau.
Münster, Arno 2013, *Utopie, écologie, écosocialisme. De l'utopie concrète d'Ernst Bloch à l'écologie socialiste*, Paris: L'Harmattan.
Ní Dhúill, Caitríona 2010, *Sex in Imagined Spaces: Gender and Utopia from More to Bloch* Oxford: Legenda.
Pollmann, Anna 2020, *Fragmente aus der Endzeit. Negatives Geschichtsdenken bei Günther Anders*, Göttingen: Vandenhoeck & Ruprecht.
Rehmann, Jan et al. (eds.) 2018, special issue of *Das Argument*, 325.
Riedel, Manfred 1994, *Tradition und Utopie. Ernst Blochs Philosophie im Licht unserer geschichtlichen Denkerfahrung*, Frankfurt am Main: Suhrkamp.
Schmidt, Alfred 2012 [1962], *The Concept of Nature in Karl Marx*, translated by Ben Fowkes, London: Verso.
Schmidt, Burghart 1982, *Ernst Bloch*, Stuttgart: Metzler.
Theophil, Manuel 2019, 'About the Decapitation of Corpses: Reflections of Ernst Bloch's *Ungleichzeitigkeit* in the Novels of Klaus Mann (including a Glimpse into the Present)', *Colloquium: New Philologies*, 4, 3: 129–48.
Thompson, Peter and Slavoj Žižek (eds.) 2013, *The Privatization of Hope: Ernst Bloch and the Future of Utopia*, Durham and London: Duke University Press.
Warnke, Camilla 2000, '"Das Problem Hegel ist längst gelöst": Eine Debatte in der DDR der fünfziger Jahre', in *Anfänge der DDR Philosophie: Ansprüche, Ohnmacht, Scheitern*, edited by Volker Gerhardt and Hans-Christoph Rauh, Berlin: Ch. Links.
Weigand, Karl-Heinz 1998, 'Ernst Bloch. Une introduction', *Revista Filosófica de Coimbra*, 13: 71.
Weigand, Karl-Heinz 2007, *Bloch. Eine Bildmonographie*, Berlin: Suhrkamp.
Zetkin, Clara 1920, *Revolutionäre Kämpfe und revolutionäre Kämpfer 1919*, Stuttgart: Spartakus.
Zipes, Jack 2019, *Ernst Bloch: The Pugnacious Philosopher of Hope*, London: Palgrave Macmillan.
Zudeick, Peter 1987, *Der Hintern des Teufels. Ernst Bloch – Leben und Werk*, Moos: Elster.

CHAPTER 2

Will There Be Nothing Rather Than Something? Ernst Bloch's Overcoming of Gnosticism

Agata Bielik-Robson

What has no shadow has no strength to be.[1]

∴

It is necessary to reduce things to their nothingness in order to restore them to their true nature.[2]

∴

The purpose of this chapter is to put Ernst Bloch's philosophy to a test suggested by Hans Blumenberg in *The Legitimacy of the Modern Age*.[3] According to Blumenberg, modernity constitutes the second – and one successful – attempt at overcoming Gnosticism, after the first attempt, undertaken by Christianity, had failed. However – Blumenberg argues – it was not modern philosophy but science that had managed to escape Gnosticism's ontological trap of viewing the world as an illusion bordering on nothing. Modern metaphysics proved unable to liberate itself from the powerful pull of the Gnostic rejection of being, in spite of all philosophical efforts to affirm the existence of material reality. Even when claiming to be materialist, it had at its core remained suspicious of matter as an imperfect and privative mode of being.

In the twentieth century, when the Gnostic dilemma was addressed (mostly due to Blumenberg's critical enterprise, which in 1966 made explicit the problem that had previously implicitly undermined materialist philosophy), the intellectual development of many thinkers can indeed be said to fall under the rubric of *trying to overcome Gnosticism*: an initial strong attraction to the

---

1 This is the last line of Czesław Miłosz's poem 'Faith'; my translation.
2 Scholem 1995a, p. 242.
3 See Blumenberg 1985.

Gnostic model first begins to wane and is subsequently replaced by an attempt to exit the negative paradigm towards the re-affirmation of worldly existence. Such was the path of Franz Rosenzweig, Bloch's contemporary. Initially influenced by the theologies of Karl Barth and Adolf von Harnack with its Marcionite Gnostic traits, he went on to devise – in *The Star of Redemption* (written 1918–9; published 1921) – an entirely new philosophical system intended, precisely, to escape the power of ontological negation.[4] The same pattern can be found in Hannah Arendt, whose early fascination with the Christian acosmism characteristic of Weimar theology eventually gave way to an openly declared *amor mundi*, or love of the world.[5] Hans Jonas – who in his seminal *Gnosis und spätantiker Geist* [Religion of Gnosis, 1934] argued in favour of Gnosticism as a legitimate philosophical position (as in the works of such prominent thinkers as Martin Heidegger) – devoted himself after the Second World War to creating a *via affirmativa*, a project that culminated in his decidedly pro-cosmic 'philosophy of responsibility'. Gershom Scholem, the great twentieth-century historian of Jewish religious thought, likewise began as an uncompromising Marcionite and eventually shifted his position towards the more dialectical 'Jewish Gnosis' of Isaac Luria, while Walter Benjamin, under Scholem's influence, followed a similar trajectory. Leo Strauss, in his early years smitten by Karl Barth, also spent the rest of his life elaborating a new metaphysical category of *physis* as a conceptual weapon against the nihilising tendencies of Gnosticism.[6] All of them were combatting the Gnostic syndrome they had acquired in their youth, trying to find a cure and *failing*, or at least – to put it in Samuel Beckett's terms – *failing better*. Yet in spite of all their efforts, they never entirely managed to lift Blumenberg's 'curse', which had doomed modern philosophy to remain structurally entrapped in the Gnostic denigration of matter.

My aim in what follows is to locate Bloch within this late modern constellation of attempts to overcome Gnosticism, reading his *Avicenna and the Aristotelian Left* as an attempt to counteract his early Marcionite tendencies, manifest above all in *The Spirit of Utopia*. There is an ongoing debate among Bloch scholars concerning the importance of Gnostic motives in his thought. Whereas some see such motives as decisive, others view them as of minor significance, especially in Bloch's later years, which were marked by the impact of Engels's dialectical materialism. The perspective I wish to propose here has the

---

4 See Pollock 2012 and 2014.
5 *Amor mundi* – love of and faith in the world – is the title Arendt originally wanted to use for her *magnum opus*, which was eventually called *The Human Condition*.
6 On the different strategies of overcoming Gnosticism in Jonas, Scholem and Strauss, see above all Lazier 2012.

advantage of reconciling these two positions. While emphasising the lasting importance of Gnosis for Bloch, it also points to his struggle with the Gnostic negation of matter, which, as I will argue, cannot be regarded as fully successful, yet at the same time should not simply be dismissed. Hence my use of Beckett's phrase *failing better* – 'fail, fail again, fail better' – which is perhaps the best that modern philosophy can offer. Initially taken by the Gnostic 'Evangelium of the Alien God'[7] to the point of being called a 'Jewish Marcionite',[8] Bloch later on attempts to ground his 'political Gnosis' in a more robust materialism. Without abandoning his sympathy for the revolutionary aspects of Gnostic negation – as is evident particularly from the late *Atheism in Christianity* – he shifts the radical *no* from the metaphysical realm, where it involves a rejection of being, to the political realm, where it entails a rejection of all sovereign – 'pharaonic' – forms of power.[9] Yet there remains the question of whether this transformation of Gnosticism – its translation from the metaphysical into the political – is fully successful. It is my contention that even *Avicenna and the Aristotelian Left*, which was supposed to overcome Marcionite anti-materialist dualism once and for all, is the locus of the most stubborn Gnostic return in Bloch's later writings.[10]

1 A Perfect Symmetry

According to Hans Jonas, the paradigmatic modern philosopher most affected by the syndrome of the Gnostic return is Martin Heidegger. Heidegger's being-towards-death [*Sein-zum-Tode*] executed in the harsh conditions of thrownness [*Geworfenheit*], as well as the stark contrast he draws between authentic life and life spent in the anonymous mode of 'the they' [*das Man*], clearly points to the Gnostic understanding of human existence as a constant struggle between the pneumatic and the material, in which the latter eventually emerges as 'non-authentic', as the illusory results of the metaphysical Fall and Error.

---

7   See Harnack 1924.
8   In his essay 'Walter Benjamin – ein moderner Marcionit?', Jacob Taubes, putting Bloch in the company of Benjamin and Simone Weil, even goes so far as to accuse him of being a Marcionite who 'had bought all this metaphysical anti-Semitism' – and not a Jewish Marcionite, but the subtler hybrid he detects in Benjamin, especially in the latter's *Theologico-Political Fragment* (Taubes 2006, p. 55).
9   Bloch 2009, pp. 60–1.
10 See O'Regan 2001.

In Jonas's account, Gnostic metaphysics, though seemingly dualistic, is actually based on a radical asymmetry. The true being – the only being worthy of that name – is of a purely pneumatic nature, while matter turns out to be the fake creation of an Archon, a minor apostate deity who made this fallen world by merely imitating the divine creative power. Thus, while from the point of view of material entities the true being *appears* as nothing (a 'no-thing' whose mode of existing cannot be compared to that of cosmic beings), from the point of view of the true being the created world simply *is* nothing.

Jonas detects the same asymmetry in Heidegger's relation between Being and beings, in which he sees a modern philosophical variant of the antagonism between the Great Life and the created world as known from Valentinus, the second-century Alexandrian Gnostic and the presumed author of *The Gospel of Truth*, the foundational text of Gnostic metaphysics. While the Great Life is a pure spirit [*pneuma*] – living in a state of fullness [*pleroma*], knowing no matter, time or decay – the lower world, created by the Error [*plane*], or the personified demiurgic power of deviation, is a cosmic mistake, doomed to suffer in the material condition of becoming and perishing. Material life is therefore not just a pale copy of the Ideal of Life, as it is in Plato: it is a *wrong* copy, an erroneous quasi-imitation of Life, which, in Valentinian thought, is by definition indestructible and immortal. Thus, just as the Valentinian Great Life feels wrongly projected 'into the affliction of the worlds', so does Heideggerian Being 'object' to the presencing of beings by immediately withdrawing from them, as if in disgust:

> All we wish to say here is that in both cases 'to have been thrown' is not merely a description of the past but an attribute qualifying the given existential situation as determined by that past. It is from the gnostic experience of the present situation of life that this dramatic image of its genesis has been projected into the past, and it is part of the mythological expression of this experience. 'Who has cast me into the affliction of the worlds, who transported me into the evil darkness?' asks the Life; and it implores, 'Save us out of the darkness of this world into which we are thrown'. To the question the Great Life replies, 'It is not according to the will of the Great Life that thou hast come there': 'That house in which thou dwellest, not Life has built it': 'This world was not created according to the wish of the Life'.[11]

Yet despite Jonas's diagnosis, Heidegger can also be regarded as belonging to the constellation of thinkers who attempted to overcome Gnosticism. After

---

11   Jonas 2001, p. 63.

his post-war turn or *Kehre*, Heidegger attempts to recast the relation between Being and beings in a more symmetrical manner, so as to neutralise the effects of radical negativity by which the Great Life or Being rejects the ontological product in the form of beingness [*Seiendheit*] as unworthy of its dwelling. This change has been pointed out by Giorgio Agamben, who in *The Use of Bodies* directs our attention to Heidegger's crucial auto-correction in the later edition of *What Is Metaphysics?*:

> What is in question here is nothing less than the metaphysical problem of the ontological difference between Being and beings ... As sometimes happens, the cruciality and the difficulty of the decision is attested in Heidegger in an easily overlooked textual detail: the correction of one word in a sentence of the *Nachwort* added in 1943 to the fourth edition of *What Is Metaphysics?* Where in the 1943 text we read: 'It belongs to the truth of Being that Being certainly [*wohl*] is without beings, and that by contrast beings are never without being', the fifth edition (1949) *corrects the 'certainly' into 'never'*: 'It belongs to the truth of Being that Being is never without beings and that beings are never without Being'. While in the first version the connection between Being and beings is broken from the side of Being, which consequently appears as nothing, the second edition affirms that *Being can never be separated from beings*.[12]

For Agamben, this seemingly innocuous change announces an epochal transformation: from a total asymmetry, where Being is still in the position of the traditional Absolute and as *ab-solutus* can be ontologically detached from the beings it produces, to a *perfect symmetry*, where Being is no longer an Absolute and cannot be thought without beings, which now belong to the intrinsic truth of Being and exist as 'truly' as Being itself. While the Absolute could earlier represent the highest – most intense, true, essential – being, in the light of which the existence of all other beings appeared merely relative and close to nothing, now, after the turn, the relationship is more equal. Gone is the image of the Great Life or Being rejecting the affliction of the worlds with scorn.[13]

---

12   Agamben 2015, pp. 163–4. Agamben's translation of the German word *wohl* is actually somewhat misleading: *wohl* means 'probably', at a stretch 'almost certainly', but not simply 'certainly'. Yet this only strengthens Agamben's argument about Heidegger's hesitation as to how to solve the mystery of the ontological difference.

13   According to Adorno, the issue of symmetry versus asymmetry is actually as old as metaphysics itself, and if Heidegger encounters this problem, it is because he participates in the Western metaphysical tradition inaugurated by the debate between Plato and Aristotle. In his lectures on metaphysics, Adorno claims that the original locus of this tension

The new metaphysical model, then, does not allow for a separate and self-sufficient Absolute; indeed, it shifts the very intuition of a true existence to finite beings that are no longer judged as privative – as diminishment of the higher mode of being – but as existing per se. Here, 'finitude is not privation'.[14] That is to say, it is conditioned, not by an Absolute, but rather by what Derrida calls the 'unconditional without sovereignty',[15] an origin which can never detach – or absolve – itself from what it originates. Hence, Heidegger writes the new name of *Seyn/Beyng* as a crossed-out word. This way of writing 'Being' is meant to indicate not a negative theology, in which 'nothing' is one of the names of *hyperessentia*, but rather what we might call a metaphysics of origination or coming-into-being marked by the perfect symmetry of *never without*. Understood in this way, *origin* is not a hyper-being disguised as nothing. Rather, it conditions beings in the mode of *es gibt*, which, while giving, immediately withdraws for the sake of beings that solely can be said to exist. Hence, what appears as the world is not a diminution of the highest creative being; the withdrawal of Being [*Entzug des Seins*] is a different operation – not so much an occlusion of the light as giving a place. Beings emerge *in-stead*: in the place of the origin and as a replacement of the origin which constantly displaces itself to let beings be.

Heidegger was not the first thinker to conceive the ontological difference in such a non-absolutist manner. The primacy in this respect belongs to Hegel, who first used the concept of nothing with reference to the origin in the literal sense by depriving it of the superessential halo of negative theology. In the *Science of Logic*, the beginning is defined strictly as non-existing and as merely 'reaching out to being' in a manner reminiscent of Jacob Böhme, who described the abyssal origin as *seinshungrig*, or craving for being:

> As yet there is nothing, and something is supposed to become. The beginning is not pure nothing but a nothing, rather, from which something is

---

   is to be found in Plato's *Parmenides*: 'In it Plato puts forward what might be seen as the implicitly very dialectical thesis that, however little the Many amount to without the One – the Many refers to the scattered things, as opposed to the one Idea under which each thing in a genus is subsumed – *however little this Many may be without the One, without its Idea, just as little is the One, the Idea, without the Many*' (Adorno 2001, p. 17; emphasis added).

14   Nancy 1997, p. 29.
15   In 'Epoche and Faith' – an exchange with Yvonne Sherwood, Kevin Hart and John D. Caputo – Derrida says: 'One has to dissociate God's sovereignty from God, from the very idea of God. We would have God without sovereignty, without omnipotence' (Derrida 2005, p. 42).

to proceed; also being, therefore, is already contained in the beginning. Therefore, the beginning contains both, being and nothing; it is the unity of being and nothing, or is non-being which is at the same time being, and being which is at the same time non-being. Further, being and nothing are present in the beginning as *distinguished*; for the beginning points to something other – it is a non-being which refers to an other; that which begins, as yet *is* not; it only reaches out to being. The being contained in the beginning is such, therefore, that it distances itself from non-being or sublates it as something which is opposed to it. But further, that which begins already *is*, but *is* also just as much *not* yet. The opposites, being and non-being, are therefore in immediate union in it; or the beginning is their *undifferentiated unity*.[16]

While Böhme can be credited with the radical demotion of the once most sublime 'nothingness' which, in his mystical vision, fell from the superlative heights to the abyssal depths of privation and craving for being, Hegel sublates Böhme's theosophy into a neutral philosophical idiom which for the first time formulates the metaphysics of perfect symmetry: when the beginning points to something other as a non-being which refers to an other, then it cannot be thought without beings that arise from the *Aufhebung* of the non-being inherent in the origin. On the other hand, because of the never complete act of sublation, the beings thus emerged perpetuate the non-being in themselves and as such are still 'not yet' beings in the evolutionary dialectical process of becoming.

Ernst Bloch often declared that he participates in this new evolutionary transformation of metaphysics, directed against the asymmetrical arrangement of the Gnostic or Neoplatonic scheme of emanation as diminution / privation of light / being. His choice of Aristotle and *a fortiori* of the Aristotelian Left can be explained by his desire to oppose the absolutist system of the privileged Origin, which engenders beings more or less accidentally and sets the unchanging point of reference for any redemptive act of *restitutio ad integrum*. In accordance with Hegel's pro-symmetrical innovation, Bloch writes: 'When the Primordial-One which is the Beginning is thought of as creative, what comes after it must thereby seem smaller. To proceed from so lofty a source is *ipso facto* to diminish'.[17] And with reference to theories of emanation he states:

---

16   Hegel 2010, p. 51. Cf. Mondin 1963, pp. 88–9.
17   Bloch 2009, p. 201.

> The Neo-Platonists, and later on the Gnostics, did not believe in creation by a primordial Father but in emanation from a primordial Light. These emanations, however, were at the same time downward falls; the farther they receded from the Light, the weaker they became, and their only goal was to climb back through the world to their source. This *Alphastress* [the emphasis on the origin] goes back to Plato, though already in the earlier Academy Speusippos had reversed matters, with his evolutionary stress on the Way which leads away. Right from Aristotle to Leibniz and Hegel, then, *emanation was opposed by evolution, which saw the Primordial-One in all its perfection as the end-product and not the starting point of development.* The beginnings of growth took place, on the contrary, in a very vague and imperfect realm indeed: one which stood closer to Plato's questing Eros than to a perfect world of Ideas beyond all growth.[18]

While I endorse Bloch's intentions in stressing the primacy of evolution over emanation – or, in Heideggerian terms, the primacy of symmetry over asymmetry – my aim here is to assess whether his theory lives up to them. My critique will circle around two fundamental questions. First, is Bloch's *Omega-point* – the ultimate goal of the evolution of being – indeed different from, and superior to, the *Alpha*, given that he nonetheless has recourse to the Gnostic topos of 'homecoming'? Second, and relatedly, is his speculative materialism truly materialist and not another Neoplatonic or Gnostic variant of *materia spiritualis* in Marxist disguise?

2 *Materia ultima*: To Be or Not to Be?

For Bloch, the final goal of metaphysical evolution is the *humanisation of nature* – a term he borrows from Marx's early utopian manuscripts – in which the natural world sheds the necessitarian form of mechanical objectivity and shows itself in the paradisiac glory of a place free of antagonisms:

> Humanization of nature – that would mean the opening-up of the cosmos, still closed to itself, to be our Home: the Home once expressed in the mystical fantasy of new heaven and new earth, and echoing on through the beauty and quality of nature as these have found expression in painting and poetry, with the great leap out of the realm of necessity draw-

---

18   Ibid. Emphasis added.

ing ever closer to man. Not to mention that out-and-out qualitative, all-shattering horizon of *apocalypsis cum figuris* kept open not in antiquity but in the Christianity of Dürer's day, at least in the realm of fantasy ... *Vivant sequentes*. Marxism, and the dream of the unconditioned, follow the same path and the same plan of campaign. A *Humanum* free from alienation, and a World into which it could fit – a world as yet still undiscovered, but already somehow sensed: both these things are definitively present in the experiment of the Future, the experiment of the World.[19]

A similar vision concludes the last book to appear during Bloch's lifetime, a study devoted to the notion of the 'experiment of the World', his *Experimentum Mundi* of 1974:

> *Naturalisation of humankind, humanisation of nature.* Neither can be thought without the most-driven immanence [*höchst fortgetriebene Immanenz*] as something closest to the human cause and the world-cause alike, which must be brought about from the existential darkness ... Then, the enlightenment *ex fine* and the proximity to the face [*die Nähe zum Gesicht*] will no longer be mere a slogan [*Lösewort*], they will step forwards as a fully meaningful watchword [*Losungswort*]: *Natura naturata nos ipsi erimus*.[20]

Bloch describes the advent of *materia ultima* by means of an array of concepts and rhetorical figures, most of them taken from religion and Marxist materialism. *Naturalisierung des Menschen, Humanisierung der Natur* is explained through images related to the Christian Apocalypse as the 'enlightenment *ex fine*' [from the end] – the future reign of Jerusalem Golden after the shattering of the 'hindering realm' [*der schädliche Raum*] of objectified nature – as well as the Kabbalistic *tikkun*, in which humanised nature will have shown *das Gesicht*, a friendly face, already 'almost there', hidden in the folds of the evolving material immanence. The final words of *Experimentum Mundi* evoke Saint Augustine's 'On the seventh day, we will be ourselves'.[21] They suggest that on the final day of creation, when the material world will have achieved a fully realised form, the shell of the natured nature will break and release the no-longer hindered spark of what Bloch calls the Real-Possible: the energetic and plastic aspect of existence, so far occluded by the hindering, resistant form of

---

19   Bloch 2009, pp. 255–7.
20   Bloch 1975, p. 264.
21   Dies septimus etiam nos ipsi erimus (Augustine 2011, 23:30).

material objects and manifest only in human subjectivity. *We* – the collective human subject of what Marx calls species beings, or *Gattungswesen*, as opposed to isolated individuals – will finally become *ourselves*; that is, what we truly are, a pure creative *natura naturans*, free of the objectified 'obstructing realm', which will give way to a *Goldraum*, the time space of Jerusalem Golden, or (in Kabbalistic terms) the triumph of time over space: 'the New Jerusalem will come forth as an intrinsically grown antidote to the infinity of the cosmos, as a truly centred universe, comprising All in a Golden Realm, the very opposite of the inflationary All'.[22] The *Drehung*, which inaugurates the turn towards the realisation of the Omega, would thus consist in the radical inversion of the ontological tendency: from the expansion of *in-sich-Sein*, which produces the infinite extension of dead matter, to the intensity of *für-sich-Sein*, in which *das Daß* – the brute fact of mere existence, or *quodditas* – finally finds an answer to the question of its identity and purpose and becomes conscious of its *Was*, its *quidditas*. This reversal therefore announces a full turnabout of the entire material universe: matter, so far merely multiplying in the extensive mode, will turn reflexively on itself and begin to grow in the intensive mode of consciousness, searching to find the answer to the question, 'what am I?'.

On this metaphorical seventh day, 'the question of the world about itself [*die Frage der Welt nach sich selber*]' will finally have found the answer. The world, the self-experiment of being, now knows *what* it is: an eternal energy destined for happiness and joy [*Glück*]. This destiny is ultimate because happiness and joy are autotelic: once the possibility of a full enjoyment of one's existence emerges, there is no need to ask, as Valentinus did, *where-to* and *where-from*. The darkness of our *Seinsfrage* becomes enlightened by the *dies novissima*, or the newest day, in the light of which all striving and all desire of all beings that ever existed are finally satisfied by the promise of eternal joy. Hence, the Omega-*tikkun* is also a time space of universal *theosis*, the true *Heimat* of liberated existence, no longer struggling to survive in a hostile environment – *sicut Dei*, happy, fateless [*schicksallos*] and beyond harm. From this day on, everything will be able to participate in the divine *modus essendi*, filled with an autotelic joy of being *what* it is and *that* it is.

This Kabbalistic emphasis on the recuperation of the absolute *jouissance* of being – originally enjoyed only by the divine *Ein-Sof*, but in the end shared by

---

22   Bloch 1975, p. 245. Cf. Edith Wyschogrod's Kabbalistic description of the cosmic Sabbath – that is, the Seventh Day of Creation – as the ideal goal, which 'expresses the turning of space into time, the respite from creation as the temporal self-articulation of identity-in-difference' (Wyschogrod 1986, p. 546).

all beings[23] – distinguishes Bloch's (secularised) eschatology from the visions of Eckhart, Böhme and Schelling, where the metaphysical finale announces the return of *Ruhe*, the peace of an original pleroma that rediscovers its lost harmony. Bloch's *Ultimum* is to be envisaged as 'without the metaphysical rest-in-peace of a mere being-at-the-end [*ohne metaphysische Pensionsruhe eines bloßen Am-Ende-Seins*]' and 'without the melancholy of fulfilment [*ohne Melancholie der Erfüllung*]'.[24] It will be full of life: the Great Life that finally came to itself, understands itself as Life and, because of that, no longer produces the shards of *natura naturata* destined for death. 'What has not yet appeared cannot pass in the same way as what has appeared; it is precisely to this core which has not yet appeared and remains exterritorial to death that the hopeful sentence *Non omnis confundar et non omne confunditur* [I will not perish wholly and nothing will] refers in its full cosmological sense'.[25]

As Johan Siebers points out, 'the *Ultimum* comprises a necessity of confrontation with death as the strongest anti-utopia'.[26] Indeed, the challenge of death is met by Bloch's ingenious theory of phenomenality. What does not appear cannot go the way of all appearances, the passive products of the appearing force [*das Erschienene*]; what stays *in potentia* [both potentiality and power] as *das Erscheinende* does not fall under the rule of becoming and perishing, which is the fate of all actualised reality. Juxtaposing these two Latin formulae – *Natura naturata nos ipsi erimus* and *Non omnis confundar* – we might say that there will arise a vision of a new nature as *natura naturans* without *natura naturata*, a new nature still energetic and full of life, yet now conscious of itself and thus remaining *für sich* – that is to say, for its own sake and not for sake of the natured products which are doomed to rise and perish. *Alles wird sein wie hier – nur ein klein wenig anders* [All will be the same, just slightly different]: this sentence from Bloch's *Spuren* [Traces, 1930] outlining the messianic process of a 'slight adjustment' implies that the new nature is not going to be a radically new creation.[27] Rather, it will be the same world, but in a different mode of

---

23 Here, Bloch might be following one of the Kabbalistic schools which imagined the life of the primordial Infinite, or *Ein-Sof*, as 'the joy, delight and pleasure – in Hebrew *schi'a-schu'a*', as Gershom Scholem puts it in 'Die Sprachtheorie Isaak des Blinden' (Scholem 1973, p. 53; my translation).
24 Bloch 1975, pp. 247 and 257.
25 Bloch 1975, p. 247. The German original reads: 'Was noch nicht erschienen ist, kann nicht so vergehen wie Erschienenes; auf dieses als unerschienener Kern zum Tod Exterritoriale bezieht sich der Hoffnungssatz: *Non omnis confundar et non omne confunditur*, auch und gerade kosmologisch'.
26 Siebers 2012, p. 584.
27 Bloch 2006, p. 158 (the fragment 'Invisible Hand'). On the same page, and with Gershom Scholem in mind, Bloch explains the miracle of the slight adjustment in the following way:

being – the mode that does not appear, which does not create appearances, objectifications and individual alienated *modi* of separate thing-like existence.

But is not 'the mystical fantasy of a new heaven and earth', in which matter undergoes the ultimate de-alienating transformation, in fact an oblique dream about the *destruction* of matter? The term 'apocalypsis', often used by Bloch, is inherently ambiguous precisely on this point: it is a prototype of all later variants of *schöpferische Zerstörung* [creative destruction], where total annihilation of the old becomes a necessary condition for the creation of the new. My suspicion is that Bloch wants to be like Hegel, a thinker of the evolution of being 'leading away' from its humble beginnings, but ends up like Schelling, who inverts the developmental process and ultimately affirms an *involution* of the material world as an error of creation, thus advocating a variant of the Gnostic *reversio* (even if Bloch tries to distance himself from the Schellingian *ultimum* in the 'rest-in-peace' model of a retired deity enjoying its eternal *Pensionsruhe*).[28] Hence, although Bloch is deliberately vague in his messianic prophecy of the humanisation of nature, he is nonetheless close to those thinkers who openly saw the Omega Point as the 'spiritualisation of matter'.[29] The idea of 'opening-up the cosmos, still closed to itself, to be our Home'[30] has a stronger ring of Gnostic-anamnetic homecoming to it than he would like to admit.

Part of the problem is that Bloch adheres to the doctrine of alienation and de-alienation, which constitutes one of the remnants of the asymmetrical metaphysics of the Fall, and hence *nolens volens* reproduces the theosophic motives of the Grand Return to the unspoiled pleromatic origin – what Scholem calls the 'retrospective utopia' of *restitutio in integrum*.[31] Although declaratively pro-evolution (in favour of the Omega Point) and against anamnesis (the nostalgic Alpha Stress), Bloch's system proves to be aporetically engaged with many residues of the metaphysics of radical asymmetry. The final transformation of matter conceals a secret dimension of destruction and de-

---

'Another rabbi, a true Kabbalist, once said: To bring about the kingdom of freedom, it is not necessary that everything be destroyed, and a new world begin; rather, this cup, or that bush, or that stone, and so all things must only be shifted a little. Because this "a little" is a hard thing to do, and its measure so hard to find, humanity cannot do it in this world; instead this is why the Messiah comes'.

28   On the Gnostic elements of Schelling's 'odyssey of the spirit' as a variant of the Valentinian *nostos* / homecoming, see Bielik-Robson 2019.

29   On the affinities between the Russian messianists and Bloch, all fervent readers of Dostoevsky, see Okłot 2016 and Smith 2010.

30   Bloch 2009, p. 255.

31   Scholem 1995a, p. 4.

alienation, suggesting a 'homecoming', even if to a home we never yet had: perhaps the ultimate matter will be able to know *what* it is, but will it be able to confirm *that* it is?

3 Against the 'Creation Myth': Persistent Marcionism

The main obstacle to Bloch's materialism seems to be his lifelong opposition to the 'creation-myth', an opposition which first manifested itself in his affirmative recovery of Marcion in *The Spirit of Utopia*, where this second-century Christian Gnostic was praised as the teacher of the God of Exodus as opposed to the God of Creation – a motif repeated almost verbatim in the much later *Atheism in Christianity*.[32] Bloch extolls Marcion as the first thinker to reinterpret Christianity in the Gnostic dualistic manner. Instead of the one God responsible for both creation and redemption, Marcion proposed the existence of two separate deities: the minor God of creation (called Archon Jehova), who made this irredeemably fallen material world of birth and decay, and the major God of redemption or Exodus (called Jesus), a wholly 'alien God' who comes from the outside to rescue the souls captured in the 'iron cage' of created reality. Yet is it possible to be materialist and Marcionite at the same time? Whereas it is relatively easy to see how a theological materialism might result from the creationist doctrine as a secularisation of the affirmative attitude towards the created material world (God's *ki tov*, 'and that was good'), it is rather more difficult to understand how any affirmation of matter might come out of the vehement rejection of the creation myth. Writing about the milieu of the Christian Gnostics, to which Marcion belonged, Bloch states: 'Here creation took the place of emanation, and instead of (or at least as well as) *evolutio* there was a break-through, an Exodus into the Utterly-new. In this scheme of things, however, *the one who created the world cannot be the same as the one who leads out of it again*: even the serpent-scapegoat did not relieve the mythical Creator of responsibility for his work'.[33] His hesitation expressed in the parenthesis is telling: while he wishes to stay faithful to the metaphysics of evolution, which is based on the affirmation of created matter, he also wants to retain the antagonistic elements of discontinuity, crisis and breakthrough, which are based on the Gnostic doctrine of Exodus out of created matter.

---

32 See Bloch 2009, pp. 173–80 ('Second Thoughts about the Exodus-Light: Marcion's Gospel of an Alien God Without This World').

33 Bloch 2009, p. 202; emphasis added.

Marcion provides Bloch with a lens through which he reads and appropriates all theologico-philosophical conceptions from Saint Paul to Marx. Even the way in which Bloch reads Isaac Luria's messianic Kabbalah is Marcionite: it is the very opposite of the Hegelian evolutionary appropriation of the doctrine of *tsimtsum* – the divine contraction – as a gentle withdrawal of the origin, which Hegel, as we have seen, interprets philosophically as 'the beginning pointing to something other'. Bloch's Marcionite dislike for the idea of the created world runs so deep that all he can see in God's contraction is a severe limitation, which he immediately associates with an imprisonment from which only a radical Exodus offers release. Thus, whereas Gershom Scholem in his account of the Lurianic Kabbalah accentuates the ambiguity present in the concept of *tsimtsum* (which on the one hand appears to condemn the world to a 'universal exile', yet on the other 'liberates creation' and sends it on its own evolutionary path),[34] Bloch interprets the *galut* [exile] motif in an unambiguously negative-Gnostic manner, rejecting any possible positive appraisal of the act of creation. The messianic God of Exodus has nothing to do with the God who 'imprisoned' himself and us and who is wrongly praised by 'the solemn hymn of Genesis':

> Even in later extended creation mysticism, which then in the Cabbala became a gnostic mysticism of emanation, the god of exodus and promise never lost the final power ... One of the greatest Cabbalists, Isaac Luria (1534–72), introduced the idea of exile even into the teaching of the creation itself and thereby changes it completely; *bereshith, the beginning, the word with which the Bible opens, thus became the beginning not of a creation but an imprisonment.* The world came into being as a contraction (*tsimtsum*) of God, is therefore a *prison from its origin*, is the captivity of Israel as of the spiritual sparks of all men and finally of Yahweh. Instead of the glory of the alpha or morning of creation, the wishful space of the end or day of deliverance presses forward; *it allied itself to the beginning only as to a primal Egypt which must be set aside.* Little though such ramifications

---

34 Bloch's interpretation of Luria stands in stark contrast to the 'Hegelian' reading of the Lurianic heritage offered by Scholem, notably in 'The Seventh Lecture: Isaac Luria and His School' in *The Major Trends of Jewish Mysticism* (Scholem 1995b, pp. 244–86). There, Luria is presented less as a fundamentally negative Gnostic than as a theosophic precursor of the dialectical method, which, instead of rigidly opposing no-being and being in a rigid antithesis, includes negativity into the evolutionary process of being. On the dialectical / positive interpretation of Luria's *tsimtsum*, see also Scholem 1976, p. 283: 'A being that is not God could only become possible and originate by virtue of such a contraction, such a paradoxical retreat of God into himself. By positing a negative factor in Himself, God liberates creation'.

of Mosaism accord with the solemn hymn of Genesis, they correspond precisely to the original God of exodus and the *Eh'je asher eh'je*, the God of the goal.[35]

I have evoked the difference between Bloch's and Scholem's readings of Isaac Luria for a purpose. My objection to Bloch draws heavily on Scholem's critique of Martin Buber's controversial use of Hasidic mysticism. Scholem famously charges Buber with the deliberate neutralisation of the annihilating moment for the sake of a visionary affirmation of the living world made of intense 'I and Thou' encounters. That is to say, where Buber sees the messianic intensification of Life *in* the world, Scholem detects an acosmic destruction and a mystical evacuation *out of* the world. Where Buber seeks affirmative pro-cosmic redemption, Scholem discovers only the apocalyptic fire, which destroys and redeems at the same time or, more precisely, which *redeems through destruction*. Where Buber senses a higher material mode of being, alive and free, Scholem sees no matter at all: while the material shards disappear, the sparks of spirit can be fully released from their carnal imprisonment and return to their pleromatic origin. By way of illustration, Scholem cites the following Hasidic story:

> The Baal Shem once asked an outstanding scholar about his relation to prayer: 'What do you do and where do you direct your thoughts when you pray?' He answered: 'I bind myself to everything of individual vitality which is present in all created things. For in each and every created thing there must be a vitality which it derives from the divine effluence. I unite with them when I direct my words to God in order by my prayer to penetrate the highest regions'. Then the Baal Shem said to him: '*If that is what you do, you destroy the world*, for in extracting its vitality and raising it to a higher level, you leave the individual created things without their vitality'.[36]

According to Scholem, Buber is the one who does not know that if he longs to extract the sparks of the Great Life from things, he also longs for the destruction of the world. Gnostic negativity, inherent in the idea of radical redemption / Exodus, cannot be easily eliminated. It remains an integral part of the doctrine which in its core was devised as anti-creationist and anti-cosmic:

---

35   Bloch 1986, vol. 3, p. 1237; emphasis added.
36   Scholem 1995a, p. 242.

The Hasidic authors obviously did not believe that they had in any way broken with the Gnostic tradition of the Kabbalah and, little as Buber wants to admit it, they wrote clearly and plainly as Gnostics ... The teaching of the uplifting of the sparks through human activity does in fact mean that there is an element in reality with which man can and should establish a positive connection, but the exposure or realization of this element simultaneously annihilates reality, insofar as 'reality' signifies, as it does for Buber, the here and now ... The Hassidics do not teach us to enjoy life as it is; rather, they advise us – better: demand of us – to extract, I am tempted to say distill, from 'life as it is' the perpetual life of God. But this is the salient point: the 'extraction' is an act of abstraction ... For precisely in that act in which we let the hidden life shine forth we destroy the here and now, instead of – as Buber would have it – realizing it in its full concreteness.[37]

Bloch seems to be trapped in a similar aporia. While he attempts to use – and simultaneously overcome – his Marcionite Gnosticism for the sake of material reality by facilitating its Exodus out of the creation myth towards the promised land of 'concrete utopia', he downplays the destructive moment of the messianic redemption. Just as Buber, he believes that he can neutralise the destruction of the world and transform it into a radical revolution of the material *modus essendi* that would realise matter in its full concreteness. But will this still be a mode of *being*, crowning the 'experiment of the world' – or will it rather be, as Scholem suggests, a mode of *non-being* resulting from the regressive withdrawal from the *experimentum mundi*? And is there a way in which these two modes can be told apart – to be, or not to be?

4   Metaphysics of Potentiality

It is precisely this aporetic double image – seemingly pro-cosmic, deep down anti-cosmic – which I now want to relate to Bloch's materialist manifesto, his work on the Aristotelian Left which constitutes the concluding part of the *Das Materialismusproblem, seine Geschichte und Substanz* [The Problem of Materialism: Its History and Substance, 1972], a series of lectures on which Bloch started to work as early as 1936. In Bloch's case, the apocalyptic ambivalence – the fluid zone of indeterminacy between redemption and annihilation –

---

37   Scholem 1995a, pp. 240–1.

seems even more troubling than in the case of Buber, who merely glosses over the destructive tendency inherent in the Hassidic 'earthly mysticism of everyday life'. Bloch actually sides with this tendency against the creation myth and *yet* insists on being a materialist: a speculative, mystical, Gnostic one, but a materialist all the same. It is therefore even more pertinent to ask of Bloch the questions Scholem asks apropos of Buber's selective use of Kabbalistic Gnosis: is the 'new heaven and earth' still heaven and earth or nothing at all? Is this a proleptic evolution which gradually works through the world of material actuality, or rather an involution to the state of 'being-in-possibility' which will no longer need any actualisation?

In Bloch's reading of the two representatives of the Aristotelian Left – Avicenna and Averroes – the 'leftist' inversion of the classical Aristotelian paradigm involves two major steps: first, granting the highest metaphysical privilege not to actuality but to potentiality, which instead of representing a merely passive principle, as it still does in Aristotle, now acquires prerogatives of active and creative potency; second, enriching the concept of matter according to the above transformation, which eventually leads to Avicebron's identification of God with matter and subsequently to Spinoza's *deus sive natura*. Bloch downplays the influence of *kalam* (Islamic theology) on Avicenna and Averroes, whom he would like to see as representatives of an almost secular *falsafa*, or philosophical wisdom, with the former giving rise to the Aristotelian Right and the latter to the Aristotelian Left. This, however, is a deliberate anti-theological misreading, for such a profound change of the category of potentiality would not have been possible without the theistic doctrine of extreme voluntarism grafted by *kalam* theologians onto the Aristotelian system.

Due to the fusion of these two very different horizons – a fusion brought about by the teaching of the first Mutasilites, the more rationalistically minded group of *kalam* thinkers – Aristotle's *Metaphysics* and the Abrahamic religion of God capable of voluntary creation were combined into a new system, which radically transformed the meaning of both *theion* and *hyle*.[38] In the former, the Unmoved Mover was the ultimate pure form, being in its highest actuality, but precisely because of that could not be conceived as a creator, as a *theion* capable of contemplating things in their not-yet actualised status of potentiality. Instead of making things new, he could only attract the other beings as constantly moving towards their perfect state of *entelechia*. In other words, it was the notion of voluntary creation that radically changed the picture, requiring as

---

38 On the *kalam* transformation of the concept of potentiality into sovereign form of potency and its later theologico-philosophical consequences, see Agamben 2000, especially pp. 245–53 ('The Scribe, or On Creation').

it did a transvaluation of the two principal Aristotelian categories – the primacy of potentiality/potency, now no longer passive but marking the highest 'capacity to act', over the static and already realised actuality. The Aristotelian Left subsequently projected the image of God as an omnipotent will onto matter as potentiality: the equivocation of Aristotle's *dynamis* – meaning both passive possibility and capacitating potency – became fused into the single and no longer ambiguous notion of the material, active substance, vividly creating new forms of being from within and, as Bloch would often emphasise, guided by a highly willed *Natursubjekt*, the subject that is nature: 'Now form does not remain external to matter, as the scholastics of the Right had taught, but rather: *matter and form, the capacity to become and the capacity to act, appear bound up in the same natura naturans*. If anything, they implicate themselves in a reciprocity in which the passive and the active potency ultimately collapse into one, according to their nature'.[39]

On Bloch's account, this deliberate ambiguation radically changes matter's ontological status: it is no longer seen as a passive receptacle that receives forms from beyond through an imprint or imposition (as, say, in Plato's *Timaeus*, where the Demiurge stamps the primal *hyle* with the eternal paradigms). Matter is now a medium and a message: it is inherently predisposed towards in-formation which it actively prepares in itself. All it needs is an awakening impulse, an *eductio formae* which, left to the initiative of the divine spirit or God's will, brings out and actualises a 'being-after-possibility' [*kata to dynaton*] out of the potential 'being-in-possibility' [*dynamei on*]. Eventually, however, even this last remnant of transcendence disappears, giving way to a fully immanentised form which, like Giordano Bruno's 'helmsman to the ship', works through and leads matter from within: 'As for us, we call it the "internal artificer", because it shapes matter, forming it from inside like a seed or root shooting forth and unfolding the trunk, from within the trunk thrusting out the boughs, from inside the boughs the derived branches, and unfurling buds from within these'.[40]

---

39 Bloch 2019, p. 65. Bloch often stresses the fortunate ambiguity of potence / potentiality, which was affirmatively embraced by the Aristotelian Left. By way of example, see p. 39 ('This occurs thanks to the sea change introduced by Avicenna, one that reveals the form of matter to be inherently both potential and potent, both potent and potential') and p. 54 ('Hence, Averroes, far from inscrutable equivocation, thoroughly embraced the passive-active double meaning of dynamis-matter. Precisely the specific "potency" of form development now pulsates within the general "potentiality" of matter and makes dynamis-matter the womb of the undeveloped yet maturing configurations of form').

40 Cited in Bloch 2019, p. 63; for the original, see Bruno 2004, p. 38.

Yet such promotion of potentiality/potency as the higher and now privileged mode of being is not without consequences, not least for the concept of the actual. In *kalam*, God is granted the absolute power, which is understood more in terms of potential ('what He can yet do') than in terms of actual achievement ('what He had already done').[41] Later, the nominalist scholastics directly influenced by Asharite *kalam* (the non-rationalistic theology hostile to the Mutasilite party) will define *potentia absoluta* solely as infinite potentiality and *oppose* it to actuality. Due to this theological reversal, the actual is demoted from the highest being of *I Am That I Am* (as in Thomas Aquinas, who remains much closer to the original Aristotelian tradition) to a 'hindrance', an obstacle on God's way to manifest His unbound *potestas*. While potentiality is promoted to the very essence of the divine, actuality is downgraded to the status of an obstacle in the form of being interested only in its self-preservation at the expense of the not-yet realised creative possibilities.

Bloch follows *kalam*-inspired nominalist theology when he states, in his conversation with Adorno, that 'there is a very clear interest that has prevented the world from being turned into the possible' and that 'the *hindering element* is also in the possible'.[42] Similarly, in his work on the Aristotelian Left – and while praising the Romantic artist for being capable of seeing into the dynamic living heart of *natura naturans* and disregarding the shards of *natura naturata* – Bloch writes:

> Fully in line with the tradition of pregnant form and painting toward the idea of liberating matter, one of [Gotthold Ephraim] Lessing's observations is apropos. The painter in [Lessing's 1772 play] *Emilia Galotti*, who brings the prince a commissioned painting, speaks Lessing's own

---

41 For instance, William Ockham, very much under the influence of Asharite *kalam*, says in *Quodlibeta* 'Deus multa potest facere quae non vult facere [God does not want to do many of the things He can do]', which Blumenberg interprets as an expression of the infinite rift between the always larger creation *in potentia* and the much more limited creation *in actualitas* (cf. Blumenberg 1985, p. 609). The Asharite/nominalist model of the divine potence/potentiality then travels via Reformed theology into the heart of secular modernity. It is at the heart of Nietzsche's will to power, which speaks of itself in Ockhamian idiom: 'Whatever I may create and however I may love it – soon I must oppose it and my love, thus my will wants it' (Nietzsche 2006, pp. 89–90). It also informs the idea of the Romantic genius, well articulated in Agamben's musings on Glenn Gould's genius of playing *as if not* playing: 'even though every pianist necessarily has the potential to play and the potential to not-play, Glenn Gould is ... the only one who can not not-play, and, directing his potentiality not only to the act but to his own impotence, he plays, so to speak, with his *potential to not-play*' (Agamben 2007, p. 35).

42 Bloch 1988, pp. 6 and 17; emphasis added.

thoughts and, indeed, in words that recall Aristotle, or rather Avicenna-Averroes: 'Art must paint the picture as Plastic Nature – *if there is such a thing* – imagined it: without the falling off that recalcitrant matter makes unavoidable, without the decay with which time attacks it'. The resistant matter is the material of 'what-is-after-possible', *taken as a disruption or constraint* [*Störung und Hemmung*]; the conjectured plastic nature, however, thinking its own image, this is the material of 'what-may-become-possible', which the artist further actualizes ... The modern artist thus now steps into the scene as both the liberating and perfecting force, such that he clearly and distinctly brings out, exposes, the shape of matter predisposed within matter.[43]

The actuality which is *nach-der-Möglichkeit* or *kata to dynaton* emerges both according to [*kata*] and after [*nach*] what is possible, by realising only one of the possible paths: once it is established in actual existence, it blocks the realisation of other alternatives. As the secondary effect of the potential, it is an objectified reality – the interest of which is to remain in its constituted form and in this manner repress the other possibilities by preventing them from coming to the ontological fore.

However, is such an *overestimation of possibility*, coupled with the *underestimation of actuality*, not a particularly worrying consequence for a materialist? If Neoplatonism suffers from an all too negative view of actual creation as merely privative, and if the Aristotelian Right demotes the material world to the role of ontological vassal, the Aristotelian Left – from Avicenna via Bruno to Bloch – does not appear to fare any better. By overestimating the material 'being-in-possibility' it turns the actual *natura naturata* into a mere negation of the former. 'Instead of the self-realization of many world-forms in matter itself, the pure active form rules on high, and its annex, the world, is at best a vassal'.[44] This objection, which Bloch levels against the Aristotelian Right, could actually be made of Bloch himself, whose declaratively pro-cosmic speculat-

---

43   Bloch 2019, pp. 43–4; emphasis added, translation modified (for the German original, see Bloch 1952, p. 76). Loren Goldman and Peter Thompson translate *kata to dynaton* as 'what-is-considered-possible', which reflects Bloch's subjective approach to the wilful aspect of *Natursubjekt* – a will to progress entangled in a conflict with the will to remain. I have reverted to Thompson's earlier suggestion to translate *kata* simply as *after*, both in terms of the temporal sequence (actuality *post* potentiality) and in terms of 'taking after' something as a model. In accordance with Bloch's nominalist tendency, the constituted actuality is no longer perceived as an active achievement (as in traditional Aristotelianism), but rather as a secondary effect, an epiphenomenon.
44   Bloch 2019, p. 25.

ive materialism may not be as welcoming to the *actual* material world as he believes. The world as a *vassal* is precisely what he is against, yet the sources he draws upon tend towards the world's vassalisation, albeit not in an explicit manner. Seemingly without a contrastive transcendence, immanence splits again according to the old hierarchical pattern: naturing nature detaches itself from natured nature, which appears as a deadened product of the vibrant *All-Leben* [All-Life], to be discarded as soon as it emerges.[45]

The idea that this creative matter may in fact *detest* any stable form which it itself produces and may wish to remain in its potentiality as 'an eternal womb of creation' – the pattern established by Valentinian Gnosticism, whereby Great Life rejects the 'affliction of the worlds' – appears in Giordano Bruno, whom Bloch praises for realising the full potential of the Aristotelian Left: 'Bruno's glowing naturalism, which brings Avicenna, Avicebron, and Averroes fully to the world, is so capacious that he even views the Aristotelian concept of the drive of matter toward form (as something molding its shape) as being inconsistent with the *autarchy of matter (as an eternal womb of creation)*'.[46] Bloch cites Bruno:

> [Matter] does not desire those forms which daily change on its back ... There is as little reason to say that matter desires form as that it hates it ... By the same line of reasoning, according to which it is said to desire what it sometimes receives or produces, it can also be said to abhor whatever it throws off or rejects. In fact, it detests more fervidly than it desires, for it eternally throws off that individual form after retaining it a very short while. The source of the forms cannot desire what is already within it, for one does not desire what one already possesses.[47]

---

45 The extreme form of such ontological oscillation can be found in Gilles Deleuze, whose speculative materialism in many ways resembles that of Bloch (even though Deleuze ultimately rejects the idea of a 'subject of nature'). Just as for Bloch, for Deleuze life must be a Great Life: pure, immediate, pleromatic, unmarked by alienation. Beneath the deadened, rigid, territorialised forms of life bound/imprisoned, there flows a life full and uncastrated, a pure unbound flux of constant self-overcoming and self-transformation which does not stand or rest even for a second and where 'everything springs up only to disappear immediately'. And while death is inscribed into the natured bound forms, the explosive 'pure fluxes of desire' belong to the 'sphere of virtuality', which is the pure living matrix of all actual life and as such a late avatar of the Gnostic/nominalist *potentia inordinata* (Deleuze 2004, p. 44).

46 Bloch 2019, p. 32; emphasis added.

47 Ibid. The original can be found in Bruno 2004, p. 86.

Having equated the finitude of natured nature with the death caused by the hatred of naturing nature towards any forming compulsion, Bruno is fully prepared to side with the infinite potentiality of the matter-womb, now detached from its products and no longer coerced to bring them forth in an actualised manner: the way they are already 'possessed' by matter's potentiality/potency ('possession' being yet another term belonging to the family of words centred round *potestas*) is sufficient in itself. To force the womb of matter to give birth to separate entities goes against the rule of matter's autarchy, which should allow matter to be what it is and as it is, with no pressure, which is always an external factor of discipline, imposed on the matter to produce beings. Bloch, however, is not entirely happy with such an outcome. Although he rejects the idea of the pressure from without – the disciplining divine rule extolled by the Aristotelian Right – he nonetheless expects matter to have a will and desire of its own, a will which will exercise an inner pressure, not allowing matter to rest on its laurels, as it were. In *Experimentum Mundi*, he articulates his dissatisfaction with Bruno in the following way: 'From the perspective of the philosophy of nature, there emerges a question: parallel to the working subject which produces a history, is there a subject of nature, which could be a motor of the dialectics of nature?'[48] The issue of *internalised pressure* – an idea that stands in stark contrast to Bruno's total autarchy of matter as the right to stay as a pure womb no longer obliged to give birth to forms – is crucial here. Thus enters *das Natursubjekt* [the subject that is nature], or *der Subjektkern der Natur* [the subject core of nature].

5 To Be and Not to Appear: *natura naturans* without *natura naturata*

Bloch cannot but reject Giordano Bruno's autarchy of matter. After all, to accept Bruno's immanentist naturalism of substance, which – as Hegel remarked apropos Spinoza – does not yet know the subject, would mean to abandon the ambition to 'finish the world'. Bloch only flags up this problem towards the end of his book, where he invokes the Hegelian dialectic as being able to transform the speculative materialism of the Aristotelian Left into a properly dialectical one whereby goal-orientated subjectivity emerges as one of the crucial forms educed from matter. Bloch views this *eductio formae* as a historical process which, though not simply teleological and not unproblematically progressive, is at least ordered temporally, evolving according to its 'objective

---

48   Bloch 1975, p. 218.

fantasy', which expresses the hidden desire of matter and which can come to the fore and become truly active only in the subjective forms of being, capable of carrying and kindling the spark. 'We and we alone, then, carry the spark of the end through the course ... And the spark is still open, full of unarbitrary, objective fantasy'.[49] The subject, therefore, in which the latent tendency of the humanisation of nature reaches its *Ultimum*, is a privileged form where matter achieves a higher level of plasticity, malleability and possibilisation. It is thus closer to the 'matter's utopia', in which it will have shed for good its previous mechanical appearance.[50] Writing about Bruno, Spinoza and their vitalist aftermath, Bloch states:

> And yet the human in the *natura naturans* is missing in it; the entire aspect of the labor and history that effects the progress of nature is missing; above all, character – limited by class status as well as the completed Pan of Pantheism – is missing: *an unfinished world* ... Therefore we can now say: Hegel is important because of the dialectical method (and everything connected with it), but Aristotle and his Left are important because of their concept of matter. Not only Hegel; the Aristotelian matter-concept and its radicalizing (penetrating to the roots) Avicenna-Bruno metamorphosis are alive in dialectically conceived materialism, an especially noteworthy ferment. They promote the development of the world-image, better yet, the true *meta*-physics of activity and hope, in contradistinction to the purely or impurely mechanical, that of stasis and the absence of qualities. Spirit, moreover, as the highest bloom of organic matter, would not be able to arise from it [that is to say, from matter] and transform existence if it were not required and called forth by it, thus, if it were not predisposed within it, and lastly, autochthon-

---

49 Bloch 2000, p. 227.
50 The complex relationship between the telos of history, the *Novum* and the *Ultimum* in Bloch's system is explained well by Johan Siebers: 'The *Novum* is only possible as an attempted *Ultimum* at the Front of history; the *Ultimum* is a new attempt of something that never yet existed and not a mere repetition of a lost origin ... At the end of his reflections on the notion of the *Ultimum*, Bloch uses the term "promised land": the realm of freedom – he says – is a "land promised by the process". By resorting to religious language, Bloch wants to emphasise that the relation between history and its end goal depends on the way it manifests itself in creation and on hopeful expectation rather than on effective or even teleological causality, even if it constantly calls for continuous revolutionary progress ... But the process itself does not produce the solution, and the end goal remains exterritorial to it. What mediates this paradox [of simultaneously effecting and *not* effecting the end goal – ABR] is, precisely, the category of hope' (Siebers 2012, pp. 583, 588).

ous ... Rather, the problem facing the Left Aristotelians, still unsatisfied, remains more pressing than ever: how, in material events and their forms, transformations are not to lose the Topos, in which colors as well as the qualities of things do not become corrupted, in which life, consciousness, the path of human history, and its creations have a place against and within this enormous inorganic background. In one gesture, we can say *that material utopia is not really a paradox, that dynamei-on matter implies a total concrete-utopian content, and we can hold its latent form as a foundation*. Avicenna and Averroes themselves, having unbound themselves and embraced transformation, had bestowed on their *eductio formarum ex materia* not only a hylozoist but also *hylokryphe*, thus latent form, an 'incomplete entelechy'. For all formations are attempts to shape the not yet-actualized treasury of matter itself – without an inert mechanical block standing against it and without a prime mover floating above it. This is, or rather this is helped by, *the speculative materialism of the Aristotelian Left, which is certainly not yet at its end, despite all its talk of the completed seventh day and its pantheistic claims that we have reached our final day of rest in the dynamei-on itself, as though Pan were both good and all that were needed*. Yet there is no way out of this closed system, in particular in its surplus dimensions: *eschatological profundity* cannot be fulfilled without Bruno and Spinoza, and without this other thing, namely, a conscience that is turned outward against both subjectivism and mechanistic dogma.[51]

This seems to be the crux of the *Materialismusproblem*, the problem of materialism itself: a triple intersection between mechanicism, whereby matter is perceived as a senseless *Klotz*, or lump, given over to external forces (at first the will of God and then the force-fields described by Newtonian science); Bruno's autarchic pantheism, which liberates matter from the necessity to produce forms; and Bloch's own subjective form of vitalism, which requires an almost personified concept of a willing *Natursubjekt*, coinciding with *natura naturans*, in order to guarantee the forward movement of matter [*Materie nach vorwärts*]. Bloch's solution, which emphasises the leading role of the *Natursubjekt*, avoids the extreme positions of mechanicism and Bruno's pan-vitalism by fostering the vision of the spirit as internalised by matter, intrinsic to its own desire. In *The Principle of Hope*, Bloch insists that one should not approach the subject of nature as something 'psychical prior to *natura naturata*', but rather as a 'creat-

---

51   Bloch 2019, pp. 65–7; emphasis added.

ive form of matter' deriving from the teaching of Averroes.[52] At the same time, however, such decisive subjectivisation of matter tends to dissolve all the hard contours of material existence, leaving us with a living flux, dangerously reminiscent of the *materia spiritualis* from Plotinus's *Enneads*.[53] What, then, happens with matter when it becomes so thoroughly 'subjectivised' and 'humanised'?

Let us have another look at the 'promised land' of the *Ultimum / Omega Point* against the backdrop of Bloch's emphasis on *Natursubjekt* or *natura naturans*. If this is the *hylokryphe* [the ultimate, latent tendency of universal matter], then material history would indeed resemble a kind of a Schellingian odyssey, where creation – the emergence of beings as *natura naturata* – constitutes only one passing episode in the circuitous journey of the spirit returning to itself, to a restful eternity (Bruno's 'eternal womb of creation') no longer disturbed by the necessity to create. Despite all Bloch's declarations to the contrary, the Gnostic anamnetic pattern of homecoming, heavily present in Schelling, dominates the scene of the 'seventh day': the goal which is to *heal* God / matter-womb / *natura naturans* from the erroneous desire to create asserts itself in Bloch, too. Granted, it is not the *anamnesis* of a straightforward *restitutio in integrum* as a simple return to the once wounded and now healed pleroma of pure poten-

---

52 'In this stratum therefore, in the materially most immanent one that exists at all, lies the truth of that which is described as the subject of nature. Just as the old concept of *natura naturans*, which first of all signified a subject of nature, is of course still half-mythical ... but by no means posits (in an idealistic way) a psychological element as prior to *natura naturata*. On the contrary, the concept of *natura naturans* was from the very beginning, from its originator, the "naturalist" Averroës onwards, applied to creative matter. Even if the remnants of mythology cited above are not lacking, which may return as a pantheistic bogeyman, and which have long accompanied the problem of the subject of nature at least as a secularized Isis' (Bloch 1986, vol. 2, pp. 673–4).

53 Writing about Avicebron's *materia universalis*, a concept that led him to equate God with matter, Bloch rightly derives it from Plotinus: 'Thus Avicebron's highest matter composes itself within universal matter: the *materia spiritualis*, taken directly from Plotinus, namely his *hyle noetike*, spiritual or intelligible matter (*The Enneads* 2.4.1–5), high above, with the One. *In Plotinus's system of emanations, from the One down into the darkness of common matter, the very principle of matter he otherwise vilifies is surprisingly ennobled.* This happened because matter became linked with the second-highest thing in Plotinus's world, *nous*, or World Spirit, and so, in the heavenly sphere, lay at the feet of the Highest, the One. And indeed, this was accompanied by the emphatically positive reversal of its absolutely miserable connotation in the lowest world: to be an empty, dark abyss. *Precisely this emptiness, impersonal and without quality, could serve as a foil to the most sublime emptiness, qualityless, impersonal, of the One*' (Bloch 2019, p. 57; emphasis added). Clearly, Bloch is convinced that by emphasising the idea of spiritual matter, itself marginal and ambivalent in Plotinus's system, he is already rescuing the materialist element in the Neoplatonic scheme of emanation. It is precisely on this point that I disagree.

tiality. Rather, as in Schelling, where the spirit eventually comes to itself by recognising its nature and thus finding its home, Bloch outlines an odyssey of matter which in the end comes to itself and recognises its nature in (as Blake puts it) energy as eternal joy, forever liberated from the error of self-misprision from which results nothing but failure, futility and nullity: *Scheitern, Umsonst, Nichts*.[54] Just as Schelling's God, emerging out of the unconscious into self-consciousness, goes through the ordeal of creation, so does Blochian matter go through the still unconscious 'ferment' of producing *natura naturata*, which in the end turns out to be merely a hindrance and an obstacle, *Störung und Hemmung*, not being proper. And just as in Schelling the creation of worldly material existence is but a transitional error, so is in Bloch – in spite of misleading materialist phrases such as 'turn to the worldly' – the World as Actualised only a 'betrayal' of potentiality, 'detested' by the active forces of *natura naturans* and thus destined to perish.

Bloch's *die Realisierung des Realisierenden* [the realisation of the realising], in which the *experimentum mundi* culminates, cannot therefore be understood as Aristotelian *Aktualisierung* [actualisation]. Rather, it is an expression of potentiality/potency *as such*. It is *das Realisierende* without the passive result of *das Realisierte*, a power which no longer exhausts itself in any external production that betrays its living energetic nature. The *dies novissima* of the *ultima materia* is conceived here as the messianic day of pure *natura naturans*, which will have finally recognised the error of self-objectification and learned the mode of being just *für sich*, for itself and for its own sake. In spite of Bloch's appeal to the Hegelian-Marxist dialectic and the *Natursubjekt*, this vision does not really differ from the one painted by Bruno: the 'seventh day' is indeed the day of matter's independence, on which it is finally allowed to return to the state of autarchy as an eternal womb of creation.[55]

Bloch is adamant in emphasising that the *Ultimum* does not entail a standstill or a 'rest in peace' of being at its end. On the contrary, it is pure *Bewegung*,

---

54 Bloch 1972, p. 469.
55 Since, for Bloch, art is the best approximation of the concrete utopia in its attempt to portray *natura naturans* only, it is quite possible that he would find it best 'embodied' (if this is the right word) in Kazimir Malevich's principles of suprematism, laid out in his manifesto-painting *White on White* (1918). If, for Agamben, Glenn Gould is the perfect musician who plays *as if* he were not playing, Malewicz is the perfect painter who paints *as if* he were not painting, allowing the Gnostic-iconoclastic tradition to find a paradoxical iconic expression. The white square which comes forward from the white background in an almost imperceptible manner represents a creative potentiality / potency, which refuses to be fully actualised. This affinity between suprematism and Bloch's 'Gnosticism of the Left' was first noticed by Michael Pauen; see Pauen 1994.

the movement of matter liberated from all *Störungen* [hindrances], slowing down its free *Gärung* [fermentation] now 'without limits'. As Bloch puts it in his *Tübinger Einleitung in die Philosophie*, 'there are no limits to this self-activating possibility. Always new shapes come from the forming material womb, from the matter which, as a Substance, remains conditioned, but as possibility is limitless and inextinguishable'.[56] There will therefore be no 'completion' [*Gelungenheit*] crowned by absolute peace. Rather, what we are dealing with – Bloch maintains – is the liberation of the process itself which, freed from the necessity to actualise itself in a reified manner, will have obtained perfect spontaneity.[57] And if the matter's spirit of utopia incarnates itself best in the human spirit and its Marxian readiness to change the world, it is also the 'self-consciousness of the working man' that allows the closest approximation of the will driving the *Natursubjekt* or *natura naturans* of the *Materie nach vorwärts*. Work, after Marx, should no longer be conceived as a *homo faber* activity, orientated towards the production of external things that merely add to and perpetuate the view of matter as *ein ahistorischer Klotz*, an unhistorical lump.[58] Rather, it should be a transformation of nature, fusing with its most progressive fluid tendencies from within. Once again elaborating on Marx's double prophesy – humanisation of nature, naturalisation of man – Bloch writes:

> In history it is the self-consciousness of historical actors as working people, whereas in nature it is the realisation of that which was hypothetically called *natura naturans* or the subject of material movement, which constitutes a problem that until now has hardly even been touched upon, although it clearly belongs to the expectation comprised in Marx's slogan of the 'humanisation of nature'.[59]

---

56 Bloch 1970, p. 232. The German reads: 'der so sich aktivierenden Möglichkeit sind keine Grenzen gesetzt. Immer neue Gestalten kamen und kommen aus dem bildenden materiellen Schoß, aus der Materie als dem Substrat stets bedingter, doch noch nie begrenzter, erschöpfter Möglichkeiten'.

57 The liberation of the *Natursubjekt* / *natura naturans* from the necessity to create is, perhaps, the only solution to the otherwise aporetic vision of the *Ultimum*, which Bloch himself sees as extended between 'the crucial pair of concepts: *Novum* – Completion (finished becoming, peace)' (Bloch 1972, p. 116). In his discussion of Bloch's concept of *spekulativer Materialismus*, Hans Heinz Holz also points to this aporia; see Holz 2012, p. 507.

58 Bloch 1970, p. 227.

59 Bloch 1972, p. 235. The German original reads: 'In der Geschichte ist sie die Selbstergreifung des geschichtlichen Täters, als des arbeitenden Menschen; *in der Natur ist sie die Verwirklichung dessen, was man hypothetisch natura naturans oder Subjekt der materiellen Bewegung genannt hat*, ein noch kaum berührtes Problem, obwohl es ... in der Verlängerungslinie der Marxschen "Humanisierung der Natur" liegt'; italics added.

In the Omega Point, therefore, *actus purus* and *materia ultima* – the two concepts that Bloch borrows from the Thomistic scholastics – should finally coincide, as Hans Heinz Holz correctly observes: 'Only in the *materia ultima* – the eschatological frontier concept – the modes finally coincide, matter and form become one, and essence and appearance are identical'.[60] Indeed, one way of understanding this coincidence is to see form as so intrinsic to matter that it no longer forces matter to appear as formed, as no longer a step forward in the series of natured products. Just as Agamben's *forma-di-vita* [form-of-life] is to such a degree internal to life that it is no longer disciplining and rigidifying the spontaneous living flux,[61] Bloch's 'form-of-matter' will be so perfectly fused with the material substance that it will no longer generate alienated results. Once all the remnants of the *eductio* of matter from without and above are removed – from God's creative *fiat* to the demiurgic making of forms out of passive matter – the only material way of being will consist in an infinite and uninhibited *eductio* or *Hervorbringen*, forming strictly from within and hence without the alienating effect of isolated appearances. The true meaning of *nos ipse erimus* – the final, prophetic phrase of *Experimentum Mundi* – is therefore: *to be and not to appear*.

But what does this really mean? Is it at all possible to be and *not* to appear, especially if our ambition is to construct a pro-cosmic materialist metaphysics, which would no longer resort to the concept of the spiritual Absolute, as in the case of the Gnostic Great Life? Even if we are willing to ignore the aporias intrinsic to Bloch's concept of the *Ultimum* and grant it metaphysical validity, we still cannot be sure of *what matter really wants* or what the true content of its 'objective phantasy' is: the question remains as 'dark' as the living moment of our present *ich bin* [I am], which Bloch describes in the opening section of *The Spirit of Utopia*. Is the *hylokryphe* – the hidden tendency of matter – tinged with the Gnostic *reversio*, which dreams about *natura naturans* without *natura naturata*, without the compulsion to create? Does, deep down, in its deepest latent tendency, matter dream of its own redemptive annihil-

---

60 Holz 2012, p. 503.
61 See above all Agamben 2013, where the Franciscan 'perfect life' is derived from the same progressive scholastic formation advancing the notion of *natura naturans* and the world's immanent vitality. This affinity also demonstrates that Bloch, despite his reservations with regard to Bruno's autarchy of matter, remains captivated by the latter's idea of matter refusing to step out of the mode of potentiality. Yet whereas for Agamben such refusal – the gesture of Herman Melville's Bartleby ('I would prefer not to') – allows for a relaxed regression into a state of *impotenza*, for Bloch it only announces an intensification of the power / potency aspect of *natura naturans*, which can finally achieve a status of pure 'unbound' energy, unhindered by its 'bound' product limitations.

ation, the way it was envisaged by Scholem? Habermas's characterisation of Bloch as a 'Marxist Schelling' would then appear to be apt if taken to be pointing to the Schellingian therapeutic scheme underlying Bloch's philosophy of process, but arguably wrong in attributing to Bloch a genuinely Marxian materialism.[62]

So perhaps, in spite of his investment in Marx's and Engels's dialectical and speculative materialism, with which he sought to overcome his early spiritual leanings, Bloch is not a materialist at all. Perhaps his attempt at self-correction failed, his later *failing-better* compromise of a *Gnostic materialism* – the transformation of the Marcionite hatred against the creation myth into a rejection of *natura naturata* – remaining one of the most fascinating yet simultaneously impossible figures of late modern metaphysics. Hence, if one of the most significant metaphysical mutations responsible for the modern turn towards the worldly is the one observed by Agamben in Heidegger's self-correction – a seemingly innocuous shift from a total asymmetry to an equally perfect symmetry in the relation between Being and beings – then Bloch does not participate in this change. In spite of all his criticisms of Neoplatonism and the Aristotelian Right, he still maintains a fundamentally hierarchical asymmetry between *natura naturans* and *natura naturata*, which renders the speculative-materialist concept of a 'vibrant matter' one-sided. Instead of overcoming Gnosticism, Bloch merely transposes the asymmetrical relation between the Great Life and the afflicted worlds, the life spiritual and the life material, onto the plane of matter itself.

But what if matter is what it *is*, not at all that vibrant, as well as what it *could be*, and not so mechanistically determined either? If so, then the elimination of the former, not-so-vibrant aspect would mean simply the elimination of matter itself: the ultimately desired humanisation of nature would lead to the disappearance of nature. To put things as simply and succinctly as possible, Bloch seeks to distinguish the concept of matter from its mechanistic reduction – but what if this attempt goes too far and what we are left with in the end is no longer materialism, but just idealist speculation?

As in the case of all Jewish messianists plagued by the Gnostic syndrome – and Bloch is definitely one of them – the apocalyptic destruction of the world and the redemption of the world form a zone of fluid indeterminacy. This moment of indeterminacy is captured well by Catherine Moir in her otherwise sympathetic account of Bloch's position:

---

62 See Habermas 1969/70, pp. 324–5.

The mistake of physicalism, according to Bloch, is to reduce matter to simple *Klotzmaterie*, inert, passive, and static: simply there. Indeed, in Bloch's speculative materialism *there is no meaningful sense in which matter is "there" at all*, except as "incomplete precisely in its there-ness". The point is rather that if we conceive of the fundamental unity of reality as radical potentiality, as Bloch does, *the philosophical distinction between the material and the ideal all but dissolves*.[63]

Following in the footsteps of Scholem, Jacques Derrida identified the fatal error of the religious Absolute that also characterises the Gnostic syndrome: the mistake of loving life so much that nothing actually living appears worthy of being called properly living apart from the absolute Great Life which, precisely because it is now deprived of any negativity, is no longer a life.[64] This is the very flaw that is at the heart of Bloch's treatment of matter, which attempts to eliminate everything negative, most of all death, the entropic factor of anti-utopia: by trusting in matter's vital Real-Potential, Bloch rejects all the elements of material existence that inhibit the utopian process as belonging to *der schädliche Raum* [the obstructing realm], so that, ultimately, he ends up with nothing but pure spirit. If Derrida is right, then all the negative features of the Fall that appear in Bloch's system – alienation, exile, dispersion, the inertial lumpness of the *Klotzmaterie* – are the indispensable attributes of material being as such, which 'certainly contains also failure, futility, nullity'[65] and last, but not least, death. For 'what has no shadow has no strength to be'.

Bibliography

Adorno, Theodor W. 2001, *Metaphysics: Concepts and Problems*, translated by Edmund Jephcott, London: Polity Press.

Agamben, Giorgio 2000, *Potentialities*, translated by Danie Heller-Rozen, Stanford: Stanford University Press.

Agamben, Giorgio 2007, *The Coming Community*, translated by Michael Hardt, Minneapolis: The University of Minnesota Press.

Agamben, Giorgio 2013, *The Highest Poverty: Monastic Rules and Form-of-Life*, translated by Adam Kotsko, Stanford: Stanford University Press.

---

63   Moir 2013, p. 134; emphases added.
64   See Bielik-Robson 2018, 79–94, where I explain Derrida's deconstructionist argument in detail.
65   Bloch 1972, p. 469.

Agamben, Giorgio 2015, *The Use of Bodies: Homo Sacer IV/2*, translated by Adam Kotsko, Stanford: Stanford University Press.

Augustine 2011, *De Civitate Dei*, Charleston: Nabu Press.

Bielik-Robson, Agata 2018, 'Religion of the Finite Life? Messianicity and the Right to Live in Derrida's Death Penalty Seminar', *Political Theology*, 19, 2: 79–94.

Bielik-Robson 2019, *'The Story Continues* ... Schelling and Rosenzweig on Narrative Philosophy', *International Journal of Philosophy and Theology*, 80, 1–2: 127–42.

Bloch, Ernst 1952, *Avicenna und die Aristotelische Linke*, Frankfurt am Main: Rütten und Loening.

Bloch, Ernst 1970, *Tübinger Einleitung in die Philosophie*, Frankfurt am Main: Suhrkamp.

Bloch, Ernst 1972, Das Materialismusproblem, seine Geschichte und Substanz, Frankfurt am Main: Suhrkamp.

Bloch, Ernst 1975, Experimentum Mundi. Frage, Kategorien des Herausbringens, Praxis, Frankfurt am Main: Suhrkamp.

Bloch, Ernst 1986 [1954–9], *The Principle of Hope*, 3 Volumes, translated by Neville Plaice, Stephen Plaice and Paul Knight, Cambridge, Mass.: MIT Press.

Bloch, Ernst 1988, 'Something Missing: A Discussion between Ernst Bloch and Theodor W. Adorno on the Contradictions of Utopian Longing', translated by Jack Zipes and Frank Mecklenburg, in *Utopian Function of Art and Literature: Selected Essays*, Cambridge, MA.: MIT Press.

Bloch, Ernst 2000 [1918; 2nd, extended ed. 1923], *The Spirit of Utopia*, translated by Anthony Nassar, Stanford: Stanford University Press.

Bloch, Ernst 2006 [1930], *Traces*, translated by Anthony Nassar, Stanford: Stanford University Press.

Bloch, Ernst 2009 [1968], *Atheism in Christianity: The Religion of the Exodus and the Kingdom*, translated by J.T. Swann, London: Verso.

Bloch, Ernst 2019 [1952], *Avicenna and the Aristotelian Left*, translated by Loren Goldman and Peter Thompson, New York: Columbia University Press.

Blumenberg, Hans 1985 [1966], *The Legitimacy of the Modern Age*, translated by Robert M. Wallace, Cambridge, Mass.: MIT Press.

Bruno, Giordano 2004 [1584], *Cause, Principle and Unity: Essays on Magic*, translated by Richard J. Blackwell, Cambridge: Cambridge University Press.

Deleuze, Gilles 2004, *Desert Islands and Other Texts 1953–74*, translated by Michael Taormina, Los Angeles and New York: Semiotext(e).

Derrida, Jacques 2005, 'Epoche and Faith', in *Derrida and Religion: Other Testaments*, edited by Yvonne Sherwood and Kevin Hart, New York: Routledge.

Habermas, Jürgen 1969/70, 'Ernst Bloch – A Marxist Romantic?', *Salmagundi*, 10–1: 311–25.

Hegel, Georg Wilhelm Friedrich 2010, *The Science of Logic*, translated by George di Giovanni, Cambridge: Cambridge University Press.

Holz, Hans Heinz 2012, 'Spekulativer Materialismus', in *Bloch-Wörterbuch. Leitbegriffe der Philosophie Ernst Blochs*, edited by Beat Dietschy, Doris Zeilinger and Rainer E. Zimmermann, Berlin and Boston: de Gruyter, 483–507.

Jonas, Hans 2001, *The Gnostic Religion: The Message of the Alien God and the Beginnings of Christianity*, Boston: Beacon Press.

Lazier, Benjamin 2012, *God Interrupted: Heresy and the European Imagination between the World Wars*, Princeton, NJ: Princeton University Press.

Moir, Catherine 2013, 'The Education of Hope: On the Dialectical Potential of Speculative Materialism', in *The Privatization of Hope: Ernst Bloch and the Future of Utopia*, edited by Peter Thompson and Slavoj Žižek, Durham: Duke University Press.

Mondin, Battista 1963, *The Principle of Analogy in Protestant and Catholic Theology*, New York: Springer.

Nancy, Jean-Luc 1997, *The Sense of the World*, translated by Jeffrey S. Librett, Minneapolis: University of Minnesota Press.

Nietzsche, Friedrich 2006, *Thus Spoke Zarathustra: A Book for All and None*, translated by Adrian Del Caro and Robert Pippin, Cambridge: Cambridge University Press.

Okłot, Michał 2016, 'Apocalypse Left and Right: Bloch's and Rozanov's Renunciation of the Future', *Poetics Today*, 37: 387–413.

O'Regan, Cyril 2001, *The Gnostic Return in Modernity*, Buffalo, NY: SUNY Press.

Pauen, Michael 1994. *Dithyrambiker des Untergangs. Gnostizismus in der Ästhethik und Philosophie der Moderne*, Berlin and Boston: de Gruyter.

Pollock, Benjamin 2012, 'On the Road to Marcionism: Franz Rosenzweig's Early Theology', *Jewish Quarterly Review*, 102, 2: 224–55.

Pollock, Benjamin 2014, *Franz Rosenzweig's Conversions: World Denial and World Redemption*, Bloomington: Indiana University Press.

Scholem, Gershom 1973, *Judaica 3. Studien zur jüdischen Mystik*, Frankfurt am Main: Suhrkamp.

Scholem, Gershom 1976, *On Jews and Judaism in Crisis: Selected Essays*, edited by Werner Dannhauser, New York: Schocken Books.

Scholem, Gershom 1995a, *The Messianic Idea in Judaism and Other Essays in Jewish Spirituality*, New York: Schocken Books.

Scholem, Gershom 1995b, *The Major Trends of Jewish Mysticism*, New York: Schocken Books.

Siebers, Johan 2012, 'Das Ultimum', in *Bloch-Wörterbuch. Leitbegriffe der Philosophie Ernst Blochs*, edited by Beat Dietschy, Doris Zeilinger and Rainer E. Zimmermann, Berlin and Boston: de Gruyter.

Smith, Oliver 2010, *Vladimir Solovyev and the Spiritualization of Matter*, Boston: Academic Studies Press.

Taubes, Jacob 2006, *Der Preis des Messianismus. Briefe von Jacob Taubes und Gershom*

Scholem und andere Materialien, edited by Elettra Stimili, Würzburg: Königshausen & Neumann.

von Harnack, Adolf 1924. *Marcion: Das Evangelium vom fremden Gott. Eine Monographie zur Geschichte der Grundlegung der katholischen Kirche*, Leipzig: J.C. Heinrichs'sche Buchhandlung.

Wyschogrod, Edith 1986, 'Crossover Dreams', *Journal of the American Academy of Religion*, 54: 543–7.

CHAPTER 3

Art, History and the Language of Death: Bloch's *The Spirit of Utopia* between Hegel and Derrida

Ivan Boldyrev

In his *Derrida, an Egyptian* – a long obituary framed as a historical contextualisation – Peter Sloterdijk invokes Ernst Bloch as having put forward a messianic hermeneutics of dreams. According to Sloterdijk, the founding figure of this hermeneutics is the biblical Joseph, the Jewish outcast in Egypt, the chosen one who is at the same time hated for his gift and condemned to marginality. As an interpreter of dreams, Joseph, as depicted by Thomas Mann, blends into Freud, and Sloterdijk casts Derrida in a similar role: that of someone coming from a different land – in his case, Algeria – and gaining widespread recognition for being able to decipher what remains incomprehensible to others. Derrida the philosopher is an Egyptian because he follows Freud in searching for radical otherness within cultural forms; that is to say, for something that those forms seek to suppress, which yet persists irreducibly within them as their secret element, just as Egypt remained with the Jews even after they believed they had left it behind following the Exodus.

Sloterdijk, then, characterises Derrida's critical project as *Egyptian*, though he adds a striking twist: '"Egyptian" is the term for all constructs that can be subjected to deconstruction – except for the pyramid, that most Egyptian of edifices. It stands in its place, unshakeable for all time, because its form is nothing other than the undeconstructible remainder of a construction that, following the plan of its architect, is built to look as it would after its own collapse'.[1] In other words, Sloterdijk describes Derrida as an interpreter who ultimately still wishes to see *something that he is unable to deconstruct further*, something that resists even his own, most destructive reading.

How does Bloch fit into this scheme? For Sloterdijk, Bloch's hermeneutics is situated somewhere in between Freud and Derrida; that is to say, in between what Sloterdijk calls the first and third waves of dream interpretation. Freud's *Moses and Monotheism* demonstrates the ambiguous persistence of the Egyptian among the Jews in spite of their desire to rid themselves of Egypt and reach

---

1 Sloterdijk 2009, p. 27.

the Promised Land. Derrida radicalises this psychoanalytic reading by showing 'how the signs of *being* never provide the wealth of meaning they promise'.[2] Bloch – Sloterdijk believes – is preoccupied with 'a mass interpretation [that is, an interpretation focused on the masses rather than on representatives of an elite] of dreams', whereby 'the proletarian and traditional dreams of a better life [are] elevated to a political productive force'.[3] He makes *traces* – the almost imperceptible elements of the past and the present – legible in the light of a future utopia, the communist society to come.

In what follows, I will try to show that Bloch's early philosophy provides – in the same seemingly unmotivated way that Bloch intrudes into Sloterdijk's text – a new perspective on the issues discussed by Derrida reading Hegel and in turn read by Sloterdijk. These issues concern above all the power of critical reading and the resistance to it. I will address them by exploring the role that imagery related to Egypt and its past plays in Bloch's *The Spirit of Utopia*, as well as the question of how, in this light, we can read the great *monument of the past* that is speculative dialectics, with Hegel as its architect.

1 The Spirit of Utopia: *Inwardness and Petrification in the World Tearing Apart*

It is not simply my arbitrariness as a reader that brings these thinkers together. The arguments and metaphors employed in Bloch's first major book, *The Spirit of Utopia*, are inspired by Hegel and are similar to those invoked by Derrida and Sloterdijk. Not least, Egypt figures prominently in these early aesthetic and political reflections by Bloch. The book's starting point – 'The Production of the Ornament', its first extended chapter – is a discussion of modern art and the different ways in which it can be organised. Here, Bloch discusses the fundamental – and, as he sees it, near irreconcilable – opposition '[b]etween … constructions pretending to be art by sliding over into the monumental or Egyptian, and something entirely different coming due in our time: purely spiritual, musical expression that aspires to be *ornament*'.[4] He thus juxtaposes the dead, unchanging forms of aesthetic and political conservatism with a possible symbolic alternative: *construction* versus *ornament*. At issue is not what is often called highbrow art, but *Kunstgewerbe* – 'applied art', something produced for

---

2 Ibid. Italics added.
3 Sloterdijk 2009, p. 25.
4 Bloch 2000, p. 14. All references are to the English translation based on the final, definitive version of Bloch's book.

the everyday life of large collectives, accompanying the bodies and souls of the many. Hence, we are already moving beyond the dreams of the Pharaoh, deciphered by Joseph, to Sloterdijk's second wave of dream interpretation.

Bloch proposes a radical separation of technique and expression, a separation that should release the energies of the new ornamental art. Machine, technique and mechanism are too formal to grasp the interior reality of subjectivity. Anticipating Bloch's call for two Marxist streams,[5] this idea means maximum *unburdening*, the subordination of the *lower needs* to the perfectly rational technical structures and unleashing the inner and inward for the most sublime aims of the art to come. Bloch concedes that traditional ornamentality all too often served as a way to over-stabilise the soul – that is, subjectivity – and to degrade applied art to 'wealthy, feudal, theocratic, pontifical luxury'.[6] Applied art tended to decorate, and hence hide, political stasis. What is needed, therefore, is not a 'stagnant carpet', but a new, true carpet 'pointing beyond' the present towards 'the possibility of an anti-luxurious [that is to say, a non-contemplative, politically activist] Expressionism'.[7]

Bloch then proceeds to develop what amounts to a full-blown reconsideration of the entire history of art. His narrative is not constructed as a logical argument. Rather, it is a speculative survey – supported by bold claims and a remarkable intensity of imagery – of the development of Western aesthetic sensibility and of absolute spirit, of which it is a moment. Unlike Hegel, however, whose aesthetics moves from the 'symbolic' via the 'classical' to the 'romantic' epoch, Bloch begins with classical art. Yet the logic of his presentation seems to follow another triad – namely, the joyful fullness of life, followed by death and resurrection.

Greek art and the Greek way of life are interpreted as being too superficial, as not able to counter the *Ernstfall* [the moment of crisis], not equal to the task of confronting the deadly seriousness of the historical *kairos*.[8] In Bloch's account, Greek art is simply not revolutionary enough in its attempt to produce harmony and equilibrium. It stays *horizontal*, faithful to the symmetry and serenity of

---

5   In *Heritage of Our Times* (1935), Bloch distinguishes between a sober, *cold-stream* Marxism, which provides the analytics of capitalist factuality, and a utopian, *warm-stream* Marxism aimed at formulating visions of the future and transcending the given social, political and aesthetic order. Both types of Marxism, he argues, are needed: each would be directionless without the other.
6   Bloch 2000, p. 17.
7   Bloch 2000, pp. 17, 13. Cf. Benjamin Korstvedt's extensive commentary on Bloch's notion of the carpet as an artwork going beyond the limitations of mere functionality and abstract transcendence (Korstvedt 2010).
8   Cf. Bloch 2000, p. 20, and Bloch 1964, p. 32.

pure aesthetic satisfaction. Bloch calls Greek style (as well as its later Renaissance incarnation) *indecisive*: it lacks the political energy of decision, fleeing instead into (bad) utopian worlds of plastic beauty and security. He finds this style unacceptable in its blissfulness and merely 'epidermal' organicity, which can never experience the mystery of inner life.[9]

Bloch's critique makes it clear how strongly interconnected aesthetics, politics, philosophy and hermeneutics are in his work. His early notion of utopia underpins, and is in its turn underpinned by, a political activist reading of art history. While describing and evaluating the succession of art forms, he reads history and politics as the awakening of a new utopian *subjectivity* – the 'soul' – and as energy set free in the final struggle of aesthetic styles.

Bloch inverts the standard chronological order by making what he terms Egyptian 'constructedness' the next step of the argument. But he also interprets this approach to art – and indeed to life as whole – as an *ever-present danger to any aesthetic form*. This danger consists in the temptation of complete externalisation, the production of *das völlige Außen*: 'Man ... sees his future here, but sees himself dying, hides himself in the grave'.[10] What the Egyptians produce is the restatement of their pervasive fear of death by literally setting it in stone and silencing inner life. Their art is *the volition to become like stone*. This stone, which is the pyramid, conceals – as a huge grave – not the interiority of the soul, but rather something dead. In this 'most uncanny chamber' one sees not life's intensity (a word Bloch associates with the power of subjectivity), but rather the contrast to the overwhelming static splendour of Ra. Death envelops death and conceals nothing else.[11] The movement of Egyptian art is the movement outwards and, at the same time, of 'the mastery of death' – of Hegel's 'absolute master'.[12]

'Only Christian life truly breaks through the stone'.[13] Bloch frames the move away from Egyptian art forms as an Exodus towards Christian art, which has as 'its sole, foundationally *a priori* object the now still loose and flowing ornamentation and signature of the immediate human being'.[14] He synthesises the various forms of Gothic art, but also – somewhat problematically – of African art and Nordic art, into an 'endless line' which acquired, with Christianity, a

---

9 Bloch 2000, p. 23.
10 Bloch 2000, p. 20; cf. Bloch 1964, p. 32.
11 Bloch 2000, p. 21.
12 Bloch 2000, p. 24.
13 Bloch 2000, p. 22.
14 Bloch 2000, p. 26.

transcendent direction.¹⁵ Human life is brought back into the dead forms of purely objective art, and the complete static of death and finitude are transformed in view of the *soul* venturing beyond the given external form.

Bloch then links the elements of this new art to the artistic 'drive toward expression' in his own time.¹⁶ He endorses 'painting inwards' (by which he means the emphasis on 'self-projection' even in the most abstract art) and proclaims the rise of *Kunstgewerbe* as art which transcends its purely functionalist logic by moving towards 'the self-encounter within painted objects and with them'.¹⁷

Bloch's idea of Expressionism involves finding in different forms of art, including the Gothic one, '*expressive*-descriptive *sigillary signs* for the unconsummated mystery of the We and of the ground, for a spontaneously animated, unconsummated, functional, in itself still symbolic ornamentalism and symbolism': the ornament becomes the way of expressing 'externalized interiority'.¹⁸ Note the 'unconsummated' here: what makes the ornament so important for Bloch's aesthetics is its openness and flexibility. Bloch associates with these 'organic' forms both the utopian potential and its related uncertainty: what he calls the 'Gothic line' contains an 'agitation' – that is to say, it is restless and never fully identical with itself.

The inherent instability he sees in this new art explains how one can overcome the danger of the deathly coldness immanent in any act of construction. The new utopian aesthetics demands radical expression: 'We have become more individual'.¹⁹ The self-encounter that is required can be observed in van Gogh's and Cézanne's paintings, which perform this remarkable operation when we – the viewers – suddenly recognise and approach ourselves in the outer world. Cézanne's still lives embody the 'intensity in small things', and herein lies their real historical significance.²⁰ Their world becomes the inner world of the spectator: 'Suddenly I see my eyes, my ears, my state: I myself am this drawer and these fish, I am these fish of a kind that lies in drawers; for the difference vanishes, the distance lifts between the artistic subject and the artistically represented object'.²¹ What Bloch is describing here is the new speculative synthesis of subject and object – a synthesis which, importantly, is only

---

15   Bloch 2000, p. 25.
16   Bloch 2000, p. 27.
17   Bloch 2000, pp. 29, 30.
18   Bloch 2000, pp. 24, 25.
19   Bloch 2000, p. 27. The German reads: 'Wir sind ichhafter geworden' (Bloch 1964, p. 41).
20   Bloch 2000, p. 32.
21   Ibid.

possible in the moment that *The Spirit of Utopia* wants to conjure up, with pictures that can appear 'like magical mirrors where we glimpse our future, like the inmost ornaments of our inmost shape, like the finally perceived, adequate fulfilment, self-presence of what has eternally been meant, of the I, of the We, of the *tat twam asi* [thou art it too], of our glory vibrating within mystery, of our secret divine existence'.[22] The resurrection of the soul in this aesthetics – an aesthetics which Bloch calls Expressionist – becomes the experience most adequate for the new utopian philosophy and hence for our ability to deal with history and politics. It enables us to overcome the peril of 'construction', the dead static of Egyptian pyramids.

2   Hegel's Traces on the Pyramids

Bloch's reference to the I and the We evokes Hegel's famous definition of spirit – '"I" that is "We" and "We" that is "I"'.[23] The historical succession of art forms, the interplay of the subjective and the objective, of the inward and the outward, the interconnections between the structures of art and the structures of life – all these motifs point to the Hegelian background of Bloch's narrative.[24] Indeed, Bloch explicitly acknowledges that Hegel's treatment of Egyptian art constitutes the starting point for his own interpretation. In Hegel's *Aesthetics*, the interaction of the inner and the outer is the general theme, with pyramids being the first expression of the inner that is also a first move outwards, in the form of death. The pyramids 'put before our eyes the simple prototype of symbolical art itself; they are prodigious crystals which conceal in themselves an inner meaning and, as external shapes produced by art, they so envelop that meaning that it is obvious that they are there for this inner meaning separated from pure nature and only in relation to this meaning'.[25] We find a similar description associating the dead form with its dead content in the *Phenomenology*: 'The crystals of pyramids and obelisks, simple combinations of straight lines with plane surfaces and equal proportions of parts, in which the incommensurability of the round is destroyed, these are the works of this artificer of rigid form … [T]he works receive Spirit into them only as an alien, departed

---

22   Ibid.
23   Hegel 1977, p. 110. The German reads: '*Ich, das Wir, und Wir, das Ich ist*'.
24   The same, incidentally, is true of Georg Lukács's contemporaneous *Theory of the Novel* (1916/20), which itself was heavily influenced by Hegel's philosophical aesthetics.
25   Hegel 1975, vol. 1, p. 356; cf. vol. 2, pp. 650–4.

spirit that has forsaken its living saturation with reality and, being itself dead, takes up its abode in this lifeless crystal'.[26] For Hegel, the emergence of pyramids marks the first understanding of the difference between the spiritual and the non-spiritual, as well as an attempt to fix – to physically as well as symbolically stabilise – the remains kept inside. The artificer [*Werkmeister*] externalises himself, exposes his inwardness. This is an important step towards the symbolic representation of absolute spirit. What is still missing is an expression of spiritual self as self – what Hegel calls *language*. Hegel's pyramids thus lack the power and the dynamics of subjectivity, and in this Bloch's aversion to Egyptian art echoes Hegel.

Derrida likewise structures his famous essay 'The Pit and the Pyramid: Introduction to Hegel's Semiology' around the movement of externalisation and the analysis of linguistic signs.[27] His starting point is a metaphor in the *Encyclopaedia*, where Hegel compares a sign with a pyramid, 'in which the alien soul is ensconced and preserved'.[28] In Hegel's semiology, Derrida argues, the temporality of the sign – indicating something different from itself – becomes a re-appropriation of presence, a *referral* or detour, necessary for the spirit to come to itself.[29] Hegel's speculative dialectics *is* therefore the science of signs, tracing what the spirit signifies: the speculative effort consists essentially in creating and maintaining the connection between the inner (meaning) and the outer (its representation). In Hegel's more specific theory of language in the *Encyclopaedia*, intelligence draws from the 'night pit' the images conserved there and, in its higher form of 'productive imagination', externalises itself in signs, which in their contradictory unity (of the internal and the external) turn out to be manifestations of the dialectical movement as such – the embodied sublation of spatial intuition in time.[30]

Continuing his interpretation of (or comments on) Hegel, Derrida maintains that the same unity can be rephrased and reconstituted as both an animated body and a tomb:

---

26   Hegel 1977, pp. 421–2.
27   The essay can be found in Derrida's *Margins of Philosophy* (Derrida 1988, pp. 71–108). Its title is a pun on Edgar Allan Poe's 1842 short story *The Pit and the Pendulum*.
28   Hegel 1978, p. 177. Derrida's translation of – and linguistic comment on – Hegel's 'die *Pyramide*, in welche eine fremde Seele versetzt und aufbewahrt ist' (Hegel 1978, p. 176) reads: 'conveyed [transposed, transplanted, translated: *versetzt*; *versetzen* is also to place on deposit; *im Leihause versetzen*: to place in the pawn shop], and where it is conserved (*aufbewahrt*: consigned, stored, put in storage)' (Derrida 1982, pp. 83–4).
29   Derrida 1982, p. 72.
30   Derrida 1982, pp. 79–80, 88–9.

The tomb is the life of the body as the sign of death, the body as the other of the soul ... But the tomb also shelters, maintains in reserve, capitalizes on life by marking that life continues elsewhere ... The body of the sign thus becomes the monument in which the soul will be enclosed, preserved, maintained, kept in maintenance, present, signified.[31]

In other words, there is a soul, an inner, which is protected by an outer. It is this outer which, by signifying, *resists the duration of time*.[32] The aspiration to externalise, the *sine qua non* of the speculative, the landmark of any aesthetic effort, is symbolised by a depository for the deceased.

Following Hegel, Derrida then moves from sign to language and to voice (or tone) as realisations of this negative movement, making the inward outward, 'the movement of the spirit relating itself to its own interiority and hearing itself speak'.[33] It is at this point that he puts forward the now famous thesis that Hegel's semiology is built upon the primacy of tone as the idealising movement of a double negation – negating the spatial sensibility of the material and then negating itself and evaporating. The externality of stone, the silence of death and the mechanics of the universal linguistic machine constitute the trace of the unsublatable, haunting the movement of the speculative. It is this 'pyramid' that Derrida the Egyptian is ultimately interested in: it becomes the horizon of his deconstructionist enterprise.

Let us return to Ernst Bloch. Bloch sees the danger of mortification in the building of closed, self-sufficient works of art and in the striving for completion with regard to any intellectual edifice – a development culminating in Hegel.[34] Indeed, *The Spirit of Utopia* criticises Hegel for being preoccupied with 'an enchantment of *construction* all too remote from the self and all too freed of subjective participation'.[35] That is to say, Hegel, too – in spite of his dialectical dynamics, in spite of his desire to leave behind the shell of the sign, the deaf mortality of the surface – is ultimately an Egyptian architect of death who

---

31   Derrida 1982, pp. 82–3. This is a particularly important topos in Derrida. Elsewhere, he plays with various meanings of this deadly silence, as in this well-known statement: 'The *a* of *différance* ... is not heard; it remains silent, secret and discreet as a tomb: *oikesis*' (Derrida 1982, p. 4).
32   Cf. Bloch's later commentary: 'The wall of leaves, the roof of blossoming branches, how soon they are yellow, the winter destroys them. Life is too frail for building: whereas what is dead lives here, because it lasts' (Bloch 1986, vol. 2, p. 721).
33   Derrida 1982, p. 95.
34   On Lukács's early praise for Hegel in this context, as well on Bloch's attitude to Lukács, see Chapter 2 in Boldyrev 2014.
35   Bloch 2000, p. 181; emphasis added.

lacks the sense of true inwardness. His speculative system remains a purely 'external' form, neutral or indifferent vis-à-vis our existential concerns: 'we lose ourselves completely here; nothing about us is answered or resolved. Whether we suffer, whether we can be blessed, whether we are immortal as individual, existing human beings – the concept does not care'.[36] In other words, Bloch views Hegel's philosophy as an intellectualistic project, an exercise in closure, as lacking the true dynamics of utopia, the normative dimension of the future. It is mere *anamnesis*, a recollection of something that has already been, an elimination of true conflict and contradiction in favour of a detached theoretical enterprise. It offers an all too comfortable reconciliation with the *status quo*.

Bloch's solution is 'to let Kant burn through Hegel' so that Kantian inwardness may 'overtake' the *Encyclopaedia*.[37] 'Kant ultimately stands above Hegel as surely as *psyche* above *pneuma*, Self above Pan, ethics above the *Encyclopedia*, and the moral nominalism of the End above the still half cosmological realism of Hegel's world-idea'.[38] At the same time, Hegel supplements Kant: his 'constructions' provide a necessary step in making utopian aspiration total and eventually in expanding the soul to the external world so that it becomes the *world* of the soul. The utopian subjectivity that Bloch associates with Kant, the existential, 'moral-mystical' reality of the self-encounter, needs to be accompanied by a more pragmatic, 'objective', outwardly orientated view, and it is here that Hegel becomes relevant. He furnishes an historical and political perspective: his emphasis on the intersubjective space of human realisation ensures that the analysis does not remain focused exclusively, and hence one-sidedly, on inwardness and the subjective intensity of time.

Whereas Bloch confronts Hegel by invoking the existential intensity of individual utopian experience – an inwardness which in his view is never reducible to the speculative totality of subject and object – Derrida arguably does the opposite. He confronts Hegel's speculation with something it can never grasp – namely, 'the machine defined in its pure functioning, and not in its final utility, its meaning, its result, its work', the machine which would function 'without ... being governed by an order of reappropriation', such as, precisely, Hegelian *dialectical economy*, the ability of dialectics to grasp and assimilate any heterogenous discourse or cultural form by transforming it into a mere

---

36   Bloch 2000, pp. 179–80.
37   Bloch 2000, p. 187. The section on Kant and Hegel in *The Spirit of Utopia* is entitled 'Kant and Hegel, or, Inwardness Overtaking the Encyclopedia'.
38   Ibid.

'moment' in the unfolding of totality.[39] In other words, whereas Bloch leaves the machine behind, making the technical a precondition of the emancipation of inwardness, Derrida views the machine, the mechanism, as a limit to Hegelian dialectics. From a Derridean perspective, therefore, there is no reason to turn inwards, since the machine is a pure formal externality: it functions as an 'outside', as something strictly separated from any 'subject'.

3 History and the New Immediacy

How should we assess Bloch's position historically and philosophically? What does his contribution to our understanding of ourselves and the world around us consist in? I would argue that his attempt to account for the inner life (which he often calls 'soul') makes him a precursor of Derrida, but *also* opens up a genuinely new, specifically Blochian dimension.

Let us recall Derrida's reading of Hegelian semiology. It involves the movement from the pit – the storage of unconsciously preserved sensual material – to the pyramid, the sign, the site of the spirit's autonomous action relating itself to itself. In Sloterdijk's interpretation invoked at the outset of this chapter, it is here that we find the final horizon of the deconstructionist enterprise: it is the pyramid – the temple of death, the triumph of externality – that is the undeconstructible remainder, radical otherness. We find a similar idea – or fear – in Hegel himself, when, in his early work, he speaks about positivity and alienation: what if the external remains a lifeless surface?[40] What if the inner intention – be it a work of an artist or a political institution – becomes distorted and perverted by its very realisation, because of its realisation?

Bloch's Hegel is a thinker who himself falls victim to this reification by prioritising the overall construction over subjective intention, by making the inner dependent on the outer, the intention dependent on its systematic realisation and externalisation in a totality as the unity of subject and object. For Bloch, however, the inner self, this pit, which needs to be externalised, *is still in the making*. It is not predetermined and cannot become a 'moment', a mere element in the overall process of construction. Rather, it is a promise, a trace of the not-yet. As such, it emerges from the lack – indeed, the impossibility – of total externalisation. The 'soul' is the image of this radical incompleteness.

---

39 Derrida 1982, p. 107.
40 See, for example, his 1795/96 *The Positivity of the Christian Religion* (Hegel 1996).

Bloch views art or, more precisely, applied art (or design) as staging or enacting such 'open' practices of non-identity and anticipation. But these practices can also be thought of as expressions of a *new immediacy* preventing the synthesis of Kant and Hegel – of subjective experience on the one hand and historical, political and intersubjective awareness on the other – from becoming another Egyptian system; that is to say, from becoming alienated, distorted and perverted with respect to the original purpose. *The Spirit of Utopia* itself seeks to enact such existential practices of seeing and hearing, of the utopian *souci de soi*, and in so doing to end our fixation on death – an empty form, a soulless edifice – and instead make us witness the 'signature of the immediate human being'.[41] The community envisioned by Bloch, the *We* he invokes with both persistence and impatience, is based on this self-encounter, on the sudden recognition of oneself amidst unending ornamentality, on the inexhaustibility of utopian transcending paired with – and incessantly referring to – 'the intensity in small things'.

Bloch's deconstruction of Hegel stretches beyond the idea of the 'pure question', of something resisting the ready-made answers of the kind that Hegel (in Bloch's view) was inclined to advance.[42] Bloch's position has a specific *historical and political index* that prepares him – unlike, say, the Greeks (whom Bloch considered too light-hearted, as we saw earlier) – for the critical moment that is the *kairos* and which sharpens his utopian sensitivity, his ability to notice and precipitate radical change in our world, the world of the soul. The utopian impulse, even in its most elementary form of everyday aestheticisation, is only activated at specific moments in time. That is why one particular motif – a motif somewhat obscured by Bloch's idiosyncratic aesthetic speculation – is centrally important to his narrative: namely, the apocalyptic feeling that 'the visible world seems to be crumbling anyway'.[43] The epoch in which Bloch was writing was, not unlike ours, a time of apocalyptic anticipation.[44] The experiences of the new art, of music and of wonder are precisely the ways to make one vigilant in a world in which every fold of time is, in Benjamin's parlance,

---

41   Bloch 2000, p. 26.
42   Bloch insists that we need 'to grasp the question about us purely as question and not as the construed indication of an available solution' (Bloch 2000, p. 197).
43   Bloch 2000, p. 32.
44   'Only the good, anamnestic person holding a key can draw forth the morning from this night of annihilation: if those who stayed impure do not weaken him, and if his call to the Messiah is illuminated enough to rouse the saving hands, to secure the grace of arrival for himself, to awaken the inspiriting, gracious powers of the Sabbath kingdom, consequently to engulf and immediately to vanquish the brutal, satanically dispiriting flashpoint of the Apocalypse' (Bloch 2000, p. 273).

the strait gate through which the Messiah might enter. This historical, messianic dimension is present in the short aesthetics developed at the beginning of *The Spirit of Utopia*; it characterises much of what is said further on in the book; it energises Bloch's later utopian hermeneutics; and – last but not least – it gives us an idea of how one might try to revolutionise one's dreams, turn them into emancipatory practice *without* adopting Hegelian teleology and thus move beyond the pit and the pyramid.

4   The Cunning of Reason

I would like to end with an important caveat. Both Bloch and Derrida reject the identifying movement of closure they detect in Hegel, and instead seek to find a radical alterity, a non-identity immune to the teleological movement of dialectics. Both deploy the idea of the *trace* as marking an experience of non-identity, expressed as the not-yet in Bloch and as the non-achievability of full presence, as a non-sublatable negativity, in Derrida.[45] Ironically, however, in carrying out this project, Bloch falls prey to the very Hegelianism he is critiquing. He wishes to *enact* his utopian philosophy and, since he eschews system building, his own narrative escapes systematic representation. Yet to the extent that this narrative possesses logical coherence (and without any such coherence it would simply be incomprehensible), the logic is essentially Hegelian in nature. The repertoire of aesthetic forms Bloch draws upon, the vocabulary he uses to discuss them and indeed the very idea of the externalisation of the inner, the interplay of the self and the thing – these are all inherited from Hegel.[46] Moreover, the intention of letting Kant burn through Hegel looks suspiciously like an attempt at Hegelian speculative synthesis. Overall, Hegel's dialectics, with its orientation towards mediation and totality, appears to be a necessary element in Bloch's attempt to give intersubjective meaning to his speculations about utopian art and to synthesise his aesthetic sensibility with his political aspirations.

Sloterdijk links the deconstructionist attempt to avoid final characterisations with Derrida's ambiguity towards his own post-mortal fate – expected oblivion and, *simultaneously*, survival. This duality, I argue, evokes the Hegelian scheme of negation qua *Aufhebung*. Was being *aufgehoben* – being *both*

---

45   Aptly summarised by Lévinas in an essay to which Derrida refers in *Of Grammatology*: the trace 'signifies without making appear' (Lévinas 1963, p. 620).

46   For example, Bloch portrays pyramids as crystals; see Bloch 2000, p. 25, as well as the explicit reference to Hegel in Bloch 1986, vol. 2, p. 722.

negated and preserved in the history of philosophy – not precisely what Derrida eventually wished for himself? After all, a deconstructionist reading Hegel is to a hair close to Hegel, for Derrida is, as Sloterdijk remarks, in 'constant danger of falling in love with the objects of deconstruction'.[47] Hence, for all their insistence on a wholly alternative philosophy, both Bloch and Derrida face the same challenge: that of grasping and overcoming Hegel before they are themselves grasped by him. Their style reveals this unwanted affinity – an affinity we should be aware of when discussing their critiques of Hegelian dialectics.

Bibliography

Bloch, Ernst 1964 [1918, 2nd version 1923], *Geist der Utopie*, Frankfurt am Main: Suhrkamp.

Bloch, Ernst 1986 [1959], *The Principle of Hope*, 3 Volumes, translated by Neville Plaice, Stephen Plaice and Paul Knight, Cambridge, Mass.: MIT Press.

Bloch, Ernst 2000 [1918, second version 1923], *The Spirit of Utopia*, translated by Anthony A. Nassar, Stanford: Stanford University Press.

Boldyrev, Ivan 2014, *Ernst Bloch and His Contemporaries: Locating Utopian Messianism*, London: Bloomsbury.

Derrida, Jacques 1982 [1972], *Margins of Philosophy*, translated by Alan Bass, Brighton: Harvester Press.

Hegel, Georg Wilhelm Friedrich 1975 [1842], *Aesthetics: Lectures on Fine Art*, 2 Volumes, translated by T.M. Knox, Oxford: Clarendon Press.

Hegel, Georg Wilhelm Friedrich 1977 [1807], *Phenomenology of Spirit*, translated by A.V. Miller, Oxford: Oxford University Press.

Hegel, Georg Wilhelm Friedrich 1978 [1830], *Hegel's Philosophy of Subjective Spirit*, 3 Volumes, translated by M.J. Petry, Dordrecht and Boston: Reidel.

Hegel, Georg Wilhelm Friedrich 1996 [1795/6], 'The Positivity of the Christian Religion', in *Early Theological Writings*, translated by T.M. Knox, Philadelphia: University of Pennsylvania Press.

Korstvedt, Benjamin M. 2010, *Listening for Utopia in Ernst Bloch's Musical Philosophy*, Cambridge etc.: Cambridge University Press.

Lévinas, Emmanuel 1963, 'La Trace de l'autre', *Tijdschrift voor Filosofie*, 25, 3: 605–23.

Sloterdijk, Peter 2009 [2006], *Derrida, an Egyptian: On the Problem of the Jewish Pyramid*, translated by Wieland Hoban, Cambridge and Malden, Mass.: Polity.

---

47   Sloterdijk 2009, p. 59.

CHAPTER 4

Between Dialectics and Metaphysics: Critical Reflections on Bloch's *Subjekt-Objekt*

Henk de Berg

Ernst Bloch (1885–1977) was one of the most important representatives of what has come to be called Western Marxism, the type of Marxism that rejected the Soviet-style economistic and deterministic interpretation of Marx's work and highlighted instead the role of human consciousness, thought and action in historical development.[1] As with other Western Marxists, notably his contemporaries Theodor W. Adorno and Georg Lukács, the strongest influence on Bloch, after Marx himself, was Hegel. In 1951, Bloch published *Subjekt-Objekt. Erläuterungen zu Hegel* (Subject-Object: Explanations of – or, alternatively, Comments or Commentaries on – Hegel), a tome of well over 500 pages that seeks to establish both the sum and substance of Hegel's ideas and their continuing relevance to philosophy and social thought. It is a supremely erudite and surprisingly lucid study of Hegel, though hardly an easy read: its lucidity is relative to the subject matter and, even at his best, Bloch is an extremely challenging writer.[2] The book also provides, as Douglas Kellner remarked many years ago, an excellent entrance point into Bloch's own philosophy.[3] Oddly enough, it has so far not been translated into English and is largely ignored in Bloch studies.[4] My aim in what follows will be twofold: to offer a historically

---

1 On the relationship between Bloch and Western Marxism, see Douglas Kellner's chapter in this volume, as well as Boldyrev 2015 and Ujma 1995. The standard life-and-work studies of Bloch are Münster 2004 and Zudeick 1987; Markun 1977 offers a shorter, straightforwardly biographical overview. Geoghegan 1996 provides a lucid English-language introduction to Bloch's philosophy. More recent critical discussions can be found in Thompson and Žižek (eds.) 2013.
2 Cf. Adorno's famous statement that 'in the realm of great philosophy, Hegel is arguably the only one with whom at times one literally does not know, and cannot determine with any degree of certainty, what he is talking about' (Adorno 1993b, p. 89; translation modified). Characterisations of Bloch's writing range from 'opaque' to 'impossible to follow'. To cite only one example: 'If his style prefigures utopia in its imaginative brio, it also does so in its obscurity. Rarely has St Paul's remark about seeing the kingdom of God through a glass darkly been more apposite' (Eagleton 2017, p. 91).
3 Cf. Kellner 1983, p. 282.
4 Only 40 pages out of a total of 520 are available in English: Chapter 9 on 'The Dialectical Method' (Bloch 1983) and Chapter 25 on 'Dialectic and Hope' (Bloch 1976). A Spanish transla-

contextualised close reading of *Subjekt-Objekt*, and to establish the strengths and weaknesses of the arguments it puts forward. In this way, I hope to throw new light on Bloch's overall philosophy, which is currently experiencing a renaissance.[5]

1   Structure and Context

Aside from a two-page preface and an equally short postscript to the 1962 edition, Bloch's *Erläuterungen zu Hegel* is in three parts: 'Der Zugang' [The Way In, ca. 40 pages]; 'Die Philosophie' [The Philosophy, ca. 320 pages], which offers a critical examination of Hegel's oeuvre from the *Phenomenology of Spirit* to the posthumously published lectures on the philosophy of history, the history of philosophy, aesthetics and the philosophy of religion; and 'Die Aufhebung' [Sublation, ca. 145 pages], which explores the criticisms made of Hegel by a number of post-Hegelian thinkers, above all Feuerbach, Schelling, Kierkegaard and Marx, while also introducing central elements of Bloch's own philosophy. All three parts are composed of multiple chapters, each of which is followed by key citations from Hegel's texts.

In the preface, Bloch stresses that his study 'does not claim to be a book about Hegel, but rather one that thinks towards him, with him and through and beyond him [*erhebt nicht den Anspruch, ein Buch über Hegel zu sein, sie ist eher eines zu ihm, mit ihm und durch ihn hindurch*]', because with Hegel's thought there is 'something not yet settled in the essential question it poses, and something unfinished in the proposed solution [*ein Unerledigtes in seiner wesenhaften Frage, ein Unabgegoltenes in deren versuchter Lösung*]'.[6] I will return to this issue – the principal element of Bloch's reading of Hegel – later on. There is another reason why Bloch refuses to write some kind of manual, a reason he addresses at the very beginning of 'The Way In': genuine understanding requires the ability to think for oneself, critically, lest one ends up 'repeating

---

tion was published as early as 1949. A good example of the neglect of *Subjekt-Objekt* in the secondary literature is Hassan Givsan's *Nach Hegel*, which mentions Bloch's study exactly once (Givsan 2011, p. 212).

5   Cf. Cat Moir's introduction to the present volume as well as her recent revaluation of Bloch's ontology, epistemology and politics (Moir 2020).

6   Bloch 1962, pp. 11–12. In order to avoid cluttering the text with footnotes, subsequent references to *Subjekt-Objekt* will be placed immediately after the citations. Unless indicated otherwise, all translations in this chapter are my own. I have rendered Bloch's stylistically idiosyncratic and at times almost untranslatable German fairly freely, supplying the original where I deemed this helpful.

what others have repeated, following a single terminological line [*im Gänsemarsch der Phrase*]' (17).[7] Bloch does not elaborate on this, but the target of his words is not hard to identify: in the Eastern bloc, philosophy was dominated by dogmatic-orthodox Marxism, which tended to view Hegelianism, or anything that even looked like a defence of Hegel, as a dangerous manifestation of bourgeois *idealism* (in the philosophical sense of the term). As early as 1924, Bloch's old friend Georg Lukács had experienced first hand the Soviet style of doing philosophy, when his Hegelo-Marxist collection of essays *History and Class Consciousness* was vilified at the Fifth Congress of the Communist International as an instance of left-wing deviationism, forcing the Hungarian master thinker into a humiliating recantation-cum-autocriticism.[8] Bloch, who in 1949 had settled in East Germany and was only too aware of the continued existence of this type of Party pressure, strove to resist the petrification of philosophy there – until the building of the Berlin Wall in 1961, when he gave up and opted to accept a Chair in the West German city of Tübingen.

Things were not much better in the English-speaking world, with which Bloch had become intimately familiar during his decade-long exile in America (1938–49), where between 1945 and 1947 he wrote the first draft of *Subjekt-Objekt*. The influence of anti-idealist and 'anti-metaphysical' movements more generally, such as logical positivism, remained strong, and for many even the mention of Hegel's name was a provocation. Karl R. Popper, in his two-volume *The Open Society and Its Enemies* (1945), had just launched an all-out attack on Hegelian philosophy, which in his view was nothing but 'bombastic and mystifying cant', a kind of pseudo-reasoning that cheated its way to its so-called insights by a combination of 'jargon', 'gibberish', 'equivocation' and the 'merely verbal trick' of the dialectic.[9] Worse, Hegel put this procedure to work 'to pervert the ideas of 1789', the ideals 'of reason, freedom, equality, and the other ideas of the open society'; his world view was in essence that 'of modern totalitarianism'.[10] The following year, in 1946, Bertrand Russell's best-selling *History of Western Philosophy* made much of the same points. Hegel's basic approach –

---

7 The appeal to Kantian Enlightenment values is emphasised on the next page through the implicit opposition of *mündig* [mature] and *Gängelband* [leading strings for children]. Like Adorno, Bloch frequently makes philosophical points by means of linguistic allusion.

8 As late as 1980, the orthodox communist Robert Steigerwald found it necessary to condemn Lukács's book as the 'Pandora's box of modern revisionism' (Jung 1989, p. 95). Cf. also Lukács's posthumously published self-defence, *Chvostismus und Dialektik*, the English translation of which includes an introduction by John Rees and a postface by Slavoj Žižek (Lukács 2000).

9 Popper 1945, vol. 2, pp. 26, 38 and 43.

10 Popper 1945, vol. 2, pp. 40, 47 and 75.

his idealist logic – was fundamentally mistaken, 'and from this mistake arose the whole imposing edifice of his system'.[11] Consequently, 'almost all Hegel's doctrines are false'.[12] His philosophy of history, for instance, 'required, if it was to be made plausible, some distortion of facts and considerable ignorance', but luckily (or unluckily) 'Hegel ... possessed both these qualities'.[13] Believing that 'wherever there is law there is freedom', Hegel espoused 'a very superfine' ethics, but unfortunately one that 'does not mean that you will be able to keep out of a concentration camp'.[14] Finally, 'Hegel's doctrine of the State', Russell said, 'justifies every internal tyranny and every external aggression that can possibly be imagined'.[15]

Bloch, then, had his work cut out for him. But before we turn to the various ways in which he deals with the supposedly unproductive nature of Hegelian philosophy, it is worth noting that the critical perspective I have just outlined is by no means entirely a thing of the past. Specialist research may have relegated most of the traditional criticisms incontrovertibly to the realm of fiction, or rather of prejudice, but beyond the circle of Hegel scholars many of the old 'myths and legends'[16] have proved remarkably persistent. To give only one example, the leading Enlightenment scholar T.J. Reed contended as recently as 2015 that Hegel's philosophy 'lacks intellectual underpinning and expressly rejects all counterargument'.[17] According to Reed, Hegel even refuses to accept 'the Enlightenment's distinction between fact and value, the way the world is and the way the world ought to be' and 'bad-mouths anyone who questions the status quo': his intellectual position is 'a kowtowing to reality' underpinned by 'sophistries'.[18] Indeed, even Hegel scholars are not immune to the pull of this anti-Hegelian tradition, as can be seen from Glenn Alexander Magee's widely used *Hegel Dictionary*, which states that '[f]or Hegel, it makes about as much sense to "critique" society as it does to "critique" nature'.[19]

---

11 Russell 1961, p. 715.
12 Russell 1961, p. 701.
13 Russell 1961, p. 705.
14 Russell 1961, p. 711.
15 Ibid.
16 Cf. Stewart (ed.) 1996.
17 Reed 2015, p. 56.
18 Reed 2015, pp. 57 and 56. Six years earlier, in a book with a similar-sounding title but different content, Reed had formulated an even fiercer critique, which accuses the German thinker of philosophical swindle and rhetorical legerdemain and concludes, after referencing Orwell's *Nineteen Eighty-Four*, that Hegel's way of philosophising 'discourages, and was probably meant to discourage, all fresh, mature thought and action that wishes to change things as they are' (Reed 2009, p. 194).
19 Magee 2010, p. 179.

2   Language and Style

It is not surprising that Bloch should start his revaluation with an analysis of Hegel's language and philosophical style. These are both, after all, the first things any reader of Hegel is confronted with and – as we have seen – favourite objects of critique. Now, according to Bloch, we are dealing here with two levels of complexity: a linguistic one and a conceptual one. Let us start with the first level, which in Bloch's view includes: the regular lack of a clear connection between sentences; violations of grammatical rules; convoluted Latinate constructions; regionalisms and other demotic forms of expression; tantalising and evocative but ultimately obscure metaphors; and (shading into the second level) ambiguous terminology. This is a good characterisation of Hegel's stylistic peculiarities, though it does somewhat overstate their frequency. Interestingly, it is also an accurate description of Bloch's style. His defence of Hegel's way of writing is thus simultaneously an explanation of his own approach to philosophy: thought should capture the essence of reality, and if that essence happens to be opaque, indeterminate or fractured, then the German will be difficult to understand, ambiguous or broken too:

> The precise expression of something obscure is very different from the obscure expression of something straightforward. ... In poetry, this distinction is well known: the obscurity of Goethe's 'Winter Journey in the Harz' or 'Wanderer's Storm-Song' resides primarily in the subject-matter, and in the language only insofar as it expresses this fermenting and dawning material [*den gärend-dämmernden Stoff*] (20–21).

The reference to poetry is misleading when it comes to Hegel, whose overall narrative logic remains resolutely discursive, but it is well suited to Bloch, who often writes in a highly literary manner. Towards the end of *Subjekt-Objekt*, Bloch explicitly, albeit in passing, mentions Joyce as a writer who 'can ... teach the philosophers what does not fit their Procrustean bed [of logical analysis] ... by bringing in a "prelogical", experienced [including unconsciously experienced, hence also *intuited*] reality which is disintegrated and yet hangs together [*durch die Aufnahme zerfallen-aneinanderhängender "prälogischer" Erlebniswirklichkeit*]' (470–71). As is well known, Bloch had already made this point in the 1930s during the *Expressionismus/Realismus-Debatte*, a series of discussions about the relative merits and demerits of Expressionism (attacked by Alfred Kurella, Georg Lukács and others as being, if not a direct forerunner of fascism, then at least a manifestation of bourgeois decadence and mere subjectivism) and Realism (extolled, above all by Lukács, as being capable of rendering visible both the ills of modern society and the progressive march of history towards its pregiven socialist telos).[20] In a number of perspicacious contributions to the debate – articles that were later included in the second, 1962 edition of *Erbschaft dieser Zeit* [Heritage of Our Times, 1935] – Bloch mounted a spirited defence of Expressionism, stating among other things:

> Lukács presupposes everywhere a closed coherent reality ... in which ... [we find] the uninterrupted 'totality' which has flourished best in idealist systems, including those of classical German philosophy ... But perhaps Lukács's reality, that of the endlessly mediated, but coherent total context [*die des unendlich vermittelten Totalitätszusammenhangs*], is not so objective at all; perhaps his conception itself still contains classical-systemic features; perhaps *genuine* reality is also interruption. Lukács has an objectivistically closed concept of reality, and that is why he opposes ... every literary and artistic attempt to chop to pieces any picture (even capitalism's picture) of the world; that is why he detects nothing but subjectivistic corrosion in all literature and all art which, starting from the *real* corrosion of the surface of reality, seek to discover something new in the hollow spaces; and that is why he looks at literary and artistic experiments aimed at piercing and chopping up a fragmented and decaying reality as if they were themselves instances of decay ... But ... is there no dialectical relationship between decline and ascent? Is what is unclear, unripe and incomprehensible automatically, in all cases, part of bourgeois decadence? Can it not also ... be part of the transition from the old world into the new?[21]

---

20 The issue was obviously of topical importance for *émigré* writers, who wanted to wage an intellectual war on Nazi Germany and were thus faced with the question as to which parts of the country's literary, artistic and philosophical past they should embrace (or 'inherit', *erben*) and which parts they should reject – the so-called heritage problem or *Erbeproblem*. The debate is documented in Schmitt (ed.) 1973. Some of the key texts in English translation can be found in Benjamin et al. 2007.

21 Bloch 1991, pp. 246–7; translation modified. Although Lukács had paid particular, indeed almost exclusive, attention to the Expressionists' poetological statements, largely ignoring their actual literary texts and paintings, it is Bloch who comes much closer to Expressionism's self-understanding. See, for example, Kasimir Edschmid's 1917 manifesto 'Über den dichterischen Expressionismus': 'No one believes that what is real coincides with the external reality which appears to us ... Hence the Expressionist's space becomes a vision. He does not merely see – he envisions [*Er sieht nicht, er schaut*] ... Facts have meaning only insofar as the writer's hand, penetrating through them, grasps what lies behind them' (Edschmid 1986, p. 28).

Seen through this lens, Expressionism gave voice to a yearning for a different, better world, an un-alienated humanity. What Lukács saw as its purely negative, nihilistic attitude was actually 'directed towards the humane; it orbited, almost exclusively, what is genuinely human and the form of expression of its incognito'.[22]

I have quoted so extensively from Bloch's reflections on Expressionism not only because they explain – as mentioned above – his own way of writing, but also because they underpin his approach to cultural artefacts generally. The Nazi, Bloch says with an Adornian turn of phrase, finds in the cultural past 'only the kitsch that he is himself',[23] but the dogmatic-orthodox Marxist detects in it little else than a reflection of the dominant ideology, a form of false consciousness – whereas the aim of a more subtle hermeneutic should be to bring out the dual character of culture as *both* reflective of broader and deeper economic trends *and* expressive of a resistance to them, a dreaming beyond them. Hence Bloch's use of the German words *Schein* and *scheinen* in this context: literature, art, film and so on constitute both the ideational *appearance* of a materialist praxis and the *shining*, the lighting up and illumination, of utopian trends and tendencies within that praxis.[24]

Let us now move on to the conceptual challenges posed by Hegel's language and style. On this second level of philosophical complexity – Bloch says – the reader is faced with: highly abstract specialist terminology; fuzzy concepts, or concepts that constantly seem to change in meaning; statements that are completely counterintuitive and often appear simply counterfactual; and

---

22 Bloch 1991, p. 248; translation modified. Cf. again 'Über den dichterischen Expressionismus': 'the landscape of Expressionist literature is the great Paradisiacal one, is that of God's original creation, which is more beautiful, more colourful and more infinite than the one that our eyes, in their empirical blindness, perceive ... [In this landscape] man ... *becomes human*' (Edschmid 1986, pp. 28–9). In fairness to Lukács, it should be pointed out that the literary-theoretical principles underlying his plea for Realism are by no means outlandish: (i) his basic proposition that humans are narrative beings with a strong desire for 'proper' story-telling is not at all implausible; (ii) his suggestion that avant-gardisms ineluctably end up in a vicious circle of forced innovations is not without empirical merit; and (iii) his warning that all forms of literary and artistic non-conformism tend to be recuperated quickly by the powers that be, leaving only a *faux* revolutionism which all too often acts as a substitute for genuine political action – this warning should be taken seriously. For a defence of Lukács along those lines, see Dannemann 1997, especially pp. 31–42 and 78–80.
23 Bloch 1991, p. 240.
24 The specifically Blochian term for the forward-pointing function of culture is *Vor-Schein*, which has variously been rendered as 'pre-appearance', 'shining ahead', 'anticipatory illumination' and 'ontological anticipation'. On Bloch's dialectical view of art and literature, see Jameson 1971, pp. 116–59; cf. also Kessler 2006.

the semantic inversion of key words, so that, for example, *abstract* means concrete, and *concrete* comes to denote something abstract. What are the reasons for these peculiarities, so often seen as instances of sloppiness, ignorance or even charlatanism and as such used to discredit Hegel (and Bloch as well, for here too their approaches are not dissimilar)? First, there is Hegel's attempt to put philosophy on a new footing, and this explains the use of typically Hegelian terminology, including its neologisms. Second – though this is an argument that emerges only in the later chapters of *Subjekt-Objekt* – the 'scientific' [*wissenschaftlich*] nature of Hegel's philosophy requires a special conceptual apparatus. Having to delve more deeply than mere empirical observation would allow, yet unwilling to accept any transcendent framework, Hegel demands – Bloch says – 'that reason follow its own course, produce its own categories' (159). Bloch, then, places Hegel firmly in the rationalist tradition of Descartes and the Enlightenment with their systematic 'doubt vis-à-vis the hitherto accepted teachings of the Church' (157), highlighting the Hegelian version of Kant's *Sapere aude!* in Hegel's 1818 inaugural lecture in Berlin: '*The courage of truth* and *faith* in the *power of the spirit* is the primary condition of *philosophical study* ... the closed essence of the universe *contains no force* which could withstand the force of cognition'.[25] In other words, Bloch's Hegel 'dissolves through the *humanum* of reason ... any supernatural content of the concept of God' (317; cf. 323–4).[26] It is this double thrust – against mere empiricism *and* against theology – that explains the conceptual innovations and intricacies of Hegelian philosophy.

But why does Hegel reject straightforward empiricism? Bloch's answers to this question take us to the third and fourth reasons for Hegel's conceptual approach. Central to Hegelianism, Bloch says, is the conviction that *no thing* is ever just what it seems (what it 'is' from a crudely empirical perspective)

---

25 Cited on p. 110; Hegel 1999, p. 185. The preceding sentence, which Bloch does not quote, reads: 'the one thing I shall venture to ask of you is this: that you bring with you a trust in *science, faith* in *reason*, and *trust and faith in yourselves*'.

26 On this reading of Hegel, cf. Bloch's *Atheismus im Christentum* [Atheism in Christianity, 1968]; the recent English edition contains a helpful introduction by Peter Thompson. For reasons of space, I cannot deal with this topic here and will just point to one thing that, as far as I know, has gone unnoticed in the secondary literature – namely, the significant parallels between Bloch and Roger Garaudy's Marxist study *Dieu est mort. Étude sur Hegel*, first published in 1962, which puts forward the thesis that, while as a person Hegel may not have been an atheist, the God that appears in his oeuvre 'n'est rien d'autre que l'homme saisi dans la totalité de son histoire' and as such is a kind of work in progress: 'Dieu est en mouvement, en travail, en genèse. L'univers entier de la nature et de l'histoire n'est que l'enfantement de Dieu' (Garaudy 1962, pp. 280 and 103).

because *every thing* is part of a larger whole, and as such it acquires, or rather always already has, an additional, different signification than what it *appears as* on the surface. This is not merely a matter of subjective interpretation: 'paradox is ... the voice of the object itself' (27). Hegel seeks to express this complex relation of surface and depth, of appearance and essence, and that is the third reason why his texts pose such conceptual challenges. Once again, Bloch illustrates his point with reference to literary writers, most notably G.K. Chesterton. Perhaps marginally more convincing than his own, not particularly strong examples, might be *The Man Who Was Thursday*, Chesterton's most famous novel, in which a poet-policeman (a paradox in itself) infiltrates a group of anarchists, only to discover that all the other members of the group are police infiltrators too.[27]

Because of the centrality of this holistic, dynamic-relational method to Hegelianism, Bloch returns to the issue in two later chapters, 'Hegel und der Empirismus' (pp. 109–20) and 'Die dialektische Methode' (pp. 121–54). There, Bloch argues that empiricism – or, to use the other term he employs in this context, positivism – 'takes things as they supposedly are' and as such constitutes 'a veneration of so-called facts', whereas Hegel's approach is 'the exact opposite' (109). Identifying himself with this Hegelian position, Bloch stresses that 'what is needed is to reject the formalism that remains stuck in the "correctness" of A=A and to become familiar instead with the material force of thought, which is the ability to cognise actual interrelations [*reale Zusammenhänge zu erkennen*]' (110); 'positivism, by contrast, is ... the art ... of never learning to philosophise' (110–11). The immediate givenness of facts is an illusion, as is, therefore, the absolute nature of sense perception, because reality is a dynamic ensemble which through its interrelations determines the nature of its constituents, so that no object is ever exhausted by its empirical appearance, its essence being the 'product of an extensive network of socio-historical and natural-historical mediations' (113). Nothing is ever merely immediate, because nothing is ever not mediated. As Hegel puts it in the *Science of Logic*: 'there *is* nothing in heaven or nature or spirit or anywhere else that does not incorporate immediacy and mediation alike, so that both these determinations prove to be non-separate and non-separable and the opposition between them null and void'.[28]

It is this philosophical requirement that will become foundational for Marx's thought, Bloch adds – the requirement to see social reality as 'a product ... not ... in the sense of an abstract commodity, but [as one that] all the time refers

---

[27] The novel is replete with such paradoxes; see as one further instance the inversion of *prosaic* and *poetic* in Chapter 1 (Chesterton 1987, pp. 12–13).

[28] Hegel 2015, p. 46; translation modified. Bloch himself does not quote this passage.

back to the production process in which it originates and, above all, continues to transform itself' (113). Bloch could have employed one of Marx's favourite tropes here, though he does not do so: if you cut an object, human blood will come out.[29]

'The truth', then, 'is the whole',[30] and this whole is a process. But this process is not some calm, continuous flow; rather, it is highly dynamic and tension-laden. It is *dialectical*. That is to say, reality is the evolving sum total of competing strivings and opposing trends – a process which continually negates its constitutive elements and, through these (negations of) negations, continuously creates a *new* reality. Hence nothing is ever stable, everything is perpetually in motion, each segment of the natural and social world is always already something else. Bloch is keen to stress the radical nature of this dialectical process:

> A world of struggle appears, a world split within itself never coming to a standstill. It is the storminess, the rhythm of respiration in the overthrow of the given which runs right through Hegel's dialectic; it derives from the French Revolution ... Hence the subversive aspect of the dialectic ... negation ... is most extraordinar[il]y energetic [*rührig*]. It puts everything petrified to the sword [*läßt jede Gewordenheit über die Klinge springen*]. It is the shattering and the destruction which break open a path for the new; Hegel presents the dialectic as an uninterrupted process of *breakthroughs*. The unity or synthesis which forms at each point is not merely a harmonized unity of contradictions, which is a feature of all previous dialectic up to Hegel. Hegel calls this unity, using an intentionally offensive expression, 'unity of unity and contradictions'; shot through with contradiction itself and no harmonious compromise, it continues in its explosive motion. It moves as a series of abrupt changes and leaps [*von Umschlägen und Sprüngen*], as a prepared and mediated series certainly, but one which has nothing to do with the fatal category of gradualness or peaceful development as adjustment to something given. Sudden qualitative change takes place, the wave breaks, when a defin-

---

29 Cf., for example, the following citations from Volume 1 of *Capital*: 'A great deal of capital which appears today in the United States without any certificate of birth was yesterday, in England, the capitalised blood of children'; 'If money, according to [Marie] Augier [in *Du crédit public et de son histoire*, 1842], "comes into the world with a congenital blood stain on one cheek", capital comes dripping from head to foot, from every pore, with blood and dirt' (Marx 2010f., pp. 744 and 748).
30 Hegel 1977b, p. 11; translation modified.

ite quantity is attained it is transformed. The new grows within the old, then its hour has come, when the time is ripe, it tears itself loose from the old with a leap; it advances dialectically, decisively, suddenly (123–5).[31]

I will explore this dimension of Bloch's interpretation more fully later on. What is relevant here is that Bloch points to the dialectic as the fourth reason for the conceptual complexity of Hegelian philosophy: it explains – he says – the fuzzy nature of Hegel's terminology. 'It is ... the *fluidity* of the concepts ... in which the Hegelian dialectic lives' (122). This, too – the precise nature of the relationship between reality and thought – is something to which we will have to return. For the moment, suffice it to say that according to Bloch the dialectic is also behind Hegel's conceptual contradictions, such as his idea that *being* and *nothing* are identical: every *Sein* is always already something else and as such has perished, passed into *Nichts*. Or, to give an example on which Bloch dwells a little longer, Hegel's inversion of the terms *abstract* and *concrete*: it is the uneducated – Hegel says – who think in an abstract manner, for their focus on 'concrete' people and events *abstracts* isolated parts from what is really a much larger whole. By way of explanation, Bloch cites a passage from Hegel's short essay 'Wer denkt abstrakt?' [Who Thinks Abstractly?, 1807], including its final paragraph, thereby implicitly, but no doubt intentionally, bringing out a further subversive element in Hegel's thinking: 'Among the Austrians, a soldier may be beaten, he is canaille; for whoever has the passive right to be beaten is canaille. Thus the common soldier is for the officer this *abstractum* of a beatable subject with whom a gentleman who has a uniform and *porte-épée* must condescend to interact – and that could drive one to surrender to the devil' (31).[32]

---

31 I have given the passage as rendered by John Lamb (Bloch 1983, pp. 286–7). The beginning conveys an even more strongly revolutionary message in the original German: 'Eine Welt des Kampfes erscheint, eine in sich selbst entzweite, nirgends stockende. Es ist Märzhaftes [an allusion to the post-Hegelian March Revolution of 1848 and conceivably also to the Ides of March] in Hegels Dialektik, der Atem [cf. the *ruach* – breath, wind or spirit – of God in Genesis 1: 2] der Umwälzung [one of Engels's favourite terms] des Bestehenden [*the given*, perhaps, but with strong overtones of *the existing social order*], von der Französischen Revolution her, geht durch sie hindurch'.

32 Hegel 1966, p. 465; translation modified. The final sentence alludes to Goethe's *Faust*, from which Hegel quotes, imprecisely, in both the *Phenomenology of Spirit* (Hegel 1977b, p. 218) and the *Philosophy of Right* (Hegel 2006, p. 16), as follows: 'Do but despise reason and science, / The highest of all human gifts. – / Then you have surrendered to the devil / And must surely perish' (cf. *Faust: Part One*, lines 1851–2 and 1866–7). As he does elsewhere,

Fifth, and last, there is a didactic aspect to Hegel's conceptual approach – namely, the attempt to break the readers of their habit of viewing things from a common-sense perspective. On a larger scale, this method is of course familiar: the entire structure of the *Phenomenology of Spirit* is aimed at demonstrating that ordinary consciousness is, in a variety of ways, limited and must transform itself into the more encompassing and more penetrating mode of thought that is the dialectic if the individual's and society's awareness is to supervene the one-sided views, irrational *idées reçues* and flawed categories and determinations (as well as the social realities that go with them) of the past. As Hegel puts it:

> The familiar *tout court*, precisely because it is familiar, is not cognitively understood. The most common way in which we deceive ourselves and others is by assuming something as familiar and accepting it on that account; for all its arguing and without realising it, such [an attempt at] knowing never really gets off the ground. Subject and object, God, nature, understanding, sensibility and so on are uncritically treated as known quantities and used as a valid framework, and as such function as fixed starting- and end-points. While these remain unmoved, the knowing activity goes back and forth between them, thus moving only on their surface ... Hence the task nowadays consists ... in freeing determinate thoughts from their fixity.[33]

The *Phenomenology* requires us to 'walk on our heads', so that, in viewing everything from 'this unwonted posture', we find ourselves on a journey that shakes all our certainties and convictions – 'the path of *doubt* or, more precisely ... the path of despair'.[34] Now, on a smaller scale – Bloch says – Hegel's way of conceptualising things seeks to produce just this kind of defamiliarisation. By disrupting the well-rehearsed modes of both everyday and philosophical discourse, Hegel enables us to abandon our habitual, often unconscious attachment to folk theories and theoretical fallacies. Finally, Bloch once again hints

---

 Bloch cites from Hegel's *Werke*, published in 1835; the original text of 1807 has 'Prussians' instead of 'Austrians': in Prussia, the corporal punishment of soldiers was abolished only in the context of Scharnhorst's and Gneisenau's military reforms of 1807–14.

33   Hegel 1977b, pp. 18 and 19–20; translation modified. Bloch himself (p. 79) only cites the first sentence.
34   Hegel 1977b, pp. 15 and 49; translation modified. The walking-on-one's-head image explains the celebrated phrase of both Marx (in the 1873 afterword to Volume 1 of *Capital*) and Engels (for instance, in *Ludwig Feuerbach*) that Hegel's dialectic is standing on its head and must be turned upside down again for it to be demystified.

that this is not merely a matter of epistemology, but something that has sociopolitical implications, for the final citation that he employs in this context, which comes from Hegel's *Lectures on the History of Philosophy*, reads as follows:

> What people call common sense is often far from sensible. Common sense comprises the maxims of its time. Before Copernicus, for example, it would have been against all common sense if anyone had said that the earth went round the sun ... In India, in China, [the idea of] a republic is contrary to common sense. This is the mode of thinking which contains all the prejudices of its time, and we are ruled by these thought-determinations [*Denkbestimmungen*] without being aware of it.[35]

Having looked at Bloch's defence of Hegel's – which in many ways also means Bloch's own – linguistic and conceptual style, we are now in a position to examine his interpretation of Hegel's substantive philosophy. There would be little mileage in providing a point-by-point treatment of Bloch's reading of each of Hegel's individual works. Instead, I will organise my discussion around two interrelated themes: the relation between idealism and materialism, and the birth of modernity.

3   Idealism and Materialism

According to Hegel, the 'stuff' of our everyday experience is reality's surface appearance [*Erscheinung*]. But what is its essence [*Wesen*]? How does Hegel view what one might call the ultimate nature of reality? Bloch's answer to this question is twofold: Hegel is an idealist; and Hegel is a crypto-materialist.

Hegel's idealism – Bloch says – consists in his 'panlogism, in the total equation of real being with true thought [*Panlogismus, in der restlosen Gleichung von wahrem Denken und wirklichem Sein*]' (135; cf. 195). His ontology is a 'mythology of concepts [*Begriffsmythologie*]' which posits a 'spurious life of abstractions [*Scheinleben von Abstraktionen*]' (136 and 159). The problem with Hegel's philosophy is therefore not, as some have argued, that it postulates the existence of a God or God-like being that is somehow external to empirical reality (the infamous Hegelian 'Spirit', with a capital 'S'). 'The real objection ... is ... that [Hegel's philosophy] reduces everything to concepts [*verbegrifflicht*] ...

---

[35]   Cited on pp. 31–2; cf. Hegel 1995, vol. 1, p. 379.

In Hegel, the process of negation appears far too much by the book; it is not infrequently imposed on the course of events instead of being elicited from it' (135). This rigid conceptual schematism finds its most visible expression in Hegel's attempt to force a triadic structure on every subject matter and culminates in such fantastical statements as the proposition that 'the stars as fixed points "possess merely the abstract identity of light", whereas sun, planet, moon and comet "constitute up in the sky, outside one another, the moments of the concept"' (135).[36] Bloch elaborates the point by using the terminology of medieval scholasticism: Hegel's concepts are *universalia ante rem*. As such, their logical structure precedes their worldy instantiations, which merely follow a pre-existing script. Seen through this lens, Hegel is a 'neo-Platonist' (161).

As a result, there is a tension between Hegel's *dialectic* as a Mephistophelean devil that forever denies (cf. 153), stopping at nothing and bowing before no one, and his *idealist ontology*, which entails the actualisation of a 'world-plan *ante rem*' (161) with, as we will see, a clear historical telos. The picture that Hegel's philosophy offers is thus one of 'processual restlessness and premature peace [*Prozeßunruhe und verfrühter Frieden*]' (185). In a few isolated passages scattered throughout his study, Bloch explains this dual character socio-economically, as the ideological reflection of the tension between feudalism and nascent capitalism. On this point, his perspective dovetails with the conclusion reached by Georg Lukács, who wrote in *The Young Hegel* (1948):

> We have seen that the social preconditions of Hegel's philosophy forced it into an idealistic mould from the outset, and at the same time they set definitive limits to his understanding of the laws governing society and history, limits which only intensified the tendency towards idealism.[37]

It should be added, however, that Bloch's position here is not entirely clear. On the one hand, he seems to be saying that it is the resurgence of feudalism – the

---

36   Bloch citations come from part 2 of the *Encyclopaedia* (Hegel 2004a, pp. 90 and 80; translation modified).

37   Lukács 1975, p. 395. Towards the end of 'The Way In', Bloch briefly discusses Lukács's study, which he praises as an excellent guide to Hegel's early philosophy. Yet Lukács *over-emphasises*, Bloch says, the direct philosophical links between Hegel and Marx, while *de-emphasising* the indirect ones by minimising or ignoring any element in Hegel that does not fit the straightforward rationalism of existing Marxism – thereby missing an opportunity to open up Marxist thought to other traditions. The latter is, of course, the very thing that Bloch himself wishes to achieve through his work, including his studies of Thomas Münzer, Christian Thomasius, the medieval Islamic philosophers Avicenna and Averroes, and indeed Hegel.

post-revolutionary Restoration of Europe – that paralyses Hegel's philosophy, stopping the dialectic in its tracks, as it were (cf. 54–5).[38] On the other hand, he posits that Hegel's historical-philosophical optimism, his reconciliation with the present, 'reflected ... the ascent of the bourgeoisie in Germany': whereas 'Schopenhauer's will to life was the bourgeoisie's metaphysically demonised existence, Hegel's world-spirit was its metaphysically idealised existence' (196 and 236; cf. 228). What is clear, however, is that Bloch, in a manner not dissimilar to Feuerbach, views Hegelianism as a system that both *reifies* history and *is reified* by it.

According to Bloch, Hegel's philosophy is not straightforwardly idealist, but also possesses a more or less hidden *materialist* dimension. This is hardly surprising – Bloch says, taking up a criticism originally put forward by Schelling – because if this were not the case, there would be no need for any kind of empirical process: if the world is in essence pure logicality, self-sustaining and complete from the start, then why should the logos undertake an arduous historical journey? Who or what would start it on its way? Hegel famously states in the preface to the *Phenomenology*: 'Of the absolute it must be said that it is essentially a *result*, that only in the *end* is it what it truly is'.[39] But, Bloch says 'this cannot be derived from Hegel's panlogism' (137). In other words, if we are to take seriously Hegel's remark about 'the seriousness, the suffering, the patience and the labour of the negative'[40] and indeed if we look at his actual analyses, we see that his idealist dialectic is often *de facto* – and here Bloch uses a near untranslatable, though not specifically Blochian term – *Realdialektik* (137), a dialectic of/as reality. Hegel's understanding of himself is therefore a form of 'self-deception' (140); and because his schematism is so often vanquished by his realism, it could be said that 'Hegel is not a Hegelian' (458).[41]

What does this 'crypto-materialism' or 'crypto-praxis' (199, 370, 374 and *passim*) consist in? Here, again, we encounter a certain ambiguity, or ambivalence.

On the one hand, Bloch has a tendency to detect in Hegel the very things that are constitutive of his own philosophy. Thus, Bloch states that 'even before hav-

---

38 In addition, Bloch mentions (cf., for example, pp. 60, 66–7, 125–6 and 227) the strong orientation towards the past in Hegel's time – especially the emergence of a conservative type of historical sensibility, the *historische Schule* – but the logic of his argument requires that this factor itself be seen as related to larger socio-economic developments.
39 Hegel 1977b, p. 11; translation modified.
40 Hegel 1977b, p. 10; cited by Bloch on p. 136.
41 The allusion is, of course, to Marx's well-known remark to his son-in-law Paul Lafargue, made apropos of a certain type of contemporary French 'Marxism' and reported by Engels: 'ce qu'il y a de certain, c'est que moi je ne suis pas marxiste'.

ing been turned upside down again' (103).[42] Hegel identifies a lack of something, and a drive or tendency to fill this gap, as the motor of historical development; Bloch characterises this dimension in terms of 'need', 'want', 'hunger' and 'hope' (137–9). He links this crypto-materialism to Hegel's concept of *Totalität*, or, more precisely, to the fact that Hegel must somehow make this concept work. The whole is immanent in all of its parts, but the parts are not from the start fully actualised manifestations of the whole. As such, they do not yet cohere as parts of, and do not yet adequately express, that whole. It is this fundamental contradiction that dynamises the relation between the whole and its parts, turning the latter into what Hegel calls *Momente* [key elements, decisive moments] of a progressive series of negations. Bloch writes:

> Every merely partial fulfilment, every evolutionary formation [*Bewegungsgestalt*] or historical society that has become deficient, begets the foundation [*zieht in ihrem Schoß die Träger ... groß*] of a need which goes beyond it, and of a more highly developed capability to fulfil this need. Both this need and this active capability contradict the old form of existence; hence, they become explosive, carrying within them the call to the future, to the (historically relative) sublation of the contradiction (138).[43]

Two pages further on, Bloch again stresses that:

> ... in some parts of Hegel's work, need constitutes the fundamental contradiction to any existing barrier; this dynamic state of not being adequate to the immanent totality feeds the dialectic of coming to be and passing away. It is the simultaneity of the presence and non-presence of the whole, of the *totum* – this *utopian* type of presence, as it were – that drives 'finitude' into opposition against its current state (140).

This interpretation, with its emphasis on utopian hope as the core of the dialectic, is more Bloch than Hegel.[44] Thus, Bloch states in the preface to his magnum opus, the three-volume *Das Prinzip Hoffnung* [The Principle of Hope, 1949–59]: 'Expectation, hope, intention towards possibility that has not yet

---

42   Cf. note 34 above.
43   Bloch 1983, p. 298; translation modified.
44   Interestingly, John Lamb's translation of the passage cited above omits precisely the Blochian phrase 'des Totum oder Alles, es ist diese gleichsam utopische Art von Anwesenheit' (Bloch 1983, p. 300).

become: this is not only a basic feature of human consciousness, but, concretely corrected and grasped, a basic determination within objective reality as a whole'.[45] And towards the end of the second part of volume one, in a section entitled 'The Not in Origin, the Not-Yet in History, the Nothing or Conversely the All at the End', he provides the following précis:

> What is happening in itself and immediately as 'now' is – in this [initial] shape – still empty. The that [*das Daß*; i.e., the fact *that* something is happening] in the now is hollow, is initially undetermined, a fermenting *not* – the not with which everything starts up and begins, around which every something is still built. The not is not there, but, being the not of a there, it is not solely and simply not, but also the not-there. As such, the not cannot stay with itself; rather, it is actively orientated towards the there of a something. The not is both the lack of something and the flight from this lack: it is a driving [*Treiben*] towards what is missing. Hence, it is with a not[-yet] that the *driving* in living beings takes shape: as drive [*Trieb*], need, striving and primarily as hunger.[46]

Not for nothing was Paul Ackermann's refrain '[b]ut something is missing [*Aber etwas fehlt*]' from Brecht's *Rise and Fall of the City of Mahagonny* one of Bloch's favourite lines.[47]

On the other hand, however, Bloch at times reads what he sees as Hegel's crypto-materialism as a kind of proto-Marxism. This is because Bloch also interprets historical development in Hegel (or at least the dimension of it that he – Bloch – finds convincing) as the manifestation of the dialectical-transformative power of human labour. Thus, 'the dialectical movement is posited purely theoretically in the *Phenomenology* and yet also [i.e., in the very same text] takes place as the real interaction, in the form of labour, between human beings and objects, with the re-worked objects working back on the human beings' (423). In this sense, Bloch says, Hegelian negation is not an abstract concept, but the 'real transformation of objects and human beings

---

45 Bloch 1996a, vol. 1, p. 7; translation modified.
46 Bloch 1996a, vol. 1, p. 306; translation modified. The German original is less grating than its English equivalent. The first sentence, for example, reads in German: 'Was an sich und unmittelbar als Jetzt vor sich geht, ist so noch leer'. The terms *an sich* and *unmittelbar* are, of course, Hegelian.
47 Cf. Bloch 1991, pp. 232–3, as well as the chapter 'Etwas fehlt ... Über die Widersprüche der utopischen Sehnsucht' – a radio discussion between Bloch and Adorno – in Bloch 1985, pp. 350–68.

through labour' (374). This interpretation differs from the Blochianising reading discussed in detail above. It hones in not on a kind of ontological *dreaming ahead* (to use Bloch's term),[48] but on *the ensemble of the social relations* (to use Marx's phrase) arising from people's productive activity. Moreover, it equates Hegel's materialism with human activity and rejects his view of nature as idealistic.

Of course, the two interpretations are not diametrically opposed. After all, people work in order to quench their thirst and still their hunger, to be free from want, to satisfy their material and immaterial needs. Also, labour requires planning, a thinking ahead; it also implies a desire, a wanting ahead, as it were. In other words, there is a clear link between not-yetness and human labour. It is through their transformative praxis that people change their world, and hence their circumstances and their room for manoeuvre, while also already changing themselves in the process (an aspect that Hegel develops in the *Phenomenology*, as Bloch – like Marx before him – highlights), thereby generating a dialectical sequence of human and social self-actualisations on the way to what Bloch, with the final word of *The Principle of Hope*, calls 'home'.[49] Nonetheless, a tension between the two interpretations remains – a tension that, as I will show in the final section of this chapter, is reflective of the oscillation in Bloch's own philosophy between utopia as an ontological category and utopia as the result of human praxis.

It seems to me that the first, Blochianising reading of Hegel is an instance of *Hineininterpretieren*, a kind of overidentification with the subject matter. But the second, Marxianising reading is problematic too. It not only reduces the 'bad' (idealist) Hegel to a hopeless metaphysician. It also limits the scope and focus of the 'good' (materialist) Hegel to one area of society, one type of human activity – labour. Here, Bloch clearly takes his cue from Marx himself, who wrote in his *Economic-Philosophical Manuscripts*:

> ... the outstanding achievement of Hegel's *Phenomenology* and of its final outcome, the dialectic of negativity as the moving and creating principle, is ... that Hegel views the self-creation of man as a process, objectification [*Vergegenständlichung*] as subjectification [*Entgegenständlichung*],

---

48 Bloch himself calls this 'Lenin's phrase' (cf. the fifth section of *What Is to Be Done?*), but, as with all concepts he borrows from other thinkers, it is placed fully in the service of his own conceptual framework.

49 Bloch 1996a, vol. 3, p. 1376. Peter Thompson has coined the apt term *Gattungswerden*, or species-becoming, as opposed to *Gattungswesen*, or species-being, for humanity as seen by Bloch; see Peter Thompson's preface to Bloch 2009, p. xx, and Thompson 2012.

as externalisation [*Entäußerung*] and as sublation of this externalisation; in other words, that he grasps the essence of *labour* and understands concrete – true, real – man as the result of his *own* labour.[50]

Marx then goes on to say that, unfortunately, '[t]he only labour that Hegel knows and recognises is *abstract-mental* labour'.[51] Now, this idea – that Hegel takes no account of people's *real, sensuous labour* – is incorrect, and it is to Bloch's credit that he recognises this. Yet, like Marx, Bloch reduces Hegel's realist dimension to a focus on labour, and we must now explore why this approach is indeed reductive.

Let us start with a general question: what was Hegel trying to achieve? What was it that one might term his *project*? The best way to answer this question, I believe, is by approaching it historically. Now, the first thing that strikes one about Hegel's early texts – written between 1793 and 1800, when he was a *Hofmeister*, or private tutor, in Berne and Frankfurt – is how much they are concerned with social, political and, above all, religious matters.[52] Hegel does not address specialised philosophical problems, but he wants to know: how can people today feel at home in the world?[53] Writing immediately after the French Revolution, and the Terror that followed it, and with nascent modernity all around him – the birth of the modern individual, the early stages of industrial capitalism and so on – he asks: how can we be parts of a whole, not isolated individuals, and yet remain autonomous agents?[54]

---

50 Marx 2010c, pp. 332–3; translation modified.
51 Marx 2010c, p. 333; translation modified. The more famous expression of this idea can be found in Marx's first thesis on Feuerbach.
52 This is evident already from their titles, such as *The Positivity of the Christian Religion* (1795/96) and *The Magistrates Should be Elected by the People* (1798). Almost all of these texts remained unpublished during Hegel's lifetime. There also appears to have been an extensive commentary on the German translation of James Steuart's 1767 *An Inquiry into the Principles of Political Economy*; but that manuscript is lost.
53 This praxis-orientated starting point is typical not only of Hegel but also of his fellow 'idealists' Fichte and Schelling, and it is regrettable that so much of today's philosophy tends to ignore it. A good example is Manfred Frank's otherwise very useful *Einführung in Schellings Philosophie* (Frank 2016), which manages to reduce Schelling's entire early philosophy to epistemology.
54 As no biographer fails to mention, every *quatorze juillet* Hegel drank a glass of wine to commemorate the French Revolution, which in his *Lectures on the Philosophy of History* he hails as follows: 'Never before, from the moment the sun stood in the firmament and the planets revolved around it, had this been witnessed: man acting to stand on his own head, his own thinking [*sich auf den Kopf, d.i. auf den Gedanken stellt*], and shape reality in accordance with his thinking ... This, then, was a glorious dawn. All thinking beings joined in to celebrate this epoch-making event' (Hegel 2004b, p. 447; translation modified).

Hegel's early intellectual trajectory consists in his exploring and then rejecting a range of possible solutions. The collectivist harmony of classical Greece – he comes to realise – is no longer possible and indeed no longer desirable under the conditions of modernity. The binding force of the Church, of 'positive' – official, dogmatic – Christianity, is equally repressive, while religion as purely individual, feeling-based faith possesses no integrating power. Alternatives such as Robespierre's *culte de l'Être suprême* or a new type of *Volksreligion* that Hegel toyed with for a while turn out to be unsatisfactory as well. Finally, the merely aesthetic creation, or recreation, of existential harmony (or the attempt to turn the very hopelessness of that undertaking into a sign of the longing for such harmony), as practised by Hegel's friend Hölderlin, is – for Hegel himself – ultimately an admission of defeat. It is at this point that Hegel launches his own solution. We must develop, he says, not an artificial way out of modernity, but a way into it. What is needed is an approach that allows us to comprehend and embrace the modern world in its full complexity, including its most fundamental feature – our potential for critical, rational reasoning and our ability to assess, and hence to accept or reject, the constituent elements of our social existence. The way Hegel fulfils this requirement is by historicising both the structure of the world and the categories (theories, conceptions and the like) we use to understand this structure; that is to say, by transposing Kant's concept of reason – reason as impervious to history and removed from the vagaries of life – onto history and society. Thus, Hegel, after moving from Frankfurt to Jena to take up a university lecturing post, writes in his first academic text, the *Difference between Fichte's and Schelling's Systems of Philosophy*:

> When the might of union vanishes from the life of man and the oppositions have lost their living connection and reciprocity and gained independence, the need for philosophy arises. In this sense, there is a contingent element to all this [i.e., with respect to the precise form that the oppositions take], but given that such division [*Entzweiung*] exists, [philosophy] is the necessary attempt to sublate the dichotomy between a rigidified subjectivity and a rigidified objectivity and to comprehend the historical existence [*das Gewordensein*] of the intellectual and the real world as a becoming, its being as a product [and simultaneously] as a producing.[55]

---

55   Hegel 1977a, p. 91; translation modified.

In short, philosophy for Hegel is *cultural analysis*, and his core conviction is the idea that getting a theoretical, practical and existential grip on the world (a world that very much includes us and our cognising activity) means rendering visible the internal dynamics of that world.

It is here that Hegel's concept of *Geist* [spirit] comes in. It designates social life as a whole; indeed, *Geist* is in many ways the conceptual successor to what Hegel in his early writings calls *Leben* [life]: it occupies – on a theoretically higher, more reflective level – the same structural-discursive position as that older concept. Moreover, *Geist* designates social life in its interrelations and tensions, as a unity which is both that unity and its disunited elements, as what Hegel in his study of Fichte and Schelling calls 'the identity of identity and non-identity';[56] in this sense, *Geist* is also the successor to Hegel's other early key concept, *Liebe* [the love between two people who form one couple]. Finally, it designates social life as a process, as an entity which produces and reproduces itself and thus generates a history as and through the continuous transformation of the relations between the disunited elements and between these elements and the whole. Hence the following description from the *Phenomenology of Spirit*, which Hegel completed in 1806, at the very end of his Jena period:

> The simple substance of life is therefore the splitting-up of itself into shapes [*Gestalten*] and at the same time the dissolution of these existing differences; and the dissolution of the splitting-up is in its turn a splitting-up, a forming of new structures [*ein Gliedern*]. So that the two sides of the whole movement – both the existence of the shapes in the general medium of independence and the process of life – coincide. The process of life is just as much the production of shapes as the sublation of shapes ... It is this cycle that constitutes life: ... the developing whole that [continually] dissolves its development[al stages] and in this way sustains itself.[57]

Spirit, then, is social reality in its dynamic interconnectedness: it is the whole of that reality, and it is nothing but that reality. 'Spirit is ... self-supporting, absolute, real being'.[58] It is 'the movement of positing itself, or ... the mediation of its self-othering with itself'.[59] Hence, spirit is not God, not a ghost, not a cosmic

---

56 Hegel 1977a, p. 156.
57 Hegel 1977b, p. 108; translation modified.
58 Hegel 1977b, p. 264.
59 Hegel 1977b, p. 10.

mind and not a cosmic principle or metaphysical life-force. It is not the hidden agent behind historical change. It is not an independently existing something ('x') that underlies an independently existing something else, such as empirical reality ('y'). In philosophical terms, it is not a substratum and it has no substratum. It is not 'behind' anything and nothing is 'behind' it. *Spirit is social reality in permanent dialectical motion.* And it is the task of philosophy to render visible these dialectical workings. What is therefore required is an approach that penetrates reality's observable, thing-like appearance [what Hegel calls its *unmittelbar*, or immediately given, dimension] and brings out the historical tensions [reality's *mittelbar*, or mediated, dimension] generating, shaping, interrelating and driving these social 'facts'.

The point here – and it is easy to miss – is that in this view *Erscheinung* [appearance] and *Wesen* [essence], the dialectic of which is rendered visible by philosophy, are one and the same: appearance *is* essence, and essence *is* appearance. As Hegel puts it: there 'is nothing in the appearance that is not in the essence and, conversely, there is nothing in the essence that is not in the appearance'.[60] Appearance is what the essence seems to be (it is the way the essence appears) when looked at from a common-sense or crudely empirical perspective; and essence is the appearance looked at from a dialectical perspective.[61] To illustrate this point with an example, Western Europe in the late 1810s, just after the Congress of Vienna, may have *appeared* to many contemporary observers as a neo-feudal entity, comprehensibly dominated by the restoration, but its *essence* was its course towards a capitalist class society.

Epistemologically, Hegel's approach means that the dichotomy between subject and object disappears or rather is sublated. There is no longer simply a cognising ego on the one hand and an external reality on the other, an opposition which then gives rise to such constructions as Kant's thing-in-itself, but phenomena and noumena are instead *aufgehoben* in spirit as the over-arching reality encompassing both subject and object. Ontologically – and this is more important in the present context – Hegel's approach implies the sublation of the dichotomy between idealism and materialism. As the whole of social reality in its dynamic interconnectedness, Hegel's spirit is actually not something spiritual as against something material, but is rather the multiplicity of the mediations of the ideational and the material. Spirit is thus not, to put it in

---

60 Hegel 1986, p. 84; translation modified.
61 Hegel sometimes, and somewhat misleadingly, calls this dialectical perspective *speculation*, by which he means a method that is able to sublate the reified contradictions (say, between subject and object, or between the individual and the collective) in which his predecessors, such as Kant, were stuck.

Marx's terms, people's 'consciousness' as opposed to their 'social being'; it is not ideology as opposed to praxis; and it is not philosophy or thought as opposed to economics. It is all of these together – as well as education, law, art and literature, fashion, leisure, consumerism etc. – as *Realdialektik*.

Admittedly, putting things like this is perhaps somewhat misleading. First, spirit as relevant to philosophy is not *literally* all social reality, but rather that reality without its purely accidental features. If I cross the road and am run over by a car, or if I marry Viv instead of Jo, then that is something contingent (although even in those instances what one might call substantive reality plays a role in terms of, say, technological progress and road safety, or marriage laws); and Hegelian philosophy does not concern itself with mere coincidence, 'appearance without essence [*wesenlose Erscheinung*]'.[62] This is what Hegel means when he says that 'philosophy paints its grey in grey'.[63] As Dudley Knowles puts it, Hegelian philosophy does not aim to 'explain every detail and facet of the social world', which is 'multicoloured', but to bring out 'its monochromatic core, painting a grisaille painting which captures the essential elements'.[64]

Second, the social world also contains elements that are no longer in keeping with the times and as such are doomed to perish, elements that Hegel calls *untrue*. This does not mean that they are somehow not there; they exist just as much as do traffic accidents and marriages. But their existence is irreversibly undermined; the dialectic has already moved beyond them. When Hegel defines spirit as 'everything actual, in so far as it is true',[65] he does so in order to highlight the critical edge to his conception; that is to say, in order to make it clear that his approach is very much not 'a kowtowing to reality' (to use T.J. Reed's phrase cited at the beginning of this chapter). Hegel's explanation makes this explicit:

> Truth in the deeper sense consists in the identity between objectivity and the concept. It is in this deeper sense of truth that we speak of a *true* state or a *true* work of art. These objects are *true* if they are as they ought to be; i.e., if their reality corresponds to their concept. Viewed from this perspective, to be untrue is the same as to be bad. A bad man is an untrue man, a man who does not behave in the way his concept or vocation requires. Admittedly, nothing can exist if it were *wholly* devoid of iden-

---

62 Hegel 2006, p. 25.
63 Hegel 2006, p. 23.
64 Knowles 2002, p. 70.
65 Hegel 2005, p. 275.

tity with its concept. Even bad and untrue things have being, in so far as their reality still, somehow, conforms to their concept. Whatever is thoroughly bad and contrary to the concept is for that very reason on the way to ruin.[66]

Hegel's approach, then, implies neither the naïvely optimistic position that 'whatever is is right' nor the cynical view that 'might is right'. I will return to this issue further below.

The reference to *the concept* in the citation above takes us to the third and final caveat that we must bear in mind: Hegel's sublation of the dichotomy between idealism and materialism does not imply that life is a process without structure – what Hegel, taking a swipe at Schelling's *Identitätsphilosophie*, calls 'the night in which, as the saying goes, all cows are black'.[67] Let us look at this point in a little more detail. *Geist*, I said, encompasses social life in its manifold interactions. In this sense, Hegel would not have disagreed with Marx's statement in *The Eighteenth Brumaire of Louis Bonaparte* that '[m]en make their own history, but ... not ... under circumstances chosen by themselves, but under circumstances directly encountered, given and transmitted from the past'.[68] People transform the world in which they live, and in so doing they transform themselves.[69] But the world that is being transformed works back on them, impeding or accelerating what has been achieved, thereby limiting or extending their room for manoeuvre. And Hegel deals with a great many of these transformative actions and events: with changes in political structure; shifts in ideological mentality; scientific discoveries, such as the invention of gunpowder, of the printing press, and of the compass; religious revolutions such as the Reformation; the advent of capitalism and its repercussions; the development of art and literature; and major historical events such as the French Revolution – to name but a few. Now, essential to Hegel's thought, and of course to Marx's thought, is the idea that not all types of interaction have the same weight. But whereas Marx singles out the economy as the form of life that 'in the final instance' (to use Engels's phrase) is the most influential,[70] Hegel high-

---

66   Hegel 2005, p. 276; translation modified.
67   Hegel 1977b, p. 9.
68   Marx 2010e, p. 103.
69   Hegel's most famous expression of this position can be found in the section 'Independence and Dependence of Self-Consciousness: Lordship and Bondage' in the *Phenomenology* (Hegel 1977b, pp. 111–19).
70   This is not to deny that Marx had a sophisticated understanding of the interconnectedness of social spheres. In fact, it is to presuppose such understanding. Marx's occasional one-sidedness in stressing the role of economics – his occasional tendency to ignore the

lights the determining role of the drive for freedom, a drive that finds expression not only in people's way of thinking but also in their actions and indeed in their social institutions and structures. It is Hegel's central conviction that there is an internal logic to the world's dialectical development and that this logic has its basis in humanity's potential for self-awareness, self-criticism and self-determination. We have the capacity to be free, and history – despite its periods of stasis, despite its detours and setbacks, its horrors and traumas – is the actualisation of that potential for freedom. This is what Hegel means when he talks about *der Begriff*, the concept or the notion, which encompasses not only 'theoretical concept' and 'conceptual thinking', but also 'the rational potential of reality itself' – our ability to think, to think conceptually and critically, and to act on this basis and hence to be self-determining and, in this sense, *free* agents. Equivalent terms that Hegel uses in this context are the idea [*die Idee*], thought [*der Gedanke*] and reason [*die Vernunft*]. Hegel explains the kind of historical development he has in mind with two analogies:

> The child ... has only the capacity for, the real possibility of, reason ... and, since he cannot yet do anything rational, has no rational consciousness. Thus what man is at first implicitly [*an sich*] becomes explicit [*für ihn*] ... To come into existence is to change and yet remain one and the same ... The plant, for example, does not lose itself in mere indefinite change ... The driving force is the contradiction that as germ the plant remains implicit [*an sich*] and yet is not supposed to be like that ... [T]he whole of what is brought forth is already contained in the germ ... in a latent form, *virtualiter*.[71]

It is this unfolding that we observe with regard to history, Hegel says: our potential to be rational, self-determining, free agents is 'baked into' the world from the start. In other words, Hegel firmly rejects the belief that there is no rhyme or reason to humanity's evolution. The point of his argument is precisely that there is indeed an immanent logic to historical development, and that this logic plays itself out in the tensions within and between the ideational and the material.

---

importance and relative autonomy of other factors, evident most clearly from his preface to the *Critique of Political Economy* – must be seen as resulting from a desire to correct the existing neglect of that key factor and to redress the balance.

71 Hegel 1995, vol. 1, pp. 21–2; translation modified.

To put things theoretically once more, the world according to Hegel advances dialectically; that is to say, it moves through contradiction. Its course is based on the

> ... principle that negation is also something positive; that a clash of contradictions is not a zero-sum game and does not dissolve into abstract nothingness, but produces the negation of a *particular* content; that [in other words] such a negation is not negation *tout court*, but the negation of a *specific state of affairs*, which [then] dissolves, and is therefore determinate negation; so that the result essentially [*wesentlich*] retains that from which it derives ... As the result, the negation is a determinate negation, it has a *content*. It is a new concept [*Begriff*], but a higher, richer concept than the preceding one, because it is enriched by its ... opposite: it contains its opposite, but also more than that opposite, and [in this sense] is the unity of itself and its opposite.[72]

This is what Hegel means when he says that world history is 'the self-propelling of the concept', *die Selbstbewegung des Begriffs*: 'it is the content in itself, *the dialectic which it possesses within itself*, which moves the subject matter forward'.[73] As I outlined above, this *Realdialektik* – these manifold clashes of contradictions in/as reality – takes place between different philosophies, but also between philosophy, or cultural criticism, and the existing social order, as with Socrates. It takes place in the form of religious transformations, as with the arrivals of Christianity and the Reformation, and in the form of other major historical events, such as the French Revolution; it takes place between classes, as in the dialectic of lordship and bondage; and so on. Of course, the various contradictions of the *Realdialektik* are intertwined in multiple ways. Also, what types of conflict and conflict resolution gain particular historical significance at a specific time is an empirical question, but they are all different manifestations of the self-movement of the concept, and '[i]t is this difference which is decisive in the diversification of world history'.[74] More and better education means deeper self-awareness for more people; more political participation means more self-determination; and scientific discoveries make people less dependent on nature. But the dialectic can also become all but frozen and produce periods of stasis. It can overshoot the mark, as it were, as when the French Revolution engendered the 'absolute freedom' that led to the Terror; and it can

---

72 Hegel 2015, p. 33; translation modified.
73 Hegel 1977b, p. 44, and Hegel 2015, p. 33; translation modified.
74 Hegel 1995, vol. 1, p. 21; translation modified.

generate violent opposition to newly acquired forms of freedom. The central idea – the point bears repeating – is this: there is a direction to history; this direction is the dialectic of spirit; and this dialectic is not an idealist one but involves the material just as much as the ideational dimensions of life.

Let us now return to Marx and Bloch. In a way, it is perhaps odd that Marx should view Hegel as an exponent of idealism. After all, Hegel explicitly takes account of different manifestations of spirit: individual human consciousness (what he calls *subjective spirit*); politics, economics and social organisations (*objective spirit*); and religion, music, art, literature and philosophy as the modes in which spirit comprehends itself (*absolute spirit*). Yet Marx does view Hegel as an idealist, as we have seen. It is one of Bloch's strengths that he recognises that this aspect of Marx's thought is wrong. Without stating explicitly that his great predecessor is mistaken, Bloch takes a view which is the exact opposite of that put forward by Marx. Bloch writes:

> The following ... remains of fundamental importance in Hegel: he understands the seemingly theoretical relation between subject and object as a transformative-practical one; that is, *as a relation in the form of labour*. After all, the development described in the *Phenomenology* only takes place in the form of such a reciprocal reshaping [*Umbilden*] of the subject by the object and of the object by the subject. In other words, the dialectical movement is posited purely theoretically in the *Phenomenology* and yet also takes place as the real interaction, in the form of labour, between human beings and objects, with the re-worked objects working back on the human beings. And this happens in such a way that the changes on the level of theory themselves take place, and cannot but take place, as part of the overall transformative labour process: a transformation of knowledge generates a transformation of social existence, [and] a transformation of social existence in its turn transforms knowledge and consciousness. This is comparable to Marx's third thesis on Feuerbach: 'The [vulgar-]materialist doctrine according to which human beings are the products of social circumstances and education, and different human beings therefore the products of different social circumstances and education, overlooks the fact that it is human beings themselves who change these circumstances, that the educators themselves must be educated' (423–4).[75]

---

[75] Bloch cites from Engels's version of the thesis, which is slightly longer than Marx's original text.

In contrast to Marx himself, then, Bloch sees Hegel and Marx as having essentially the same stance on this issue. Interestingly, and not entirely convincingly, Bloch then immediately reverts to a more traditional Marxist position by stressing that this stance, though inherent in Hegel's dialectical method, is an 'anomaly' (426) as far as Hegel's overall system is concerned. More importantly, while Bloch appears to capture the Hegelian dialectic in its full complexity, he in reality reduces it to human labour. Even more problematically, his focus on the ensemble of man's social relations does not stretch beyond the true but sociologically unspecified insight that history is the arena of human interaction. Herein lies the main weakness of Bloch's philosophy – its lack of sociological specificity. I will return to this criticism in the final two sections. First, we must explore Bloch's interpretation of Hegel's view of historical development in more detail.

4   Modernity

At the heart of Bloch's interpretation of Hegelian historiography is the conviction that 'for Hegel, history comes to an end in or around 1830' (226): from then on, time is 'dead' (234) and the world 'completed' (360). This does not mean that Bloch sees Hegel as a reactionary. He points to the 'love of humanity and yearning for freedom' (248) in Hegel's early writings and, in sharp contrast to his contemporaries Popper and Russell (as well as many earlier and later critics), brings out the progressive political aspects of the *Philosophy of Right*, including its implicit plea for a host of things that were nowhere to be found in Hegel's Prussia, such as the equality of all people before the law, the administration of justice in open court and right to a jury trial, and the freedom of the press. In addition, Bloch highlights Hegel's scathing criticism of the highly influential anti-Enlightenment thinker Karl Ludwig von Haller, whose *Restauration der Staatswissenschaft* [The Restoration of Political Science, 1816] extolled the supposedly divine foundations of feudalism and the nobility.[76]

---

[76]   Bloch (250) quotes from an extended footnote in the *Philosophy of Right*, as follows: it is 'the harshest thing that can happen to man to have strayed so far from thought and reason, from respect for the laws and from the insight that it is infinitely important that the duties of the state and the rights of the citizen be determined by law, [to have strayed so far from all this] that absurdity comes to be seen as the word of God' (Hegel 2006, p. 281). Terry Pinkard describes von Haller as providing 'the Prussian king and the nobles with a framework in which they could defend their old rights' and hence with 'the rationale for a complete restoration of the pre-Napoleonic Prussian order' (Pinkard 2000, p. 460).

Even more perspicacious is Bloch's discussion of Hegel's much-maligned *Doppelsatz* that what is rational is real and that what is real is rational.[77] Referring to Hegel's own subsequent (but even today all too often ignored) elaboration – 'existence is in part mere appearance, and only in part [actual] reality'[78] – he points out that Hegel knows very well that the world around us is in many ways irrational, permeated with 'things that are bad, that should not be' (253). What is more, Bloch stresses the *dynamic* nature of Hegel's concept of reality: for Hegel, the world is an ever-active, forward-thrusting process, and that is why he cannot be seen as a conservative 'in the sense of political quietism' (253). Here, Bloch invokes the authority of Marx, citing from his September 1843 letter to Arnold Ruge: 'Reason has always existed, but not always in a rational form' (271–2).[79]

Yet all this does not alter the fact that Bloch believes that Hegel brings history to a standstill, as it were. Nor does it change the fact that Bloch believes that, if there is any openness towards the future left in Hegel's historiography, it is because of his dialectical method, which militates against his substantive interpretation of history. This, then, is for Bloch the essential weakness of Hegelian philosophy: that it accepts – indeed, presents as permanent – a world still permeated with alienation. It proceeds 'as if externalisation [*Entäußerung*, the social exteriorisation of human subjectivity] and objectification [in the sense of reification] ... were simply synonymous and any [possible] world simply [a manifestation of] alienation' (101). This is why Hegel is unable to see alienation as a problem: if, as Hegel seems to assume, a loss of autonomy is our fate under any social dispensation, then how could the existing heteronomy at the supposed end of history appear as problematic?

In short, Bloch maintains that in Hegel's philosophy 'all pressing matters vanish, and everything that is constitutive of the world of today and human decision-making [*die Welt der Aktualität wie der Entscheidung*] disappears' (39), to the extent that even art and literature lose their transcendent function – their role as what Bloch calls *Vor-Schein* and (quoting St. Augustine) *praeludium vitae aeternae* (cf. 289–91).[80] However, is it actually true that Hegel 'negated the future' (12)?

---

77   Cf. Hegel 2006, p. 20.
78   The citation comes from paragraph 6 of the *Encyclopaedia* (Hegel 2005, p. 9).
79   The letter was first published in the *Deutsch-Französische Jahrbücher*; see Marx 2010a, p. 143.
80   Bloch, pp. 289–91. The reference is to St Augustine's *De musica*, VI.2; cf. Bloch 1996a, vol. 2, p. 833. The only exception, Bloch argues in an interesting interpretation of Hegel's *Aesthet*

It is certainly correct to say that Hegel rejects the view of history as a series of coincidences, a chaotic, merely chronological progression without rhyme or reason, or as a kind of circular movement in which there is nothing new under the sun. 'It is important that we should recognise', he says, 'that the development of the spirit is a form of progress, for although this idea is widespread enough, it is just as frequently attacked'.[81] Of course, Hegel is not taking the (patently absurd) position that history constitutes an uninterrupted upward development. He explicitly acknowledges that 'there have been several extended periods which have come to an end without any apparent continuation; in which, rather, all substantial cultural gains were destroyed, with the unfortunate result that everything had to start again from the beginning'.[82] Nor is he blind to the countless cataclysms that over the centuries have engulfed so many, often in the most brutal ways. On the contrary, Hegel is only too aware of history's many horrors. In a particularly pessimistic passage, he compares history to a slaughterhouse, 'an altar on which the happiness of nations, the wisdom of states, and the virtue of individuals' are sacrificed to evil 'needs, passions, interests, etc.', such that 'we are moved to profound pity'.[83] Yet these moral catastrophes do not turn history into a pointless and aimless succession of more or less random events. Hegel writes that

> ... world history moves on a higher plane than that to which morality properly belongs, for the sphere of morality is that of private convictions, the conscience of individuals and their own particular will and mode of action; and the latter have their value, imputation, or reward or punishment within themselves. What is required and accomplished by the ultimate end of the spirit ... takes place on a more abstract level than the obligations, liability, and responsibility which attach to individuality in an ethical sense.[84]

To illustrate this passage with an example, the rationality of the French Revolution does not reside for Hegel in the event's 'moral goodness' (he was fully conscious of the manifold revolutionary crimes, not to mention the regime of

---

    ics, is humour: not in the form of subjectivistic Romantic irony, but as the 'transcending humour' in writers such as Cervantes, whose light-hearted farewell to the past has a contagiously liberating effect (cf. 291–4).

81   Hegel 1975, p. 125.
82   Hegel 1975, p. 127; translation modified.
83   Hegel 1975, pp. 68–9.
84   Hegel 1975, p. 141; translation modified.

Terror that followed the initial revolt),[85] but rather in the fact that it established the principle of political freedom; this is a development that, in Hegel's eyes, is to be welcomed, but that does not provide a retrospective moral justification for everything that took place and certainly does not somehow redeem the individuals who engaged in wrongdoing.

Yet in spite of its many horrors, history for Hegel is 'the development of the spirit's consciousness of its own freedom and of the consequent realisation of this freedom'.[86] Hence, it is not 'an eternally recurring cycle' as one may observe 'in the natural world', but 'progress towards a better and more perfect condition'.[87] This is so because history develops dialectically; that is to say, because historical negation is always determinate negation, which does not simply eliminate the previous stage, but sublates it. Moreover, far from being merely quantitative in nature, this process has a distinct goal – human freedom. Indeed – Hegel says – we have in many ways already reached this 'ultimate end of the world'.[88] Yet every time Hegel talks about such an endpoint, he immediately appears to backtrack. Thus, he limits the current realisation of freedom to post-1789 Western Europe, and even here – he says – freedom is not yet fully realised.[89] What, then, are the problems and obstacles that he believes still exist?

First, he points to the influence of still powerful feudal and nascent capitalist structures on modern legal and political processes. In England, for example, many 'particular interests' of the landed aristocracy still 'have positive [i.e., officially ratified] rights attached to them which date from the antique times of feudal law'.[90] Second, 'this utterly inconsistent and corrupt state of affairs' – that is to say, the extent to which private interests threaten to undermine the independence of the judiciary and political decision-making – is aggravated by a growing trend towards economic and political 'liberalism' based on 'the atomistic principle'.[91] Shared values and concerted action are increasingly being displaced by a particularism oblivious to, and destructive of, people's sense of a common destiny. Freedom, in other words, threatens to unleash 'the sway of individual wills'.[92] It is this lack of mediation – between individuals and

---

85 Cf. Hegel 1977b, pp. 355–63.
86 Hegel 1975, p. 138.
87 Hegel 1975, p. 124.
88 Hegel 1975, p. 44.
89 Cf., for example, Hegel 1975, p. 197, and Hegel 2004b, p. 442.
90 Hegel 2004b, p. 454; translation modified.
91 Hegel 2004b, pp. 455 and 452; translation modified.
92 Hegel 2004, p. 452.

between individuals and society as a whole – that constitutes a barrier to freedom: because unbridled liberalism, or atomistic freedom, ultimately *reduces* people's sense of freedom and indeed their actual freedom.

This is visible most clearly in the problem of poverty, an issue which preoccupied Hegel early on. Already in his Jena period he remarks that capitalism creates a 'contrast between great wealth and great poverty', such that the former 'makes itself into a force ... [that is to say] a point of attraction', as a result of which a 'huge population is thrown into helpless poverty'.[93] He returns to the issue in the *Philosophy of Right*, pointing out that while poverty may be the result of personal failings, it is more often caused by 'contingent physical factors and circumstances based on external conditions'.[94] If production is shifted overseas, for instance, workers lose their jobs through no fault of their own. The ensuing poverty impacts directly on their objective freedom: 'they are more or less deprived of all the advantages of society, such as the ability to acquire skills and education in general, as well as of the administration of justice, health care, and often even of the consolation of religion'.[95] In addition, it impinges on their subjective freedom and hence on their feeling of self-worth: 'that feeling of right, integrity ... and honour which comes from supporting oneself by one's own activity is lost'.[96] In the most extreme case, this leads to the emergence of 'a rabble', which 'is created ... by inward rebelliousness against the rich, against society, the government, etc.'[97] And all of this is not some natural disaster, not an act of God, but results from the workings of capitalist society. 'No one can assert a right against nature, but within the conditions of society hardship at once assumes the form of a wrong inflicted on this or that class'.[98]

What is striking about Hegel's discussion of the obstacles to freedom is that he offers no real solutions. With regard to the 'important question of how poverty can be remedied', he toys with a number of possible answers, but only in order to arrive at the less than helpful conclusion that it 'is one which agitates and torments modern society especially'.[99] As regards liberalism in general, he merely states that this 'collision [between the interests of the individual and those of the collective], this nodus, this problem, is that with which history

---

93 Hegel 1983, p. 140; translation modified. In what follows, Hegel critically alludes to Matthew 13:12 ('For whosoever hath, to him shall be given, and he shall have more abundance: but whosoever hath not, from him shall be taken away even that he hath').
94 Hegel 2006, p. 265.
95 Ibid.
96 Hegel 2006, p. 266.
97 Ibid.
98 Hegel 2006, pp. 266–7.
99 Hegel 2006, p. 267.

is now preoccupied and the solution of which it will have to work out in the future'.[100] This should not come as a surprise. After all, in the preface to the *Philosophy of Right*, Hegel famously stresses that 'each individual ... is a *child of his time*; thus philosophy, too, is *its own time comprehended in thoughts*. It is just as foolish to imagine that any philosophy can transcend its contemporary world as that an individual can overleap his own time or leap over Rhodes'.[101]

Bloch, then, is wrong to claim that there is no openness towards the future in Hegel. But he is right to say that Hegel thinks that history has reached a kind of endpoint. That endpoint is the realisation that human beings are autonomous individuals possessing reason – the capacity for criticism and moral judgement – as well as particular life goals, opinions, a conscience and a sense of self-worth. Yet in actualising this freedom, both individuals and society as a whole keep running into a host of problems, as freedom begins to develop a logic of its own that threatens to undermine the driving force behind it. For Hegel, therefore, his own time is not simply an end, but also a beginning – the beginning of modernity.

In other words, what is left according to Hegel is to address the many serious challenges of modernity practically, here and now. To quote once more from the preface to the *Philosophy of Right*: if anyone's 'theory does ... transcend his own time ... then it certainly has an existence, but only within his opinions – a pliant medium in which the imagination can construct anything it pleases'.[102] Yet this is precisely what Bloch claims we *ought to* and indeed *can* do. Is he right? Does Bloch's philosophy reach beyond modernity in a manner that is more than mere opinion and imagination? This is the question to which we must now turn.

5   Beyond Modernity?

Let us briefly recall the central tenets of Bloch's philosophy. According to Bloch, historical development possesses two aspects – that of matter, and then that of sociality in both its conscious and unconscious dimensions. These aspects cannot be seen in isolation from one another but are two sides of one and the same coin. By way of initial orientation, one might say that they are Bloch's version of the Marxian interplay of objective historical factors (not least – though

---

100   Hegel 2004b, p. 452; translation modified.
101   Hegel 2006, pp. 21–2.
102   Hegel 2006, p. 22.

by no means exclusively – economic ones)[103] and subjective historical factors (such as the emergence of the proletariat's awareness of its own position). Yet whereas Marx displayed little interest in the world's pre-social evolution, Bloch views history in far more encompassing terms – as the development of matter. Through a series of erudite, if at times eclectic and idiosyncratic, readings of thinkers ranging from Aristotle via Avicenna, Averroes, Giordano Bruno and Baruch de Spinoza to Friedrich Engels, he interprets humanity's present and future as the outcome of natural – that is to say, overarchingly matter-based rather than merely social – processes. His aim is perhaps most akin to that of Engels, whose *Dialectics of Nature* was, as Cat Moir puts it, an attempt to explain human history from a Marxist perspective 'as simultaneously continuous with and yet irreducible to natural history'.[104]

The key to Bloch's speculative materialism is his concept of matter as a dynamic category. 'Matter, this is not the mechanical lump [*der mechanische Klotz*] but ... active being [*bewegtes Sein*] ... being which has not yet been delivered; it is the soil and the substance in which our future, which is also its own future, is delivered'.[105] In other words, already nature per se, and not just its emergentist level that is the social world, tends towards the actualisation of latent possibilities, towards a kind of fulfilment or completion. 'Expectation, hope, intention towards possibility that has not yet become [*Intention auf noch nicht gewordene Möglichkeit*]: this is not only a basic feature of human consciousness, but, concretely corrected and grasped, a basic determination within objective reality as a whole'.[106]

For Bloch, then, being is in its very essence a becoming, but not simply in the sense that it realises its pregiven potential. Rather, its very potential is a historical category. Hence, it is not merely the actualisations that are continually new, but the possibilities themselves. Being possesses a potential for potentialities: it contains within itself possibilities that do not yet exist. To put it differently, matter is simultaneously both process and product, but the relation between the two is the opposite of – to take the classic example – that between the acorn and the oak tree. Matter develops towards ever higher forms (including an understanding of itself in human consciousness) and indeed towards a kind of completion or fulfilment, and yet we cannot know exactly what is being completed or fulfilled, nor exactly how this process will take place.

---

103 Cf. note 70.
104 Moir 2020, p. 39; for the similarities and dissimilarities between Bloch and Engels, see especially pp. 69, 73 and 83.
105 Bloch 1996a, vol. 3, p. 1371; translation modified.
106 Bloch 1996a, vol. 1, p. 7.

This is the chutzpah, or scandalon, of Bloch's philosophy: the idea that history, not just human history but even natural history, tends towards something that is not yet known. Bloch posits a directionality to history while acknowledging that the question as to the telos – the direction-towards-what-exactly – is impossible to answer. Or rather, it can only be answered in terms that hover somewhere between vagueness, metaphor, analogy and vision: things will be as they should be; what is missing will no longer be absent; there will be universal harmony – and a host of other images ranging from God's Kingdom on Earth to Marx's realm of freedom, and from *Heimat* to utopia. What is more, we cannot even be certain that we will ever get to this 'there', because, as Bloch keeps reminding his readers and listeners, hope can be disappointed.[107]

Bloch's philosophy confronts us with a paradox not unlike that posed by Heidegger's philosophy: it posits a relationship between matter-as-producing and matter-as-product without being able to make the relationship explicit. More than that, Bloch stresses that the relationship by definition cannot be explicated by traditional science or analytical philosophy, which are unable to see, or speculate beyond, this basic question: how can there *be* a not-yet-become? This is Bloch's version of Heidegger's 'ontological difference' between *Sein* and *Seiendes* – not least (as I will argue extensively further below) in that it erects similar barriers to social analysis.

The not-yet-become [*das Noch-Nicht-Gewordene*] has its subjective correlative in the not-yet-conscious [*das Noch-Nicht-Bewusste*], humanity's anticipatory awareness of a something else, something better, which 'is' (as a) not yet. Since this future can only ever be glimpsed or intuited, Bloch speaks of the darkness of the lived moment [*das Dunkel des gelebten Augenblicks*].[108] Yet people's 'dreams of a better life'[109] are not, or at least need not be, mere flights of fancy or hallucinations. Genuine glimpses or intuitions of a better

---

107   This is the topic of Bloch's 1961 inaugural lecture at the University of Tübingen.
108   Bloch's phrase was almost certainly inspired by the early Lukács's *Anarchie des Helldunkels*, or 'anarchy of light and dark' (Lukács 1971, p. 151). A further source of inspiration might have been the rather obscure phrase *Nacht der Welt*, or 'night of the world', from Hegel's Jena manuscripts. When we look at something – Hegel seems to be saying – it becomes an image or representation in us. However, the relationship between human consciousness and the world is not straightforward, because the image is not necessarily a clear and conscious one, so we often remain in the dark as to what it represents. Such unconscious images might rise up out of the darkness into dreams or unbidden thoughts (cf. Hegel 1983, p. 87). Slavoj Žižek discusses Hegel's phrase in several books, including *Less Than Nothing* (Žižek 2012, pp. 353–4). A selection from Žižek's work in German translation was published as *Die Nacht der Welt. Psychoanalyse und Deutscher Idealismus* (Žižek 1998).
109   This is the phrase Bloch originally wanted to use as the title for the book that became *The Principle of Hope*; cf. Zudeick 1987, p. 170.

future are possible – Bloch claims – because they are, and insofar as they are, grounded in the actual forward movement of history. Such hope 'illuminates the concept [*Begriff*] of a principle in the world'.[110] At each stage of its development, the world generates 'objectively real' [*objektiv-real*] possibilities, which in the Anthropocene provide the foundation for realistic subjective hope. In other words, the utopian can-be [*Kannsein*] that is at issue 'is a future-laden definiteness in the real itself'.[111] It is here that Bloch's distinction between the 'abstract' and 'concrete' varieties of utopia comes into play.[112] Abstract utopian thinking is removed from reality in that it ignores – that is to say, abstracts from – the essence [*Wesen*] of historical development, extrapolating the future from isolated surface phenomena [*Erscheinung*]. By contrast, concrete utopian thinking – Bloch claims – penetrates the outward appearance of empirical phenomena and locates the future in the historical tendencies generating both these natural and social 'facts' and their surplus potentialities.

A significant part of Bloch's oeuvre is devoted to such images of hope, or *Hoffnungsbilder*. From the early *Spirit of Utopia* to the late *Atheism in Christianity* and beyond, Bloch traces the manifold ways in which human beings across cultures and throughout the ages have expressed their longing for a better world. The three massive volumes of *The Principle of Hope*, in particular, offer such an exploration of anticipatory consciousness, ranging from everyday wishes, dreams, daydreams and fantasies via fairy tales and popular culture to literature, art and music, myth, religion and philosophy. They seek to elucidate how people have intuited, and given voice to, the progressive arc of history, but also how the utopian impulse has often been misinterpreted and distorted (as in Christianity's theistic eschatology) or hijacked and perverted (as in the Nazis' appropriation of the hope for a community beyond class antagonisms and economic exploitation).

Bloch's focus, then, is less on the material embeddedness of subjective and cultural superstructure phenomena than on their potential historical surplus. His hermeneutics is a secularised version of *anagogical exegesis*, the interpretation of the Bible in the light of the Life to come.[113] Indeed, Bloch's interpretations themselves tend to assume mythical or quasi-religious forms and hence produce an anagogical surplus.

---

110   Bloch 1996a, vol. 1, p. 7.
111   Bloch 1996a, vol. 1, p. 235.
112   Bloch uses the terms 'abstract' and 'concrete' in the sense of Hegel's essay 'Who Thinks Abstractly?'; cf. pp. 94–5 above.
113   In addition to biblical exegesis, Jewish Kabbalah and Weimar Classicism were the main sources of inspiration for Bloch's hermeneutics.

One of the most striking aspects of Bloch's project is the sheer number of philosophical concepts he develops. In addition to the ones we have looked at already, there are *latency* (the present's hidden, as yet unrealised, future possibilities), *non-contemporaneity* (the synchronous presence of old-but-still-existing, present and future possibilities), *the novum* (the genuinely – 'transcending' – new, as opposed to mere modernisations of the given), *the ultimum* (the arrival, or perhaps the hope for the arrival, of the genuinely new that is utopia or *Heimat*) and *extraterritoriality* (the idea that utopia or *Heimat*, which is the fulfilment or completion of history, also constitutes a qualitative leap out of the historical development human beings are familiar with and as such is 'extraterritorial' to history). In fact, these are just a few examples; the list is much longer.

This takes us to the major problem of Bloch's project. Perhaps more than any other thinker, Bloch has developed a philosophy that frequently appears removed from social reality. Of course, a new way of seeing the world requires a new conceptual apparatus. This we discussed in section 2. In Bloch's case, however, the gap between philosophical edifice and empirical praxis is worryingly wide. All too often, not merely the precise meaning of the concepts he employs, but also their relation to concrete social developments remains entirely unclear. This applies not least to his distinction between 'abstract' and 'concrete' utopianism – to the extent that one wonders if the latter is in any way substantially different from the 'true socialism' witheringly criticised by Marx and Engels, a half-literary, half-metaphysical system 'representing, not true requirements, but the requirements of Truth ... the interests of Human Nature, of Man in general, who ... exists only in the misty realm of philosophical fantasy'.[114] It is hard to disagree with J.K. Dickinson, who in his review of *The Principle of Hope* characterises Bloch as a 'logocrat' producing 'the illusion of being in control' by creating a linguistic universe which, though 'connected at various points to reality', replaces the mental penetration of the world with a 'mastery of words'.[115]

Bloch has little to say about what Hegel calls *objective spirit*, society's institutional, economic, moral, legal and political structures. He deals with *subjective spirit* in terms of people's everyday wishes, dreams, daydreams and the like, and he addresses the 'hope-contents' expressed in the manifestations of *absolute spirit* that are the arts, religion and philosophy. Yet when it comes to the analysis of (to use Marx's phrase) *the ensemble of the social relations*, his philosophy

---

114 Marx and Engels 2010, p. 511.
115 J.K. Dickinson, 'Ernst Bloch's *The Principle of Hope*: A Review of and Comment on the English Translation', *Babel* 36, 1, 1990: 7–31 (pp. 30 and 15); cited in Geoghegan 1996, pp. 43–4.

is of little value. In other words, in his attempt philosophically to transcend the empirically given, Bloch effectively abandons Hegel's and Marx's level of socio-economic and socio-political reflection, ending up with an essentially Feuerbachian view of sociality which lacks sociological specificity.[116] His study *Natural Law and Human Dignity*, for example, develops a vision of a socialist society virtually without positive law and jurisprudence and instead based on the (correct) psychological disposition of its citizens[117] – a dubious political-philosophical approach when viewed against the backdrop of the Stalinist perversion of Marx's ideas.

It might be objected that it is not Bloch's job to provide such concreteness. His thought, it might be argued, should be read in conjunction with Marx's ideas. Indeed, Bloch himself often presents his philosophy in this way: as the 'warm stream' of moral sensibility, utopian imagination and hope complementing the 'cold stream' of materialist suspicion, empirical analysis and sobriety.[118] It might also be argued that his philosophy remains Marxist at its core in that – as Cat Moir puts it – 'for Bloch, the labour of the imagination is itself a historical force'.[119] The problem is that such arguments only work if one can specify the interrelations between Bloch's and Marx's conceptual apparatuses. This, however, is impossible, precisely because Bloch simply overleaps the whole area of social mediations. Tendency, latency, the objectively real, the novum and so on – they all retain an essentially metaphysical immediacy. Here, again, Bloch is closer to Feuerbach than he is to Hegel and Marx. While acknowledging the dialectic of historical phenomena, he assumes that on a deeper level historical development is somehow beyond such empirical vulgarity and can therefore be explored – or at least sensed, intuited – sui generis.

Accordingly, a large proportion of Bloch's oeuvre, including almost the entirety of *The Principle of Hope*, is devoted to fictional texts (in the broadest sense of both terms). There are two aspects to this. First, there is the idea that such texts provide a unique kind of access to the world: that they have the capacity to register social shifts and anticipate social developments in ways that remain closed to science and other forms of positivist knowledge. Now, the assumption that feeling and fantasy are forms of knowledge is neither unusual nor unreasonable.[120] But it does open the door to highly subjective interpretations,

---

116   Both Feuerbach and Bloch were heavily influenced by Giordano Bruno, Jacob Böhme and Spinoza.
117   See Bloch 1996b; cf. Bloch 1996a, vol. 1, p. 173.
118   Cf., for example, Bloch 1996a, vol. 3, pp. 1365–70.
119   Moir 2020, p. 8.
120   To give only one example, Freud famously states that 'creative artists are valuable allies

which in the case of Bloch are then cloaked in the garment of social analysis. Second, the 'distanciated'[121] nature of such fictional approaches to social reality is used by Bloch to absolve himself from the irksome task of establishing specific sociological links between writer, text, context and readership and to escape instead into the realm of presumed anthropological constants. Nowhere is this more visible than in his reading of the Bible as a transhistorical document: its liberationist message – Bloch says – 'speaks to so many people as though it had grown up with them', resonating 'through the ages and across the lands'.[122]

This type of criticism is not new. Georg Lukács, for example, wrote in one of his contributions to the *Expressionismus/Realismus-Debatte* 'that Bloch … expresses the notion that the subject-matter and the composition of works of literature depend on man's relationship to objective reality. So far so good. But when Bloch comes to demonstrate the historical legitimacy of Expressionism and Surrealism, he ceases to concern himself with the objective relations between society and the active men of our time … Bloch fails to make reality his touchstone and instead uncritically takes over the Expressionist and Surrealist attitude towards reality, and translates it into his own richly imaginative language'.[123] Part of the orthodox Marxist disavowal of Bloch in the GDR from 1956 onwards – however narrowly dogmatic and personally disingenuous much of it may have been in uncritically toeing the party line – also honed in on the subjectivist nature of Bloch's philosophy.[124] More recently, Terry Eagleton likewise castigated Bloch's 'contempt for the empirical':

> As one who railed against what he called 'the malnutrition of the socialist imagination' … Bloch is at risk of a conceptual obesity of Rabelaisian

---

and their evidence is to be prized highly, for they are apt to know a whole host of things between heaven and earth of which our philosophy has not yet let us dream' (Freud 1990, p. 34; the allusion is to *Hamlet* 1.5.174–5). The word *philosophy* is here used by Freud to designate *science*.

121 On this concept, see Ricoeur 1981, especially pp. 131–64.
122 Bloch 2009, pp. 10–11. In an odd Eurocentric twist, he adds that, by contrast, the teachings of 'Lao-Tse … and Buddha … cannot be taken out of their own countries' (p. 11; translation modified).
123 Lukács 2007, p. 42.
124 In spite of earlier criticisms, Bloch had been awarded the GDR's prestigious National Prize and made a member of the East German Akademie der Wissenschaften in 1955. The following year, Party leader Walter Ulbricht published an editorial in *Neues Deutschland* entitled 'Was wir wollen und was wir nicht wollen [What We Want and What We Do Not Want]', in which he effectively declared Bloch a philosophical outlaw. For a measured discussion of this period in Bloch's life, see Zudeick 1987, pp. 186–245.

proportions ... Yet the paradox of this stunningly diverse body of work is its fundamentally monotone quality. Its prodigal range exemplifies again and again the same rather slender set of concerns ... The repetitiveness of his writing is astonishing. *Totum* and *Ultimum* are also *Optimum* and *summum bonum*, while *Heimat*, Being, the All, *eschaton* and *pleroma* are more or less interchangeable. Apart from the fact that all these terms gesture to a future state of peace, freedom and classlessness, they are notably low on content ... One might claim that Bloch's writing is at once too little Marxist and too much so – too eager to assume that almost every historical phenomenon, however remote from modern politics, can be milked for its emancipatory value, yet too intent on funnelling this prodigious mass of material into the mold of historical materialism ... Is finding evidence of proto-Marxism everywhere one looks a question of being open-minded or tunnel-visioned?[125]

While such criticisms are justified, they do not fully come to grips with Bloch's philosophy. Its real problem goes deeper, lying less in its empirical inadequacy per se than in its essentially metaphysical dimension. Exploring that dimension will give us a better understanding of Bloch's project and will also expose its fundamental weakness more clearly.

6   Between Dialectics and Metaphysics

Bloch's core philosophical conviction is the idea that the arc of history bends towards utopia – that history will engender a state of freedom and justice which goes beyond the mere accumulation of previous forms of progress. This is not a fanciful notion in itself. After all, history often moves in leaps and bounds. The emergence of industrial capitalism is one example; the birth of the modern individual is another. It is precisely this insight that is at the heart of Hegelian and Marxist dialectics. Yet Bloch's claim – or hope – only makes sense if it does indeed rely on the analysis of historical development as a dialectical process. It is here that we encounter a fundamental ambiguity in his philosophy: it continuously oscillates between dialectics and metaphysics. This is not a contingent feature of his thought, not a flaw that could be remedied – it is constitutive of his entire approach. And it is both the principal attraction (for his admirers, that is) and the principal weakness of his philosophy.

---

125   Eagleton 2017, pp. 104 and 93–4.

It is my contention that there is a structural homology here with Heidegger's philosophy.[126] Just as Heidegger moves back and forth between positing a connection between *Sein* and *Seiendes* (because without this link Being would be but an empty concept) and disavowing such connection (because the moment Being is linked intimately to empirical reality it loses its transcendent function), so Bloch oscillates between utopia-as-history and utopia-as-extraterritoriality. This homology has not been explored by secondary literature; existing studies of the relation between Heidegger and Bloch, which are few and far between in any case, are therefore of little use.[127] Instead, I will take my cue from Adorno's critique of Heidegger's *Fundamentalontologie*, and my aim in what follows will be to adapt and apply Adorno's insights to the critical analysis of Bloch's philosophy.[128]

To begin with, let me reiterate what I said earlier: when looked at from a philosophical vantage point, there is nothing wrong with Bloch's concept of utopia per se. One may reject his utopianism as excessive or even counterproductive from an anthropological, psychological, sociological or political standpoint,[129] but the idea of a qualitative historical leap is not in itself illogical or contradictory. Nor is it empirically unfounded. The philosophical problem does not reside in Bloch's concept in general; it resides in the generality of his concept. Bloch decouples *utopia* to such an extent from Hegel's *das, was ist*[130] that it becomes a reality sui generis. This metaphysical hypostatisation, which appears in a variety of guises in Bloch's work – mystical intuition, literary evocation, religious faith and other 'dreams of a better life'[131] – sits ill with his claim to philosophical analysis. Yet this metaphysical dimension is not – as critics from Lukács to Eagleton would have it – simply an analytical weakness; that is to say, it does not just signify a lack of empirical concreteness which introduces a high degree of subjectivity into Bloch's thought. Rather, it is the structural,

---

126   I use the concept of *homology* to highlight the fact that I am not presupposing some kind of elective affinity between Bloch's and Heidegger's projects. On this conceptual issue, cf. Titzmann 1993.

127   The most extensive study is Becker 2003; the special issue on Bloch and Heidegger of *New German Critique* (45, 1988) treats the two thinkers largely separately. Other discussions include Hudson 1982, pp. 90–3, 124 and 155; Münster 1987; and Riedel 1994, especially pp. 225–8, 230–1 and 263–7.

128   Cf. Adorno 1973, 2007 (especially part one, pp. 61–131), 2008 (pp. 37–9, 62–4, 67–8 and 199) and above all 2019. Adorno's 1960 analysis of the revised edition of Bloch's *Traces* hints at some of the same points (Adorno 1993a).

129   Cf. de Berg 2012, which criticises utopianism in general (i.e., not specifically the Blochian variety) from these perspectives.

130   'To comprehend *what is* is the task of philosophy' (Hegel 2006, p. 21).

131   Cf. note 109 above.

or rhetorico-structural, vehicle of a specific philosophical modus operandi. By claiming utopia as a historical category, Bloch validates, or rather appears to validate, his materialist credentials; and by positing utopia as a post-historical – 'extraterritorial' – category, he obviates, or rather appears to obviate, the need for a proper dialectical analysis of the ensemble of the social relations that drive historical development. To put it polemically, the metaphysical hypostatisation of the telos enables him to engage in a kind of philosophical double-dealing. Bloch's *dialectics* makes his approach seem sufficiently empirically concrete to render the abstract nature of the historical novum all but invisible, while his *metaphysics* makes his approach seem sufficiently conceptually abstract to render any questions about the concrete nature of the novum irrelevant. What results is a peculiar rhetorical back-and-forth between concretion and abstraction: before one side of the equation finds itself at risk of scrutiny, Bloch has already moved to the other side.

Rather than illuminating the relation between his Marxism and his metaphysics, Bloch hides their precise contours in an analytical twilight zone.[132] This puts a particular strain on his use – and indirectly on his concept – of language, which continually hovers between explanation (of what is) and evocation (of what might be). Incapable of theorising utopia by discursive means, Bloch keeps falling back on language as revelation, a way of speaking which no longer designates its object dialectically but conjures it up as an un-mediated presence. True language becomes the language of Truth; words become the Word. Now, this may work as theology, but Bloch does not wish to be a theologian. Stripped of its religious dimension, and hence of the faith-based extra-linguistic reality that both underpins it and is underpinned by it, his language has to carry the entire referential weight of his philosophy by itself. This is why it keeps morphing from a (failed) explication of utopia into an embodiment of it. In Bloch, language acquires a semi-ontological status: it becomes a stand-in for empirical reality. This is the structural reason for what Eagleton has called Bloch's 'conceptual obesity'.[133] The world that Bloch claims to analyse is ultimately a world of words, of words which no longer possess sociologically identifiable referents but summon – or, perhaps it would be better to say, aim to create *ex opere operato* – what they are supposed to refer to. Philosophy has turned into magic.

There is a curious paradox about this metaphysical approach: it constitutes a real problem and yet explains much of Bloch's popularity – for what makes

---

132 Its existential correlative is the 'darkness of the lived moment'; cf. note 108 above. I will return to this concept further below.
133 Cf. pp. 123–4 above.

his project appear so convincing to so many is that it manages to portray this methodological weakness as a strength. The impossibility of discussing utopia discursively is presented as evidence of its genuinely new, transcending nature. That is to say, rather than simply claiming that it is impossible to extrapolate and delineate the novum dialectically, Bloch transforms this very claim, this very impossibility, into the positive content of his philosophy. This is the basic metaphysical structure of his thought, which seeks to reach beyond history by dialectical means and keeps failing – inevitably so, because the transcendence that is the novum cannot be captured by the analysis of empirical reality. The dialectic is a worldly phenomenon; there is no leap out of the immanent. Bloch responds to this quandary with a double move. First, he stresses that the transcendence that is at issue is not supernatural, but immanent in nature. Of course, even an immanent transcendence is still a transcendence, a place (or no-place, utopia) beyond thought. Thinking cannot transcend thinking. So – in a second move – Bloch turns this methodological problem into a philosophical solution by reclaiming the dialectical ineffability of the novum as the theoretical foundation of utopia as (post-)historical otherness. The attempt to capture the postulated utopian transcendence in positive terms fails, as it must; but this very failure confirms – so the implicit argument goes – that we are dealing with the genuinely new and not merely an improvement of the current state of affairs. The impossibility of theorising utopia becomes proof of the existence of utopia.

This metaphysical structure reveals the essentially Romantic – and thus un-Marxist – core of Bloch's philosophy. It relies on a mode of thought that Hegel characterises as the *unhappy consciousness* of Romanticism, an approach that

> ... does not *relate* itself as a *thinking* consciousness to its object, but, though it is indeed *in itself* a pure thinking individuality ... is only a movement *towards* thinking and hence is [ultimately a form of] devotion. Its thinking as such is no more than the hollow [*gestaltlos*; lit., formless, shapeless] sound of church bells or a mist of warm incense, a musical thinking that does not reach the level of the concept [*Begriff*], which would be the sole immanent, objective mode of thought. This infinite, pure inner feeling does indeed come into possession of its object; but this does not make its appearance in conceptual form, not as something comprehended, but as something alien.[134]

---

134   Hegel 1977b, p. 131; translation modified.

What we are dealing with is – in Hegel's phrasing – 'the movement of an infinite yearning', because the essence that the Romantic reaches for 'is the unattainable *beyond* which, in being laid hold of, flees, or rather has already flown'.[135] Hegel explains this with an allusion to the Crusaders' search for the burial place of Jesus and quest for the Holy Grail:

> Where that 'other' is sought, it cannot be found, for it is supposed to be, precisely, *a beyond*, something that can *not* be found … Consciousness therefore can only find as a present reality the *grave* of its life. But because this grave is itself an *actual existence* … the presence of that grave, too, is merely the struggle of an enterprise doomed to failure.[136]

The fascination that Bloch exerts as a thinker resides precisely in his philosophical Romanticism. Unable to theorise utopia dialectically, and unwilling to explore the tension between his materialist and his metaphysical claims, he offers a Romantic surplus – a pledge that is its own redemption. By replacing sociological analysis with infinite yearning while couching (and covering) this longing in an array of quasi-analytical concepts, he stages a discursive forward movement that de facto rotates around its own axis.

In his critique of Heidegger, Adorno calls this kind of approach 'aureolatic' because it 'promises at every moment to be more than it is'.[137] Now – Adorno goes on to say – Heidegger's project undoubtedly arose in response to a real intellectual and spiritual need. However, 'having proved incapable of satisfying this need in the particular [i.e., genuinely philosophical] form in which it undertook to address it, this thinking was obliged, in accordance with its very structure, to perform a kind of turnaround [*Volte*; also, sleight-of-hand], which consists in renouncing the satisfaction of the need, since that cannot be satisfied, while simultaneously acting as if it did satisfy it'.[138] I would argue that the same applies to Bloch's project. Countless people are looking for hope, for a way out of capitalism's manifold contingent and structural forms of injustice and inequality. At the same time, more traditional, sociologically based Marxist analyses – however trenchant they may be in their critique of contemporary society – are felt by many to have too little to say about a possible post-capitalist

---

135   Ibid.
136   Hegel 1977b, pp. 131–2; translation modified.
137   Adorno 2019, p. 102. The English translation has 'hallowed', not 'aureolatic', but the German terms *aureolisch* and *Aureole* are clearly meant to designate inferior versions of Benjamin's *auratisch* and *Aura*.
138   Adorno 2019, p. 143; translation modified.

future, while more practical, politically based approaches are often considered manifestations of craven reformism. This leaves an intellectual and spiritual gap, which Bloch's principle of hope appears to fill, even though all it factually does is to present its own methodological cul-de-sac as the way out that it fails to supply.[139] Today, in a world that is becoming increasingly neoliberal, the yearning for utopia is growing too. This development goes a long way towards explaining the renaissance of interest in Bloch's philosophy. However – to cite Adorno – '[t]he fact that an intellectual and spiritual need exists does not guarantee the possibility of its fulfilment'.[140]

In Bloch, then, the never-ending preoccupation with the infinite yearning, or 'hope', for a perfect post-capitalist world takes precedence over and ultimately displaces the immanent, objective analysis of the dialectical relationship between present and future. This is the central problem of his philosophy. The metaphysical overvaluation of utopia devalues the exploration of contemporary actuality. Accordingly, Bloch effectively abandons Marx's orientation towards the real world with its *specific* economic, political and social 'relations in which man is a debased, enslaved, forsaken, despicable being'.[141] The entire arena of social mediations falls into the sphere of the merely empirical, an immanence too sullied by the imperfections of everyday human actions and institutions to engender the purity of a genuinely new future. The birth of utopia requires an immaculate conception. The 'principle of hope' can therefore never rely on the analysis of what is, but only on the aureola of what might be. This is the structural reason why Bloch in the final analysis places the burden of 'genuine' progress on the development of dynamic matter, just as Heidegger claims that Being 'clears its own space', 'unconceals itself' and the like.[142]

Viewed from this perspective, Bloch's 'darkness of the lives moment' turns out to be a highly ambiguous concept. It can be taken – and no doubt was authentically (in classical Marxist terminology, subjectively) meant – as an acknowledgement of the complexity of historical development and as a warning against the belief in social engineering inherent in dogmatic-orthodox Marxism. But its effective – objective – function in Bloch's philosophy is rather that of cover for a certain kind of intellectual defeatism. In Bloch, rational illumination is ultimately a jack-o'-lantern, because it remains, by definition, stuck

---

139   Cf. Adorno 2019, p. 144.
140   Adorno 2019, p. 143; translation modified.
141   Marx 2010b, p. 182.
142   Cf. Adorno 2019, p. 72.

in the given, the immanent. Indeed, to insist on the *ultima ratio* of critical thinking distorts and demeans utopia, which, by definition, lies *beyond* critical thinking.

Bloch keeps switching between dialectics (reason) and metaphysics (faith), but the final step towards the principle of hope can only be taken by 'transcending' reason – that is to say, by relinquishing it. This abandonment of reason is not merely an intellectual defeat. It also has implications for politics. Regardless of Bloch's personal political preferences, according to his *philosophy* we can only see things through a glass darkly: his philosophy offers few pointers, if any, that might guide our practical behaviour. His study of natural law and human dignity, to which I referred in the previous section, is a case in point.[143] If the goal is utopia, and if utopia is the unknown and indeed unknowable beyond, what could or should we do to get there? What preparatory work can we possibly do if the dialectic of the empirical here and now provides no bridge to the elysian hereafter? All that is really left is a secular – yet equally vague – version of St Paul's 'meanwhile redeeming the time, because the days are evil'.[144] In the final analysis, Bloch transfers the power of human praxis to a hylozoistic concept of matter, just as Heidegger transfers it to a hypostatised concept of Being.[145] He disregards Marx's admonition in the eighth thesis on Feuerbach: 'All social life is essentially *practical*. All mysteries which lead theory to mysticism find their rational solution in human practice and in the comprehension of this practice'.[146] Adorno's conclusion with regard to Heidegger's *Fundamentalontologie* therefore also applies to Bloch's philosophy:

> this whole form of thought is to be seen as mythological in a questionable sense ... When I speak of a reversion to mythology, I am really referring to the revocation of freedom, the cancellation of that aspect of freedom through which the subject has wrested itself from the blind, opaque context of nature, from the sway of fate or destiny ... I would add that ... what is ascribed [by Heidegger] to Being ... bears all the hallmarks of irrationality. In other words, Being is characterized as something utterly obscure [*etwas ganz Dunkles*] that may somehow be sensed and venerated, but about which nothing substantive [*nichts Inhaltliches*] can ever be said.[147]

---

143 See p. 121 above.
144 Ephesians 5: 16; cf. Colossians 4:5.
145 In a few places, Adorno actually uses the term 'hylozoism' with regard to Heidegger; see Adorno 2019, pp. 72, 76 and 229.
146 Marx 2010d, p. 5.
147 Adorno 2019, pp. 175 and 177; translation modified.

In the end, then, Bloch leaves the world pretty much as it is. We may dream beyond it, but the lived moment is too dark to grasp its workings, while the extraterritorial bliss that is utopia lies outside our empirical bailiwick. Dialectics has yielded to metaphysics.

Bibliography

Adorno, Theodor W. 1973 [1964], *The Jargon of Authenticity*, translated by Knut Tarnowski and Frederic Will, Evanston: Northwestern University Press.

Adorno, Theodor W. 1993a [1960], 'Ernst Bloch's *Spuren*: On the Revised Edition of 1959', in *Notes to Literature*, Volume 1, translated by Shierry Weber Nicholson, New York: Columbia University Press.

Adorno, Theodor W. 1993b [1963], *Hegel: Three Studies*, translated by Shierry Weber Nicholsen, Cambridge, Mass.: MIT Press.

Adorno, Theodor W. 2007 [1966], *Negative Dialectics*, translated by E.B. Ashton, New York: Continuum.

Adorno, Theodor W. 2008 [2003], *Lectures on Negative Dialectics*, translated by Rodney Livingstone, Cambridge and Malden, MA: Polity Press.

Adorno, Theodor W. 2019 [2002], *Ontology and Dialectics*, translated by Nicholas Walker, Cambridge and Medford, MA: Polity Press.

Adorno, Theodor W., Walter Benjamin et al. 2007, *Aesthetics and Politics*, translated by Rodney Livingstone et al., London and New York: Verso.

Becker, Ralf, 2003, *Sinn und Zeitlichkeit. Vergleichende Studien zum Problem der Konstitution von Sinn durch die Zeit bei Husserl, Heidegger und Bloch*, Würzburg: Königshausen und Neumann.

Bloch, Ernst 1962 [1951], *Subjekt-Objekt. Erläuterungen zu Hegel*, slightly enlarged ed., Frankfurt am Main: Suhrkamp.

Bloch, Ernst 1976 [1951], 'Dialectic and Hope', translated by Mark Ritter, *New German Critique*, 9: 3–10.

Bloch, Ernst 1983 [1951], 'The Dialectical Method', translated by John Lamb, *Man and World*, 16: 285–313.

Bloch, Ernst 1985, *Tendenz – Latenz – Utopie*, Frankfurt am Main: Suhrkamp.

Bloch, Ernst 1991 [1935; 2nd, enlarged ed. 1962], *Heritage of Our Times*, translated by Neville Plaice and Stephen Plaice, Oxford: Polity Press.

Bloch, Ernst 1996a [1949–59], *The Principle of Hope*, 3 Volumes, translated by Neville Plaice, Stephen Plaice and Paul Knight, Cambridge, Mass.: MIT Press.

Bloch, Ernst 1996b [1961], *Natural Law and Human Dignity*, translated by Dennis J. Schmidt, Cambridge, Mass., and London: MIT Press.

Bloch, Ernst 2009 [1968], *Atheism in Christianity: The Religion of the Exodus and the Kingdom*, translated by J.T. Swann, London and New York: Verso.

Boldyrev, Ivan 2015, *Ernst Bloch and His Contemporaries: Locating Utopian Messianism*, London and New York: Bloomsbury.
Chesterton, G.K. 1987 [1908], *The Man Who Was Thursday: A Nightmare*, Harmondsworth: Penguin.
Dannemann, Rüdiger 1997, *Georg Lukács*, Hamburg: Junius.
de Berg, Henk 2012, 'Warum wir keine Utopien brauchen', in *Berliner Debatte Initial*, 23, 4: 5–17.
Eagleton, Terry 2017 [2015], *Hope without Optimism*, New Haven and London: Yale University Press.
Edschmid, Kasimir 1986 [1917], 'Über den dichterischen Expressionismus', in *Expressionismus und Dadaismus*, edited by Otto F. Best, Stuttgart: Reclam.
Frank, Manfred 2016 [1985], *Eine Einführung in Schellings Philosophie*, Frankfurt am Main: Suhrkamp.
Freud, Sigmund 1990, Delusions and Dreams in Jensen's 'Gradiva', translated by James Strachey, in *The Penguin Freud Library*, Volume 14, Harmondsworth: Penguin.
Garaudy, Roger 1962, *Dieu est mort. Étude sur Hegel*, Paris: PUF.
Geoghegan, Vincent 1996, *Ernst Bloch*, London and New York: Routledge.
Givsan, Hassan 2011, *Nach Hegel. Kritische Untersuchungen zu Hegels Logik, Schellings 'positiver' Philosophie und Blochs Ontologie*, Würzburg: Königshausen und Neumann.
Hegel, Georg Wilhelm Friedrich 1966, 'Who Thinks Abstractly?', in *Hegel: Reinterpretation, Texts, and Commentary*, translated and edited by Walter Kaufmann, London: Weidenfeld and Nicolson.
Hegel, Georg Wilhelm Friedrich 1975, *Lectures on the Philosophy of World History: Introduction*, translated by H.B. Nisbet, Cambridge; Cambridge University Press.
Hegel, Georg Wilhelm Friedrich 1977a, *The Difference between Fichte's and Schelling's System of Philosophy*, translated by H.S. Harris and Walter Cerf, Albany: State University of New York Press.
Hegel, Georg Wilhelm Friedrich 1977b, *Phenomenology of Spirit*, translated by A.V. Miller, Oxford: Oxford University Press.
Hegel, Georg Wilhelm Friedrich 1983, *Hegel and the Human Spirit: A Translation of the Jena Lectures on the Philosophy of Spirit (1805–6)*, translated by Leo Rauch, Detroit: Wayne State University Press.
Hegel, Georg Wilhelm Friedrich 1986, *The Philosophical Propaedeutic*, translated by A.V. Miller, Oxford: Basil Blackwell.
Hegel, Georg Wilhelm Friedrich 1995, *Lectures on the History of Philosophy*, 3 Volumes, translated by E.S. Haldane and Frances H. Simson, Lincoln and London: University of Nebraska Press.
Hegel, Georg Wilhelm Friedrich 2004a, *Philosophy of Nature: Part Two of the Encyclopaedia of the Philosophical Sciences (1830)*, translated by A.V. Miller, Oxford: Oxford University Press.

Hegel, Georg Wilhelm Friedrich 2004b, *The Philosophy of History*, translated by J. Sibree, Mineola, NY: Dover.
Hegel, Georg Wilhelm Friedrich 2005, *Logic: Part One of the Encyclopaedia of the Philosophical Sciences (1830)*, translated by William Wallace, Oxford: Oxford University Press.
Hegel, Georg Wilhelm Friedrich 2006, *Elements of the Philosophy of Right*, translated by H.B. Nisbet, Cambridge: Cambridge University Press.
Hegel, Georg Wilhelm Friedrich 2007, *Political Writings*, translated by H.B. Nisbet, Cambridge: Cambridge University Press.
Hegel, Georg Wilhelm Friedrich 2015, *The Science of Logic*, translated by George di Giovanni, Cambridge: Cambridge University Press.
Hudson, Wayne, 1982, *The Marxist Philosophy of Ernst Bloch*, London and Basingstoke: Macmillan.
Jameson, Fredric 1971, *Marxism and Form: Twentieth-Century Dialectical Theories of Literature*, Princeton, NJ: Princeton University Press.
Jung, Werner 1989, *Georg Lukács*, Stuttgart: Metzler.
Kellner, Douglas 1983, 'Introduction to Ernst Bloch, "The Dialectical Method"', *Man and World*, 16: 281–4.
Kessler, Achim 2006, *Ernst Blochs Ästhetik. Fragment, Montage, Metapher*, Würzburg: Königshausen und Neumann.
Knowles, Dudley 2002, *Hegel and the Philosophy of Right*, London and New York: Routledge.
Lukács, Georg, 1971 [1911], *Soul and Form*, translated by Anna Bostock, Cambridge, Mass.: MIT Press.
Lukács, Georg 1975 [1948], *The Young Hegel: Studies in the Relations between Dialectics and Economics*, translated by Rodney Livingstone, London: Merlin Press.
Lukács, Georg 2000 [1996], *A Defence of 'History and Class Consciousness'*, translated by Esther Leslie, London and New York: Verso.
Lukács, Georg 2007 [1938], 'Realism in the Balance', in Walter Benjamin et al., *Aesthetics and Politics*, translated by Rodney Livingstone, London and New York: Verso.
Magee, Glenn Alexander 2010, *The Hegel Dictionary*, London and New York: Continuum.
Markun, Sylvia 1977, *Ernst Bloch*, Reinbek bei Hamburg: Rowohlt.
Marx, Karl 2010a, 'Marx to Ruge [letter of September 1843]', in *Marx and Engels Collected Works*, Volume 3, London: Lawrence and Wishart.
Marx, Karl 2010b, 'Contribution to the Critique of Hegel's Philosophy of Law: Introduction', in *Marx and Engels Collected Works*, Volume 3, London: Lawrence and Wishart.
Marx, Karl 2010c, 'Economic and Philosophic Manuscripts of 1844', in *Marx and Engels Collected Works*, Volume 3, London: Lawrence and Wishart.

Marx, Karl 2010d, 'Theses on Feuerbach', in *Marx and Engels Collected Works*, Volume 5, London: Lawrence and Wishart.

Marx, Karl 2010e, 'The Eighteenth Brumaire of Louis Bonaparte', in *Marx and Engels Collected Works*, Volume 11, London: Lawrence and Wishart.

Marx, Karl 2010f., Capital, Volume 1, in *Marx and Engels Collected Works*, Volume 35, London: Lawrence and Wishart.

Marx, Karl and Friedrich Engels 2010, The Communist Manifesto, in *Marx and Engels Collected Works*, Volume 6, London: Lawrence and Wishart.

Moir, Cat 2020 [2019], *Ernst Bloch's Speculative Materialism: Ontology, Epistemology, Politics*, Chicago, IL: Haymarket Books.

Münster, Arno 1987, 'Das Totenschiff der Philosophie? Ernst Bloch und Martin Heidegger', in *Verdinglichung und Utopie. Ernst Bloch und Georg Lukács zum 100. Geburtstag*, edited by Michael Löwy, Arno Münster and Nicolas Tertulian, Frankfurt am Main: Sendler.

Münster, Arno 2004, *Ernst Bloch. Eine politische Biographie*, Berlin: Philo.

Pinkard, Terry 2000, *Hegel: A Biography*, Cambridge: Cambridge University Press.

Popper, Karl R. 1945, *The Open Society and Its Enemies*, 2 Volumes, London: Routledge.

Reed, T.J. 2009, *Mehr Licht in Deutschland. Eine kleine Geschichte der Aufklärung*, Munich: Beck.

Reed, T.J. 2015, *Light in Germany: Scenes from an Unknown Enlightenment*, Chicago and London: University of Chicago Press.

Ricoeur, Paul 1981, *Hermeneutics and the Human Sciences: Essays on Language, Action, and Interpretation*, translated by John B. Thompson, Cambridge: Cambridge University Press.

Riedel, Manfred 1994, *Tradition und Utopie. Ernst Blochs Philosophie im Licht unserer geschichtlichen Denkerfahrung*, Frankfurt am Main: Suhrkamp.

Russell, Bertrand 1961 [1946], *History of Western Philosophy*, London: George Allen & Unwin.

Schmitt, Hans-Jürgen (ed.) 1973, *Die Expressionismusdebatte. Materialien zu einer marxistischen Realismuskonzeption*, Frankfurt am Main: Suhrkamp.

Stewart, Jon (ed.) 1996, *The Hegel Myths and Legends*, Evanston, Ill.: Northwestern University Press.

Thompson, Peter 2012, 'Mensch', in *Bloch-Wörterbuch. Leitbegriffe der Philosophie Ernst Blochs*, edited by Beat Dietschy, Doris Zeilinger and Rainer E. Zimmermann, Berlin and Boston: Walter de Gruyter.

Thompson, Peter and Slavoj Žižek (eds.) 2013, *The Privatization of Hope: Ernst Bloch and the Future of Utopia*, Durham and London: Duke University Press.

Titzmann, Michael 1993 [1977], *Strukturale Textanalyse. Theorie und Praxis der Interpretation*, Munich: Fink.

Ujma, Christina 1995, *Ernst Blochs Konstruktion der Moderne aus Messianismus und

Marxismus. Erörterungen mit Berücksichtigung von Lukács und Benjamin, Stuttgart: M & P Verlag für Wissenschaft und Forschung.

Žižek, Slavoj 1998, *Die Nacht der Welt. Psychoanalyse und Deutscher Idealismus*, Frankfurt am Main: Fischer.

Žižek, Slavoj 2012, *Less Than Nothing: Hegel and the Shadow of Dialectical Materialism*, London and New York: Verso.

Zudeick, Peter 1987, *Der Hintern des Teufels. Ernst Bloch – Leben und Werk*, Moos: Elster.

CHAPTER 5

Bloch's Commentary on Marx's 'Theses on Feuerbach' in *The Principle of Hope*

Vincent Geoghegan

The Principle of Hope contains a section in which Bloch provides a number of detailed comments on the eleven 'Theses on Feuerbach', written by the young Marx and published much later with minor editing by Engels.[1] Explicitly referring to this section as a 'commentary', Bloch notes towards the beginning of the piece that '[t]here is, as far as can be seen, still no commentary on the Eleven Theses; only when there is one, arising out of the common cause itself [i.e., the historical Marxist revolutionary movement], does the continuously productive coherence of their brevity and depth also open up'.[2] The term 'commentary' is evocative; it brings to mind the rich medieval tradition of commentaries by authors such as Duns Scotus and Thomas Aquinas, who scrutinised an authoritative work such as Peter Lombard's *Book of Sentences* not just to try and understand it, but also to relate their own deliberations to the text. Of course, one cannot push this somewhat ahistorical comparison too far, and one must be mindful of Bloch's frequent pejorative usage of the term 'scholastic'. Nevertheless, Bloch can be seen to be doing something not entirely dissimilar in his own commentary on Marx's text.

Marx was of interest to Bloch early on – for example, in *The Spirit of Utopia* (1918) – but only as one thinker among others, and one with whom Bloch had significant differences.[3] By the time Bloch was writing *The Principle of Hope* (1938–47), however, he had come to view Marx as a thinker of pre-eminent importance, indeed as the fundamental theorist of modern times. Bloch seeks to bring out the central truths of the theses, but, importantly, he does so by bringing to bear on the text his own utopian system of thought, while implicitly criticising the lacunae in his predecessor's text. The present chapter aims

---

1 See Marx and Engels 1976. For the differences between the two versions, cf. de Berg and Large (eds.) 2012, pp. 6–7 and 145–9.
2 Bloch 1986, vol. 1, pp. 278 and 254.
3 I examine Bloch's changing relationship to Marx over the years in Geoghegan 1996, pp. 117–32. Boldyrev 2014 is also useful on this issue.

to provide a critical exposition of Bloch's close reading of the structure and substance of the theses. It does not in its turn claim to be a commentary, though it will explore the tensions in Bloch's reading of Marx.

1 The Beginning

Bloch begins his commentary by trying at a fairly general level to comprehend the theoretical relationship between Marx and Feuerbach. To indicate his sense of the importance of Feuerbach to Marx, and to explicate his own understanding of Marx's emerging project in the 1840s, Bloch argues that Feuerbach cannot be dismissed as a left Hegelian. On the contrary – Bloch stresses – Feuerbach critiqued and surpassed the idealism of thinkers such as Bruno Bauer and Max Stirner (even though he ultimately remained in the grip of 'bourgeois ideology') and developed (albeit inadequately) a materialism which, crucially and in sharp contrast to the 'pure materialists', recognised that a human being is a 'sensory object'.[4] Hence, 'Feuerbach's anthropological materialism ... marks the facilitated possible transition from mere mechanical to historical materialism'.[5] However, Bloch also maintains that Feuerbach in one crucial sense was not sufficiently Hegelian. 'Feuerbach could not find the path to reality; precisely the most important aspect of Hegel: the historical-dialectical method, he rejected'.[6] This combination of acceptance and rejection is apparent in Bloch's reference to Engels's 1888 reminiscence of his and Marx's Feuerbachian moment back in the 1840s: 'enthusiasm was general: we were all momentarily Feuerbachians. How enthusiastically Marx greeted the new interpretation, and how greatly – despite all critical reservations – he was influenced by it, we can read in *The Holy Family*'.[7] Bloch deploys one of his own concepts, the *Front*, to encapsulate his understanding of Marx's project in the theses. The Front – a term with conscious military connotations – is the place where present and future meet, where the world is advancing into liberating newness. Accordingly, the theses are to be viewed as 'signposts' of Marx's evolving epochal theoretical shift with its revolutionary forward glance, a journey 'out of the materialism of the base behind the lines into that of the Front'.[8]

---

4 Bloch 1986, vol. 1, pp. 252 and 253.
5 Bloch 1986, vol. 1, p. 253.
6 Ibid.
7 Bloch 1986, vol. 1, p. 250; cf. Engels 1934, p. 28.
8 Bloch 1986, vol. 1, p. 253.

Bloch treats as authoritative Engels's recollection that the theses, which the latter published in an appendix to *Ludwig Feuerbach and the Outcome of Classical German Philosophy* in 1888, were drafted by Marx in 1845 – when *The German Ideology* was being written – and were brief initial formulations not meant for imminent publication. This allows Bloch to read the text in a new, productive manner. He notes that, given the nature of their creation, it is not self-evident how the individual theses relate to one another, nor, given the clear areas of overlap, to what extent they aim to express different things. He acknowledges the usefulness of earlier attempts to group various theses together, but rejects groupings that simply follow the one-to-eleven order of Engels's published version. By way of example, Bloch mentions groupings such as 'Unity of Theory and Practice in Thought' (theses one to three), 'Understanding of Reality in Contradictions' (theses four to five), 'Reality Itself in Contradiction' (theses six to nine) and 'Location and Task of Dialectical Materialism in Society' (theses ten to eleven).[9] Here, mere sequence becomes authoritative. Instead, Bloch proposes a philosophical approach based on 'themes and contents'.[10] This generates four groups: *the epistemological group*, which is concerned with 'perception and activity' (theses five, one and three); *the anthropological-historical group*, which focuses on 'self-alienation, its real cause and true materialism' (theses four, five, seven, nine and ten); the *uniting or theory-practice group*, which deals with 'proof and probation' (theses two and eight); and *the password*, a group consisting just of thesis eleven, 'the most important' one.[11] Bloch is keen to stress the unity underlying this diversity, asserting that 'between the individual theses within each respective group there is free, complementary movement of voices; just as, between the groups themselves, continual correlation is taking place, forming a coherent unified whole'.[12] Let us now look at each of these groups in turn.

2 The Epistemological Group

Theses five, one and three establish the parameters for Bloch's treatment of Feuerbach as a materialist, with Marx both praising and admonishing Feuerbach for his relationship with materialism and idealism. Bloch also adds his own understanding of the historical-philosophical forms of these traditions to

---

9   Bloch 1986, vol. 1, p. 254.
10 Ibid.
11 Ibid.
12 Bloch 1986, vol. 1, p. 255.

fill out his conception of the nature of Marx's purpose in these pithy theses. Thesis five in Engels's version reads: 'Feuerbach, not satisfied with abstract thinking, appeals to sensuous contemplation, but he does not conceive sensuousness as a practical, human-sensuous activity'.[13] Bloch uses the first part of this thesis to portray Feuerbach as rejecting the perceived philosophical emptiness of the idealism of his day: 'Feuerbach reminded us of this at a time when every academic street-corner still resounded with mind, concept and nothing but concept'.[14] Feuerbach instead sought to give perception a materialist grounding: 'he wants his feet on the perceived ground'.[15] Bloch homes in on Marx's critique of Feuerbach's 'appeal to sensuous contemplation' to put forward his own formulation of this critique – namely, 'that with contemplative sensoriness, the only kind Feuerbach understands, his feet cannot yet move and the ground itself remains unnegotiable' – and to use the concept of contemplative sensoriness to reflect on the historical forms of the concepts of activity and work.[16] The bridge to these reflections is Bloch's endorsement of a particular theme in the first thesis; namely, Feuerbach's failure to recognise an important theoretical legacy – or 'cultural surplus', as Bloch terms this phenomenon elsewhere – in Hegelian idealism. The key section of Marx's first thesis is this:

> The chief defect of all hitherto existing materialism – that of Feuerbach included – is that the object, reality, sensuousness, is conceived only in the form of the object or contemplation but not as human sensuous activity, practice, not subjectively. Thus it happened that the active side, in opposition to materialism, was developed by idealism – but only abstractly, since, of course, idealism does not know real sensuous activity as such.[17]

To explicate this claim, Bloch provides an historical-materialist account of the different modalities of labour in the succession of modes of production from ancient slave-owning societies through feudalism to the capitalist mode of production. He speaks of the contempt felt for work by the ancient elites and the feudal aristocrats, noting that 'in Athens even sculptors were counted as philistines'.[18] Such contempt was not incompatible with the development of

---

13   Engels 1934, p. 74.
14   Bloch 1986, vol. 1, p. 255.
15   Ibid.
16   Ibid.
17   Engels 1934 p. 73.
18   Bloch 1986, vol. 1, p. 256.

materialism from Democritus to the early modern Hobbes, but this materialism was essentially 'contemplative', and it remained present in Feuerbach. With capitalism, a new concept of work was produced, but one that embodied the conflicts and dissimulations of this new mode of production. The economic imperatives of capitalism required that work be honoured, but its unequal social basis meant that it was the appearance of work, and not work itself, that was honoured. This happened morally in the form of a 'work ethic', and epistemologically in the concept of 'activity'.[19] This development in its turn entered the idealist philosophy of the time, whose crowning glory was Hegel; thus, 'rationalism, the idealism of the new age ... reflected the work process much more powerfully in epistemological terms than [did] the materialism of the new age'.[20]

Bloch states that Marx paid Hegel the ultimate historical compliment in calling the *Phenomenology* 'the standpoint of modern political economy'; Feuerbachian materialism by contrast – Bloch says – lacks '*the constantly oscillating subject-object relation called work*' ('subject-object' is a crucial category in Bloch's understanding of human and social dynamics).[21] In other words, in Hegel we glimpse the socio-economic forms of modernity, or 'the real workform of *historical genesis*', whereas Feuerbach – here Bloch's historical-philosophical criteria produce a rather brutal picture – 'occupied in epistemological terms the standpoint of slave-owning society or even of serfdom, on account of the non-active, still contemplatory element in his materialism'.[22] Yet in order to remain fair and validate Marx's critical appropriation of both Feuerbach and Hegel, Bloch also stresses – as I already hinted above – that in idealism bourgeois activity possesses only the '*appearance* of work', as the actual work is done by other classes, while entrepreneurs have an 'ultimately passive, external, abstract relationship' to a market economy.[23]

Bloch's reflections on thesis three reveal a crucial and abiding theme in his developing system of thought – a pervasive humanism which both naturalises humanity and makes it an essential dimension in the further development of the world, for 'the Being that conditions everything now itself contains active men'.[24] Let us cite the thesis in full:

---

19 Ibid.
20 Bloch 1986, vol. 1, p. 257.
21 Ibid.
22 Bloch 1986, vol. 1, pp. 257–8.
23 Bloch 1986, vol. 1, p. 258.
24 Ibid.

> The materialist doctrine that men are products of circumstances and upbringing and that, therefore, changed men are products of other circumstances and changed upbringing, forgets that circumstances are changed precisely by men and that the educator must himself be educated. Hence this doctrine necessarily arrives at dividing society into two parts, of which one towers above society (in Robert Owen, for example).
>
> The coincidence of the changing of circumstances and of human activity can only be conceived and rationally understood as revolutionising practice.[25]

Bloch detects here a critique of Feuerbach's 'mechanistic materialism'[26] – of an approach which, while seemingly elevating humanity to a precious product of nature, actually fails to appreciate the true achievements of humanity. That is to say, Feuerbach posits 'man as blossom, but in fact simply as blossom', while simultaneously degrading nature to mere surrounding stuff.[27] This notion of mere '*givenness*' ignores the fact that there is in 'the human environment hardly anything given which is not equally something worked on'.[28] According to Bloch, this mistaken train of thought (to be found, he argues, not just in Feuerbach, but also in *Vulgärmarxisten*) involves a misunderstanding of the undoubted truth of the '*primacy of being over consciousness*', a misunderstanding which buttresses mechanistic environmentalism.[29] He asserts that 'independence of being from consciousness is by no means the same as independence of being from human work'.[30] Rather, human activity is intrinsic to the development of the external objective world, with 'the subject-object-mediation ... a piece of the external world'.[31] Bloch thus sees Marx as battling both a vulgar materialist 'fatalism of being' and an idealist 'exaggerated activity-optimism', and he inserts citations from *The German Ideology* and *Capital* that testify to the endurance of this particular thrust of Marx's work.[32] Bloch's reflections on thesis three feed into a recurring theme in his Marxist theorising: the centrality of human activity in the further advance of nature. Thus, he argues that in Marx 'human activity with its consciousness is itself explained as a piece of nature, moreover

---

25   Engels 1934, p. 74.
26   Bloch 1986, vol. 1, p. 260.
27   Ibid. This criticism is a recurring theme in Bloch's oeuvre.
28   Bloch 1986, vol. 1, p. 259.
29   Ibid.
30   Ibid.
31   Ibid.
32   Bloch 1986, vol. 1, p. 260.

as the most important piece, in fact as radical practice precisely at the base of material being, which again primarily conditions the consciousness that follows'.[33]

3 The Anthropological-Historical Group

Bloch identifies theses four, six, seven, nine and ten as belonging to what he calls 'the anthropological-historical group'. His objective is to use Marx's critique of Feuerbach's ahistorical and abstract individualism to validate an historically grounded and concrete socialist humanism, and to reflect upon the religious heritage of humanity grasped (albeit inadequately) by Feuerbach. He starts with thesis four, the key sections of which read as follows:

> Feuerbach starts out from the fact of self-alienation, the duplication of the world into a religious, imaginary world and a real one ... He overlooks the fact that after completing this work, the chief thing still remains to be done.

> Feuerbach resolves the religious essence into the human essence. But the human essence is no abstraction inherent in each single individual. In its reality it is the ensemble of the social relations.[34]

Here, Bloch says, Marx is articulating the claim that Feuerbach's humanism revolves around an 'abstract genus of man, which is quite unstructured in class and historical terms' – a mere anthropological linkage grounded in a supposed natural unity.[35] Developing a theme he will explore more fully in *Natural Law and Human Dignity* (1968), Bloch links Feuerbach to the prehistory and history of bourgeois political philosophy. Ancient stoicism, natural rights, ideas of human toleration, French conceptions of the citizen and Kant's 'general humanity' – they all fed into the 'generality of bourgeois human rights with the abstract citizen above it, this moral-humanitarian generic ideal'.[36] At the same time, Bloch invokes thesis ten ('The standpoint of the old materialism is "civil society"; the standpoint of the new is human society or socialised humanity')[37]

---

33 Ibid.
34 Engels 1934, pp. 74–5.
35 Bloch 1986, vol. 1, p. 263.
36 Ibid.
37 Engels 1934, p. 75.

to show that Marx appreciated the residual strength of the concept of humanity, albeit in a necessarily transformed mode. Bloch calls this Marx's retention of the 'value-concept of humanity' and grounds it in a Marxist politics: 'the new proletarian standpoint, far from removing the value-concept of humanism, in practice allows it to come home for the very first time'.[38]

Thesis nine provides Bloch with a basis to criticise Feuerbach's understanding of the nature of religion in the modern world. This thesis states that 'the highest point attained by contemplative materialism ... is the outlook of single individuals in "civil society"'.[39] Bloch scrutinizes Feuerbach as such an individual. Feuerbach's contemplative materialism, he argues, generated an existential emptiness that was filled by 'an idealism'[40] which does not critique the *contents* of religion but merely their *transposition onto an imaginary world*. Feuerbach thus deploys 'almost a kind of non-denominational *pectoral theology*', a theology based on emotion and personal experience.[41] The result is the retention of the authoritarian ideology of Christianity in the act of dissolving the authoritarian God. Feuerbach

> ... allows almost all the attributes of the father-god to remain, in the unavoidable emptiness of his 'idealism forwards', as virtues in themselves so to speak, and only the heavenly god is struck from the list. Instead of: God is merciful, is love, is omnipotent, works miracles, hears our prayers – all that can be said now is: mercifulness, love, omnipotence, working miracles, hearing prayers are divine. Accordingly, therefore, the whole apparatus of theology remains intact.[42]

The only change is in the fact that the 'heavenly location' is replaced with 'a certain abstract region' grounded in the 'natural' basis of human individualism.[43]

By taking this approach, Feuerbach does a disservice to the 'squandered wealth' of the religious heritage of humanity, which Bloch articulates with reference to religious art: 'Who would wish to underestimate precisely the depth of humanity, the humanity of the depth in religion-charged art, in Giotto, in Grünewald, in Bach and ultimately even perhaps in Bruckner?'[44] Against

---

38 Bloch 1986, vol. 1, p. 264.
39 Engels 1934, p. 75.
40 Bloch 1986, vol. 1, p. 266.
41 Bloch 1986, vol. 1, p. 267.
42 Ibid.
43 Ibid.
44 Ibid.

Feuerbach's 'idealism forwards', Bloch recommends Marxism's *'materialism forwards, wealth of materialism'*, which 'posits the transformation of the world from within itself. Into an other world beyond hardship, which has not the least in common either with the other world of mythology, or with its master- or father-contents'.[45]

4 The Theory-Practice Group

This next group that Bloch constructs and explores consists of theses two and eight. These read in Engels's version:

> The question whether objective truth can be attributed to human thinking is not a question of theory but is a practical question. In practice man must prove the truth, i.e., the reality and power, the 'this-sidedness' of his thinking. The dispute over the reality or non-reality of thinking which is isolated from practice is a purely scholastic question.
>
> Social life is essentially practical. All mysteries which mislead theory to mysticism find their rational solution in human practice and in the comprehension of this practice.[46]

According to Bloch, it is this radical foregrounding of practice – the claim that there is 'no theoretically-immanently possible complete proof', because 'truth is not a theory relationship alone, but *a definite theory-practice relationship*' – that constitutes the world-historical novelty of Marx's thought.[47] This 'wholly creative and new' discovery of Marx renders all previous philosophy 'scholastic'.[48] Bloch then seeks to substantiate this claim with a critical survey of philosophical thinking since the time of the Greeks. Accordingly, ancient and medieval epistemology is said to 'not reflect reality', while 'bourgeois-abstract activity was not truly mediated with its object'.[49] To sustain this indictment, Bloch has to engage in some fancy rhetorical footwork so as to keep certain thinkers in the guilty tradition. Thus, while acknowledging Francis Bacon's breakthrough inductive and experimental method, he maintains that for Bacon

---

45 Ibid.
46 Engels 1934, pp. 73 and 75.
47 Bloch 1986, vol. 1, p. 268.
48 Ibid.
49 Ibid.

the theoretical truth of science is 'autarkical', such that proof does not lie in practice but is only 'the fruit and reward of truth'.[50] Likewise, Hegel – who 'comes closest to a premonition of a practice-criterion' – is deemed to be undermined by *anamnesis*, a fundamentally conservative form of recollection.[51] 'The closed-circuit thinker Hegel, the antiquarium of what is unalterably already existing, thus ultimately prevailed over the dialectical process-thinker Hegel with his crypto-practice'.[52] Finally, the left Hegelians, in whose company the young Marx cut his theoretical teeth, are condemned as exponents of Fichte's subjective idealism, and their 'practice' is unmasked as 'sharp practice'.[53]

At this point, Bloch returns to Feuerbach. He alights on the concepts of 'mysteries' and 'mysticism' in thesis eight to frame the *'pectoral practice'* – the warm inner feeling of love – he detects in this thinker.[54] Not that Bloch rejects love in the form of helping, of relating to victims and of energising hatred of exploitation, for these animate a partisanship required in socialist practice. But in Feuerbach, Bloch asserts, love is sentimentalised as an emotion between individuals. In a harsh and unpleasant phrase, he claims that Feuerbach 'effeminates humanity', sapping the will to struggle and entrenching conformity, and he accuses him of mysticism, of putting forward 'love-mysteries without clarity'.[55] Yet Feuerbach's mysteries are also said to be different from the 'idolatry of darkness' (an allusion to manifestations of irrationalism such as National Socialism) which beset the contemporary world.[56] Ultimately, 'Feuerbach lies ... on that German salvation-line which leads from Hegel to Marx, just as the German disaster-line leads from Schopenhauer to Nietzsche and the consequences'.[57]

5   The Password

This group deals with the famous thesis eleven: 'The philosophers have only *interpreted* the world in various ways; the point however is to *change* it'.[58] The heading of the relevant section in *The Principle of Hope* points to the key role that Marx's final – and, as Bloch puts it, 'most important' – thesis plays in

---

50   Bloch 1986, vol. 1, p. 269.
51   Ibid. I will return Bloch's adaptation of Plato's term *anamnesis* later on.
52   Bloch 1986, vol. 1, p. 270.
53   Ibid.
54   Bloch 1986, vol. 1, p. 274.
55   Bloch 1986, vol. 1, pp. 272 and 274.
56   Bloch 1986, vol. 1, p. 273.
57   Bloch 1986, vol. 1, p. 274.
58   Engels 1934, p. 75.

Bloch's commentary: 'The Password and Its Meaning'.[59] The opening sentence can be read as Bloch's statement of agreement between himself and Marx on the importance of the forward glance: 'It is recognized here that the future aspect is the nearest and most important'.[60] Their approach is then sharply differentiated from Feuerbach's deployment of the future, which is dismissively characterised as a ship 'which never sets sail'.[61] Feuerbach is condemned as the creator of mere bookish articulations of the principles of a better world, which the contemporary world rightly ignores. He displays the vanity of one who wishes to create a 'work' that will 'hover through the ages in ... an autarkical manner' and which is addressed to an 'equally contemplative reader'.[62] Bloch accepts that there is novel material in Feuerbach's work, but he views it as ungrounded. 'The standpoint may have been a new one, but it remained a mere vantage point; conceptual invention thus gave no instructions for real intervention'.[63] Hence Marx's pointed criticism and call to arms in thesis eleven.

Bloch also highlights the danger of misunderstanding this pithy thesis with regard to the nature of social transformation and philosophy. Thus, he warns of what he sees as the grave danger posed by the philosophical movement of pragmatism. Painting the matter in rather broad brushes, he evokes a link between American pragmatism and American capitalism which draws its energy from a highly jaundiced view of US culture and society. American pragmatism, he asserts, 'stems from a region which is utterly alien to Marxism, from a region which is hostile to it, intellectually inferior, ultimately downright disreputable', and he refers to pragmatists as thinkers who 'repeatedly subscribe to Marx's proposition, just as if it was ... American cultural barbarity'.[64] At the basis of American pragmatism is 'the view that truth is nothing more than the commercial usefulness of ideas'.[65] This one-sided statement is followed by a few words of a more nuanced nature about William James and his 1907 work *Pragmatism*, in which the US capitalist 'to a certain extent still appears to be generally human, is so to speak garnished in a humanitarian way, even in an almost life-promoting and optimistic way'.[66] However – Bloch says – this appearance is related to the particular stage of American capitalism at the time, with its distinctive forms of ideological distortion. Post-James, pragmatism is deemed to

---

59 Bloch, 1986, vol. 1, pp. 254 and 274.
60 Bloch, 1986, vol. 1, p. 274.
61 Ibid.
62 Bloch, 1986, vol. 1, p. 275.
63 Ibid.
64 Ibid.
65 Ibid.
66 Bloch 1986, vol. 1, p. 276.

have enshrined and further developed an ideology that embodied 'the final agnosticism of a society stripped of any will towards the truth'.[67] The process of degeneration receives further impetus from the two world wars, which Bloch distinguishes in terms of a 'generally imperialist' First World War and a 'partially imperialist' Second World War driven by the Nazis. Pragmatism became the form and veil for blatant self-interest. 'What served the German nation, i.e. what served German capital finance was right; what furthered the interests of life, i.e. maximum profit, and what appeared to be useful for its purposes, was truth'.[68] Worse, this approach could be presented as a form of theory practice – a grievous libel on the eleventh thesis.

In addition, Bloch identifies (without mentioning any particular thinkers by name) manifestations of what he terms *practicism* in some forms of Marxism. This current is morally different from pragmatism in that the practicists' 'will is pure, their intention revolutionary, their goal humanitarian'.[69] Yet by 'omitting the head' they succumb to 'trial and error' and 'tinkering', which methodologically connects them to pragmatism.[70] In Marx, Bloch emphasises, '*a thought is not true because it is useful, but ... useful because it is true*'.[71] Practicism thus misunderstands and indeed degrades the role of philosophy in thesis eleven, turning 'the highest triumph of philosophy' into 'an abdication of philosophy'.[72] The consequences are dire:

> Precisely that future aspect is poorly served here which no longer comes towards us uncomprehended, but to which conversely our active knowledge comes; – Ratio keeps watch on this stretch of practice. Just as it keeps watch on every stretch of humanitarian road home: against the irrational which ultimately also shows itself in any practice devoid of concept. For if the destruction of reason sinks back into the barbaric irrational, then the ignorance of reason sinks back into the stupid irrational. ... *Even banality is ... counter-revolutionary against Marxism itself*; since Marxism is the consummation (not the Americanization) of the most progressive thoughts of humanity.[73]

---

67 Ibid.
68 Ibid.
69 Ibid.
70 Ibid.
71 Bloch 1986, vol. 1, p. 277. Bloch adds a citation from Lenin's *Three Sources and Three Components of Marxism* that makes the same point: 'Marx's doctrine is all-powerful because it is true' (Lenin, 1963, vol. 1, p. 44).
72 Ibid.
73 Bloch 1986, vol. 1, pp. 277–8.

Bloch seeks to substantiate this position by a nuanced defence of the practice of authentic philosophy. Thesis eleven, he insists, is not establishing a simple antithesis between knowing and changing.[74] Rather, it is doing a great deal of conceptual work under the surface of its few words. Marx is critiquing a certain form of class-based interpretation, not philosophy as such, with 'interpretation' being linked to the 'contemplation' criticised in earlier theses. In other words, he is raising the flag of 'non-contemplative knowledge', which remains a flag of knowledge in the midst of action. Here, Bloch points to *Capital*, which 'while a clear directive for action ... is not a sort of recipe for a quick heroic deed ante rem, but stands in the middle of the res, in painstaking examination, philosophizing contextual exploration of the most difficult reality'.[75] Nor will Bloch allow Marx to be seen as having rejected all contemplative philosophy, arguing that the latter saw the continuing value of 'important philosophy from a great age'.[76] Thus, Bloch interprets the astringent language deployed in *The German Ideology* ('Philosophy is about as similar to study of the real world as masturbation is to love-making') as referring not to the work of Hegel 'and other great philosophies of the past, no matter how contemplative these were considered to be', but rather to the 'philosophical windbaggery' – in effect, non-philosophy – of post-Hegelian thinkers such as Max Stirner and the religious socialist Georg Kuhlmann: it was their work that animated Marx's tirade against 'philosophy'.[77]

Bloch implicitly links his own conceptions of cultural heritage and ideological surplus to Marx's 'creative real entry into an inheritance' in the latter's approach to Hegel.[78] Central to his analysis is Marx's 1844 'Introduction to the Critique of Hegel's Philosophy of Right'. Referring to Marx's famous assertion that 'philosophy could not be abolished without realizing it, could not be realized without abolishing it', Bloch states that 'Marx ... gives both factions of the time an antidote for their behaviour, in each case a reverse medicina mentis: he imposes greater realization of philosophy on the practical men of that time, and greater abolition of philosophy on the [mere] theoreticians'.[79] And he is happy to embrace the concept of a 'Marxist philosophy' as possessing a fundamental orientation towards a better future. It is a philosophy

---

74 As Bloch points out, the word *but* ('but the point is to change it') was inserted by Engels and is missing from Marx's original. Cf. de Berg and Large (eds.) 2012, pp. 6–7 and 149.
75 Bloch 1986, vol. 1, p. 278.
76 Ibid.
77 Marx and Engels 1975, p. 236, and Bloch 1986, vol. 1, p. 279.
78 Bloch 1986, vol. 1, p. 279.
79 Bloch 1986, vol. 1, p. 280. The German verb that Marx uses for 'abolish' is the Hegelian *aufheben*.

> ... which, with staying power, with full cultural inheritance, is well-versed in ultra-violet, that is: in the future-laden properties of reality ... [S]ound change, especially that into the *realm of freedom*, comes about solely through sound knowledge, with ever more precisely mastered necessity. Out and out philosophers have subsequently changed the world in this way: Marx, Engels, Lenin.[80]

6   The Archimedean Point

Bloch brings his commentary to a conclusion by deploying the old concept of the Archimedean point (derived from the remark attributed to Archimedes, 'Give me a place to stand, and with a lever I will move the whole world'). Referring to thesis four – which, among other things, states that the secular basis of capitalist society is self-contradictory and must be understood as such 'and then, by removal of the contradiction, revolutionized in practice' – he contends that Marx reveals how 'the old world could ... be lifted off its hinges and the new one on to its hinges'.[81] The conclusion's full title already indicates the direction in which Bloch will take this idea: 'The Archimedean Point; Knowledge Related Not Only to What Is Past, but Essentially [*wesentlich*] to What Is Coming Up'.

Central to Bloch's argument here is his adaptation of Plato's *anamnesis*, or conservative recollection. An initial textual grounding is provided by the *Communist Manifesto*: 'In bourgeois society the past rules over the present, in communist society the present rules over the past'.[82] However, wishing to fuse this Marxian framework with his own utopian philosophy, Bloch extends Marx's observation on the role of 'the present' in communist society by inserting his uniquely Blochian future-orientated concepts: 'And the present rules *together with the horizon within it*, which is the horizon of the future, and which gives to the flow of the present specific space, the space of new, feasibly better present. Thus the beginning philosophy of revolution, i.e. of changeability for the better, was ultimately revealed on and in the *horizon of the future*; with the science of the New and power to guide it'.[83]

Marx's other proposition – namely, that in capitalist society the past rules over the present – is more immediately congenial to Bloch's assumptions about ontology and epistemology in history. Deploying Marx's critique of contem-

---

80   Bloch 1986, vol. 1, pp. 280–1.
81   Engels 1934, p. 74, and Bloch 1986, vol. 1, p. 282.
82   Bloch 1986, vol. 1, pp. 282–3.
83   Bloch 1986, vol. 1, p. 283.

plative materialism, he asserts that before Marx 'all knowledge was ... related essentially [*wesentlich*] to what is past, since only this can be contemplated' and that therefore the 'New' was not properly grasped.[84] Capitalist commodification has worsened this centuries-old mode of thinking focused on a solidified past:

> Thinking in commodity-form has particularly intensified this old traditional impotence; since the way capitalism turns all men and things into a commodity not only lends them alienation, but it also makes evident: the thought-form commodity is itself the intensified thought-form Becomeness [*Gewordenheit*], Factum. On account of this Factum the Fieri [making, producing] is particularly easily forgotten, and consequently the producing element on account of the reified product, and on account of the apparent Fixum at the back of men, the openness in front of them.[85]

Bloch argues that this epistemological development has roots stretching back to ancient times, to Plato's *anamnesis*, in which – in Socrates's words – 'searching and learning are purely and simply ... memory', such that knowledge is already fully formed, and 'beingness [*die Wesenheit*]' is essentially 'Been-ness [*Ge-wesenheit*]'.[86] This contemplative approach sees merely 'chaff, wind, formlessness in the future', while putting a premium on the reassuring antiquity of the past, the further back the better: 'in the relation: knowledge-past, the Crusades permit more "scientificality" ... than both the last two World Wars, and Egypt, which is even more distant, more than the Middle Ages'.[87] Marx, by contrast, has a sophisticated approach to the past and the future. In Marxism, the past – be it the past of ancient primitive communism or that of historical class struggles – is not viewed from an antiquarian perspective, but as constituting different aspects of an ongoing process into the future. 'The dialectical-historical tendency science of Marxism is ... the mediated *future science of reality plus the objectively real possibility within it ... Only the horizon of the future, which Marxism occupies, with that of the past as the ante-room, gives reality its real dimension*'.[88] In this way, Bloch extracts from Marx's reflections a naturalist, humanist vision of human progress. His conclusion, which, significantly,

---

84 Ibid.
85 Ibid.
86 Ibid. Socrates's phrase comes from Plato's *Meno* (81B–82A).
87 Bloch 1986, vol. 1, pp. 285 and 284.
88 Bloch 1986, vol. 1, p. 285.

ends with the same word as does *The Principle of Hope* as a whole, reads as follows: 'Thus the totality of the "Eleven Theses" testifies: socialized humanity, allied with a nature that is mediated with it, is the reconstruction of the world into homeland [*der Umbau der Welt zur Heimat*]'.[89]

7   Bloch, Feuerbach and Marx

There is a genuine tension in Bloch's treatment of Feuerbach in *The Principle of Hope*. As Bloch seeks to vindicate Marx's system of ideas and affirm his own strict adherence to that system, he applauds Marx's blows against Feuerbach, even adding a few punches of his own in the process. Yet he is also palpably drawn to Feuerbach's understanding and development of Hegel's appreciation of humanity's historically grounded cultural heritage. This attraction, which is central to Blochian utopianism, is evident from his locating of Feuerbach on the 'salvation-line from Hegel to Marx'.[90] It can be observed even more clearly elsewhere in *The Principle of Hope*, as well as in some other texts. Thus, in the lengthy section on 'Religious Mystery' towards the end of *The Principle of Hope*, he notes with real enthusiasm:

> Feuerbach brought religious content from heaven back to man, so that man is not made in the image of God but God in the image of man, or more exactly of the ideal guiding images of man at any given time. As a result God as the creator of the world disappears completely, but a gigantic creative region in man is gained into which – with fantastic illusion, with fantastic richness at the same time – the divine as a hypostatised human wishful image of the highest order is incorporated.[91]

To give one further example, in *Das Materialismusproblem* he quotes Feuerbach when criticising the historicist view of heritage: 'The chariot of world history is a tiny chariot. So, just as one cannot climb into it if one is too late, one can only obtain a place if one abandons some of the commodities of the old historical household utensils – and only takes along the most unsaleable, necessary, and essential things'.[92]

---

[89]   Bloch 1986, vol. 1, p. 286.
[90]   See note 57 above.
[91]   Bloch 1986, vol. 3, pp. 1284–5.
[92]   Bloch 1988, pp. 44–5. The citation comes from Feuerbach's early *Gedanken über Tod und Unsterblichkeit* [Thoughts on Death and Immortality, 1830].

The tension in the treatment of Feuerbach bespeaks a divergence from Marx which is grounded in Bloch's early theoretical formation, a divergence narrowed but still present in *The Principle of Hope* and indeed beyond it. This is the messianic, eschatological voice that Bloch developed and refined in his interactions with Lukács and Benjamin, as evident particularly in *Spirit of Utopia* and *Thomas Münzer as Theologian of Revolution*.[93] As we saw earlier, Marx and Engels registered the importance of their Feuerbachian moment, but it was a brief moment. There was no notion of a still living religious legacy: for them, religion had a past, but no future. They viewed religion as an instrument of oppression and an arena for the yearnings of the oppressed for a better existence, but not as part of the solution, which lay in the struggle against the socio-economic structures generating the conditions for religion. Hence their relatively few remarks on religion after the 1840s – decline and extinction was to be its fate. For Bloch, on the other hand, the religious legacy of humanity, understood atheistically ('Only an atheist can be a good Christian; only a Christian can be a good atheist'), was to be a potent force in the utopian transformation of reality.[94] His appropriation of Marx was therefore always going to be partial.

There is also the question of the role of philosophy. Bloch, as we saw, passionately believes in the necessity of philosophy; in his commentary, he views Marx as in an important sense the continuer, as well as the destroyer, of past philosophical concerns. Thus, while fully endorsing Marx's radical project of praxis, he in effect presents Marx as a *philosopher* of radical practice; hence the contrast between the philosophical salvation line Hegel-Feuerbach-Marx and the disaster line Schopenhauer-Nietzsche. We also noted Bloch's characterisation of Marx, Engels and Lenin as 'out and out philosophers' who changed the world.[95] Moreover, Bloch was drawn to Marx's early 'Towards a Critique of Hegel's *Philosophy of Right*: Introduction', which speaks of the emancipation of Germany in terms of the emancipation of human beings such that 'the *head* of this emancipation is *philosophy*, its *heart* is the *proletariat*. Philosophy cannot be made a reality without the abolition of the proletariat, the proletariat cannot be abolished without philosophy being made a reality'.[96] However, many philosophers have been uneasy about the notion of Marx as

---

93 Cf. the extensive discussion in Boldyrev 2014.
94 Bloch 2009, p. viii.
95 Bloch 1986, vol. 1, p. 281.
96 Marx and Engels, 1975, p. 187. The final sentence reads in the original German: 'Die Philosophie kann sich nicht verwirklichen ohne die Aufhebung des Proletariats, das Proletariat kann sich nicht aufheben ohne die Verwirklichung der Philosophie'.

philosopher. In the case of Richard Rorty – to give only one example – this scepticism grew out of his critique of the pretensions of philosophy in general. In his 'Philosophy as a Transitional Genre' – a title that crisply announces the article's central thesis – he argues that, after the Renaissance, religion gave way to philosophy, but that philosophy in its turn has been giving way to literature. This transition from a philosophical to a literary culture took place after Kant, in the time of Hegel's supremacy: the latter's claim that 'philosophy paints its gray on gray only when a form of life has grown old' effectively sounded the death knell of philosophical culture.[97] Rorty asserts that Hegel's remark 'helped the generation of Kierkegaard and Marx realize that philosophy was never going to fill the redemptive role that Hegel himself had claimed for it', adding that 'since Hegel's time, the intellectuals have been losing faith in philosophy'.[98]

One should also note the development of the category of the *antiphilosopher* in the works of Terry Eagleton, Boris Groys, Etienne Balibar and Alain Badiou. Antiphilosophers – Eagleton says – are 'wary' and 'nervous' of philosophy: their theoretical objective is to resist the siren call of philosophical hubris, so 'they tend to come up with ideas that are suspicious of ideas'.[99] He brings in Feuerbach to sustain this argument. Though wishing to validate philosophy, the German thinker understood the non-philosophical dimensions of humanity: 'Feuerbach wrote that any authentic philosophy had to begin with its opposite, nonphilosophy. The philosopher, he remarked, must accept "what in man does not philosophize, what is rather opposed to philosophy and abstract thought"'.[100] It is in this sense – Eagleton maintains – that 'Marx was more of an antiphilosopher than a philosopher'.[101] Groys, for his part, singles out Marx and Kierkegaard as the initiators of this trend, while Balibar claims that Marx was 'perhaps ... the greatest antiphilosopher of the modern age'.[102] Badiou, by

---

97   Rorty 2007, p. 91. The citation from Hegel comes from the preface to the *Philosophy of Right*.
98   Rorty 2007, pp. 91–2.
99   Eagleton 2011, p. 131.
100 Ibid. The citation from Feuerbach is from his *Vorläufige Thesen zur Reform der Philosophie* [Provisional Theses for the Reformation of Philosophy, 1843].
101 Eagleton 2011, p. 130.
102 Groys 2012, pp. xix–xx, and Balibar 2007, p. 2. It is true that Balibar, while noting Marx's break with 'a certain form of philosophy', also argues that 'we can at last return to Marx and, without either diminishing or betraying him, read him as a philosopher' (Balibar 2007, pp. 4 and 5). Eagleton meanwhile concedes that antiphilosophers are nervous of philosophy 'for philosophically interesting reasons' (Eagleton 2011, p. 131), while Groys talks of antiphilosophy as being 'a new branch of philosophy' (Groys 2012, p. xix). All of this admittedly lessens the gap between Bloch and the antiphilosophers.

contrast, views the matter in a way that leads us back to Bloch. He characterises Lacan, Foucault and Derrida as antiphilosophers, but sees Althusser as a practitioner and advocate of philosophy: 'not only did [Althusser] maintain that there was philosophy; he announced that there always will be. Basically he believed in *philosophia perennis*'.[103] Here, there is clearly a parallel with Bloch, who, like Althusser (or at least like Althusser as interpreted by Badiou), used Marx's work to develop a new philosophy.

8   Conclusion

Like its medieval predecessors, Bloch's commentary combines an intense scrutiny of an old text, and a very small text at that, with a lengthy, multi-faceted 'actualising' analysis which brings that text to life again. Moreover, although Marx's ideas are woven into the fabric of *The Principle of Hope*, the commentary provides the one sustained, formal engagement with the formative concepts of Marx in the entire work. In addition, it gives us a snapshot of an important stage in Bloch's development, enabling us to see the rich legacy of his early messianic utopianism structured in new ways, with Münzer meeting Marx, so to speak. Finally, with the trace of an old medieval form, Bloch's commentary on the 'Theses on Feuerbach' adds a crucial element to the inventive architecture of *The Principle of Hope*.

Bibliography

Badiou, Alain 2009, *Pocket Pantheon: Figures of Postwar Philosophy*, translated by David Macey, London and New York: Verso.
Balibar, Etienne 2007, *The Philosophy of Marx*, translated by Chris Turner, London and New York: Verso.
Bloch, Ernst 1959, *Das Prinzip Hoffnung*, Frankfurt am Main: Suhrkamp.
Bloch, Ernst 1986 [1959], *The Principle of Hope*, 3 vols., translated by Neville Plaice, Stephen Plaice and Paul Knight, Oxford: Basil Blackwell.
Bloch, Ernst 1988, *The Utopian Function of Art and Literature: Selected Essays*, translated by Jack Zipes and Frank Mecklenburg, Cambridge MA and London: The MIT Press.
Bloch, Ernst 2009, *Atheism in Christianity: The Religion of the Exodus and the Kingdom*, translated by J.T. Swann, London and New York: Verso.

---

103   Badiou 2009, p. 89.

Boldyrev, Ivan 2014, *Ernst Bloch and His Contemporaries: Locating Utopian Messianism*, London: Bloomsbury.

de Berg, Henk and Duncan Large (eds.) 2012, *Modern German Thought from Kant to Habermas: An Annotated German-Language Reader*, Rochester, NY: Camden House.

Eagleton, Terry 2011, *Why Marx Was Right*, New Haven and London: Yale University Press.

Engels, Frederick 1934 [1888], *Ludwig Feuerbach and the Outcome of Classical German Philosophy*, New York: International Publishers.

Geoghegan, Vincent 1996, *Ernst Bloch*, London and New York: Routledge.

Groys, Boris 2012, *Introduction to Antiphilosophy*, translated by David Fernbach, London and New York: Verso.

Lenin, Vladimir Ilyich 1963, *Selected Works*, 3 Volumes, Moscow: Progress Publishers.

Marx, Karl and Frederick Engels 1975, *The German Ideology*, in *Marx and Engels Collected Works*, Volume 3, London: Lawrence & Wishart.

Marx, Karl and Frederick Engels 1976, 'Theses on Feuerbach', in *Marx and Engels Collected Works*, Volume 5, London: Lawrence and Wishart.

Rorty, Richard 2007, *Philosophy as Cultural Politics: Philosophical Papers*, Volume 4, New York: Cambridge University Press.

CHAPTER 6

Natural Law in the Ideas of Bloch, Hegel and Marxism

Holger Glinka

> The spirit of the sociology of man restlessly aims at deciphering the smudged letter of freedom that is in our own minds – and which is the most proximal 'natural law' – in a rationalist-millenarian fashion, thereby enabling us to attain the open form of the invisible church against all atavistic-astral gods of fear.
>
> BLOCH, 'On the Ethical and Spiritual Leader, or the Twofold Manner of the Human Face' (1920)

∴

1 Introduction*

This chapter outlines an alternative to the interpretations of Ernst Bloch's thought that have been put forward in Marxism, theology and the philosophy of religion. Bloch has a relatively superficial understanding of Marxist social theory; indeed, he views Marxism largely as an economic theory. Moreover, he homes in on 'utopia' and 'hope' as distinctly worldly concepts. This can be seen, for instance, in Chapter 36 of his *Freedom and Order: Outline of Social Utopias*, the first published section of *The Principle of Hope*. There, he argues that the 'oldest outlines of social utopia' emerged alongside the judgement of the prophets heralded in the Old Testament: 'man overtakes, even outshines his God – that is the logic of the Book of Job, despite his apparent submission at the end'.[1] At the same time, Bloch also claims that 'Christianity is not just an outcry against deprivation, it is an outcry against death and the void,

---

* I am grateful to Andreas Arndt (Berlin) for his advice on a key aspect of this chapter.
   Translators' note: We have rendered Bloch's often obscure German fairly freely, and we have silently modified existing translations where we deemed it necessary.
1 Bloch 1966, p. 53.

and inserts the Son of Man into both. But even if the Bible contains no elaborated social utopia, it does point most vehemently, in both negative and positive terms, towards this exodus and this kingdom'.[2] And his philosophy of the *Tertium* – the dimension of being which is located between no-longer-being and not-yet-being – differs, both in terms of methodology and of the philosophy of history, from the approach taken by orthodox Marxist philosophers precisely in that it establishes an intimate connection between socialist and Christian principles.[3] This aspect has important implications for his interpretation of natural law – something that is still apparent from one of his very last explanations of how his philosophy relates to the state and to Marxism:

> The state is the institution of authority [*Gewalt*] *per se*. Marx and Engels established that, at the end of our pre-history, the state will wither away [*absterben*]; and that violence alone will not bring this about, but that this process is above all contingent on a change in the relations of production. What is striking here is that 'withering away' is an extremely non-violent, peaceful and, as it were, Christian expression. This peaceful transition failed to materialise in the bourgeois revolution, during which roles were simply reversed, with power passing from absolutism to the bourgeoisie.[4]

Against this backdrop, it is remarkable that Bloch takes account neither of Marx's and Marxism's view of natural law nor of Hegel's position on the old ('empirical') natural law and the new ('purely formal') rational law. It seems therefore appropriate to explore both, and this will be my aim in what follows. Bloch himself, by contrast, views the legal social utopia outlined in Fichte's *Der geschlossene Handelsstaat* [The Closed Commercial State, 1800] as the zenith of classical German philosophy in the realm of rational constitutional law – a slightly odd position given that Fichte's economic theory had hardly any influence on the development of socialist thought in the nineteenth century.

2   Bloch and Marxism

> Foundational for Marxism is not only economic partisanship on behalf of the exploited and oppressed, but also economic partis-

---

2 Bloch 1986, vol. 2, p. 502.
3 On the *Tertium*, cf. Albrecht 1991.
4 Bloch 1978, p. 237.

anship for the humiliated and degraded based on natural law – a partisanship that knows how to fight for human dignity as the constitutive heritage of classical natural law and which does not allow any authority [*Obrigkeit*] (to the extent that authority is necessary at all), whether hereditary or recent, to become cocky.

BLOCH, *Natural Law and Human Dignity*

∴

When the old Bloch seeks to enthuse his students in Tübingen about the 'fire and light of theory, which back then hugely motivated the three students in Tübingen [a reference to Hegel's, Schelling's and Hölderlin's joint time at the Tübinger Stift] as well as those at other universities', he remains faithful to his favourite slogan or password [*Losungswort*], Marx's eleventh thesis on Feuerbach.[5] He revises his 1918 work, *The Spirit of Utopia*, along Marxist lines in 1923; a year before this, in 1922, his *Thomas Münzer: Theologian of Revolution* appears; and *The Principle of Hope* tellingly ends with a chapter on Marx.[6] Yet the East German leadership comes to suspect *The Principle of Hope* of discrediting the 'Workers' and Peasants' State' as a mere transitional stage on the way to the realisation of Bloch's 'utopia'. From 1957 onwards – and ignoring the fact that utopian thought is present 'in every great philosophy'[7] – the GDR's Socialist Unity Party (SED) criticises Bloch's ideas on the basis of a doctrinaire Marxism-Leninism. Manfred Buhr, for example, writes the following in the East German *Deutsche Zeitschrift für Philosophie*: 'Here [in Volume Three of *The Principle of Hope*] too, Bloch finds himself on sidepaths that are far removed from the great high road that leads to social-

---

5 Bloch 1978, pp. 393–4. Bloch's own intellectual biography is thoroughly shaped by a typically 'bourgeois' systematic approach to knowledge and a corresponding educational background.

6 Bloch published only three monographs dedicated solely or largely to a single philosopher: Bloch 1962 (on Hegel), 1968 (on Christian Thomasius) and 2019 (on Avicenna). It is striking that he never wrote a separate study of Marx; cf. Markun 1977, pp. 76–7. In autumn 1959, the publisher Suhrkamp includes *Spuren* [Traces, 1930] in its publication programme. Soon afterwards, the same publisher showcases a revised edition of *Das Prinzip Hoffnung*, which omits the notorious apotheosis of Stalin that was in the earlier version. A discussion of this controversial paragraph is beyond the scope of this chapter.

7 Horkheimer and Adorno 2002, p. 93.

ism'.[8] This kind of reaction is unsurprising given the considerable tension between Bloch's complex philosophy – with its sophisticated implications for our understanding of time, technology and nature, not least the insight that 'progress does not occur as a chronological and homogeneous series ... [but] in different and overlapping temporal dimensions'[9] – and the rather more straightforward, or simplistic, position on historical progress put forward and imposed by the East German state.

Yet the chapter in Bloch's *Naturrecht und menschliche Würde* [Natural Law and Human Dignity, 1953] entitled 'Althaus, Hobbes, Grotius: Rationalized Natural Law and the New Edifice of the Law' is still conceived within the framework of Marxist historiography.[10] In addition, the 'realm of freedom' or the 'pronounced non-economy' that Bloch has been proclaiming since *The Spirit of Utopia* – and that he sees as being realised in the age of the abolition of private property – does converge with a socialist understanding of natural law in *The Principle of Hope* as well. However, Bloch views the history of natural law as holding the promise of a continuation of a social utopia in which – as Hans Dieter Schelauske puts it – 'the classless society [functions] as the goal of political endeavours'; that is to say, for him the classless society is 'the derivative of natural law'.[11] This hope presupposes a problematic distinction – yet one that Bloch clings to his whole life – between civil society on the one hand and the state as the 'executive committee of the ruling class' on the other.[12] This distinction goes hand in hand with a further one – namely, that between utopias of freedom and utopias of order, which Wilfried Korngiebel explains by pointing out that the former 'tend to be decentralised and democratically structured', whereas the latter 'tend to be centralistic and organised along authoritarian lines'.[13]

Some objections to *The Principle of Hope* really concern Bloch's overall philosophy. Thus, there are those who maintain that Bloch uncritically adopts theorems of classical German philosophy and, following in its footsteps, claims a kind of knowledge superior to that possessed by the various individual academic disciplines. This exaggerated claim, it is said, can only be explained with

---

8   Buhr 1960, p. 356. Manfred Buhr, who was Bloch's academic assistant between 1952 and 1957, completed his doctorate under Bloch's supervision in 1957. This did not prevent him from becoming one of his former supervisor's fiercest critics. He ended up as Director of the 'Zentralinstitut für Philosophie' of the East German Academy of Sciences.
9   Bloch 1970, p. 137.
10 See Bloch 1996, pp. 45–52.
11 Schelauske 1968, p. 252; cf. Valdes 1963, especially pp. 376–9.
12 Bloch 1977, p. 268.
13 Korngiebel 2017, p. 177.

reference to the time in which his philosophy emerges (i.e., the period immediately after World War I), when Marxist theory – Marxism as the 'fundamental science of history and society' – is still unproblematically attractive to the left-wing intelligentsia, and when confidence in the possibility of revolutionary social change is still strong. Accordingly, a further objection is that Bloch's deployment of Marxism, too, is uncritical and naïve. Such criticisms notwithstanding, the surprisingly strong resonance that Bloch enjoys in West Germany as early as the 1950s is not least the result of *The Principle of Hope*. He is granted political asylum there in 1961 and proceeds to organise a series of lecture evenings in Frankfurt am Main and Tübingen.[14] In the same year, his practical philosophy is published in the form of *Natural Law and Human Dignity*, which appears as Volume Six of the 'authorised complete edition' of his writings. In contrast to 'human happiness', he sees 'human dignity' as a spiritual quality – one of the many things that Bloch, as a Lask defender, inherits from classical German philosophy: 'Emil Lask, the last Neo-Kantian, went so far as to speak of the "primacy of practical reason even in logic"'.[15]

3   Marxism and Natural Law

> But Marxism can only be an instruction for action if its grasp [*Griff*] *is simultaneously a leap ahead* [*Vorgriff*]: the concretely anticipated goal governs the concrete path. Hence, even more decisive than the will to change things [*Wille zur Veränderung*] is the pathos of the basic goal, which as a rule is so instructive for the status of the old utopians and for the significance that is still due to them today and which, indeed, makes them into allies against so-called social democracy, for which since Bernstein the movement means everything but the goal nothing.
>
>   BLOCH, The Principle of Hope

∴

---

14   Cf. Zudeick 1985, pp. 246–57.
15   Bloch 1977, p. 353; cf. p. 601. Following Friedrich Engels, Bloch virtually without exception uses the term 'classical German philosophy' and avoids the established 'German idealism'. On the problems associated with the term 'German idealism', see Jaeschke 2006, pp. 269–83.

The term 'natural law' does not appear in the index of Marx's and Engels's *Collected Works*. This seems to suggest that for Marx the old, dualistic way of presenting law (legal naturalism versus legal positivism) remains unresolved.[16] Yet Marx's position on natural law is explicitly explored in early Marxist thought. Of particular importance to Bloch is the social democrat Eduard Bernstein. However, Bernstein and his followers – Bloch says – lacked

> ... trust in their own revolutionary vigour ... Everywhere else, social democracy turned away from philosophy. Petty-bourgeois 'realism' and philosophical ignorance coincide within it, the Bernsteins have moved beyond Hegel (and thereby, not unrelatedly, beyond the revolution); yet social-democratic defeatism does at least love one dialectic – the one that unfolds by itself but never arrives. This ... is the contemplative dialectic; consequently, it unfolds far above and beyond any activity and is the self-life of the idea [*das Selber-Leben der Idee*]. This is what the dialectic looked like in Hegel and this is how, among the social democrats, the most surprising Hegelians, it makes civil peace [a reference to the SPD's pro-war policies] and intellectual peace with the idealist course of necessity.[17]

Bernstein sought to provide a '*summary of the rational content of the socialist ideology of earlier times*'.[18] Looking at the matter from this perspective, one might argue that his 'modern socialism' possesses a foundation of sorts in natural law.[19] Yet there is a problem with Bernstein's approach: as Lucio Colletti remarks, it 'replaces the fundamental Marxian idea that the *conditions* and the *objective* roots for the emergence of socialism lie in the actual process of capitalist production' with an '*ethical* ideal, with the aim of a civilised humanity free to choose its own future and follow the higher principles of morality and justice'.[20] Indeed, Bernstein – following Marx – rejects any approach based on natural law as unscientific (while acknowledging the significant revisions such

---

16   Cf. Lohmann 1991, especially pp. 39–56.
17   Bloch 2000b, p. 358.
18   Bernstein 1923, p. 10.
19   Bernstein defines modern socialism as 'the summation of the political, economic and general cultural aspirations of the workers that have arrived at an understanding of their class position, as well as of the social layers on equal terms with them in countries where capitalism has developed, and the struggle to realise these aspirations' (Bernstein 1923, p. 10). His 'long view' of socialism was influenced above all by Robert von Pöhlmann's two-volume *Geschichte des antiken Kommunismus und Sozialismus* (Pöhlmann 1893/1901).
20   Colletti 1968, p. 17.

approaches underwent since the emergence of rational law in the late eighteenth century).²¹ The validity of *positive* law is judged by Bernstein and Bloch in the same way:

> The question of [rational] law emerges whenever positive law is recognised or perceived as unjust. People thereupon naturally [*naturgemäß*] resort to other guidelines ... [A]s a result, natural law has always had a humanitarian tendency and is the law for the oppressed or those who have been expropriated. By extension, it is thus at the same time revolutionary and has usually been frowned upon or rejected by the ruling powers.²²

Bernstein argues that the various approaches based on natural law were transcended only by the Marxist interpretation of socialism; and he provides a long list of English and French forerunners, including the utopians Gerrard Winstanley and Étienne-Gabriel Morelly.²³ The newly founded United States of America (1776/87), Bernstein argues, based the demand for universal human rights on natural law, the idea being that equality before the law guarantees justice. This was followed, he adds, by the French 'Constitution of 1793, which the radical French Convention created following the fall of the Girondists and which was prefaced by the declaration of human rights'.²⁴ Yet in contrast to Sylvain Maréchal ('L'Égalité! premier vœu de la nature [*Equality! Nature's first wish*]'), who took up Babeuf's principle of equality based on natural law, Bernstein demands that the universal assertion of inalienable human rights should henceforth no longer be derived from nature, which is unable to guarantee that they are realised: 'due to the fact that these systems, for all the correct ideas that they contain, consciously or unconsciously build upon an approach based on natural law, they are inherently utopian [in a pejorative sense; HG]. They overlook the fact that man is not just a product of nature, but in the course of time has also become a product of history and of social conditions that

---

21   Cf. Bernstein 1923, p. 11: 'Even in 1875, when a commission of the two German socialist parties that were in the process of unification drafted a party programme, they justified socialism in terms of natural rights and thereby earned the scorn of an extraordinarily fierce critique by Marx'. Bernstein is referring to the *Critique of the Gotha Programme*, written in 1875 and posthumously published in 1891. The Gotha programme was agreed as part of the merger between the Social Democratic Workers' Party and the General German Workers' Association into the Socialist Workers' Party of Germany.
22   Bernstein 1923, p. 12.
23   For a detailed overview, see Garaudy 1948.
24   Bernstein 1923, p. 17.

have in many cases developed in him inclinations and needs that he does not posess by nature'.[25] This position fosters a 'liberal' or 'revolutionary idea of law', according to which positive law is subordinate to historical development: 'what natural law cannot prove by itself is how an entire social order may become decrepit, ripe to be replaced by another one, whereas the socialists of [Marx's and Engels's] epoch believed that they could prove the necessity of replacing that order simply by reference to natural law'.[26]

Bernstein concludes his argument with a reference to Marx's and Engels's critique of Max Stirner's natural law-inspired work *Der Einzige und sein Eigentum* [The Ego and His Own, 1845]. Stirner – Bernstein says – does at least give communism credit for highlighting the natural human desire to work, to shape the world: 'By the principle of labour that of fortune or competition is certainly outdone. But at the same time the labourer, in his consciousness that the essential thing in him is "the labourer", holds himself aloof from egoism and subjects himself to the supremacy of a society of labourers, as the commoner clung with self-abandonment to the competition-State'.[27] For Marx himself, however, it is – as Cesare Luporini rightly points out – Hegel's *Phenomenology of Spirit* that is the decisive text, a text which Marx approaches from the perspective that (in Luporini's words) 'man is historically his own child, because he is the product of his own labour'.[28] Bloch, for his part, supplements Hegel's and Marx's concepts of labour ('concepts' in the extended Hegelian sense, which includes their various *realgeschichtlich* manifestations) with a reading of Stirner's work along the lines of contract theory: 'In short, the lone individual who only enters into the contrat social for himself is a free outsider not only in existing society but in every conceivable one'.[29]

4   Law and History in the Thought of Hegel and Bloch

Today, the Historical School's reaction to the various natural-law and rational-law conceptions put forward or critically assessed by Kant and Fichte, as well as by Hegel and Schelling in their early years in Jena, is outdated in both legal and historical-philosophical terms. Now it is possible to approach neutrally,

---

25   Bernstein 1923, p. 20.
26   Bernstein 1923, pp. 21–2. The term 'liberal' should not be misunderstood in a party-political sense; on this issue, see Glinka 2014.
27   Stirner 1907, p. 139.
28   Luporini 1974, pp. 123–4.
29   Bloch 1986, vol. 2, p. 569.

free from partisan concerns, the problems underlying this entire historical discourse, which has implications that extend beyond German legal thought.[30] In order to do so, we must render visible the specific discursive conditions in which these problems arose and were discussed – conditions which today are largely forgotten or ignored.

Rational law stands in contrast to legal positivism, which views law as the free positing [*Setzung*] of a people and a state; that is to say, as not requiring any supra-positive (ethical) justification. A law based on reason (albeit in the service of absolutism) was already championed by Christian Wolff in his doctrine of natural law.[31] Kant's rational law is set out in the 'Metaphysical Principles of the Science of Right' in his *Metaphysics of Morals*. According to the argument there, law governs people's interactions, but not their intentions or desires. For Kant, one of the features of the law is, *a priori*, the authority to compel. Thus, he defines (rational) law as the 'totality of conditions under which the arbitrary will [*Willkür*] of one can be combined with that of the other in accordance with a universal law of freedom'.[32] For Hegel, Kant's and Fichte's practical philosophies both represent a form of rational law. He first criticises Fichte's assumptions with regard to natural law in *The Difference Between Fichte's and Schelling's Systems of Philosophy* and then returns to the issue in 'On the Scientific Ways of Treating Natural Law', which addresses Kant's as well as Fichte's ideas. There, Hegel argues that, just like Hobbes's approach (which posits the lawless freedom of the state of nature), Kant's and Fichte's approaches (which put forward the idea that man's consciousness of freedom is independent of nature) remain logically and morally under-determined. That is to say, they lack a concept of consciousness (or 'intelligence', as Hegel sometimes puts it) which is characterised by the fact that it is 'capable of being absolute universality ... inasmuch as it is absolute individuality'.[33]

Bloch views Hegel's philosophy of right as having introduced 'the novum of a dialectical rational law' and as having postulated the actual existence of rational law in a (supposedly) rational state.[34] This, however, is a misunderstanding of Hegel based, among other things, on the myth – created by Rudolf Haym – of Hegel as 'the philosopher of the Prussian state'.[35] Why, then, does

---

30 Cf. Stolleis 2001.
31 The key text is Wolff's *Institutiones iuris naturae et gentium* of 1750. On the issue of absolutism, cf. Klippel 1976.
32 Kant 1907, p. 230.
33 Hegel 2007, p. 158.
34 Bloch 1996, pp. 128–9.
35 See Haym 1857 (for example, p. 359: 'Hegel's system became a scientific dwelling for the spirit of the Prussian Restoration').

Iring Fetscher assure us that Bloch defended Hegel from accusations of having been an admirer of the Prussian state and the restoration?[36] Fetscher could have been guided by two ideas. For one, Bloch's understanding of natural law is antithetical to the notion that the idea of freedom has been realised in the state; for another, Bloch's conception of utopia militates against any conservative reading of law and religion. The so-called *Vormärz* period that begins to emerge in Western and Central Europe around 1815 can be viewed as one of fundamental politicisation, in which previous conceptions of rational law are largely discarded. And even though in Germany the quest for a nation state dominates this period, the earliest manifestations of the all-encompassing politicisation of social life after Hegel's death in 1831 can be seen not in theories of the state, but rather in literature and philosophy.[37] This is evident in the work of Heinrich Heine and Ludwig Börne, as well as that of the Young German movement around Karl Gutzkow, Ludolf Wienbarg and Heinrich Laube, and also in the political disputes occasioned by their writing – from scathing criticism by reactionaries such as Wolfgang Menzel through to censorship and bans. This notwithstanding, virtually all German political thinkers of the same time – with the exception of Marx and Engels – are united in their strong emphasis on, and their great expectations with regard to, the state. Just like Hegel's philosophy of right, they view the state not only as a force to bring about order, but also as an administrative reality that could organise society. Bloch, the theorist of revolution and hope, views the *Vormärz* period as the concrete historical realisation of a 'dreaming forwards'; and when he advocates a 'human socialism', he does so on the courageous assumption that the eventual failure of the German November Revolution of 1918 is ultimately a failure of the left too.[38]

Central to Bloch's own contribution to the discussions surrounding law is his attempt to move beyond the centuries-old distinction between historical 'positive law' and transhistorical 'natural law'. He puts forward a full-blown philosophy of history that is based on natural law and its various postulates – above all that of human dignity – and which according to him culminates in Marxism. For him – that is to say, within the framework of an ontology of not-yet-being – there can be no ahistorical, immutable natural law. Yet he also recognises, perhaps more than anybody else, how natural law on the one hand had been posited [*gesetzt*] as a norm during the earliest periods of human history, but on the other hand had largely failed when it was practically applied. This understanding of natural law as a legal [*rechtsgesetzlich*] value that is always already

---

36 See Fetscher 1965.
37 Cf. the excellent discussion in Gedö 1999.
38 Cf. Fetscher 1972, pp. 469–78.

instantiated on the basis of historically variable motives forms an integral part of Bloch's philosophy of concrete utopia. Basing himself on ideas such as a sense of justice that (like Hegel's spirit) 'finds its way to itself', Bloch is seeking a genealogy of the concept of law, or, to put it differently, a genealogy of the manifestations of ethical life or *Sittlichkeit* (here, too, his approach dovetails with that of Hegel).

Bloch, then, remains faithful to Hegel insofar as the latter understands world history as a succession of political constitutions.[39] Hegel identifies the philosophical realisation of this development as the 'science of the experience which consciousness goes through [*Wissenschaft der Erfahrung, die das Bewusstsein macht*]', which includes a philosophical history of law.[40] However, insofar as Hegel's approach legitimises existing ('posited') legal relations and indeed political reality generally – that is to say, 'objective spirit' in the ephemeral forms of a specific social reality – it brings in Bloch's eyes 'the dialectic to a standstill precisely in the realm of the law'.[41] In other words, according to Bloch, Hegel's approach is antithetical to a concept 'of Being that will be, of Being that places itself in contradiction to all that is fixed. Hence ... as a position that insists upon holding on to that judicial positivity which is fixed, it is methodologically untenable: in opposition to the [supposed] non plus ultra we find [in reality] the *dialectic of a continuing world process*'.[42] Yet precisely because of the centrality of the dialectic to Hegel's philosophy, even his philosophy of right 'could give rise to sound ideas, despite all its apologias for the existing social order'.[43]

Bloch himself follows in the footsteps of Marx and Engels when he conceives positive law as a means of preserving the existing socio-economic relations. As Renate Damus puts it:

> In Bloch's judgement, the prevailing laws only have one task; namely, to protect the ownership of the means of production. Hence, the dominant category of jurisprudence is that of private property. Accordingly, Bloch believes that when private ownership of the means of production has been abolished, jurisprudence too will no longer have a function and thus wither away.[44]

---

39 Cf. Riedel 1994, especially p. 140.
40 Hegel 1977, p. 21; translation modified. *Science of the Experience of Consciousness* was the original title of the *Phenomenology of Spirit*.
41 Bloch 1996, p. 126.
42 Ibid.
43 Ibid.
44 Damus 1964, p. 88; cf. von Kempski 1987, p. 369.

Here, Bloch's understanding of what Kant called humanity's need to become mature [*mündig*] is crucial – the 'upright gait', the realisation of human dignity.[45] It is only when the hollowed-out legal formalism of the bourgeois rule of law – with its manifold old and new forms of forced immaturity and servitude – falls and socialism arrives that the actual implementation of human rights can begin.[46]

5 Hegel's 'On the Scientific Ways of Treating Natural Law'

In the essay 'On the Scientific Ways of Treating Natural Law' – which neither Bloch nor Marx specifically discusses – Hegel does not provide an analysis of natural law based on theonomy, for he finds that natural law concerns the spirit of ethical life.[47] Somewhat surprisingly, he also does not explore the history of natural law in this essay (or in the 'System of Ethical Life', which was written at the same time).[48] Indeed, he begins 'On the Scientific Ways of Treating Natural Law' by claiming that the earlier ways of dealing with natural law must be denied all significance. Thus, instead of developing his own concept from a critique of the history of natural law, Hegel takes the opposite approach: the explication of his own concept of natural law serves as a retrospective justification for his dismissal of previous views on the matter.

Hegel first distinguishes between two scientific ways of treating natural law: the 'purely formal' (Kant and Fichte) and the 'empirical' (Hobbes and Locke). It should be obvious that he himself subscribes to neither: already the essay's full title – 'On the Scientific Ways of Treating Natural Law, on Its Place in Practical Philosophy, and Its Relation to the Positive Sciences of Right' – makes it clear that he ascribes natural law to the realm of 'practical philosophy'.[49] The 'positive sciences' mentioned in the title are the legal sciences insofar as their

---

45 Cf. Münster (ed.) 1977.
46 Cf. Negt 1975. More recently, Jürgen Habermas has stressed the importance of Bloch's ideas; see Habermas 2014, p. 33.
47 In *Natural Law and Human Dignity*, Bloch touches on Hegel's 'On the Scientific Ways of Treating Natural Law' exactly once; see Bloch 1996, p. 69.
48 The following studies have expanded our understanding of the history of natural law today: Bruch 1997, Fidora, Lutz-Bachmann and Wagner (eds.) 2010, Scattola 1999 and Schröder 2004.
49 Here, Hegel draws on Aristotle's distinction between theoretical science on the one hand and practical science (the 'science of man' as the unity of ethics and politics) on the other. The substantive influence of Aristotle on Hegel's work is apparent above all from the *System of Ethical Life* and the *Philosophy of Right*.

object of study concerns 'positive' – historical, posited – law. Following on from the two opposing viewpoints – the purely formal and the empirical – that he sets out, Hegel proceeds to engage in a number of complex deliberations based on his nascent philosophy of the Absolute, which itself, however, is only adumbrated.

Hegel's critique of natural law resembles a discussion of the history of the natural sciences and the human sciences: he argues that natural law, like other disciplines, has lost its epistemological status because (pre-Kantian) philosophy – of which it was a part – assumed an overly metaphysical character. This development led to natural law being disconnected from philosophy, such that the former elevated experience [*die Erfahrung*] or the empirical [*die Empirie*] to an epistemological principle. Hegel views this as a fatal outcome for natural law, as this has now lost its *a priori* character. What remains is merely empirical knowledge about the manifold existing laws, rights, duties and so on, of which none is absolute and which are subsumed under concepts of the understanding [*Verstandesbegriffe*] that are deployed without any claim to objectivity. In line with his earlier text on *The Difference between Fichte's and Schelling's Systems of Philosophy*, then, Hegel's critique of empiricism relies on the standards of his philosophy of the Absolute: empiricism possesses its true scientific basis in the Absolute.

This does not mean that Hegel denies the possibility of a plurality of disciplines, or that he rejects empirical approaches per se. At the very outset of 'On the Scientific Ways of Treating Natural Law', he emphasises how 'every part of philosophy is individually capable of being an independent science'.[50] In order to realise 'the completion of a science', however, it is necessary 'that intuition [*Anschauung*; that is to say, sense perception] and image [*Bild*] be combined with the logical [dimension] and taken up into the purely ideal [realm]'.[51] Thus, each 'separate ... science must also be divested of its singularity [*Einzelheit*], and its principle must be recognised in its higher context and necessity'.[52] In brief, as in his other texts from this period (and later), Hegel's approach is based on the reciprocal subsumption of *Bild* and *Begriff*, of sense perception and conceptual thinking. By contrast, the one-sided activity of the understanding, which produces static concepts, is viewed as an obstacle to developing a truly philosophical science.

As mentioned earlier, the difference between the two inauthentic [*unecht*] ways of treating natural law criticised by Hegel – the empirical and the purely

---

50 Hegel 2007, p. 102.
51 Hegel 2007, p. 103.
52 Ibid.

formal – flows from their respective positions vis-à-vis the Absolute. Insofar as the practical sciences continue to mix or 'contaminate', as Hegel puts it, the universal of the understanding [*das Verstandesallgemeine*] – which is fixed in 'negative absoluteness' – with content, they remain nothing but empirical sciences. Conversely, if a science completely separates the Absolute from its content – hence degrading it to a 'Negative-Absolute' – then it is a merely purely formal science.[53] Hegel thus views previous conceptions of natural law as a side aisle of the more encompassing history of the Absolute. They reflect the reign of the Absolute, but in an incomplete, distorted form. The tradition of natural law is nothing but an early, now outdated stage of true absolute science; as such, it is of merely antiquarian interest.

Let us explore this critique of previous approaches to natural law in more detail. According to Hegel, the fundamental defect of the empirical way of treating natural law resides in the fact that the understanding finds more or less arbitrary general – that is, abstract – determinations of a phenomenon and deems these to represent its essence. Thus, 'marriage' is defined by something like having children or having community of property; and on this basis – which as the perceived essence of marriage is made into the foundation of a law – the entire organic relation that is marriage is determined and its concept becomes 'contaminated'. As Hegel will later explain in the *Philosophy of Right*:

> Marriage is essentially an ethical relationship. Formerly, especially under most systems of natural law, it was considered only in its physical aspect or natural character. It was accordingly only regarded as a sexual relationship, and its other determinations remained completely inaccessible. But it is equally crude to interpret marriage merely as a civil contract, a notion [*Vorstellung*] which is still to be found even in Kant[*'s Metaphysical Elements of Justice*, according to which 'the contract of marriage' is one in which 'man and woman will the reciprocal enjoyment of one

---

53   Hegel uses the term 'negative' here to designate the result of an 'abstraction from', a 'negation of'. Thus, the empiricist simply negates the differences between the real-world instantiations of an entity (be it a 'horse' or 'marriage') so as to arrive at some common denominator – an approach that produces the kind of mistaken notions that can be found in the Prussian General Legal Code, such as: 'The chief end of marriage is the generation and bringing up of children' (cf. the editorial note in Hegel 2006, p. 438). However – Hegel says – entities can have things in common that have nothing to do with their essence. At the same time, the formalist's disregard for, or negation of, the empirical is equally problematic: it too produces a one-sided 'Absolute' generated by abstraction. On the opposition between the 'universal of the understanding' and the 'universal of reason' in a legal context, cf. Hegel 2006, pp. 247–9.

another's sexual attributes']. On this interpretation, marriage gives contractual form to the arbitrary relations between individuals, and is thus debased to a contract entitling the parties concerned to use one another. A third and equally unacceptable notion is that which simply equates marriage with love; for love, as a feeling [*Empfindung*], is open in all respects to contingency, and this is a shape which the ethical may not assume. Marriage should therefore be defined more precisely as rightfully ethical [*rechtlich sittliche*] love, so that the transient, capricious, and purely subjective aspects of love are excluded from it.[54]

To put it differently, the problem of the empirical approach is its one-sidedness: from the perspective of totality – that is to say, the Absolute – it becomes evident that empiricism and formalism are complementary. Both pertain to the whole of their subject matter; but the empirical approach views this subject matter as 'completeness', as the totality of the manifold manifestations of reality, whereas the formalist approach sees it as a 'consequence', as the embodiment of that which follows from abstract general principles.

In the empirical approach, then, the understanding separates form from content, the universal from the particular, the necessary from the contingent. It is this – Hegel says – that makes it possible to speak of man's 'state of nature' and ignore universality, totality and the state. This in its turn generates a contradiction in the argument, a kind of logical inversion – the transformation of a projected facticity into an *a priori* normativity. The example he gives is that of Hobbes's *bellum omnium contra omnes*. Such an approach ends up presenting what is de facto a formless and superficial harmony as if it were the reality of society and the state. The understanding is thus dominant precisely where genuine sociality has vanished from reality, leaving only ruling and obeying [*Herrschen und Gehorchen*]. Conversely, the understanding is able to think of lived reality only in terms of ruling and obeying.

Hegel's critique of natural law seeks to overcome the contradictions in which the understanding remains stuck. It does so in order to discredit the principle of Hobbesian sovereignty for the sake of the idea of absolute ethical life – the true ethical life of the individual [*wahrhafte Sittlichkeit des Einzelnen*], an idea that is central to the *System of Ethical Life*, a work that was drafted at the same time but never completed.[55]

---

54 Hegel 2006, p. 201.
55 Of course, the idea – in a modified and more sophisticated form – is central to Hegel's mature writings as well.

'On the Scientific Ways of Treating Natural Law' and the *System of Ethical Life* are philosophically related in their critique of Fichte. Hegel charges Fichte, as well as Kant, with having a fundamentally defective philosophy of freedom. Both – Hegel claims – advocate a concept of law that ensures that universal freedom can only exist within a coercive framework. Hegel speaks in this regard of a 'system of ... externality [*Äußerlichkeit*]'.[56] He writes of the approach:

> ... whereby the essence of right and duty and the essence of the thinking and willing subject are totally one, [such an approach] is the main aspect of the philosophy of Kant and Fichte ... But this philosophy has not remained true to its oneness; instead, although it does acknowledge this oneness as the essence and absolute, it posits the separation into the one and the many just as absolutely, according equal dignity to both ... It is possible [in this approach] for right and duty to have reality independently, as a particular [realm] separate from the subjects and from which the subjects are separate; but it is also possible [in this approach] for the two to be linked ... On this presupposition, a system is established which aims to unite both the concept and the subject of ethical life, despite their separation (... their union is only formal and external); the resultant relation is called *coercion*. Since this externality of oneness is thereby totally fixed and posited as something absolute which has being in itself, the inner dimension [*Innerlichkeit*], the reconstruction of [what Fichte called] the lost loyalty and faith, the oneness of universal and individual freedom, and ethical life [in general] are rendered impossible.[57]

In order words, in this approach people either will what they ought to will or, if they do not will what they ought to will, they are coerced into willing it (as in the Terror that followed the French Revolution). What Hegel is aiming at here is a distinction that will become central to his mature works, especially the *Philosophy of Right* – that between morality [*Moralität*] and ethical life [*Sittlichkeit*]. Morality is merely an 'ought' [*Sollen*]; it establishes a 'demand' [*Forderung*], but does not necessarily produce a reality: 'Even if the *good* were posited in the subjective will, this would not yet amount to its implementation'.[58] After all, people

---

56 Hegel 2007, p. 132.
57 Hegel 2007, pp. 131–2.
58 Hegel 2006, p. 137.

do not automatically act on the basis of what they know is right and hence ought to do. Within the realm of morality, therefore, the only way to ensure that people do the right thing is coercion. Hence, Hegel says, we must transcend this – formal, abstract – moral perspective by supplementing it with a more encompassing one. This is *ethical life* as the 'fit' between subject and society, whereby we do the right thing not because we are coerced but because we have internalised our duties and no longer experience them as external impositions.[59]

The thrust of 'On the Scientific Ways of Treating Natural Law', then, is to move beyond a 'rights-based individualism' and 'make *Sittlichkeit* the measure of natural law'.[60] Accordingly, 'the absolute ethical totality is nothing other than a *people*'[61] – not in the sense of some biological, let alone racial, entity, but rather as a political unity. By way of example, Hegel mentions Montesquieu's *De l'esprit des lois* [The Spirit of the Laws, 1748]:

> Montesquieu based his immortal work on his perception of the individuality and character of nations [*Völker*; singular, *Volk*], and even if he did not ascend to [the height of] the most vital Idea, he certainly did not deduce the individual institutions and laws from so-called reason, nor did he abstract them from experience and then elevate them to universal status. Instead, he understood both the higher relations in the sphere of constitutional law, and the lower determinations of civil relations down to wills, laws concerning marriage, etc., solely in the light of the character of the whole and its individuality.[62]

'On the Scientific Ways of Treating Natural Law' effects a consequential epistemological reorientation: it places natural law above ethics as understood by Kant and Fichte. As Hegel sees it, such an understanding of ethics focused only on the individual and hence amounted to little more than a doctrine of virtue or 'a natural description of the virtues'.[63] But since, for Hegel, the realm of the ethical depends upon the state [*Zustand*; that is to say, condition, circumstances] of absolute ethical life, ethics can no longer specify the principle

---

59   Hegel stresses that ethical life transcends but *does not eliminate* individual morality, which has its place in cases where ethical life has become corrupted, or 'in extraordinary circumstances ... where [different duties] come into collision' (Hegel 2006, p. 193).
60   Hegel 2007, p. 289 (editorial footnote to p. 130).
61   Hegel 2007, p. 140.
62   Hegel 2007, p. 175.
63   Hegel 2007, p. 161.

behind this ethical life – only natural law as the science of absolute ethical life can. In other words, whereas Kant viewed the entirety of the 'metaphysics of morals' as having its foundation in the moral principle that is the categorical imperative, Hegel turns ethics into a sub-discipline of natural law: the task of 'natural law is to construct the way in which ethical nature arrives at its true right'.[64]

The young Hegel views Kant's and Fichte's approach – their ethics based on rational law – as a transitional stage (or even a form of decline) on the way to his own understanding of natural law as the science of absolute ethical life. This stance passes Bloch by when – in *Natural Law and Human Dignity*[65] – he seeks to distil Hegel's views on natural law from the *Philosophy of Right* and arrives at the conclusion that Hegel saw natural law as having been realised in the present, in the (already in Hegel's own time – Bloch says – outdated) Prussian state. In fact, Hegel leaves little doubt about the substantial *gap* between natural law and the idea of freedom in the Prussian state, as can be seen most clearly from his various university lectures on the philosophy of right.[66] More convincingly, Bloch does bring out the anti-utopian consequences of Hegel's position. Thus, he writes in *The Spirit of Utopia*:

> One searches in vain in Hegel for that sensibility which alone directs us upward and is aware of the danger, which manifests itself in Kant, in Fichte's words: that there must be, beyond the mere repetition of what is or was, a knowledge grounding the deed, or a vision of that world that is not but which shall be, which drives us to act; that in other words one is not supposed to endure the world by the will of God, but make it different by the will of God, which, defined existentially-morally, in complete opposition to the dialectical kind of anamnesis, is certainly not the will to restitute some already past and precisely known cultural alpha. In Kant, in other words, philosophy was a solitary light meant to burn up the night of this world. In Hegel philosophy becomes a headmaster, or indiscriminate lawyer for the Being that hired him, and the night of the world retreats into the merely ignorant subject.[67]

---

64   Hegel 2007, p. 160; cf. Siep 1979, pp. 160–1.
65   The book's working title was *Natural Law and the Philosophy of Right*; see Zudeick 1985, p. 176.
66   Cf. Riedel 1967 and 1970, especially pp. 6–14.
67   Bloch 2000a, pp. 184–5.

Finally, Bloch claims that Hegel developed his dialectic in idealist terms. In fact, Hegel already views the principle of consciousness as stuck in the alternatives of realism and idealism, and he discusses at length the one-sidedness of both outlooks.[68]

6 Bloch and Natural Law

Like Marx, Bloch does not develop a concept of natural law of his own. In *Natural Law and Human Dignity*, he first offers a historical reconstruction of natural-law theories from the ancient Greeks to his own time.[69] Following this survey – which takes up the larger part of that study – he rejects a range of ahistorical and idealist 'illusions'.[70] Thus, he rules out the idea that people are innately free and equal, because all rights are 'either acquired or must still be acquired in battle. The upright gait [*aufrechte Gang*] predisposes us to something that is yet to be won'.[71] Likewise, he rejects the view 'that *property* should be numbered among the inalienable rights', because it 'only arose as a consequence of the division of labor', when 'public property' was replaced by 'the private possession of the means of production'.[72] Equally untenable according to Bloch are positions that cling to 'the forms in which people were given their rights' – such as social-contract theories (whether conceived as philosophical fictions or historical facts) – and any '*a priori* constructions founded purely on the understanding [*Verstand*]', on 'deductions of legal norms from a final juridical principle *ante rem* (sociability, security, or the greatest possible individual freedom)'.[73] Such *a priori* constructions – Bloch says – were dealt a first blow by Kant's critique of reason and a second blow by Hegel's dialectic before they were shattered altogether by Marx's historical materialism.

Untenable, too, is in Bloch's eyes the hypothesis of a *consensus gentium*, the idea that all people, at all times and in all places, are fundamentally in agreement when it comes to judicial matters, or at least that they would be so if they were not blinded by the artificial light of priests and princes. Immutable is

---

68 On Hegel's sublation of the opposition between 'idealism' and 'realism', cf. Henk de Berg's chapter in this volume.

69 The focus is on Epicurus, Stoicism, Roman law, Aquinas, the Reformation, Althusius, Hobbes, Grotius, Rousseau, Kant, Fichte, Schelling, Hegel, Feuerbach, Savigny, Bachofen, the French Revolution, Marx and the *Bürgerliches Gesetzbuch* [German Civil Code].

70 Bloch 1996, p. 188.

71 Ibid.

72 Bloch 1996, pp. 188–9.

73 Bloch 1996, pp. 189 and 190–1.

people's 'intention of freeing themselves from oppression and installing human dignity, at least since the time of the Greeks', but 'not ... "man" and his so-called eternal right'.[74] Such a hypothesis requires the assumption of an eternal human nature (as in – Bloch says – Hobbes and Rousseau), which contradicts one of the central insights of Marxism:

> There is no such thing as an immutable human nature in Marxism, which views static and perennial determinations as nothing but reified abstractions. There is no fixed species-being 'man' with static characteristics upon which a natural law might be grounded; rather, the entire course of history is evidence of a progressive transformation of human nature ... 'Man' is fundamentally an x: historically and morally, he is a product of his social relations ... For Marxism, the *humanum* is a historical goal, not an *a priori* deductive principle. It is a non-present, but sensed utopia [*das utopische Unvorhandene und Geahnte*], not something that lies ahistorically at the basis of things as the arch-certainty of history.[75]

By the same token, there is no external correlate to this supposedly eternal human nature. That is to say, nature as a whole cannot be fetishised into a suprahistorical normative concept that somehow stands above and against social ills. Such 'judicial optimism of nature' is really a 'flight from society and history' while also functioning as a kind of collecting tank or melting pot for all manner of philosophical equivocations.[76]

Bloch draws on Herbert Spiegelberg's phenomenological distinction between 'cognitive' and 'ontological' concepts of natural law to disentangle these equivocations.[77] Cognitive concepts of natural law cast 'nature as the *mentor* of justice', while ontological concepts of justice 'try to give a definition of [the] essence [of nature]'.[78] Yet Bloch says that both conceptual categories – despite the differences between them and between their various sub-categories – have one thing in common: they are based on a juxtaposition of nature and history. However, Marx has taught us to dispense with such a 'contrastive ideology [*Kontrast-Ideologie*]': Marxism 'believes in history ... and the society which it brings about is not the actualisation of a *pre-existing matriarchate*

---

74 Bloch 1996, p. 191.
75 Bloch 1996, p. 192.
76 Ibid.
77 Cf. Spiegelberg 1935, especially pp. 259–61.
78 Bloch 1996, pp. 192–3. These two conceptual categories are then further divided into three and six subcategories respectively.

of nature that can function as a standard or homeland'.⁷⁹ There is – the point bears repeating – only one thing that remains unchanged: 'Only the inclination toward [*Intention auf*] the upright gait, toward human dignity, is invariant'.⁸⁰ Hence, the thrust of *Natural Law and Human Dignity* is analogous to that of *The Principle of Hope*:

> It is just as urgent *suo modo* to raise the problem of a heritage of classical law as it was to speak of the heritage of social utopias. Social utopias and natural law had mutually complementary concerns within the same humane space [*im gleichen humanen Raum*], marching separately, but sadly not striking together ... Social utopian thought directed its efforts toward human happiness; natural law was directed toward human dignity. Social utopias depicted relations in which people no longer *toil* and are no longer *heavy laden*; natural law constructed relations in which people are no longer *humiliated* and *insulted*.⁸¹

This analogy implies a conservation of the (Hegelian) viewpoint of the 'universal Other' – the concern of natural law – in a continuation of the focus on the 'concrete Other' to be found in social utopias. As Seyla Benhabib has pointed out, however, the end of Hegelian philosophies of a singular collective subject, as well as the turn from a critique of instrumental reason to Habermasian theories of communicative reason, have transformed the meaning of the concept of utopia in contemporary societies.⁸² Yet the leitmotif of *Natural Law and Human Dignity*, which is largely structured along historical lines, is the question of the origin and function of the state. Accordingly, the penultimate chapter of the study ends with the sentence: 'The basic tenor of radical natural law against the state is the classless society; it only grows insofar as it is a prelude [*indem es vorauswirkt*]'.⁸³ But if the state disappears, there is bound to be a gap – and

---

79   Bloch 1996, p. 194.
80   Bloch 1996, p. 186.
81   Bloch 1996, p. xxix; cf. Bloch 1985, p. 173. The allusions are to Matthew 11:28 ('Come unto me, all ye that labour and are heavy laden, and I will give you rest') and Униженные и оскорблённые [Humiliated and Insulted, 1861], Dostoevsky's first novel after his eight-year exile in Siberia.
82   Cf. Benhabib 2009.
83   Bloch 1996, p. 310; the same idea can already be found in Bloch 2000a. It is worth stressing that the philosophies of the state which developed during the early modern period cannot be reduced to mere 'fictions in the old natural law that were easily seen through' (Bloch 1996, p. xxvii). Rather, they were an integral part of the meandering debates about natural law at the time. On this, see Glinka 2012.

who or what might fill it? 'A future world management ... will not undertake any kind of state business. But it is quite conceivable that something like centralized advice provision [*zentrierte Ratgebung*] or administration of meaning [*Verwaltung des Sinns*] will remain, something that orders the people's feelings and instructs their minds to live ... again and again, in preparation and with a sense of direction [*das die Gemüter ordnet und das die Geister lehrt, um immer wieder ... in Bereitung und Richtung zu leben*]'.[84] Who or what, then, would be able to achieve this? Bloch's answer is a new kind of church, not in the sense of Blumenberg's secularisation thesis, but as a 'new ecumene', for 'the real metaphysical question will outlast the mythological, transcendent answers that are handed out by the churches of the masters'.[85] Hence the conclusion of *Natural Law and Human Dignity*:

> The new ecumene belongs to a society that is no longer essentially antagonistic, to a togetherness [*Gemeinsamkeit*, also something like 'common ground'] that can grow undisturbedly. And this ecumene, in order to live not just for the day but beyond the day, requires an arrangement that is more than the administration of things and takes seriously the friendship that runs deep and the fraternity that is so difficult. Socialism is the path to this; it is the finally realizable inheritance of what was meant by an inner emancipation and an outer peace. The red faith was always more than a private matter; there is a basic right to community [*ein Grundrecht auf Gemeinde*], to humanism, including politically and as far as the goal is concerned. This is what the demanding right [*das fordernde Recht*] was en route to, the *eunomia* of the upright gait in togetherness; art is not alone in holding the dignity of humanity in its hands.[86]

Bloch's ultimate aim was the reconciliation of a humane socialism with genuine freedom and democracy.

---

84 Bloch 1996, p. 276.
85 Bloch 1996, pp. 279 and 277. Bloch is scathing about the actual Church, which 'bristles at see-through blouses, but not at slums in which half-naked children starve, and, above all, not at the relations that hold three-quarters of mankind in misery. It damns desperate girls who abort a fetus, but it sanctifies war, which aborts millions ... It preserves misery and injustice insofar as it tolerates, then approves, the class violence that causes them; it obstructs the seriousness of liberation by postponing it to a St. Never-Ever Day, by shifting it into the beyond' (Bloch 1996, p. 278). On Hans Blumenberg's secularisation thesis, see Blumenberg 1988.
86 Bloch 1996, pp. 279–80. The allusion is to Engels's phrase (borrowed from Fourier) that under socialism 'the government of persons is replaced by the administration of things' (Engels 2010, p. 321; cf. p. 292).

Bibliography

Albrecht, Richard 1991, 'The Utopian Paradigm', *Communications: The European Journal of Communication Research*, 16, 3: 283–318.

Benhabib, Seyla 2009, 'Zur Utopie und Anti-Utopie in unseren Zeiten. Rede anlässlich der Verleihung des Ernst-Bloch-Preises', translated by Christian Volk, Ludwigshafen: Ernst-Bloch-Zentrum.

Bernstein, Eduard 1923, *Der Sozialismus einst und jetzt. Streitfragen des Sozialismus in Vergangenheit und Gegenwart*, 2nd ed., Berlin: Dietz.

Bloch, Ernst 1962, *Subjekt-Objekt. Erläuterungen zu Hegel*, extended ed., Frankfurt am Main: Suhrkamp.

Bloch, Ernst 1966, 'Der rebellierende Mensch. Gedanken über Hiob', in *Daß dein Ohr auf Weisheit achte. Jüdische Beiträge zum Menschenbild*, edited by Karl Heinz Schröter, Wuppertal and Barmen: Jugenddienst Verlag.

Bloch, Ernst 1968, *Christian Thomasius, ein deutscher Gelehrter ohne Misere*, Frankfurt am Main: Suhrkamp.

Bloch, Ernst 1970, *Tübinger Einleitung in die Philosophie*, Frankfurt am Main: Suhrkamp.

Bloch, Ernst 1977, *Philosophische Aufsätze zur objektiven Phantasie*, Frankfurt am Main: Suhrkamp.

Bloch, Ernst 1978, *Tendenz – Latenz – Utopie*, Frankfurt am Main: Suhrkamp.

Bloch, Ernst 1985 [1961], 'Naturrecht und menschliche Würde. Rundfunkvortrag 1961', *Bloch-Almanach*, 5: 165–79.

Bloch, Ernst 1986 [1954–9], *The Principle of Hope*, 3 Volumes, translated by Neville Plaice, Stephen Plaice and Paul Knight, Cambridge, Mass.: MIT Press.

Bloch, Ernst 1996 [1961], *Natural Law and Human Dignity*, translated by Dennis J. Schmidt, Cambridge, Mass. and London: MIT Press.

Bloch, Ernst 2000a, *The Spirit of Utopia*, translated by Anthony Nassar, Stanford: Stanford University Press.

Bloch, Ernst 2000b, *Logos der Materie. Eine Logik im Werden. Aus dem Nachlass 1923–1949*, Frankfurt am Main: Suhrkamp.

Bloch, Ernst 2019 [1952], *Avicenna and the Aristotelian Left*, translated by Loren Goldman and Peter Thompson, New York: Columbia University Press.

Blumenberg, Hans 1988, *Die Legitimität der Neuzeit*, 2nd ed. Frankfurt am Main: Suhrkamp.

Bruch, Richard 1997, *Ethik und Naturrecht im deutschen Katholizismus des 18. Jahrhunderts. Von der Tugendethik zur Pflichtethik*, Tübingen: Francke.

Buhr, Manfred 1960, 'Kritische Bemerkungen zu Ernst Blochs Hauptwerk *Das Prinzip Hoffnung*', *Deutsche Zeitschrift für Philosophie*, 4: 356–79.

Colletti, Lucio 1968, *Bernstein und der Marxismus der Zweiten Internationale*, Frankfurt am Main: Europäische Verlagsanstalt.

Damus, Renate 1964, *Ernst Bloch, Hoffnung als Prinzip – Prinzip ohne Hoffnung*, Meisenheim am Glan: Anton Hain.

Engels, Friedrich 2010 [1880], *Socialism: Utopian and Scientific*, in *Marx and Engels Collected Works*, Volume 24, London: Lawrence and Wishart.

Fetscher, Iring 1965, 'Ernst Bloch auf Hegels Spuren', in *Ernst Bloch zu ehren. Beiträge zu seinem Werk*, edited by Siegfried Unseld, Frankfurt am Main: Suhrkamp.

Fetscher, Iring 1972, 'Ein großer Einzelgänger. Nachwort', in Ernst Bloch, *Freiheit und Ordnung und andere ausgewählte Schriften*, Frankfurt am Main: Suhrkamp.

Fidora, Alexander, Matthias Lutz-Bachmann and Andreas Wagner (eds.) 2010, *Lex und Ius: Beiträge zur Grundlegung des Rechts in der politischen Philosophie des Mittelalters und der Frühen Neuzeit*, Stuttgart-Bad Cannstatt: Frommann-Holzboog.

Garaudy, Roger 1948, *Les sources françaises du socialisme scientifique*, Paris: Hier et Aujourd'hui.

Gedö, András 1999, 'Philosophie zwischen den Zeiten. Auseinandersetzungen um den Philosophiebegriff im Vormärz', in *Der Streit um die Romantik (1820–1854)*, edited by Walter Jaeschke, Hamburg: Meiner.

Glinka, Holger 2012, *Zur Genese autonomer Moral. Eine Problemgeschichte des Verhältnisses von Naturrecht und Religion in der frühen Neuzeit und der Aufklärung*, 2nd, revised ed. Hamburg: Meiner.

Glinka, Holger 2015, 'Partei', in *Schlüsselbegriffe der Philosophie des 19. Jahrhunderts*, edited by Annika Hand, Christian Bermes and Ulrich Dierse, Hamburg: Meiner.

Habermas, Jürgen 2014, 'Das Konzept der Menschenwürde und die realistische Utopie der Menschenrechte', in *Zur Verfassung Europas. Ein Essay*, 5th ed., Berlin: Suhrkamp.

Haym, Rudolf 1857, *Hegel und seine Zeit Vorlesungen über Entstehung und Entwicklung, Wesen und Werth der Hegel'schen Philosophie*, Berlin: Gaertner.

Hegel, Georg Wilhelm Friedrich 1977, *Phenomenology of Spirit*, translated by A.V. Miller, Oxford: Oxford University Press.

Hegel, Georg Wilhelm Friedrich 2006 [1821], *Elements of the Philosophy of Right*, translated by H.B. Nisbet, Cambridge: Cambridge University Press.

Hegel, Georg Wilhelm Friedrich 2007 [1802/3], 'On the Scientific Ways of Treating Natural Law, on Its Place in Practical Philosophy, and Its Relation to the Positive Sciences of Right', in *Political Writings*, translated by H.B. Nisbet, Cambridge: Cambridge University Press.

Horkheimer, Max and Theodor W. Adorno 2002 [1944], *Dialectic of Enlightenment: Philosophical Fragments*, translated by Edmund Jephcott, Stanford: Stanford University Press.

Jaeschke, Walter 2006, 'Idealism and Realism in Classical German Philosophy', in *Eriugena, Berkeley, and the Idealist Tradition*, edited by Stephen Gersh and Dermot Moran, Indiana: University of Notre Dame Press.

Kant, Immanuel 1907 [1797], *Die Metaphysik der Sitten*, Berlin: Reimer.

Klippel, Diethelm 1976, *Politische Freiheit und Freiheitsrechte im deutschen Naturrecht des 18. Jahrhunderts*, Paderborn: Ferdinand Schöning.

Korngiebel, Wilfried 2017, 'Das historische Fundament der Sozialutopien', in *Ernst Bloch: Das Prinzip Hoffnung*, edited by Rainer E. Zimmermann, Berlin: de Gruyter.

Lohmann, Georg 1991, *Indifferenz und Gesellschaft. Eine kritische Auseinandersetzung mit Marx*, Frankfurt am Main: Suhrkamp.

Luporini, Cesare 1974, 'Die eigentümliche Logik des eigentümlichen Gegenstandes', in *Cesare Luporini: Karl Marx – Kommunismus und Dialektik*, edited by Furio Cerutti, Frankfurt am Main and Cologne: Europäische Verlagsanstalt.

Markun, Silvia 1977, *Ernst Bloch*, Reinbek bei Hamburg: Rowohlt.

Münster, Arno (ed.) 1977, *Tagträume vom aufrechten Gang. Sechs Interviews mit Ernst Bloch*, Frankfurt am Main: Suhrkamp.

Negt, Oskar 1975, '10 Thesen zur marxistischen Rechtstheorie', in *Probleme der marxistischen Rechtstheorie*, edited by Hubert Rottleuthner, Frankfurt am Main: Suhrkamp.

Pöhlmann, Robert 1893/1901, *Geschichte des antiken Kommunismus und Sozialismus*, 2 Volumes, Munich: Beck.

Riedel, Manfred 1967, 'Hegels Kritik des Naturrechts', *Hegel-Studien*, 4: 177–204.

Riedel, Manfred 1970, *Bürgerliche Gesellschaft und Staat. Grundprobleme und Struktur der Hegelschen Rechtsphilosophie*, Neuwied and Berlin: Luchterhand.

Riedel, Manfred 1994 *Tradition und Utopie. Ernst Blochs Philosophie im Licht unserer geschichtlichen Denkerfahrung*, Frankfurt am Main: Suhrkamp.

Scattola, Merio 1999, *Das Naturrecht vor dem Naturrecht. Zur Geschichte des 'ius naturae' im 16. Jahrhundert*, Stuttgart: de Gruyter.

Schelauske, Hans Dieter 1968, *Philosophische Probleme der Naturrechtsdiskussion in Deutschland. Ein Überblick über zwei Jahrzehnte: 1945–1965*, PhD thesis, University of Cologne.

Schröder, Jan 2004, *'Gesetz' und 'Naturgesetz' in der frühen Neuzeit*, Wiesbaden: Steiner.

Siep, Ludwig 1979, *Anerkennung als Prinzip der praktischen Philosophie. Untersuchungen zu Hegels Jenaer Philosophie des Geistes*, Freiburg and Munich: Alber.

Spiegelberg, Herbert 1935, *Gesetz und Sittengesetz*, Zürich and Leipzig: Max Niehans.

Stirner, Max 1907 [1845], *The Ego and His Own*, translated by Steven T. Byington, New York: Benjamin R. Tucker.

Stolleis, Michael 2001, *Konstitution und Intervention. Studien zur Geschichte des öffentlichen Rechts im 19. Jahrhundert*, Frankfurt am Main: Suhrkamp.

Valdes, Ernesto Garzon 1963, 'Die Polis ohne Politik', in *Materialien zu Ernst Blochs Prinzip Hoffnung*, edited by Burghart Schmidt, Frankfurt am Main: Suhrkamp.

von Kempski, Jürgen 1987 [1964], 'Bloch, Recht und Marxismus', in *Materialien zu Ernst Blochs Prinzip Hoffnung*, edited by Burghart Schmidt, Frankfurt am Main: Suhrkamp.

Zudeick, Peter 1985, *Der Hintern des Teufels. Ernst Bloch – Leben und Werk*, Baden-Baden: Bühl-Moos.

CHAPTER 7

The Matter of Bloch's Philosophy of Nature in the Shadow of Idealism

Loren Goldman

> ... without the legacy of Aristotle and Bruno, Marx would not have been able to set much of the Hegelian world-idea on its feet in such a natural way[1]

∴

> The point here is not only to place Hegel on his feet, but to do so in view of objective-real possibility and matter as its substrate, which is still not grasped in [our interpretations of] Aristotle and the Aristotelian Left[2]

∴

1   Introduction

One of the most striking yet overlooked aspects of Bloch's work is his neo-Aristotelian view of nature, according to which the world's matter actively generates form out of itself. At first glance, this emergentist ontology may appear remote from Bloch's utopian preoccupations: why should someone concerned with the horizons of thought sully his hands with such mundane 'stuff'? For Bloch, however, the idea of self-generating nature is indispensable for the possibility of utopian transformation, as it is incumbent upon him to explain the realisation of a world that is by definition 'no-place' without the aid of salvific metaphysical agents like God or *Geist*. From his perspective, the standard philosophical interpretation of matter as inert substance animated from without

---

1   Bloch 1986, vol. 1, p. 208.
2   Bloch 1977a, p. 17.

makes utopia impossible, for the determinism of mechanistic causality precludes any thought of a future radically different from the present. The ontology of the not-yet-existing requires an account of the world that permits the emergence of genuine novelty, and hence an account of matter that is 'orientated forwards' and 'still open'.[3] In the 1920s, therefore, when *The Principle of Hope* and the category of concrete utopia were mere glimmers in Bloch's intellectual eye, he began sketching wide-ranging studies of materialism.[4] Against the conception of the world as static – what William James called the 'block-universe, entire, unmitigated, and complete' – Bloch takes it as dynamic and fructifying; the word 'matter', he writes, 'stems from *mater*, hence from the fecund womb of the world'.[5] In arguing that the world's possibilities are not exhausted, furthermore, Bloch aims to make plausible the eventual end of human alienation, fulfilling the early Marx's equation of communist society with a unity of humanity and nature.

This chapter will discuss Bloch's neo-Aristotelian ontology of matter and nature in four parts. Because Bloch understands his materialism to align with Marx's insight into the world as a place of human production, our discussion will begin with the intellectual context in which Marx was labouring: the problematic of the relationship between freedom and nature in post-Kantian German thought. The second part will then explore Marx's various articulations of the idea of matter-cum-nature, from the spontaneously swerving matter of his dissertation on Democritus and Epicurus to the aspirational unity of nature and humanity sketched in his *Paris Manuscripts* and the notion of metabolic mutualism in his *Grundrisse* and *Capital*. The third part will address Bloch's vital materialism, explaining it as an ontological position meant to buttress Marx's insights by extending a 'left-wing' interpretation of Aristotle to the relationship between form and matter. The fourth and final part will defend Bloch against influential critics like Alfred Schmidt and Jürgen Habermas, linking his account to ongoing concerns about capitalist exploitation and ecological sustainability.

A few provisos before the plunge. For all of the authors treated here, the question of the nature of matter is ultimately inseparable from the question of the matter of nature, as all are orientated towards resolving the post-Kantian problematic of the relationship between freedom and determinism, between

---

3 Bloch 1977a, p. 20; cf. Bloch 1977b, pp. 212–42.
4 See Zudeick 2012, p. 268; Bloch 2000; and Markun 1977, p. 62.
5 James 1977, p. 147, and Bloch 1977a, p. 17. Bloch's line echoes the first sentence of an essay he wrote when he was thirteen years old: 'Matter is the mother of all things' (Münster 1977, p. 22, cited in Klein 2008, p. 53).

autonomous and mechanistic causality, or between 'culture' and 'nature'. This thorny complex of issues can lead to interminable debates: John Stuart Mill thought that the constitutive tension between the competing philosophical meanings of nature as, on the one hand, 'all the powers existing in either the outer or the inner world and everything which takes place by means of those powers' and, on the other hand, 'only what takes place without the agency, or without the voluntary and intentional agency, of man' to be so fraught that he rejects the use of this ambiguous term altogether.[6] As Bloch, Marx and countless other modern thinkers have recognised, humans are material, natural beings, and thus all conventions are in some extended sense natural. Likewise, as Nietzsche noted, insofar as humans necessarily use conventional conceptual categories to describe nature (and themselves), any account we give of nature is ultimately cultural.[7] Indeed, the basic insight of Kant, the figure to whom all modern German philosophy is a footnote, is that the world is rendered for us according to our own understanding. In describing matter and nature, we describe ourselves, the possibilities and the limits of our world. Bloch's neo-Aristotelian concept of matter therefore both concerns the material substance of existence as such – the ultimate constitution of reality – and serves as a proxy for greater questions of human agency, ecological ethics and utopia.

2 Matter and Mechanism in the Shadow of Idealism

In Aristotle's teleological worldview, natural things, comprised of form and matter, develop towards their inner ends, or final causes, and one of the major debates among his intellectual descendants concerns just how these indwelling potentials became actual. The rise of modern science saw this teleological frame replaced by a mechanistic one in which matter is inert and lacks indwelling purpose. Philosophically pioneered by early modern thinkers like Descartes and Hobbes, for whom matter was the formless substance of pure extension,[8] the mechanistic framework gained wide acceptance in the mid-nineteenth century with the aspiration to unify scientific theories with empirical invest-

---

6 Mill 1998, p. 8.
7 See Nietzsche 2010. Bruno Latour's suggestion to dispense with the distinction and adopt the language of cultural-natural 'hybrids' is one response to this state of affairs; see Latour 1991, 1996 and 2004.
8 See Descartes 2001, II. 4 (IXb 65), and Hobbes 1839, II.8 (p. 119).

igation independent of any metaphysics of final causes.[9] Idealists thinkers resisted this surrender to the world's disenchantment, wherein nature exhibits no innate principles, no past and no potential for development.

Kant's influence on these matters was epochal. As is well known, Kant turned the lens of philosophy from the objective content of the world to the structure of the subject's cognitive apparatus. The phenomena of experience, Kant argues, appear in determinately structured ways, among which he includes existence in space and time, possession of quality and quantity and being subject to mechanistic causality. In themselves however – outside of human experience, as it were – things may not be as they appear within it. Yet although we lack insight into the true nature of reality, we can have objective scientific knowledge of phenomena as they appear to us, and we may furthermore employ certain meta-physical ideas like the systematicity of natural laws and the notion of freedom for the coherence of practice, both in scientific inquiry and moral activity.[10]

Kant's critically self-aware epistemology orientates his thinking on matter and nature, both of which he treats as correlates of the cognitive faculty in experience rather than as objective essences. His *Metaphysical Foundations of Natural Science* explains the concept of matter, defined dynamically and by its potential as 'the movable in space', as an *a priori* determination of reason, necessary for the possibility of outer intuitions in space and time.[11] As a necessary feature of the world of experience, empirical matter, as nature, accords with mechanistic causality. Yet Kant also argues that a thoroughgoing mechanicism fails to capture the apparently self-directed qualities of organised things like eyes, humans and ecosystems. For such entities, we have to appeal to 'an entirely different kind of original causality', that of inner purposiveness and final causes, not to supplant mechanicism but to supplement it as a reflective judgement of reason.[12] To invoke final causality in nature is not to make a constitutive claim about the world, but to regulate our practical orientation in activity. For Kant, assuming the purposive construction of the eye allows us to investigate and address problems of vision, for example, and the positing of human autonomy as the final end of nature in history can motivate rational moral agency.[13] The reach of regulative teleology is therefore vast, for the very

---

9   Cf. Schnädelbach 1984, especially Chapter 3.
10 See, for example, Kant 1999, A235/B294–A260/B315, A310–311/B367 and A327/B383–4.
11 Kant 2002a, p. 194. For Kant's concept of matter, see Carrier 2001a and 2001b as well as Friedman 2001.
12 Kant 2002b, 5: 388; cf. 5: 397.
13 As Kant writes in a discussion of the question as to whether the lens has the 'purpose' of focusing light on the retina, 'one says only that the representation of an end in the causality of nature is conceived in the production of the eye because such an idea serves as a

existence of naturally organised beings 'necessarily leads to the Idea of all of nature as a purposive system, an idea to which all mechanism of nature according to the principles of reason (at least in order to try to explain natural appearances) must be subordinated'.[14] Kant secures appearances by denying their objective reality; in doing so, his regulative conception of the world as an aesthetic and teleological space brings, in Bloch's words, the 'pulse of liveliness' into nature.[15]

Kant's idealist successors Fichte, Schelling and Hegel all chafed against his critical system's epistemological limitations.[16] Seeking the quick of the actual – the thing-in-itself occluded by phenomenal/noumenal dualism – Fichte posited the subject as the creative motor of reality, while Schelling and Hegel sought to establish Kant's regulative teleology as a constitutive fact about nature. Like Kant, Fichte asks how the subject comes to the object,[17] yet he gives philosophy an even more radically subjective turn. According to Fichte, the world does not merely *conform* to categories of human cognition, but instead the 'I' posits itself, an act that includes the determination of all possible relations of the subject to the world.[18] The priority of Fichte's subject is reflected in his downgrading of material nature to the passive field in which our agency plays out, nature thus becoming merely instrumental for human projects. Matter exists because the ethical subject must exist in the world, which is, Fichte writes, 'the sensualised material of our duty'.[19] Material being is accordingly secondary to the subjective spirit, an accident and effect of action rather than its foundation. As Bloch glosses Fichte, 'the actual material object-Being is merely a board [*Brett*] that the I nails in front of its head so that it bounces back upon itself'.[20]

In many ways, Schelling's view of nature stands diametrically opposed to Fichte's. Common to the numerous iterations of Schelling's thought is a desire to explain nature's self-animating essence, distinct from the critical idealists' anthropocentric schemas of human cognition.[21] Indeed, for Schelling the very

---

principle for guiding the eye's investigation' (Kant 2002b, 20: 236). On moral motivation through natural teleology, see Kant 2002b, 5: 434–6, and Kant 2006.

14   Kant 2002b, 5: 380.
15   Bloch 1977a, p. 212.
16   See Sedgwick (ed.) 2000.
17   Bloch 1977a, p. 215.
18   For this formulation, see Pippin 2000, p. 148, which challenges this psychological interpretation; cf. Sieroka 2007.
19   Bloch 1977a, p. 216; cf. Bloch 1977c, pp. 421–2. Bloch misquotes Fichte, whose original German reads, '*unsere Welt ist das versinnlichte Material unserer Pflicht*' (Fichte 1845, p. 185).
20   Bloch 1977a, p. 216.
21   For treatments of these topics in Schelling, see Grant 2008, Massimi 2017 and Le 2017.

practice of philosophising about nature requires it to be taken in terms of its separate vitality, to bring it 'out of the dead mechanicism in which it seems trapped, to enliven it, so to speak, with freedom, and to place it in its own free development'.[22] Schelling's view of nature is supported by a dynamic theory of matter transcendentally deduced as 'nothing other than spirit considered in equilibrium with its activity'.[23] This activity extends to all of nature, in fine and in gross: the organisation of 'world-bodies' like Earth, for example, is the *'outwardly developed inner essence of this world body itself* and formed through inner metamorphosis (e.g., of earth)'.[24] In some versions of his system, Schelling adds a doctrine of matter's innate potency, generating itself towards the light of a world soul, the ultimate artist of existence – he describes nature as 'a poem written indecipherably in a secret, magical script' which we can read 'if we recognise the odyssey of spirit within it'.[25] Schelling's *natura naturans*, glossed by Bloch as 'the creating essence of cognition, the producing essence of nature, the emerging essence of history, all at once',[26] thus renders the material world a manifestation of a non-sentient intelligence. As we shall see, later commentators often suggest that Bloch's work betrays a similarly sovereign natural subject. Yet it is not this neo-Platonic overflowing of ideas into reality that Bloch takes as Schelling's innovation, but the recovery of the Aristotelian doctrine of potentiality, the notion that matter contains 'the possibility of all potencies'.[27] Schelling not only recovers the Aristotelian doctrine of potentiality; he extends it 'most audaciously' to include utopian transfiguration proper by envisioning God united with the material world in a 'holy sabbath of nature' as a latent possibility of matter.[28]

Rounding out this summary is Hegel, who likewise transforms Kant's regulative natural teleology into a principle of reality. Hegel's approach to both nature and matter is propelled by an external, spiritual necessity, although

---

22 Schelling 1858a, p. 13. In his philosophical novel *Clara*, Schelling writes that '[t]he central role of philosophical science resides in scientifically explaining the contradictions and connections between nature and the spirit world' (Schelling 2002, p. 4, cited in Le 2017, p. 120).

23 Schelling 1858b, p. 453; Bloch's discussion replaces Schelling's 'viewed [*angeschaut*]' with 'glimpsed [*erblickt*]' (Bloch 1977a, p. 218). On Schelling's deduction of matter from the reciprocity of natural forces, see Schelling 1858c.

24 Schelling 1858d; cf. Bloch 1977a, p. 221.

25 Schelling 1858b, p. 628; cf. Schelling 2012.

26 Bloch 1977a, p. 223. See Schelling 1858a and Grant 2008. Bloch likens Schelling's image of nature to Novalis's 'petrified magical city' (Bloch 1977a, p. 222; cf. Novalis 1901, p. 336).

27 Ibid. For Schelling's neo-Platonism, see Schelling 1858e and 2008 as well as Grant 2008, especially Chapter 2.

28 Schelling, 1858e, p. 378; cf. Bloch 1977a, p. 223.

humankind is, crucially, the developmental agent.²⁹ Like Kant, Fichte and Schelling, Hegel transcendentally deduces both concepts out of purely logical categories.³⁰ As with almost everything in Hegel's work, furthermore, matter and nature are expressions of rational spirit or *Geist*, the world's self-positing ontological foundation, which gradually manifests itself over time in concrete reality.³¹ Indeed, like Schelling, Hegel characterises the philosophy of nature's object as the universal considered 'in its *own immanent necessity* in accordance with the self-determination of the concept'.³² The world's material dialectics accordingly reflect not so much the interaction of matter with itself as the logic of necessary mind, domesticated within Hegel's particular vocabulary; the idea, he explains, 'freely releases itself out of itself' as nature.³³ In his lectures on the history of philosophy, Hegel contrasts Aristotle's teaching of the constitutive quality of natural teleology with Kant's doctrine of regulative natural teleology, aligning his own view with the former.³⁴ In Hegel's developmental vision, newer forms are created out of the interaction of concepts and concrete material within history, and yet the dialectic of matter ultimately exists for the purposes of *Geist* rather than of the humans who effectuate its development. In Bloch's reading, Hegel makes the material of the world merely an instrument for the realisation of spiritual necessity; as Bloch writes, Hegel 'treats matter like a gothic master builder'.³⁵ And indeed, when describing organic bodies, Hegel writes that spirit 'is the existing truth of matter, that matter itself has no truth'.³⁶

---

29   Hegel could also claim to be at least passably expert in certain corners of empirical science. His 1801 *Habilitationsschrift* – the defence of which Schelling attended – is on contemporary debates about planetary orbits (see Beaumont 1954 and Depré 1998). The *Phenomenology of Spirit*'s 1807 title page identifies the author not only as a professor of philosophy at the University of Jena but also as an 'Assessor of the Ducal Mineralogical Society and member of other learned societies', presumably including the Westphalian Society for Natural Research, to which he was elected in 1804. Hegel was also a practitioner: as a mineralogical assessor, he was issued a pass by the University of Jena for a trip to the Harz Mountains for geological study. See Pinkard 2000, p. 114, and Verene 1998, p. 209.
30   Hegel 1986b, paragraphs 247 and 262.
31   For Hegel, the single notable exception to spirit's *rational* manifestation is the existence of an impoverished and alienated social 'rabble [*Pöbel*]' created by capitalism. See Hegel 1991, paragraphs 244 and 245; cf. Ruda 2011.
32   Hegel 1986b, paragraph 246.
33   The German reads: 'die *unmittelbare Idee* als ihren Widerschein, sich als *Natur* frei *aus sich zu entlassen*' (Hegel 1986a, paragraph 244; cf. Verene 1998, pp. 212–13).
34   Hegel 1986d, p. 376.
35   Bloch 1977c, p. 429.
36   Hegel 1986c, paragraph 389; cf. Bloch 1977c, p. 430.

If Hegel's philosophy of nature and matter reflects the notion that the world's future is already fully determined within its matter, and that our present task is merely to re-collect its forms in concrete reality, Bloch believes that Hegel's writings nonetheless contain 'cryptomaterialist strands'.[37] By acknowledging the processual, historical evolution of the idea in the world, Hegel's dialectical vision blurs the lines between human and object, interiority and exteriority and consciousness and being.[38] As Bloch explains, in Hegel 'the external world is *independent* from consciousness, yet it no longer exists as *unmediated* by consciousness, that is, as independent from the *process of labour* of the historical-dialectical Subject-Object relationship'.[39] Accordingly, human activity – the process of labour – is taken not as superfluous to, but as a constitutive and indeed predominant quality of, the material world; there is in matter 'not only a place, but the most esteemed place, for a true and intervening consciousness'.[40] For Bloch, it is this *material, labouring dialectic of nature* that forms the rational kernel within the mystical shell that Marx subsequently draws forth from Hegel by placing him on his feet.[41]

3 Matter and the Relationship between Humanity and Nature in Marx

As Bloch sees things, these thinkers all sought to escape the cage of Kant's critical system to grasp 'the sensual-materialistic thing in itself'; by making nature's development into a genetic logic of reality, however, they ultimately ended up in 'the strongest of idealisms'.[42] It is with Marx that philosophy is finally brought down to earth and made properly materialist.

Marx's philosophical formation occurred during an era of debate about Hegel's legacy that pitted broad camps of his followers against one another. Simplifying, one might say that the two most important camps were a conservative 'right' that emphasised the spiritual rationality of existing institutions as the culmination of history and a radical 'left' that saw the dialectic as open-ended, thereby projecting history's end – of the full realisation of

---

37 Bloch 1977c, p. 430. Bloch describes Hegel's spirit as a 'recollection-Geist [*Erinnerungs-Geist*]' rather than one whose matter is processual and 'still open' (Bloch 1977c, pp. 409–10).
38 Bloch 1977c, pp. 437–8.
39 Bloch 1977c, p. 438.
40 Bloch 1977c, p. 441.
41 Marx 1990, p. 103.
42 Bloch 1977c, p. 212.

freedom – into the future.⁴³ Marx stood in the latter camp, with a diverse group of thinkers including Bruno Bauer (his doctoral supervisor), Friedrich Engels, Ludwig Feuerbach, Moses Heß, Max Stirner and David Friedrich Strauß. He sought to establish philosophy on a thoroughgoing natural and materialist foundation, a project that built upon Feuerbach's humanist unmasking of Hegel's infinite *Geist* as a projection of finite being. As Feuerbach explained in his 1842 'Preliminary Theses on the Reform of Philosophy', 'the *true* speculation or philosophy is nothing but what is *truly and universally empirical*', a claim that led him to call for the unification of philosophy with natural science.⁴⁴ From Marx's perspective, Feuerbach's materialism does not go far enough: to say, as Feuerbach does, that '*Being* is the *subject*, *thought* is the *predicate*' presents the essential material reality as an abstract object of contemplation rather than as a result of '*sensuous human activity*'.⁴⁵ Put otherwise, materialism has thus far held that men are the product of circumstances, but it has ignored that 'circumstances are changed by men'.⁴⁶ Significantly, the human essence to which Feuerbach deflates *Geist* is not, for Marx, sui generis; instead, it is in reality 'the ensemble of social relations' in which individuals are enmeshed.⁴⁷ The materialist transformation of philosophy that Marx calls for is to be achieved not through further contemplation, but through revolutionising practical activity. Hence, according to Bloch, Marx begins 'the transformation of philosophy into the philosophy of changing the world'.⁴⁸

In his earliest work, Marx delves into the dynamic concept of matter as an ontological foundation for autonomy within a materialist frame. Unlike his idealist predecessors, he does not offer a transcendental deduction of matter, but focuses instead on a debate in classical Greek philosophy of nature. His 1841 dissertation accordingly pits the determinist materialism of Democritus against the undetermined materialism of Epicurus.⁴⁹ Both ancient thinkers thought of matter as atoms falling in a void, but Epicurus and his followers spoke further of spontaneous 'swerves' [Lat. *clinamina*] that could set atoms on new trajectories. Marx thus discovers in the Epicurean account of matter 'the first form of self-consciousness', the Archimedean point of a genuinely

---

43 David Friedrich Strauß originated this distinction, while also distinguishing a Hegelian 'centre'. For the intellectual context of the Left Hegelians, see Breckman 1999, pp. 261–3, and Moggach (ed.) 2006.
44 Feuerbach 2012, pp. 160 and 172.
45 Feuerbach 2012, p. 168, and Marx 2000a, p. 171.
46 Marx 2000a, p. 172.
47 Ibid.
48 Bloch 1977c, p. 519.
49 Marx 2006.

thoroughgoing naturalism.[50] In the then-contemporary philosophical landscape, Marx's arguments in favour of the swerving Epicurus over the determinist Democritus are salvos against the conservative passivity of the Hegelian Right's worldview. Elsewhere, Marx hints at a stronger, vitalist conception in response to the deadening gaze of scientific empiricism. In *The Holy Family*, he and Engels take English materialism to task for its Democritean mechanicism, arguing against Bacon and Locke that the most important quality of matter 'is motion, not only mechanical and mathematical movement, but still more impulse, vital life-spirit, tension, or, to use Jacob Böhme's expression, the throes of matter', and describing its primary forms as 'the living, individualizing forces of being inherent in it'.[51] While *The Holy Family* is unsystematic and polemical, it nonetheless reinforces Marx's rejection of the inert notion of matter as incompatible with the idea of wilful human activity as a constitutive fact of nature.

For Marx, matter is of *practical* philosophical importance because it is the prerequisite for the very activity of labour that (re)produces human existence in nature.[52] As he remarks in his so-called *Paris Manuscripts*, man, like other animals, is a directly natural being, instinctively enmeshed in the natural world for the satisfaction of his needs.[53] In practical activity, the two form a dialectical ensemble: man 'makes all nature his *inorganic* body – both inasmuch as nature is (1) his direct means of life, and (2) the material, the object, and the instrument of his life-activity'.[54] Furthermore, to say that 'man's physical and spiritual life is linked to nature means simply that nature is linked to itself, for man is a part of nature'.[55] The inversion of Hegel is unmistakable: rather than material nature being the manifestation of spirit, Marx makes spirit a manifestation of material nature acting upon itself. Importantly, it is not that humans realise goals of a totalising natural subject, of an immanent and infinite teleology of nature, but only, as Alfred Schmidt writes, 'the finite goals of finite, spatially and temporally limited men confronting limited areas of the natural and social world'.[56] Human labouring activity mediates and develops the natural world, a process to which humans ascribe meaning and which they strive to direct, but it does not do so with any inherent and overarching purpose.[57]

50 Marx 2006, p. 117; see also Goldman 2020, pp. 58–9.
51 Marx 2000a, p. 166.
52 Cited in Parsons (ed.) 1977, p. 122.
53 Marx 1978, p. 75.
54 Ibid.
55 Ibid. Cf. Marx 1973, p. 87.
56 Schmidt 2012, pp. 35–6.
57 Marx writes, 'as everything natural has to have its *beginning, man* too has his act of origin

What makes humans unique among natural beings is this 'spiritual' capacity of self-regard, the fact that human life activity is consciously directed – a characteristic that Marx, following Feuerbach, calls humanity's 'species-being' or 'species-essence' [*Gattungswesen*].[58] Ideally, the productive life-activity of human beings would be freely chosen, fully realising our natural-cum-spiritual species essence. Under capitalist property relations, however, humans are alienated from their species-being and nature as a whole. On the one hand, the end-in-itself of productive life activity is reduced to a mere means of bare survival; other humans, with whom one could freely engage in creative production, are reduced to competitive threats in the labour market. On the other hand, the natural world is reduced to nothing more than raw material for exploitation, an object of profitable conquest rather than a qualitatively rich space of organic self-relation.[59] Capitalism's inhumanity thus extends to both social relations and natural relations: we are a part of nature, yet we no longer recognise ourselves within it.

By abolishing private property, communism overcomes the various forms of self-alienation attending capitalism, liberating humans from the narrow vision of possessive individualism and restoring the social character of production.[60] No longer distorted by capitalist imperatives, human species-being could find expression in the full flourishing of freely associated labour, and nature would be stripped of its estranged, purely instrumental guise. In the *Paris Manuscripts*, Marx describes the ensuing dialectic between humans and nature in the romantic and idealist language of unity, suggesting that in communism 'society completes the essential unity of man and nature, it is the genuine resurrection of nature, the accomplished naturalism of man and the accomplished humanism of nature'.[61]

Later, Marx appropriates the biological metaphor of 'metabolism' from agronomy to describe the interdependent processes linking humans and nature through labour.[62] As he explains in *Capital*:

– history – which, however, is for him a known history, and hence as an act of origin it is a conscious self-transcending act of origin. History is the true natural history of man'; cited in Parsons (ed.) 1977, p. 135.

[58] Marx 1978, p. 75. For Feuerbach, thinking theologically, this *Gattungswesen* is humanity's infinite potential for goodness.

[59] See Marx 1978, pp. 75–7; cf. Marx 1973, p. 541; see also Fetscher 1973 and Järvikoski 1996.

[60] Marx 1990, p. 171.

[61] Marx 2000, p. 98, translation by David McLellan; cf. Martin Milligan's translation: 'Thus *society* is the consummated oneness in substance of man and nature – the true resurrection of nature – the naturalism of man and the humanism of nature both brought to fulfillment' (Marx 1978, p. 85).

[62] 'Metabolism' is the standard rendering of Marx's *Stoffwechsel*, a term that literally trans-

Labor is, first of all, a process between man and nature, a process by which man, through his own actions, mediates, regulates and controls the metabolism between himself and nature. Man confronts nature as a force of nature. He sets in motion the natural forces which belong to his own body, his arms, legs, head and hands, in order to appropriate the materials of nature in a form adapted to his own needs. Through this movement he acts upon external nature and changes it, and in this way he simultaneously changes his own nature. He develops the potentialities slumbering within nature, and subjects the play of its forces to his own sovereign power.[63]

Capitalism puts this metabolism out of whack, for the profit motive undermines the long-term sustainability of the natural world.[64] In its urge to exploit the earth as much as possible, capitalism opens a 'metabolic rift' between humans and nature.[65] This rift is reflected in a number of practices in search of profit: cash crops dominate, overharvesting robs the soil of nutrients and indeed the entire science of agriculture – the study of our most fundamental laboring activity, the nourishment of ourselves – becomes unrecognisable, for it 'no longer finds the natural conditions of its own production within itself, naturally, arisen, spontaneous, and ready to hand, but these exist as an independent industry separate from it'.[66] This self-alienating transformation of agriculture into industry has its developmental twin in the removal of people from the land and their concentration in cities as potential soldiers for an industrial army of wage labourers, further dissolving humanity's relationship to the earth.[67] This process is played out further downstream, in the development of an international, hierarchical division of labour into a Western core and a non-Western periphery.

In contrast to this rift – Marx says – a future society organised without private property, but instead according to the practice of free conscious activity of 'socialised man, the associated producers', would 'govern the human metabolism with nature in a rational way, bringing it under their own collective con-

---

lates as 'exchange/transformation of matter': labour transforms the raw matter of nature into human use value; see Marx 1990, pp. 198, 283 and 133. On 'metabolism' in Marx, see Foster 2000 (especially Chapter 5); Foster, York and Clark 2018; Mészáros 1995 (especially Chapter 2); and Schmidt 2012 (especially section B and the Appendix).

63   Marx 1990, p. 283.
64   See Fetscher 1973, pp. 465–6, and Sheasby 1997.
65   Marx 1993, p. 949, and Marx 1990, p. 637.
66   Marx 1973, p. 527.
67   Marx 1973, p. 497; cf. Foster 2000, p. 174.

trol instead of being dominated by it as a blind power; accomplishing it with the least expenditure of energy and in conditions most worthy and appropriate for their human nature'.[68] Under such collective control, 'working with the means of production held in common ... in full self-awareness as a single social labor force', productive activity would by definition become free conscious activity.[69] Such conditions present the possibility of sustainably and intelligently reforming the productive metabolism between humans and nature in a non-exploitative manner.[70]

4 Dialectical Matter and the Aristotelian Left

Bloch approaches matter and nature from a Marxian active-materialist perspective, albeit in characteristically idiosyncratic fashion, inflected with the particular emphasis of his concern for concrete utopia.[71] Marx's scattered reflections on dynamic matter serve his conviction that human labour develops nature's slumbering potential. Extending this insight, Bloch's neo-Aristotelian notion of a forwards-orientated, still-open matter undergirds his belief in the possibility of utopian transformation. For Bloch, utopia spells the transfiguration of human relations – not merely to a new reality [*das Neue*] but to a genuinely novel reality [*das Novum*], one that transcends the bounds of what we take to be possible.[72] It demands a different type of possibility altogether, the 'objective-real' possibility of what does not yet exist but that *may become* real. Bloch's account of matter and nature thus aims to account for the genesis of genuine novelty, to describe a world that contains processual tendencies whose essence is, in Cat Moir's words, 'yet to be fully determined in the process of its self-actualisation'.[73] For Bloch, moreover, *we* are history's actualising subjects; humans develop new forms out of the world through their activity.

To grasp Bloch's concept of matter, the distinction between *objective* and *real* possibility is key, for utopia resides only in the latter. As he explains in *The Principle of Hope*:

---

68 Marx 1993, p. 959.
69 Marx 1990, p. 171.
70 Hence the extension of Marx's insights in ecosocialism; see Burkett 2014, Foster 2000, Löwy 2015 and Wallis 2018.
71 For treatments of Bloch's concept of matter, see Holz 1975, Jäger 1978, Klein 2008 and Zudeick 1980.
72 See Siebers 2012.
73 Moir 2019, p. 132.

Objectively possible is everything whose entry, on the basis of a mere partial-*cognition* of its existing conditions, is scientifically to be expected, or at least cannot be discounted. Whereas *really* possible is everything whose conditions in the sphere of the *object itself* are not yet fully assembled; whether because they are still maturing, or above all because new conditions – though mediated with the existing ones – arise for the entry of a new Real.[74]

Objective possibility, then, refers to the scientific measure of possibility in the present, while real possibility refers to the world's emerging yet still developing potential. As Bloch writes, 'as long as the reality has not become a completely determined one, as long as it possesses still unclosed possibilities, in the shape of new shoots and new spaces for development, then no absolute objection to utopia can be raised by merely factual reality'.[75] The dead end(s) of the mechanistic conception only allows determinist possibility, and it does not permit genuine novelty – it lacks the transformative Kantian pulse of liveliness.[76] What is needed is a concept of matter that allows for the world's openness, one appropriate to real possibility, that provides space for these new shoots and developments. The matter of this real possibility is, Bloch writes emphatically, '*nothing other than dialectical matter*'.[77]

Bloch traces the philosophical origins of dialectical matter to Aristotle, drawing on his categories of form, matter, potentiality and actuality.[78] As hinted above, Aristotle takes all physical things as combinations of matter and form, the latter providing the stuff (say, wood) and the former providing the essence (say, chairness or bedness).[79] Matter exists as the power or potential [*dynamis*] to be many things; its possibilities only become actuality when instantiated in concrete form, a teleological movement Aristotle calls *energy* or *entelechy*.[80] In this combination, form is the active and actualising element, the essence rendered real through passive matter and the determinate telos towards which its energy drives.

Bloch places special weight on Aristotle's ambiguous description of material potentiality as both *kata to dynaton* and *dynamei on*.[81] As *kata to dynaton*,

---

74   Bloch 1986, vol. 1, p. 196.
75   Bloch 1986, vol. 1, p. 197.
76   Bloch 1977a, pp. 19 and 470.
77   Bloch 1986, vol. 1, p. 206.
78   Bloch 1977a, p. 223.
79   Aristotle 1984, 1032b1–2.
80   See, for example, Aristotle 1984, 1045b17.
81   See, for example, Bloch 1977a, pp. 152–64 and 479–546; Bloch 1977c, p. 439; Bloch 1986, vol. 1, p. 207 and vol. 3, p. 1371; and Bloch 2019.

or what Bloch calls 'what-is-according-to-possibility [*Nach-Möglichkeit-Sein*]', matter is concretely in-formed within historical conditions and limits, and it acts in line with the measure of the objective possibility already present in the world: it is 'mechanical matter'.[82] By contrast, as *dynamei on*, or 'what-is-in-possibility [*In-Möglichkeit-Sein*]'[83] – which Bloch reads as a synonym in Aristotle for matter – it is material potential 'not as that which is already in the process of being determined (according to the measure of the possible), but as the fermenting substrate of possibility itself'.[84] If what-is-according-to-possibility is the objective side of nature as we experience it scientifically, what-is-in-possibility is – as Moir writes – the 'subjective factor in matter, an unconscious yet active driving force that generates, produces, and creates'.[85] Seen in this light, matter is not simply passive, taking any form, but makes some forms possible, a 'self-fermenting womb of entelectic expressions'.[86]

For the categories of objective possibility of the world as we presently know it, matter is disposed as *kata to dynaton*, which contains its particular end within – it has achieved a form of the manifestation of its entelechy. The *dynamei on*, instead, is characterised by 'incomplete' or 'open entelechy', a term Bloch borrows from Aristotle's writings on motion, according to which entelechies are in a process of development.[87] Here, the open system of Bloch's speculative materialism gets its ontological basis, in the reality that matter makes possible forms that have not yet been brought to finality. The world's tendency and latency – Bloch's translation of Aristotle's *energy* and *entelechy* – anchor the hope that concrete utopia may yet arise.[88]

The 'driving tendency, entelectic latency' of matter as *dynamei on* does not arise spontaneously.[89] While the subjective force, the 'energetic something'[90] of matter's teeming real possibilities presents itself, like Marx's productive forces, as independent of human agency, Bloch holds – also with Marx –

---

82 Bloch 1977a, p. 473.
83 Loren Goldman and Peter Thompson translate *Nach-Möglichkeit-Sein* and *In-Möglichkeit-Sein* less literally, as 'what-is-considered-possible' and 'what-may-become-possible', respectively.
84 Bloch 1977a, p. 142; see also Bloch 1977b, p. 233, and Bloch 1977c, p. 438.
85 Moir 2019, p. 129.
86 Bloch 1977a, p. 475.
87 Bloch 1977a, p. 476.
88 Bloch 1977c, p. 143; cf. Moir 2019, pp. 128–9.
89 Bloch 1977a, p. 474.
90 Bloch 1977a, p. 20.

that humans are the efficient cause of activating matter's predisposed potential. Indeed, Bloch takes Marx's insight into the labour-processual relationship of man to nature as akin to the realisation that humans are 'the matter of hope [*Stoff der Hoffnung*]'.[91] Engels likewise held the thinking mind to be 'the highest blossom of organic matter'.[92] Subjects conscious of their historical-material agency labour to produce the unalienated reality of the not-yet glimpsed in the concrete imagination. As Bloch puts it, the real in history is 'the events produced by working people together with the abundant interweaving process-connections between past, present and future'.[93] More pointedly, he writes that the potential of matter works 'above all in the material relations of revolutionary and revolutionising class and its *potency*, and this corresponds objective-concretely to the real *possibility* as *potentiality* of these relations and their matter itself disposed to revolutionisability, thus towards the never has been, towards the *Novum*'.[94] The concept of matter as *dynamei on* thus ontologically underwrites the possibility that the traces of the 'concrete forward dream' exist because they are in fact 'fermenting in the process of the real itself'.[95]

Speculation, aesthetics and politics intersect in activating this dialectical matter. As Bloch puts it: 'Only controlled history, with an incisive countermove against inhibitions, with active promotion of tendency, can help essential material in the distance of art to become increasingly also appearance in the dealings of life'.[96] Matter generates form out of itself insofar as its manifestation as human consciousness both draws out and sketches further its ongoing process of this trans-formation towards its posited future.

Bloch's use of Aristotelian categories to describe matter's indwelling utopian potential is admittedly idiosyncratic. Understanding the substantive and symbolic transformations of these appropriations helps shed light on the issues Bloch seeks to disclose. Bloch describes his stance as 'Left Aristotelian' and situates it as the fruit of a long undercurrent of materialist commentary on

---

91 Bloch 1986, vol. 3, Chapter 55.
92 Bloch 1977a, p. 366; Bloch misquotes Engels as calling *der Menschengeist* rather than *der denkende Geist* this highest blossom (see Engels 1990, p. 327); cf. Holz 2012, p. 506, and Moir 2019, p. 131.
93 Bloch 1986, vol. 1, p. 198.
94 Bloch 1977a, p. 472.
95 Bloch 1986, vol. 1, p. 197.
96 Bloch 1986, vol. 1, p. 216. See also p. 186: 'the trumpet call in [Beethoven's] *Fidelio* would hardly have its piercing genuine effect without the storming of the Bastille, which provides the model and the unrelenting background for *Fidelio*'s music'. Cf. Hatch 1999.

Aristotle, the full flourishing of which Marx represents. Aristotle, Bloch avers, leaves *dynamei on* as the passive womb from which world forms emerge.[97] The dominant medieval Church scholastics emphasised this material passivity and put the ontological onus on form's separation from matter: Paul, for example, laments humanity's pathological 'bondage to decay' in earthly life.[98] By contrast, the accounts of the medieval Islamic thinkers Avicenna and Averroes revitalise *dynamei on* as the active material capacity towards form, taking matter as 'laden with energy'.[99] Bloch draws an analogy between this split among Aristotle's followers with the right/left split among Hegel's followers, with a conservative orthodoxy of theological apologetics valorising divine form over passively receiving matter pitted against the radical proponents of matter's inherent, actively churning potential.[100] This latter Aristotelian Left – Bloch also calls it pantheistic – is marked, against the Church, by an overriding concern for the worldly. Gone is the ontological breach between form and matter, for – against the Aristotelian Right's view of God's fallenness in matter – the founders of the Aristotelian Left saw the '*sublation [Aufhebung] of divine potency itself in the active potentiality of matter*'.[101] Avicenna, who, Bloch emphasises, had trained as a doctor and not, like the scholastics, as a monk, described development as the '*eductio formarum ex materia* [eduction of forms out of matter], with *materia* really as *mater*'.[102] Averroes draws this line out further; in Bloch's account, he makes matter into 'the world's treasury', already containing in its possibility 'all forms embryonically decided and collected' which are merely 'developed and extracted' by the pure act of divinity.[103] Taking matter in this way as universal potency puts paid to the idea of form as a self-sustaining and independent principle. While Avicenna and Averroes remain a long way from Marx's materially comprehended hope, they mark a turning point when it comes to the interpretation of Aristotle – the font of an underground current that develops itself forwards over the course of the Middle Ages and in which 'the potential of matter ultimately became birth and grave and new place of hope for the world-forms in general'.[104] Among others noted by Bloch in this chain of thinkers who give creative matter its due are the Jewish-Iberian poet-philosopher Avicebron (Ibn Gabirol), whose *Fons Vitae*

---

97 Bloch 1986, vol. 1, p. 207.
98 Romans 8:21.
99 Bloch 2019, p. 3.
100 Bloch 2019, p. 15 and *passim*.
101 Bloch 2019, pp. 15–16.
102 Bloch 1977a, p. 153.
103 Bloch 1977a, p. 155.
104 Bloch 1986, vol. 1, p. 207.

espouses Averroes's universal matter in neo-Platonic guise; the medieval Christian heretic David of Dinant, who posits a fully pantheistic materialism; and Giordano Bruno, who so inscribed form within restive matter that he made it reality's 'fertile mother' and 'sole substantial principle'.[105] As we have seen, this current had a lasting resonance, echoing subtly in Kant, Schelling and Hegel before its revival in Marx's labouring humanity as the literal material of hope.

The substantive philosophical differences between the Right Aristotelian and Left Aristotelian interpretations – a divergence which Bloch ascribes to the different economic conditions of medieval feudal Europe and the commercial Near East[106] – symbolise significantly different political imaginaries. While the scholastic, idealist interpretation of the essence of active form versus the passivity of matter was used to justify by analogy the Church's spiritual authority over society, the Left Aristotelian view has an anti-authoritarian bent. Because form comes not from the top down, as it were, but from the bottom up, it becomes democratised; clerics no longer possess sole and true insight into the world's tendencies. Indeed, from the perspective of high-church Aristotelianism, the list of Bloch's protagonists reads like a litany of heretics: the works of nearly all of them were at one time either banned or burned. So too the authors themselves: some, like Avicenna, Averroes and David of Dinant, were forced into exile; others, like Bruno, the Albigensians and many of David of Dinant's followers, met their fates at the stake. And just as these thinkers were heretics, so too was Bloch. His Left Aristotelian materialism likewise forced him into exile, as he was denounced in the GDR for his position that the entelechy of history remains open, not yet completed by the East German state.

Yet Bloch claimed neither unique nor total insight into reality. Unlike many of his orthodox critics, he took Marxism to be a big church. Marx complains in the 'Theses on Feuerbach' that other self-declared materialists had not taken human labouring activity as an objective or even formative fact about the world. Bloch recapitulates this critique within Marxism, complaining that other Marxists have not taken utopian aspiration as an objective and formative fact of the world. Indeed, for all of the intricacy of his anti-mechanistic position, Bloch's concept of nature as the womb of form is meant to buttress the utopian, revolutionary urge he views driving the *subjective* factor in Marxism. For him, the analysis of matter as *dynamei on* and *kata to dynaton* illuminates two distinct ways of 'being Red': a sober, analytic 'cold stream' and a visionary, prophetic 'warm stream'.[107] The cold stream bespeaks Marxism's scientific ori-

---

105 Cf. Bloch 1977a, pp. 157, 170–1 and 179, as well as Bloch 2019, pp. 30–3.
106 Bloch 2019, pp. 3–6.
107 Bloch 1986, vol. 1, p. 208.

entation, focusing on social and economic dynamics within the limits of known objective possibility; the warm stream, by contrast, is geared towards 'prospect-exploration' of the horizon.[108] In Bloch's estimation, coldness and warmth, or planning and aspiration, are not so much absolutely opposed as standing in dialectical tension, pushing the development of the not-yet forwards. Bloch's brief in favour of creative matter raised hackles in the GDR precisely because of its warmth, with the insistence on open entelechy and form from below taken – not surprisingly – by the state as a direct challenge to the Party's authoritative insight into social dynamics. The symbolic political function of *dynamei on* matter as a lubricating agent *within* Marxism thus parallels its symbolic political function against clerical authority in the Avicennan legacy in scholastic debates.

5 Natural Subject, Technology of Co-Production, Ecology

The GDR's moral failings notwithstanding, its philosophers were – on this point at least – insightful readers, for Bloch's Left Aristotelian materialism indeed overflows the orthodox frame. A materialism that posits the genuinely novel, transfigurative potential of real possibility within nature necessarily resists the presumed finalism of objective possibility's scientific gaze. The GDR was nothing if not predicated on the cold stream of Marxism, and its intellectual lights saw that Bloch was trying to bring still not-yet actualised revolutionary possibility into matter itself, a project both superfluous for and counter to the idea that the GDR had already secured the revolution once and for all.[109] For an orthodox (and cold) Marxist critic such as Rudolf Rochhausen, for instance, Bloch's reinvigoration of the subjective force in matter was a sin against the Engelsian dogma of dialectical materialism as predicated on matter as possessing eternal and unchanging form.[110] The GDR philosophers did not appreciate the self-aware partiality of the warm stream, the prospective-horizonal orientation as something to be offered in dialectical conversation with the cold stream.

A different criticism of Bloch's neo-Aristotelian materialism is the flipside of the complaint that it permits too much uncertainty and arbitrary freedom.

---

108 Ibid. Cf. Mazzini 2012.
109 On the GDR critique, see Horn (ed.) 1957, especially Horn's preface and the essay by Otto Rugard Gropp. Cf. 'Ernst Bloch – Exkommunisiert' 1960, 'Ein Tribunal gegen Ernst Bloch' 1991 and Moir 2019, p. 147.
110 Cf. Horn (ed.), p. 90.

To commentators like Alfred Schmidt and Jürgen Habermas, Bloch presents a potentially totalitarian vision of a world in which humans merely do nature's ostensible bidding, sacrificing their own purposes to the supposed purpose – and indeed, agency – of an ontologically prior and superior reality. This accusation makes Bloch out to be, in Habermas's influential characterisation, 'a Marxist Schelling', holding humans to be *merely* worldly vessels of a greater natural subject.[111] Schmidt accuses Bloch of entertaining a dialectic of nature that works itself out 'independently of human mental activity and production', thus leading to a 'pantheistic-hylozoic conception of a "nature-Subject", and hence ... to the abandonment of the materialist position'.[112] Bloch undoubtedly gives his critics ammunition at times, as when he speaks of nature as an independent and impersonal agent, writing – for example – that 'not the movement of all things and above all humans, but rather matter itself and in total represents itself as still unfinished entelechy'.[113] A strong reading of this warm comment indeed could make out an effective natural subject. A weaker reading, more in line with Bloch's intent, takes this instead as a simple (and Schellingian) acknowledgement that the world exists independently of humans and thus does not fit in perfectly, or even easily, with our own logic of expectation. While Schmidt sees a deterministic natural subject running roughshod over human purposes, Bloch is clear that human agency alone is the effective means by which the utopian not-yet may come to be. Paraphrasing and expanding on Hegel, Bloch writes that '[t]he rational can become actual, the actual can become rational; it depends on the phenomenology or history of appearances of true *action*'.[114]

A greater problem than the danger of sacrificing humanity to an impersonal natural subject is the potential for human subjectivity to run roughshod over nature, to exploit it *solely* for anthropocentric purposes. Indeed, ecological concerns suggest the continuing actuality of Bloch's Left Aristotelian concept of matter, for it offers a way of imposing limits on human activity out of a concern for sustainability. Schmidt's quasi-humanist critique of Bloch runs the risk of reifying humankind as the sovereign lord of nature without any concern for the welfare of its own natural subjects. Capitalism and socialism alike push towards the full development of the forces of production, and this imperative in and of itself puts no limits on the expropriation of nature. To argue specu-

111 Habermas 1983.
112 Schmidt 2012, p. 59. Schmidt fights a running battle with Bloch throughout this work; see, for example, pp. 37, 161 and *passim* in the footnotes.
113 Bloch 1977a, p. 20.
114 Bloch 1977c, p. 519.

latively that matter presents its own forms as open entelechies can be seen as an attempt to rein in the destructive productive tendencies of the Anthropocene.

Despite the grandiose language of *natura naturans* and the *Novum*, then, the concrete purpose of Bloch's Left Aristotelian approach to matter may be more modest, reflecting an attempt to bring balance into the human-nature relationship, a call for tempering the extravagances of a purely instrumental relationship to nature in our living and labouring activity. Bloch's concern is not how to unify nature and humanity *as such*, as the early Marx suggests, but how to tether human activity to nature in a way that foments mutually beneficial co-existence, in line with the later Marx's metaphor of metabolism. Such ecological considerations are evident when Bloch writes, in passages subsequently embraced by the German Greens, of a 'co-productivity of a possible natural subject or concrete technology of alliance' between nature and humankind, a process of coordinating human activity and matter's emerging potentials.[115] As Bloch puts it,

> The current of nature as a friend, technology as the delivery and mediation of the creations slumbering in the womb of nature, this belongs to the most concrete aspect of concrete utopia. But even just the beginning of this concretion presupposes interhuman concretizing, i.e. social revolution; until this occurs there will not be any steps, let alone a door, to the possible alliance with nature.[116]

Humans draw out nature's slumbering possibilities, and this active process is not pre-ordained. The realisation of the rational in the actual depends on the social lens through which nature is perceived and on the phenomenology of human action, action that is within our choosing and the outcome of which is open. It is an awesome responsibility to be the primary vehicle through which matter further manifests itself. This is all the more the case in an era when the human power to transform nature, and hence humanity itself, is staggering. In an arresting image from *The Principle of Hope*, Bloch notes the ambiguous parallel between the flash of an atom bomb and the light surrounding Christ on the Resurrection scene from the medieval German artist Matthias Grünewald's *Isenheim Altarpiece*.[117] It is up to humanity to determine whether our mater-

---

115 Bloch 1986, vol. 2, p. 686. For Bloch's influence on the German Greens, see Ely 1996, 146–7.
116 Bloch 1986, vol. 2, pp. 695–6.
117 See Bloch 1986, vol. 2, p. 694; cf. the strikingly similar use of Grünewald by Manhattan-Project physicist Victor Weisskopf in his poem 'I Looked at Zero Through Dark Glass'

ial powers will further the destructive or constructive tendencies presented as possibilities by nature, whether we shall continue down the abstract path of exploitation and alienation from matter, or whether we shall find our humanity in a mutualist relationship with it.[118] As Bloch puts it, 'the human is his own devil and his own God, and so the world'.[119]

Bibliography

Aristotle 1984, *Metaphysics*, in *The Complete Works of Aristotle*, edited by Jonathan Barnes, Princeton: Princeton University Press.

Beaumont, Bertrand 1954, 'Hegel and the Seven Planets', *Mind*, 63, 250: 246–8.

Bloch, Ernst 1977a [1972], *Das Materialismusproblem, seine Geschichte und Substanz*, Frankfurt am Main: Suhrkamp.

Bloch, Ernst 1977b [1963], *Tübinger Einleitung in die Philosophie*, Frankfurt am Main: Suhrkamp.

Bloch, Ernst 1977c [1951], *Subjekt-Objekt. Erläuterungen zu Hegel*, Frankfurt am Main: Suhrkamp.

Bloch, Ernst 1986 [1954–1959], *The Principle of Hope*, 3 Volumes., translated by Neville Plaice, Stephen Plaice and Paul Knight, Cambridge, Mass.: MIT Press.

Bloch, Ernst 2000, *Logos der Materie. Eine Logik im Werden. Aus dem Nachlass 1923–1949*, Frankfurt am Main: Suhrkamp.

Bloch, Ernst 2019 [1952], *Avicenna and the Aristotelian Left*, translated by Loren Goldman and Peter Thompson, New York: Columbia University Press.

Breckman, Warren 1999, *Marx, The Young Hegelians and the Origins of Radical Social Theory*, Cambridge: Cambridge University Press.

Burkett, Paul 2014, *Marx and Nature: A Red-Green Perspective*, 2nd ed., Chicago: Haymarket Books.

Carrier, Martin 2001a, 'Kant's Mechanical Determination of Matter in the *Metaphysical Foundations of Natural Science*', in *Kant and the Sciences*, edited by Eric Watkins, Cambridge: Cambridge University Press.

(Weisskopf 2017).

118 Bloch writes: 'Just as the chain reactions on the sun bring us heat, light and life, so atomic energy, in a different machinery from that of the bomb, in the blue atmosphere of peace, creates fertile land out of the desert, and spring out of ice. A few hundred pounds of uranium and thorium ... would be enough to present mankind with the energy, which would otherwise have to be obtained in millions of hours of labour, ready for use in slim containers and in highly concentrated form' (Bloch 1986, vol. 2, p. 664).

119 Bloch 1977b, pp. 252–3.

Carrier, Martin 2001b, 'Kant's Theory of Matter and his Views on Chemistry', in *Kant and the Sciences*, edited by Eric Watkins, Cambridge: Cambridge University Press.

Depré, Olivier 1998, 'The Ontological Foundations of Hegel's Dissertation of 1801', in *Hegel and the Philosophy of Nature*, edited by Stephen Houlgate, Albany: SUNY Press.

Descartes, René 2001 [1644], *Les Principes de la Philosophie*, in *Œuvres Complètes*, edited by André Gombay, Toronto: Connaught Descartes Project, and Charlottesville, VA: InteLex Corporation.

'Ein Tribunal gegen Ernst Bloch' 1991, *UTOPIE kreativ*, 15: 60–78.

Ely, John 1996, 'Ernst Bloch, Natural Rights, and the Greens', in *Minding Nature: The Philosophers of Ecology*, edited by David MacAuley, New York: The Guilford Press.

Engels, Friedrich 1990 [1883], *Dialektik der Nature*, in *Marx-Engels Werke*, Volume 20, Berlin: Dietz.

'Ernst Bloch: Exkommunisiert' 1960, *Der Spiegel*, 34: 54–7.

Fetscher, Iring 1973, 'Marx on Human Nature', *Social Research*, 40, 3: 443–67.

Feuerbach, Ludwig 2012, *The Fiery Brook: Selected Writings*, translated by Zawar Hanfi, London: Verso.

Fichte, Johann Gottlieb 1845, *Über den Grund unseres Glaubens an eine göttliche Weltregierung*, in *Sämmtliche Werke*, Volume 5, edited by J.H. Fichte, Berlin: Veit und Comp.

Foster, John Bellamy 2000, *Marx's Ecology*, New York: Monthly Review Press.

Foster, John Bellamy, Richard York and Brett Clark 2018, *The Ecological Rift*, New York: Monthly Review Press.

Friedman, Michael 2001, 'Matter and Motion in the *Metaphysical Foundations* and the *First Critique*', in *Kant and the Sciences*, edited by Eric Watkins, Cambridge: Cambridge University Press.

Goldman, Loren 2020, 'Left Hegelian Variations: On the Matter of Revolution in Marx, Bloch, and Althusser', *praktyka teoretyczna*, 35, 1: 51–74.

Grant, Iain Hamilton 2008, *Philosophies of Nature after Schelling*, London: Bloomsbury.

Habermas, Jürgen 1985 [1960], 'Ernst Bloch: A Marxist Schelling', in *Philosophical-Political Profiles*, Cambridge, Mass.: MIT Press.

Hatch, Christopher 1999, 'The Wondrous Trumpet Call in Beethoven's *Fidelio*', *The Opera Quarterly* 15, 1: 5–17.

Hegel, Georg Wilhelm Friedrich 1986a [1832–46], *Enzyklopädie der philosophischen Wissenschaften*, 3 Volumes, Frankfurt am Main: Suhrkamp.

Hegel, Georg Wilhelm Friedrich 1986b [1836], *Vorlesungen über die Geschichte der Philosophie III*, Frankfurt am Main: Suhrkamp.

Hegel, Georg Wilhelm Friedrich 1991 [1821], *Elements of the Philosophy of Right*, translated by H.B. Nisbet, Cambridge: Cambridge University Press.

Hobbes, Thomas 1839 [1655], *Elements of Philosophy*, in *The English Works of Thomas Hobbes of Malmesbury*, Volume 1, edited by William Molesworth, London: John Bohn.

Holz, Hans Heinz 1975, *Logos Spermatikos. Ernst Blochs Philosophie der unfertigen Welt*, Darmstadt und Neuwied: Luchterhand.

Horn, Johannes Heinz (ed.) 1957, *Ernst Blochs Revision des Marxismus. Kritische Auseinandersetzungen marxistischer Wissenschaftler mit der Blochschen Philosophie*, Berlin: Deutscher Verlag der Wissenschaften.

Jäger, Alfred 1978, 'Materie und Prozeß', in *Materialien zu Ernst Blochs 'Prinzip Hoffnung'*, edited by Burghart Schmidt, Frankfurt am Main: Suhrkamp.

James, William 1977 [1909], *A Pluralistic Universe*, Cambridge, Mass.: Harvard University Press.

Järvikoski, Timo 1996, 'The Relation of Nature and Society in Marx and Durkheim', *Acta Sociologica* 39, 1: 73–86.

Kant, Immanuel 1999 [1781/7], *Critique of Pure Reason*, translated by Paul Guyer and Allen Wood, Cambridge: Cambridge University Press.

Kant, Immanuel 2002a [1786], *Metaphysical Principles of Natural Science*, translated by Michael Friedman, in *Theoretical Philosophy after 1781*, edited by Henry Allison, Cambridge: Cambridge University Press.

Kant, Immanuel 2002b [1790], *Critique of the Power of Judgement*, translated by Paul Guyer and Eric Matthews, Cambridge: Cambridge University Press.

Kant, Immanuel 2006 [1784], 'Idea for a Universal History from a Cosmopolitan Perspective', in *Toward Perpetual Peace and Other Writings on Politics, Peace, and History*, translated by David Colclasure, New Haven: Yale University Press.

Klein, Manfred 2008, 'Prozess und Manifestation: Zu Ernst Blochs Ontologie des Noch-Nicht-Seins', in *Bloch-Almanach*, 27: 49–71.

Latour, Bruno 1991, *We Have Never Been Modern*, translated by Catherine Porter, Cambridge, Mass.: Harvard University Press.

Latour, Bruno 1996. *Aramis, or the Love of Technology*, translated by Catherine Porter, Cambridge, Mass.: Harvard University Press.

Latour, Bruno 2004. *The Politics of Nature*, translated by Catherine Porter, Cambridge, Mass.: Harvard University Press.

Le, Vincent 2017, 'Schelling and the Sixth Extinction: The Environmental Ethics behind Schelling's Anthropomorphization of Nature', *Cosmos and History*, 13, 3: 107–29.

Löwy, Michael 2015, *Ecosocialism: A Radical Alternative to Capitalist Catastrophe*, Chicago: Haymarket Press.

Markun, Sylvia 1977, *Ernst Bloch*, Berlin: Rowohlt.

Marx, Karl 1973 [1858], *Grundrisse: Foundations of the Critique of Political Economy*, translated by Ben Brewster, New York: Penguin.

Marx, Karl 1978 [1844], 'Economic and Philosophic Manuscripts of 1844', in *The Marx-Engels Reader*, edited by Robert Tucker, New York: Norton.

Marx, Karl 1990 [1867], *Capital*, Volume 1, translated by Ben Fowkes, London: Penguin.

Marx, Karl m1993 [1894], *Capital*, Volume 3, translated by David Fernbach, London: Penguin.

Marx, Karl 2000a, *Karl Marx: Selected Writings*, by David McLellan, 2nd edition Oxford: Oxford University Press.

Marx, Karl 2006 [1841], 'The Difference Between the Democritean and Epicurean Philosophy of Nature', in *The First Writings of Karl Marx*, edited by Paul M. Schafer, Brooklyn, NY: Ig Press.

Mazzini, Silvia 2012, 'Kältestrom – Wärmestrom', in *Bloch-Wörterbuch*, edited by Beat Dietschy, Rainer Zimmerman and Doris Zeilinger, Berlin: de Gruyter.

Moggach, Douglas (ed.) 2006, *The New Hegelians: Politics and Philosophy in the Hegelian School*, Cambridge: Cambridge University Press.

Moir, Cat 2019, 'In Defense of Speculative Materialism', *Historical Materialism* 27, 2: 123–55.

Massimi, Michaela 2017, 'Philosophy and the Chemical Revolution after Kant', in *The Cambridge Companion to German Idealism*, edited by Karl Ameriks, 2nd ed., Cambridge: Cambridge University Press.

Mészáros, Istvan 1995, *Beyond Capital: Towards a Theory of Transition*, New York: Monthly Review Press.

Mill, John Stuart 1998 [1874], 'Nature', in *Three Essays on Religion*, Amherst, NY: Prometheus.

Münster, Arno 1977, *Tagträume vom aufrechten Gang. Sechs Interviews mit Ernst Bloch*, Frankfurt am Main: Suhrkamp.

Nietzsche, Friedrich 2010 [1873], 'On Truth and Lies in a Nonmoral Sense', in *On Truth and Untruth*, translated by Taylor Carman, New York: Penguin.

Novalis 1901 [c. 1800], 'Fragmente', in *Schriften*, Volume 2, edited by Ernst Heilborn, Berlin: Georg Reimer.

Parsons, Howard (ed.) 1977, *Marx and Engels on Ecology*, Westport, CT: Greenwood Press.

Pippin, Robert 2000, 'Fichte's Alleged Subjective, Psychological, One-Sided Idealism', in *The Reception of Kant's Critical Philosophy*, edited by Sally Sedgwick, Cambridge: Cambridge University Press.

Pinkard, Terry 2000, *Hegel: A Biography*, Cambridge: Cambridge University Press.

Ruda, Frank 2011, *Hegel's Rabble: An Investigation into Hegel's Philosophy of Right*, London: Bloomsbury.

Schelling, Friedrich Wilhelm Joseph 1858a [1799], *Erster Entwurf eines Systems der Naturphilosophie*, in *Sämtliche Werke. Erste Abteilung III*, Stuttgart and Augsberg: Cotta.

Schelling, Friedrich Wilhelm Joseph 1858b [1800], *System des transcendentalen Idealismus*, in *Sämmtliche Werke. Erste Abteilung III*, Stuttgart and Augsburg: Cotta.

Schelling, Friedrich Wilhelm Joseph 1858c [1801], *Allgemeine Deduction des dynami-*

schen Processes oder der Kategorien der Physik, in Sämmtliche Werke. Erste Abteilung IV, Stuttgart and Augsburg: Cotta.

Schelling, Friedrich Wilhelm Joseph 1858d [1801], Darstellung meines Systems der Philosophie, in Sämmtliche Werke. Erste Abteilung IV, Stuttgart and Augsburg: Cotta.

Schelling, Friedrich Wilhelm Joseph 1858e [1798], 'Von der Weltseele', in Sämmtliche Werke. Erste Abteilung II, Stuttgart and Augsburg: Cotta.

Schelling, Friedrich Wilhelm Joseph 2002 [1862], Clara, or on Nature's Connection to the Spirit World, translated by Fiona Steinkamp, Albany: SUNY Press.

Schelling, Friedrich Wilhelm Joseph 2008 [1794], 'Timaeus', translated by Adam Arola, Jena Jolissant and Peter Warnek, Epoché, 12, 2: 205–48.

Schelling, Friedrich Wilhelm Joseph 2012 [1798], 'On the World Soul', translated by Iain Hamilton Grant, in Collapse VI: Geo/Philosophy, edited by Robin Mackay, Falmouth: Urbanomic.

Schmidt, Alfred 2012 [1962], The Concept of Nature in Karl Marx, translated by Ben Fowkes, London: Verso.

Schnädelbach, Herbert 1984, Philosophy in Germany, 1831–1933, translated by Eric Matthews, Cambridge: Cambridge University Press.

Sedgwick, Sally (ed.) 2000, The Reception of Kant's Critical Philosophy, Cambridge: Cambridge University Press.

Sheasby, Walt 1997, 'Inverted World: Marx on Estrangement of Nature and Society', Capitalism, Nature, Socialism, 8, 4: 31–47.

Siebers, Johan 2012, 'Novum', in Bloch-Wörterbuch, edited by Beat Dietschy, Rainer Zimmerman and Doris Zeilinger, Berlin: de Gruyter.

Sieroka, Norman 2007, 'Weyl's "agens theory" of matter and the Zurich Fichte', Studies in History and Philosophy of Science, 38: 84–107.

Verene, Donald Phillip 1998, 'Hegel's Nature', in Hegel and the Philosophy of Nature, edited by Stephen Houlgate, Albany: SUNY Press.

Wallis, Victor 2018, Red-Green Revolution: The Politics and Technology Facing Ecosocialism, Toronto: Political Animal Press.

Weisskopf, Victor 2017, 'I Looked at Zero Through Dark Glass', in Critical Assembly: Poems of the Manhattan Project, edited by John Canaday, Albuquerque: University of New Mexico Press.

Zudeick, Peter 1980, Die Welt als Wirklichkeit und Möglichkeit. Die Rechtfertigungsproblematik der Utopie in der Philosophie Ernst Blochs, Bonn: Bouvier.

Zudeick, Peter, 2012, 'Materie', in Bloch-Wörterbuch, edited by Beat Dietschy, Rainer Zimmerman and Doris Zeilinger, Berlin: de Gruyter.

CHAPTER 8

Ernst Bloch's Utopian Philosophy: From Hegel to Marx and Beyond

Douglas Kellner

The great utopian Marxist philosopher Ernst Bloch developed a philosophy of hope that expands conventional Marxian approaches to a vast array of forms of culture, politics and everyday life, while providing one of the richest treasure houses of cultural criticism and historical, philosophical and political critique, combined with wide-ranging philosophical speculation. Indeed, Bloch emerges from the ruins of the twentieth century – whose major catastrophes he lived through, reflected upon, protested against and wrote about – as a producer of a panoply of radical ideas, startling images and mind-boggling texts that shine a light into the dark recesses of life, illuminating the savagery of history and the political upheavals of the modern world. In this chapter, I want to explore the ways in which Bloch's philosophy of hope is grounded in a specific form of Western Marxism that has its roots in Hegel and German idealism and which merges historical, materialist and cultural components. My aim will be to show that Bloch contributes uniquely distinctive perspectives on Marxism, socialism and revolutionary theory.[1]

1   Hegel, Marx and Bloch's Western Marxism

While Bloch's Marxism is of great complexity and draws on an astonishing array of philosophical ideas, it can be located within the broad movement of Hegelian and Western Marxism opposed to the doctrinaire orthodoxy of socialist and communist traditions.[2] The term *Western Marxism* was first used by Soviet communists to disparage the turn to this critical approach in Western Europe,

---

1   This study draws on Kellner and O'Hara 1976 as well as on Kellner 1997. I took Bloch's seminars in Tübingen in 1969–70 and interviewed him in the mid-1970s, near the end of his life. Our conversation ranged from the upheavals in Portugal that I had just witnessed to the differences between India and China and the continuing need for the New Left to appropriate fully Hegel, Goethe and Marx.
2   On 'scientific' versus 'critical' Marxism, see Gouldner 1982.

but it was soon adopted by thinkers such as Georg Lukács and Karl Korsch to describe a Marxism free from Party dogmatism and the 'scientific' determinism of the Second and Third Internationals.[3] Perry Anderson interprets the turn from economic and political analysis to cultural theory as a symptom of the defeat of critical Marxism after the crushing of the European revolutionary movements of the 1920s and the rise of fascism.[4] Yet Theodor W. Adorno, Walter Benjamin, Ernst Bloch, Georg Lukács, Herbert Marcuse and the other Western Marxists were intellectuals who had a deep and abiding interest in social and cultural phenomena, and so it is only natural that they should have incorporated this into their theoretical reflections.

Marx and Engels had focused their energies on examining the capitalist mode of production and contemporary political struggles as well as the vicissitudes of the world market and modern societies (today theorised under the labels of globalisation and modernity). They analysed the economic structure of society as the interplay between the forces of production (the economy's technological stage and potential for development) and the relations of production (property relations) – a dynamic process that in its turn interacts with the various cultural, legal, political and other forms of life that are linked to, and as a rule serve to reproduce, the economic structure. This *base/superstructure* model provided a host of Marxist thinkers with the foundation for a critical theory of society and history, albeit often in simplified form. Instead of embracing the full complexity of the Marxian model, already the second generation of classical Marxists, ranging from German Social Democrats to Russian communists, focused narrowly on the role of economics and politics. Moreover, as the official doctrine of many European working-class movements, Marxism became tied to the requirements of the political struggles of the day.

After the Russian Revolution, a large number of European intellectuals became attracted to Marxism and began to develop less dogmatic models of Marxian theory, turning their attention to social theory and the study of cultural phenomena. The Budapest-born thinker Georg Lukács, for example, after having written important books such as *Soul and Form* (1910) and *The Theory of the Novel* (1916), converted to Marxism and briefly participated in the Hungarian Revolution of 1918.[5] In the early 1920s, he focused on elaborating the

---

3   On the history and genealogies of Western Marxism, see Arato and Breines 1979, Howard and Klare 1972 and Kellner 2005. The French philosopher Maurice Merleau-Ponty first provided the term with more positive connotations, as a form of opposition to Stalinism and orthodox Marxism; see Merleau-Ponty 1973.
4   See Anderson 1976.
5   On Lukács, see Arato and Breines 1979 and Feenberg 1981. On the relation between Bloch and Lukács, see Hudson 1982, pp. 34–9 and *passim*.

philosophical, sociological and political dimensions of Marxism before returning to cultural analysis later in the decade. He then went to Russia, where he withdrew internally from Stalinism while working on a series of literary studies that have significant but still largely under-appreciated importance for cultural studies. After the Second World War, he returned to his native Hungary.

As a (Western) Marxist, Lukács viewed history as the mediation of economy and society. By zooming in on this dialectical interaction, he was able to interpret cultural forms in their relation to socio-historical developments linked to a specific mode of production, while at the same time illuminating socio-historical developments through the prism of these cultural forms. In his most influential work, *History and Class Consciousness*, he argued that the Marxian vision of totality and its focus on economic production not only provided a methodology to analyse and critique capitalist society, but also helped understand why the revolutionary proletariat constituted a force capable of overthrowing it. Adopting the standpoint of the working class, he propounded, made it possible to see how capitalist society generated a continually expanding process of *Verdinglichung* [reification, or the transformation of human beings into thing-like objects] in all dimensions of society, from the labour process to cultural production and even sexual relations. For Lukács, all domains of modern life were becoming subject to the logic of production and hence pervaded with economic imperatives. In gaining an understanding of its position within this process, the proletariat would achieve a class consciousness enabling it both to grasp this historical development and to organise to overcome it, thus becoming – as Lukács put it in a Hegelian formulation – the 'subject-object' of history.

In Germany, following the abortive German Revolution of 1918, the political activist and theorist Karl Korsch also developed a Hegelian-inspired critical version of Marxism.[6] His *Marxism and Philosophy* stressed that Marxism was above all a dialectical theory that – here Korsch's approach dovetailed with *History and Class Consciousness* – provided both the tools to *interpret and criticise bourgeois society* and the historical awareness that in itself constituted a force to *transform it*. For Korsch, this unity of theory and practice was the criterion for authentic Marxism. Constructing Marxism along these lines as the revolutionary theory of the working-class movement, he developed a concept of 'practical socialism'. In his *Karl Marx*, he highlighted the principle of *historical specificity* as a key criterion of Marxian theory: Marx – Korsch said in a clear rejection of

---

6 On Korsch, see Kellner 1977. I do not know whether Korsch and Bloch had any significant interaction, although they both lived in the United States for many years.

all forms of dogmatic Marxism – never formulated transhistorical truths, but he put forward historically specific critiques of historically specific phenomena, and he did so in circumstances that were themselves historically specific and which must therefore be analysed as such.

Ernst Bloch also responded positively to the Russian Revolution and European revolutionary movements of the 1920s, but he developed a more messianic and utopian version of Marxism.[7] His early works, such as *The Spirit of Utopia* (1918), combined a heterodox view of Marxian revolutionary theory with theology and German Romanticism, presented in an Expressionist literary style. The book also includes a number of provocative reflections on Hegel as well as examinations of 'the socialist idea', religion, nature, death, metempsychosis and apocalypse, in a wide-ranging interrogation of the relationship between Marxism and religion.

As his thought matured through his intense study of the classics during the turbulent era of the First World War, Weimar, the rise of fascism and the Second World War, Bloch increasingly grounded his major works in an idiosyncratic appropriation of Hegel and Marx. *Subjekt-Objekt. Erläuterungen zu Hegel* (1951) makes this debt explicit. Written during Bloch's exile in America in the 1940s and completed in the German Democratic Republic after the Second World War, it provides both an excellent study of Hegel and one of the best introductions to Bloch's own philosophy. After remarks on Hegel's language, mode of thought and basic ideas, the text interrogates Hegel's major works from the early writings to the *History of Philosophy*. Bloch then analyses Hegel's relation to Kierkegaard, Schelling, Feuerbach and Marx, before developing Hegel's thought in a new, original direction. The chapter 'The Dialectical Method', in particular, showcases Bloch's philosophical erudition and his ability to make the most complex philosophical ideas come alive.[8] In his typical aphoristic, gnomic and suggestive style, Bloch introduces Hegelian dialectics dialectically. He demonstrates how Hegel's philosophical categories emerged from a dialectical appropriation of the classical philosophical tradition, and he illustrates the

---

7   On the complex history of Bloch and Marxism, see Hudson 1982. Curiously, in a later article on 'Bloch and a Philosophy of the Proterior', Hudson reads Bloch in relation to German Romanticism, and the Marxian dimensions fall away; see Hudson 2013. I am trying to bring Bloch back home to Marxism in this chapter by showing how deeply rooted he is in the Hegelian and Marxian tradition, though I would not deny that many more traditions and flowers bloom in his immense oeuvre.

8   For an English translation of this chapter, see Bloch 1983, pp. 285–313, along with Kellner 1983, pp. 281–4. For a critical discussion of *Subjekt-Objekt* as a whole, see Henk de Berg's chapter in the present volume.

central categories of dialectics with examples from Hegel, other philosophers and his own thought. I know of no better introduction to dialectical thinking and the basic categories of dialectics.

Part of Bloch's project in *Subjekt-Objekt* was to show the Hegelian roots of Marxian dialectics, the similarities between Hegel's and Marx's modes of thought and the advances in Marx over Hegel. Yet the book brought him into conflict with the ideological commissars of the German Democratic Republic because of its deep sympathy for Hegel, which the party ideologues felt represented an 'ideological deviation', and he was widely attacked.[9] Eventually, Bloch emigrated from the GDR in 1961 after the building of the Berlin Wall and lived in Tübingen until his death in 1977 at 92. He became one of the most influential philosophers in Germany, although his work never had the same impact as that of Adorno, Benjamin, Heidegger, Marcuse or even Lukács.

Bloch's *Tübinger Einleitung in die Philosophie* articulates a Hegelian-Marxian philosophy of the future based on a reading of Hegel and Goethe's *Faust*.[10] For Bloch, Hegel's *Phenomenology of Spirit* presented the history of spirit as a journey through stages of consciousness to absolute knowledge and as such exhibited the importance of travelling through stages of life, with an emphasis on work and practice as key determinants of human life, motifs taken up in a materialist dialectic by Marx. Bloch reads the *Phenomenology* as an 'educational manual' that presents the odyssey of spirit's maturation and development through the six steps of sense-certainty, perception, self-consciousness, reason, spirit and absolute knowledge. In this subject-object dialectic, 'the decisive theme of *labor* is added to the motif of travelling (and also learning and teaching) in the *Phenomenology*'.[11] Labour is a central mode of people's work on objects, and the production of forms of society and history became central to Marx, as Bloch stresses, citing from the Paris Manuscripts: 'The outstanding achievement of Hegel's *Phenomenology* and of its final outcome ... [is] that Hegel conceives the self-creation of man as a process, conceives objectification as loss of the object, as alienation and as transcendence of this alienation; that he thus grasps the essence of labor and comprehends objective man – true, because real man – as the outcome of man's own labor'.[12]

Bloch's philosophy is grounded in a philosophical vision of an emancipated humanity and is described by him as a 'philosophy of hope'. Following the

---

9 See Hudson 1982, p. 14.
10 A partial translation of the *Tübinger Einleitung in die Philosophie* can be found in Bloch 1970.
11 Bloch 1970, p. 48.
12 Ibid.

young Marx, Bloch sees the human being as a species-being [*Gattungswesen*], containing as yet unsatisfied needs and unrealised possibilities, which he posits as the motors of human self-activity and historical struggle. Art, philosophy, religion and other major forms of culture are for Bloch the repository of potentialities striving for expression; they give us clues as to what the human being is and can be. Bloch's work represents the magnificent project of decoding the Western cultural heritage in order to restore the human potential to oppressed individuals and create a freer and more just society. This concept of the 'not-yet' [*Noch-Nicht*] is directed against the notion of an innate, ahistorical human essence: our species – Bloch maintains – has not yet become what it can be and thus has not yet realised its true humanity.

Bloch also calls his work a 'philosophy of the future', a philosophy that depicts 'what is not, building into the blue that lines all edges of the world: this is why we build ourselves into the blue and search for truth and reality where mere facticity vanishes – *incipit vita nova*'.[13] The task of philosophy is to interpret what is not-yet-realised and to change the world in accordance with what could be. Bloch calls this ontological foundation of his theory 'Left Aristotelianism'.[14] Aristotle's concept of matter as activity and potentiality suggests an ontological priority of possibility over actuality and necessity. Following Aristotle, Bloch conceives of reality as a dynamic process latent with possibility directed toward the realisation of its potentialities that provide its *telos* and *entelechia*. All is not fullness and ripeness in this metaphysical scenario, for the not-yet is permeated with a constitutive *not*: 'The not is the lack of something and the flight from this lack; hence, it is drives toward that which is lacking. With the not, drives are modelled in the living being: as drive, need, striving and primarily as hunger'.[15] Humans are above all beings with a desire to satisfy this ontological hunger.

In Bloch's three-volume master work, *The Principle of Hope*, his philosophy receives systematic articulation. Written during his exile from fascist Germany in the United States from 1938 until 1949, the text offers an ambitious and unique Hegelian-Marxian-inspired survey of the emancipatory elements of Western culture. Supported by his wife Karola, who worked as an architect, Bloch laboured mightily to produce this encyclopaedia of hope and dreams for a better life.[16]

13   Bloch 1971, p. 43.
14   On his Aristotelianism, see Bloch 1963.
15   Bloch 1967, p. 42.
16   Interviews with Ernst and Karola Bloch in Tübingen during the summer of 1974.

2   Bloch's *Principle of Hope*

The Principle of Hope provides a systematic examination of the ways in which fairy tales, myths, literature, theatre and popular culture as well as political and social utopias, philosophy and religion – cultural expressions dismissed as derivative superstructure phenomena by many a Marxist – contain emancipatory moments projecting visions of a better life that put in question the organisation and structure of life under capitalism (or state socialism). In other words, Bloch sets forth a critical hermeneutic that renders visible how cultural history points to socialism as the realisation of humanity's deepest dreams and hopes – a hermeneutic that encourages us to look for the progressive and emancipatory (rather than merely ideological) content of cultural artefacts.

Bloch developed a cultural theory quite different from, and more nuanced than, Marxian models that present *Ideologiekritik* as the demolition of bourgeois culture and bourgeois ideology and which therefore conflate, in a reductive manner, culture and ideology. Bloch is more sophisticated than the 'critical' thinkers who simply denounce all ideology as false consciousness or stress the positive features of socialist ideology only. He sees emancipatory utopian elements, as well as deceptive and illusory qualities, in *all* ideologies. For him, ideology is invariably Janus-faced, two-sided: it contains errors, mystifications and techniques of manipulation and domination, but also a utopian residue or surplus that can be used for social critique and the advancement of progressive politics. Such a dual hermeneutic can better illuminate what is deficient and lacking in this world and what should be fought for than any merely negative, 'critical' form of interpretation. Furthermore, Bloch detects ideology in phenomena often neglected by Marxists and other ideology critics, such as daydreams, popular literature, architecture, department-store displays, sports and clothing. For him, *Ideologiekritik* should be a critique of everyday life as well as a critique of political texts and positions or of the blatant political ideologies of certain films, television series and other forms of mass-mediated culture.

Bloch, then, rejects a merely denunciatory approach to ideology critique as 'half-enlightenment': *genuine* enlightenment renders visible and criticises the ideological dimension of cultural expressions *but then goes on to read those expressions for their emancipatory potential*. Half-enlightenment deludes itself by thinking that genuine insight can be obtained solely by eliminating error, without offering anything positive and productive. Indeed, Bloch believes that part of the explanation for the defeat of the left by the right in Weimar Germany resides in the fact that the left tended to focus on the negative – on social and political criticism, on the denunciation of capitalism and the bourgeoisie – whereas fascism provided what in the eyes of many people at the time was a positive vision and an attractive alternative to the problems they experienced.

The Principle of Hope consists of three volumes, a trichotomy that roughly corresponds to Hegel's division of his system into interrogations of subjective, objective and absolute spirit. The first of Bloch's volumes examines 'Little Daydreams', 'Anticipatory Consciousness' and 'Wishful Images in the Mirror' (which analyses the utopian dimensions of fashion, advertising, display, fairy tales, travel, film, theatre, jokes and other cultural phenomena). The second volume depicts 'Outlines of a Better World', focusing on social and political utopias, including technological, architectural and geographical ones, as well as quests for world peace and a life of leisure, while the third volume discusses 'Wishful Images of the Fulfilled Moment', including morality, music, images of death, religion, morning-land of nature and the highest good.

Just as Hegel's philosophy articulated the odyssey of spirit through history and culture, so Bloch's philosophy charts the shifting vicissitudes of hope – a hope that permeates everyday consciousness and its articulation in cultural forms, ranging from the fairy tale to the great philosophical and political utopias. Individuals are unfinished, they are animated by utopian longings for fulfilment, by what Bloch calls *dreams of a better life*. This 'something better' for which people yearn is the subject-matter of *The Principle of Hope*. The book invites its readers to grasp the three dimensions of human temporality: it offers us a dialectical analysis of the *past* that illuminates the *present* and can direct us to a better *future*. The past (what has been) contains both the sufferings, tragedies and failures of humanity (what to avoid and what to redeem) and its unrealised hopes and potentials (what could have been and can yet be). History is a repository of possibilities that are living options for future action: what might have been can still be. The present moment is thus constituted in part by latency [*Latenz*] and tendency [*Tendenz*]: the unrealised potentialities that are dormant in the present and the signs and foreshadowings that indicate the direction and movement of the present into the future. This three-dimensional temporality must be grasped and activated by an anticipatory consciousness [*antizipierendes Bewusstsein*] that simultaneously perceives the emancipatory potential in the past, the latencies and tendencies of the present and the hopes of the future. In brief, Bloch develops a philosophy of hope and the future, a dreaming forward, a projection of a vision of a kingdom of freedom. It is his conviction that only when we project our future in the light of what is, what has been and what could be can we engage in the creative practice that will produce a world in which we are truly at home.

3 Everyday Life, Human Beings and Psychology

Certain versions of Marxian theory err, Bloch maintains, by failing to see the importance of culture in everyday life. A rationalistic *Ideologiekritik* believes that it can motivate people to action simply by exposing error. According to Bloch, such a belief both overestimates the power of one-sidedly rational enlightenment and underestimates the importance of hopes, desires and fantasies. Properly understanding human psychology and motivation requires taking seriously this sub-rational dimension.

Bloch's philosophy is rooted in this humanistic anthropology. It starts from the hoping, wishing and needy human being and then zooms in on the question of what stands in the way of the fulfilment of this longing and the question of how these obstacles can be removed. Bloch's thought is therefore inherently revolutionary: it provides both a standard for critique and an impetus for political action and social change.[17]

There are a number of important similarities and dissimilarities between Bloch's anthropology, with its emphasis on human psychology, and the ideas of Wilhelm Reich – author of *The Mass Psychology of Fascism* (1933) and *The Sexual Revolution* (1936) – and other Freudo-Marxists.[18] Reich urged the communists to pay more attention to people's unconscious wishes and fears and their sexual needs and desires. But he exaggerated the role of sexuality in human psychology and motivation while downplaying things such as the need for security and community, which Bloch believed the fascists (in their own, perverted way) had addressed with more success than the left.[19] Even more telling is the contrast between Bloch's ideas and Freud's own theory. In *The Principle of Hope*, Bloch carries out an extremely interesting appreciation and critique of Freud, developing his own psychological views in opposition to Freudian psychoanalysis. It seems to me that Bloch's views can productively be used to develop a Marxian social psychology today; in any case, I would argue that his approach is significantly deeper and more illuminating than the Freudo-Marxist approaches associated with the Frankfurt School and with French theory (Deleuze and Guattari, for instance, or Lyotard). Briefly examining Bloch's criticism of Freud will allow us to see how he is able to identify a thinker's ideological tendencies often overlooked by standard Marxist ideology critique, and how he is, if anything, a good deal more critical and devastating in

---

17   Bloch's version of Marxism could be compared to Dunayevskaya 2000.
18   See Reich 1972. On French Freudo-Marxism, see Poster 1975.
19   See the analysis of fascism in Bloch 1991.

his attack on ideologies than are orthodox Marxist critics. This examination will also help us to understand Bloch's distinctive anthropological-psychological perspective better.

How, then, does Bloch distinguish his theory of subjectivity from psychoanalysis? He starts off by grounding psychological tendencies in the needs of the human body, primarily hunger, rather than in instincts and the unconscious. He also conceptualises 'man as a quite extensive complex of drives',[20] emphasising cravings, wishing, desiring and hoping for a better life as opposed to the Freudian emphasis on castration, repression and the conservative political economy of the instincts, which is characterised by repetition, excitation release and ultimately entropy (the death instinct). Bloch summarises: 'In short, we realize that man is an equally changeable and extensive complex of drives, a heap of *changing* and mostly badly ordered wishes. And a permanent motivating force, a single basic drive, in so far as it does not become independent and thus hang in the air, is hardly conceivable'.[21] Rather, there are *several* basic drives, which emerge as primary at different times in social and individual life depending on the conditions prevailing at the time.

> The unconscious of psychoanalysis is ... *never a Not-Yet-Conscious*, an element of progressions; it consists rather of regressions. Accordingly, even the process of making this unconscious conscious only clarifies What Has Been; i.e. *there is nothing new in the Freudian unconscious*. This became even clearer when C.G. Jung, the psychoanalytic fascist, reduced the libido and its unconscious contents entirely to the primeval. According to him, exclusively phylogenetic primeval memories or primeval fantasies exist in the unconscious, falsely designated 'archetypes'; and all wishful images also go back into this night, only suggest prehistory. Jung even considers the night to be so colourful that consciousness pales beside it; as a spurner of the light, he devalues consciousness. In contrast, Freud does of course uphold illuminating consciousness, but one which is itself surrounded by the ring of the id, by the fixed unconsciousness of a fixed libido. Even highly productive artistic creations do not lead out of this Fixum; they are simply *sublimations* of the self-enclosed libido.[22]

Bloch's position is nuanced. He favours Freudian enlightenment rationalism over Jungian irrationalism, yet he also puts up a spirited defence of man's 'irra-

---

20   Bloch 1986, vol. 1, p. 47.
21   Bloch 1986, vol. 1, p. 50.
22   Bloch 1986, vol. 1, p. 56.

tional' dimension. At the same time, this position does not prevent him from carrying out a critique of the reactionary tendencies in irrationalist ways of thinking, especially those connected with fascism. This can be seen particularly clearly from his critique of Freud's disciple Alfred Adler (1870–1937), which links the latter's *Individualpsychologie* to specific socio-historical developments. Adler's emphasis on the *will to power* as a key human drive is related – Bloch argues – to the competitive capitalist desire to move from the bottom to the top, while his concepts of *neurosis* and the *inferiority complex* reproduce the feelings of those strata of capitalist society that have failed economically and blame themselves for their failures.

> Because Adler therefore drives sex out of the libido and inserts individual power, his definition of drives takes the ever steeper capitalist path from Schopenhauer to Nietzsche and reflects this path ideologically and psychoanalytically. Freud's concept of libido bordered on the 'will to life' in Schopenhauer's philosophy; Schopenhauer in fact described the sexual organs as 'the focal points of the will'. Adler's 'will to power' conversely coincides verbally, and partly also in terms of content, with Nietzsche's definition of the basic drive from his last period; in this respect Nietzsche has triumphed over Schopenhauer here, that is to say, the imperialist elbow has triumphed over the gentlemanly pleasure-displeasure body in psychoanalysis. The competitive struggle which hardly leaves any time for sexual worries stresses industriousness rather than randiness; the hectic day of the businessman thus eclipses the hectic night of the rake and his libido.[23]

Bloch goes on to say that the hectic nature of modern life and the structural anxiety that permeates capitalist society – which submits the population to the vagaries and uncertainties of the market – produce tendencies toward escape and regression, especially among the middle and lower *petit-bourgeois* strata. Thus, Adler's celebration of a will to power – which implicitly summons one to muster one's energies for production and competition – increasingly loses its appeal as it becomes more and more difficult to succeed in the marketplace: 'the path to the so-called heights lost some of its interest and prospects, in exact proportion to the decline of free enterprise, as a result of monopoly capitalism'.[24] As a result, the class strata that had previously followed the calls

---

23   Bloch 1986, vol. 1, p. 58.
24   Bloch 1986, vol. 1, p. 59.

of Nietzsche, Adler and others to scale the heights of competition and worldly success began to look backward towards 'the so-called depths, in which the eyes roll instead of aiming at a goal'.[25] Hence the increased appeal of Jung, 'the fascistically frothing psychoanalyst' who 'posited the frenzy-drive in place of the power drive'.[26] I cite the following passage in its entirety to provide a sense of Bloch's power as a critic as well as of his rhetorical vigour:

> Just as sexuality is only part of this Dionysian general libido, so also is the will to power, in fact the latter is completely transformed into battle-frenzy, into a stupor which in no way strives toward individual goals. In Jung, libido thus becomes an archaically undivided primeval unity of all drives, or 'Eros' per se: consequently it extends from eating to the Last Supper, from coitus to unio mystica, from the frothing mouth of the shaman, even the berserker, to the rapture of Fra Angelico. Even here, therefore, Nietzsche triumphs over Schopenhauer, but he triumphs as the affirmation of a mescalin Dionysus over the negation of the will to life. As a result, the unconscious aspect of this mystified libido is also not contested and there is no attempt to resolve it into current consciousness as in Freud. Rather the neurosis, particularly that of modern, all too civilized and conscious man, derives according to Jung precisely from the fact that men have emerged too far out of what is unconsciously growing, outside the world of 'elemental feel-thinking'. Here Jung borders not only on the fascist version of Dionysus, but also partly on the vitalistic philosophy of Bergson.[27]

Those inclined to dismiss Bloch as an irrationalist should consider this critique of German and other irrationalist thought as well as of fascist ideologies. After criticising Adler, Jung and Bergson, Bloch goes after 'sentimental penis-poets like D.H. Lawrence', 'complete Tarzan philosophers like Ludwig Klages', the celebrator of Neanderthal man Gottfried Benn and the *petit-bourgeois* mystifier Martin Heidegger.[28] While Bergson's vitalism at least contained some progressive moments, Lawrence, 'and Jung along with him, sings the wildernesses of the elemental age of love, which to his misfortune man has emerged from; he seeks the nocturnal moon in the flesh, the unconscious sun in the blood. And

---

25 Ibid.
26 Ibid.
27 Ibid.
28 Bloch 1986, vol. 1, pp. 59–72. Bloch was a consistent critic of Heidegger, early on perceiving the link between Heidegger's philosophy and National Socialism. Cf. Faye 2009.

Klages blows in a more abstract way on the same bullhorn; he does not only hark back like the early Romantics to the Middle Ages, but to the diluvium, to precisely where Jung's impersonal, pandemonic libido lives'.[29] Bloch's criticism rivals Georg Lukács's dissection of bourgeois-philosophical irrationalism in *The Destruction of Reason*, but surpasses it in offering a philosophy of hope that is still relevant today.

4 Socialism, Revolution and the Red Arrow

Ernst Bloch sets forth a paradigm of immanent (intra-historical) transcendence, in which utopian elements are anchored in a cultural tradition and historical situation and yet point to a better future in which humanity's dreams of freedom, happiness and justice can be realised. As the Obama era showed, hope can become part of the political discourse of the day, and in his theory of utopia, Bloch provides a particularly rich philosophical and political foundation of hope.[30] As I have made clear, Bloch finds anticipatory dreams not only in the social and political utopias of the great philosophers, but also in a variety of technological, architectural and geographical utopias as well as in painting, opera, literature and other forms of art. This quintessentially human hope projects images and visions of supreme fulfilment, culminating in the figure of the individual who 'has grasped himself and established what is his, without exploitation and alienation', and in this situation, 'in real democracy, there arises in the world something which shines into the childhood of all and in which no one has yet been: homeland'.[31]

This is not, Bloch stresses, wishful thinking in any superficial sense of the phrase. We are not dealing with an *abstract* but rather a *concrete* utopia, one grounded in historical reality: all cultures contain traces of *red arrows* that migrate through history looking for realisation in more human and social forms of society. In other words, cultural artefacts are never merely ideological reflections of what *is*; they contain a surplus, a critical and emancipatory potential, that points to what *ought to* and *might* be. In this sense, they are *ungleichzeitig*,

---

29 Bloch 1986, vol. 1, pp. 59–60.
30 For my take on the Obama phenomenon and the insurrections of 2011, from the North African Uprisings to the Occupy movements (all of which help explain the candidacy of socialist Bernie Sanders in the 2016 US presidential election, showing that there are grounds for hope even in the belly of the beast), see Kellner 2012.
31 Bloch 1986, vol. 3, p. 1376.

non-contemporaneous or non-synchronic with the present.[32] Admittedly, such *Ungleichzeitigkeit* can take negative forms, as is the case with traditions and residues from the past that, though completely archaic and historically surpassed, continue to be effective in the present (such as the fascist primitivism blended with unrestrained market capitalism and conservatism during the Reagan and Bush administrations, or the atavistic discourse of Donald Trump and his followers). But there is also a positive variety of *Ungleichzeitigkeit*, one that anticipates developments and hence points to an as yet unrealised future. For Bloch, ideology and utopia are thus never simply opposites, because utopian elements appear in ideologies, just as utopias are permeated with ideological mystification. It is the task of the Blochian critic to separate the wheat from the chaff – to discern and unfold history's progressive potential and to relate it to the struggles of the present and the possibilities of the future. Bloch's cultural hermeneutic is therefore inherently political: his cultural theory is intimately bound up with political practice.

Bibliography

Anderson, Perry 1976, *Considerations on Western Marxism*, London: New Left Books.
Arato, Andrew and Paul Breines 1979, *The Young Lukács and the Origins of Western Marxism*, New York: Seabury.
Bloch, Ernst 1963 [1949], *Avicenna und die Aristotelische Linke*, Frankfurt am Main: Suhrkamp.
Bloch, Ernst 1967, 'Zur Ontologie des Noch-Nichts-Seins', in *Ernst Bloch. Auswahl aus seinen Schriften*, Frankfurt am Main: Fischer.
Bloch, Ernst 1968, *Tübinger Einleitung in die Philosophie*, Frankfurt am Main: Suhrkamp.
Bloch, Ernst 1970, *A Philosophy of the Future*, translated by John Cumming, New York: Herder and Herder.
Bloch, Ernst 1971, 'Karl Marx, Death and Apocalypse', in *Man on His Own: Essays in the Philosophy of Religion*, translated by E.B. Ashton, New York: Herder and Herder.
Bloch, Ernst 1972 [1951; 2nd, enlarged edition 1962], *Subjekt-Objekt. Erläuterungen zu Hegel*, Frankfurt am Main: Suhrkamp.
Bloch, Ernst 1983 [1972] 'The Dialectical Method', translated by John Lamb, *Man and World*, 16: 285–313.
Bloch, Ernst 1986 [1954, 1955 and 1959], *The Principle of Hope*, 3 Volumes, translated by Neville Plaice, Stephen Plaice and Paul Knight, Cambridge, Mass.: MIT Press.

---

32 See the discussion of non-contemporaneity and dialectics in Bloch 1991, pp. 97–117.

Bloch, Ernst 1991 [1935], *Heritage of Our Times*, translated by Neville Plaice and Stephen Plaice, Berkeley: University of California Press.

Bloch, Ernst 2000 [1918; 2nd, revised edition 1923], *Spirit of Utopia*, translated by Anthony A. Nassar, Stanford: Stanford University Press.

Daniel, Jamie and Tom Moylan (eds.) 1997, *Not Yet: Reconsidering Ernst Bloch*, London: Verso.

Dunayevskaya, Raya 2000 [1958], *Marxism and Freedom: From 1776 Until Today*, New York: Humanity Books.

Faye, Emmanuel 2009 [2005], *Heidegger: The Introduction of Nazism into Philosophy*, translated by Michael B. Smith, New Haven: Yale University Press.

Feenberg, Andrew 1981, *Lukács, Marx and the Sources of Critical Theory*, Totowa, NJ: Rowman and Littlefield.

Gouldner, Alvin W. 1982, *The Two Marxisms: Contradictions and Anomalies in the Development of Theory*, New York: Seabury.

Howard, Dick and Karl Klare 1972, *The Hidden Dimension: European Marxism since Lenin*, New York: Basic Books.

Hudson, Wayne 1982, *The Marxist Philosophy of Ernst Bloch*, New York: St. Martin's Press.

Hudson, Wayne 2013, 'Bloch and a Philosophy of the Proterior', in *The Privatization of Hope: Ernst Bloch and the Future of Utopia*, edited by Peter Thompson and Slavoj Žižek, Durham and London: Duke University Press.

Kellner, Douglas 1977, *Karl Korsch: Revolutionary Theory*, Austin: University of Texas Press.

Hudson, Wayne 1997, 'Ideology, Culture and Utopia in Ernst Bloch', in *Not Yet: Reconsidering Ernst Bloch*, edited by Jamie Daniel and Tom Moylan, London: Verso.

Hudson, Wayne 2005, 'Western Marxism', in *Modern Social Theory: An Introduction*, edited by Austin Harrington, Oxford: Oxford University Press.

Hudson, Wayne 2012, *Media Spectacle and Insurrection, 2011: From the Arab Uprisings to Occupy Everywhere*, London and New York: Continuum and Bloomsbury.

Kellner, Douglas and Harry O'Hara 1976, 'Utopia and Marxism in Ernst Bloch', *New German Critique*, 9: 11–34.

Lukács, Georg 1971 [1916], *The Theory of the Novel: A Historico-Philosophical Essay on the Forms of Great Epic Literature*, translated by Anna Bostock, Cambridge, Mass.: MIT Press.

Lukács, Georg 1980 [1954], *The Destruction of Reason*, translated by Peter Palmer, London: Merlin.

Lukács, Georg 1991a [1910], *Soul and Form*, translated by Anna Bostock, New York: Columbia University Press.

Lukács, Georg 1991b [1923], *History and Class Consciousness: Studies in Marxist Dialectics*, translated by Rodney Livingstone, Cambridge, Mass.: MIT Press.

Merleau-Ponty, Maurice 1973 [1955], *Adventures of the Dialectic*, translated by Joseph Bien, Evanston, Illinois: Northwestern University Press.

Poster, Mark 1975, *Existential Marxism in Postwar France: From Sartre to Althusser*, Princeton: Princeton University Press.

Reich, Wilhelm 1972, *Sex-Pol: Essays 1929–1934*, translated by Anna Bostock, Tom DuBose and Lee Baxandall, New York: Vintage.

CHAPTER 9

What Can We Hope For? Reading Ernst Bloch with Antonio Gramsci

Jan Rehmann

After the Hungarian Uprising of 1956, the party and state leadership of the GDR branded Ernst Bloch a dissident and declared his philosophy utopian, idealistic, mystic-pantheistic and hence un-Marxist. In December 1956, Walter Ulbricht, in an article in *Neues Deutschland*, castigated Bloch (without mentioning his name) for assuming 'that we can understand the tomorrow only from the point of view of the day after tomorrow', which according to Ulbricht revealed how far certain philosophers had alienated themselves from the people and their struggle for a socialist society.[1] In 1957, Bloch was forced into retirement, which motivated him to emigrate to West Germany in 1961 and to teach in Tübingen.

Against the backdrop of this oppressive marginalisation, it is astonishing to see how many of the stereotypical arguments used to justify Bloch's state-socialist exclusion from Marxism have resurfaced in recent scholarship. Whatever the corresponding value judgment, Bloch's philosophy is again being portrayed as 'idealistic', 'eschatological', 'metaphysical', 'mystical' and 'speculative'. Whereas Bloch tried to 'inherit' the utopian impulses of religion from the perspective of a 'transcending without any heavenly transcendence but with an understanding of it',[2] this *rescuing critique* (to use Walter Benjamin's phrase) is once again pulled back into the orbit of religious enthusiasm. This happens, for example, when scholars as diverse as Hans Heinz Holz and Hans Jonas agree that we are dealing with a 'secularised eschatology'.[3] Similarly, Hans-Ernst Schiller attributes to Bloch a 'utopian, metaphysical-religious philosophy' with eschatological characteristics.[4] For Terry Eagleton, Bloch's philosophy is just 'mystical materialism', which 'has smuggled quasi-divine properties into [matter]'.[5] As Beat Dietschy aptly summarises, there is a widespread tendency

---

1 Cited in Zudeick 1987, p. 232.
2 Bloch 1986, vol. 3, p. 1288.
3 Holz 1975, p. 212, and Jonas 1984, p. 313.
4 Schiller 2017, p. 35.
5 Eagleton 2015, pp. 98–9.

to transform 'what Bloch had held in suspense or considered as an open horizon of problems' into something unambiguously theological or teleological: 'When he spoke of *possibilities* of nature, with which human purposes can ally or which social praxis could set free, this was interpreted as an objective teleology of the world process'.[6]

Against such manifold attempts to sever one of the most creative of Marxist philosophers from the traditions of Marxism, I will argue that Bloch's approach is best understood as an original contribution to a *philosophy of praxis*. This term was coined by Antonio Labriola, who developed a praxis-centred understanding of Marxist philosophy in order to oppose the widespread tendency that 'our doctrine' would become again a 'new inverted ideology', in particular in the shape of determinism.[7] It was then developed further by other thinkers, most notably Antonio Gramsci. Both Labriola and Gramsci started out from Marx's 'Theses on Feuerbach', according to which 'all previous materialism' had conceived reality 'only in the form of the *object, or of contemplation*, but not as a *sensuous human activity, practice*, not subjectively'.[8]

It is no coincidence that Bloch, too, develops his concept of materialism – which is explicitly directed against a static understanding of matter [*Klotzmaterie*, matter as a 'mechanical clod'] – not only from Aristotle and what Bloch called the 'line' of 'Leftist Aristotelianism',[9] but also from the 'Theses on Feuerbach'. Bloch stresses that Marxism has its Archimedean point in 'working man', in his 'social modes of satisfying needs' and his relations 'with people and with nature'.[10] Accordingly, Bloch's comprehensive concept of matter incorporates 'consciousness' and 'spirit',[11] which traditional philosophy, including Marxism-Leninism, treats as the opposite of matter. As soon as one reads Bloch from this praxis-philosophical angle, one encounters numerous similarities and intersections with Gramsci. This is all the more surprising as the two thinkers were not familiar with each other's works.

Even though dogmatic Marxism-Leninism has excluded and persecuted all kinds of praxis philosophy as a deviation, it is of course a current *within* Marxism and furthermore a particularly vibrant one that has survived the downfall of state socialism. Bloch develops his philosophy in the political context of the

---

6 Dietschy 1988, p. 88.
7 Labriola 1966, pp. 126–7. Cf. the reconstruction of Labriola's philosophy of praxis in W.F. Haug 2018.
8 Marx 1976a, p. 3.
9 See, for example, Bloch 1986, vol. 1, p. 208, and Bloch 1985a, p. 481. For a detailed analysis of Bloch's Left Aristotelian concept of matter, see Queiser 2018.
10 Bloch 1986, vol. 1, p. 286.
11 See, for example, Bloch 1985e, p. 234.

dramatic development and crisis of Marxism after the death of its founders, a crisis marked by the worldwide split between social democracy and the Communist International, the subsequent rise of fascism in Italy and Germany, and – within Marxism itself – by what Bloch perceives as a loss of utopian perspectives.

My argument divides into two main parts. In the first part, I will demonstrate the fruitfulness of a praxis-philosophical re-reading of Bloch. I will argue that his concepts of anticipation and the not-yet-conscious are underpinned by a materialist, body-centred theory of agency; that his daydream analyses can be combined with Gramsci's concept of good sense; and that his ontology of the not-yet depicts a complex interaction between a strong teleology and what I propose to call a *weak teleological force of open possibilities*. In the second part, I will use this praxis-philosophical interpretation to identify several weak points in Bloch's philosophy. The utopian-far goals he posits should not be formulated – I will argue – in terms of an identity without contradictions, while some of his essentialist and teleological assumptions need to be modified with the help of a Gramscian analysis of the hegemonic conditions for hope and hopelessness.

1   A Praxis-Philosophical Re-Reading of Bloch

1.1 *Darkness of the Lived Moment and Anticipation*

What makes interpreting Bloch so difficult is that the major concepts of his philosophy reach back far into his pre-Marxist early work yet take on a new and specific meaning after his encounter with Marxism. A careful analysis of his work needs to take both these aspects into account. The widespread method of reading the *Principle of Hope* through the lens of the early texts, or of the philosophers that the young Bloch was reading, is reductive. Ironically, it reverses Bloch's own discovery of the *Novum* [or 'genuinely new'], turning it into its archaising opposite.[12] It ignores, in particular, the specific novum of Bloch's encounter with Marxism, which started around 1923 under the influence of Georg Lukács. The immersion in Marxism 'significantly increased the relevance of Bloch's research, both challenging and setting free the power of his thought and language'.[13]

---

12   For an analysis of this concept, see Siebers 2012a. Bloch himself jibed at the attempts to demonstrate his dependency on Schelling, Plato or Aristotle: it might be more productive 'to direct the strongest attention to what is genuinely new' (Bloch 1975, p. 262).

13   W.F. Haug 2012, p. 252.

This applies, for example, to the starting point of Bloch's anthropology, the 'darkness of the lived moment', which can be traced through his entire oeuvre from the *The Spirit of Utopia* to *Experimentum Mundi*. It means that what appears to be unmediated cannot be experienced while it is ongoing. 'Only once this moment is passed or before, when it is still expected, do we have an inkling of it'.[14] 'There is no light at the foot of the lighthouse', says a German proverb quoted by Bloch, indicating that what makes up the life in our living body and drives us from within – the inner urge, the 'push within us', the beating heart, blood's circulation – cannot be sensed in an un-mediated fashion, but only before or after the lived moment.[15] 'The blood runs, the heart beats without us being able to sense what has set the pulse in motion. In fact, if there is no disturbance, then nothing under our skin can be felt at all ... Healthy life sleeps, weaving within itself. It is completely immersed in the juice in which it is stewing'.[16]

It is of course possible to derive this notion from Hegel's insight that what is known is not yet understood, from Husserl's phenomenology or from William James's 'fringes of consciousness'.[17] But the decisive turn is to be found in the context of Marx's sixth thesis on Feuerbach, according to which the 'essence' of the human being is 'no abstraction inherent in each separate individual', but rather 'the ensemble of social relations'.[18] This is of course a radical anti-essentialist definition of 'essence', which completely subverts its traditional meaning. When Bloch describes the human 'starting out' as 'empty', 'dark', 'hollow' and as something that 'cannot stay within itself', he emphasises that social individuals need to set off into an 'outside', into their specific historic-societal conditions, where they appropriate their potential 'essence'.[19] The interior must 'come out of itself [*aus sich heraus*]', it moves and experiences itself outside, and it is only 'via this outside that it can experience its own interior'.[20]

The complementary pole of Bloch's anthropology – the concepts of anticipation and the not-yet-conscious – can likewise be traced back to his early works and hence associated with Messianic, mystical, Romanticist, Goethean or neo-Kantian traditions.[21] Yet any attempt to pinpoint the specific intellectual origins of these concepts runs into the difficulty that it is usually not

---

14   Bloch 1985g, p. 386.
15   Bloch 1986, vol. 1, pp. 45, 48 and 295.
16   Bloch 1986, vol. 1, p. 287.
17   Cf. Jung 2012, pp. 51–2; Schiller 2017, p. 31; and Pelletier 2017, p. 74.
18   Marx 1976a, p. 4.
19   For example, Bloch 1985e, p. 14, and Bloch 1986, vol. 1, p. 21.
20   Bloch 1985e, p. 13.
21   Cf. Rehmann 2012, pp. 3–5.

clear whether Bloch actually draws on the literature he refers to or whether he merely refers to it to back up his already developed concept of the not-yet-conscious, which, according to his own account, struck him in 1907, at the age of twenty-two.[22] However, when he then proceeds, in the *Principle of Hope*, to develop the different aspects of anticipatory consciousness into a systematic concept of his anthropology, his understanding of Marxism plays a decisive role. Bloch quotes Marx's famous portrayal of the worst human architects, who are distinguished from the best of bees in that they build a cell in their mind before they construct it in wax. 'At the end of every labour process, a result emerges which had already been conceived by the worker at the beginning, hence already consisted ideally'.[23] According to Bloch, it is 'precisely at this point' that wishes and daydreams are formed.[24] Rather than establishing an omni-historical – 'bourgeois' – anthropological notion of human essence of the kind criticised by official GDR-Marxism,[25] Bloch is referring to the phylogenetic preconditions that allow humans to take an active part in the ensemble of society. The Berlin school of Critical Psychology around Klaus Holzkamp and Ute Holzkamp-Osterkamp has conceptualised the capacity of anticipation as part of humans' 'societal nature' or 'natural potentiality to sociality' that developed over a long time alongside the emergence of human labour, cooperation and language.[26] It is true that elementary capacities to anticipate future events can be observed in the non-human animal world as well, but these anticipatory capacities received a new quality and scope in cooperative human practices.[27]

It is in the tension between the 'incognito' of the lived moment and the anticipation of the not-yet that Bloch unfolds his theory of affects. The affects ascend from urging to longing to wishing to a wanting that has already actively decided about preferential options – in other words, the affect is a 'wanting to do'.[28] Contrary to a wide array of psychoanalytical approaches (from Freud to Jung and Adler) that consider drives as autonomous forces, Bloch reconstructs them from the point of view of the body: the human being is 'an equally changeable and extensive complex of drives, a heap of *changing*, and mostly badly ordered, wishes', often moving like 'opposing winds around a ship', but 'present throughout is only the body which wants to preserve itself'.[29] Accord-

---

22   Bloch 1975, p. 300.
23   Marx 1976, p. 284.
24   Bloch 1986, vol. 1, p. 76.
25   Cf. the summary in Müller-Schöll and Vidal 2017, pp. 18–20.
26   Holzkamp 1985, p. 180.
27   Holzkamp 1985, pp. 142–51 and 260–83.
28   Bloch 1986, vol. 1, pp. 46–7.
29   Bloch 1986, vol. 1, pp. 49–50.

ing to Eberhard Braun, this methodological decision to start from practices of self-preservation, which are both somatically conditioned and historically variable, marks Bloch's break with idealist speculation.[30]

The quality and scale of anticipation also help distinguish the 'expectant' emotions from short-term 'filled' emotions.[31] Bloch's ascending line then culminates in *hope*, which is 'the most human of all mental feelings'.[32] Some critics question the methodological grounds on which Bloch prioritises hope over, say, anxiety or fear.[33] They suggest that Bloch merely projects his political views onto his anthropology and thus subjugates it to a teleology coming from the outside. What is overlooked in this critique is that Bloch founds his argument on a concept of agency directed towards the world. This methodological starting point, which is also at the core of his dispute with Freud, is inspired by Spinoza's *Ethics*, in particular Spinoza's distinction between feelings to which we are passively subjected [*passiones*] and self-determined feelings driven by an enlargement of *potentia agendi*, of our capacity to act.[34] Viewed from this perspective, anxiety is not an ontological existential, as Heidegger would have it, but a 'suffering, oppressed, unfree' emotion imposed on us.[35]

The linchpin of Bloch's anthropology is the development of cooperative agency. On the very first page of the *Principle of Hope*, he propounds that hope 'goes out of itself, makes people broad instead of confining them': it 'requires people who throw themselves actively into what is becoming [*sich ins Werdende tätig hineinwerfen*], to which they themselves belong. It will not tolerate a dog's life which feels itself only passively thrown into What Is'.[36] This emphasis on people's active engagement [*sich hineinwerfen*] is obviously directed against Heidegger's *Geworfenheit*, or thrownness. Whereas Heidegger generalises and ontologises anxiety, elevating it to a path towards true existence, Bloch develops the notion of *docta spes*, of learned and comprehended hope, which can be corrected by observation and analysis.[37]

---

30   Braun 1983, p. 130.
31   Bloch 1986, vol. 1, p. 74.
32   Bloch 1986, vol. 1, p. 75.
33   For example, Gekle 1986, pp. 28–31 and 73–4; Schiller 2017, pp. 50–1; and Fahrenbach 2017, pp. 285, 322 and 325–6.
34   For a discussion of Spinoza's concept of power as *potentia agendi*, see Rehmann 2019, pp. 244–7. Bloch's critique of Spinoza as 'the most unequivocal of all rationalists' refers to a different aspect of Spinoza's philosophy – namely, to the dismissal of hope as powerless and passive wishing (Bloch 1986, vol. 2, p. 850).
35   Bloch 1986, vol. 1, p. 75.
36   Bloch 1986, vol. 1, p. 1.
37   Bloch 1986, vol. 1, p. 7.

1.2 From People's Daydreams to the Concrete Utopia of Marxism

Bloch proposes the 'learning' of hope as the way to overcome our 'confusion' and 'state of anxiety'.[38] This approach is similar to Gramsci's project of working on the coherence of our common sense, which is characterised by its contradictory and 'bizarre composition', containing 'Stone Age elements and principles of a more advanced science, prejudices from all past phases of history ... and intuitions of a future philosophy which will be that of a human race united the world over'.[39] With a congenial intuition, Ernst Bloch, in *Heritage of Our Times*, describes such historical discrepancies as contradictions of *Ungleichzeitigkeit*, or non-contemporaneity, which point to different pasts and open up different futures. Whereas objective non-contemporaneity refers to the continuing influence of older forms of production, subjective non-contemporaneity appears as 'accumulated rage'.[40] According to Bloch, it is such non-contemporaneous contradictions – specifically, medieval thought forms among peasants and the middle classes, resentments against capitalist modernity and antagonisms between town and countryside as well as between young and old – that were exploited by the Nazis and turned against the labour movement and parliamentary democracy in the Weimar Republic.[41] Since these contradictions are replete with undischarged futures in the past, the socialist labour movement has to learn to deal with these non-contemporaneous contradictions as well. What is needed is a multi-layered and multi-temporal dialectics able to understand and to rescue 'the subversive and utopian elements, the repressed matter of this not-yet-past'.[42]

Both Gramsci and Bloch are searching for anchor points in everyday life from which to transform contradictory common sense and to overcome its incoherence. Gramsci considers these anchor points as parts of 'good sense [*buon senso*]', the healthy nucleus of 'common sense' characterised by direct observation and an open sense of experimentation.[43] The subaltern classes need to develop their own 'organic intellectuals' able to connect their philosophy of praxis with this realistic and creative 'good sense' so that they can help elevate people's common sense to a more coherent level.[44] Bloch uses the two terms in a similar way when he states that undialectical *common sense* is not sound at

---

38 Bloch 1986, vol. 1, p. 1.
39 Gramsci 1971, p. 324.
40 Bloch 1991, p. 108.
41 Bloch 1991, pp. 97–108; cf. Dietschy 2018.
42 Bloch 1991, pp. 113–5.
43 Gramsci 1971, pp. 328 and 348; and Gramsci 1975, Q10, § 48, pp. 1334–5, and Q11, § 12, p. 1380. Cf. Rehmann 2014, pp. 130–1.
44 Gramsci 1971, p. 326; Gramsci 1975, Q11, § 12, p. 1378.

all, but rather full of petit-bourgeois prejudices, whereas *good sense* is a 'mark of fullness, of truly sound sobriety', which 'does not rule out any perspectives, except that which could lead to things which bring no blessing'.[45]

For Bloch, the specific anchor points of good sense are people's daydreams, by which 'everybody's life is pervaded'.[46] He connects his concept of daydreams to the young Marx, who in the *Deutsch-Französische Jahrbücher* (1844) famously stated 'that the world has long dreamed of possessing something of which it has only to be conscious in order to possess it in reality'.[47] Quoting this statement in his review of Georg Lukács's *History and Class Consciousness*, Bloch adds the enthusiastic comment that it attributes to human thought 'the highest constitutive force and also the highest responsibility for the world, the commission of the seventh day of creation'.[48] It is this Marxian insight that propels his project to decipher humanity's dream history in the *Principle of Hope*, which ascends from the roasted pigeons of the land of Cockaigne to social utopias and natural-right theories, poetry, architecture, music and religion. What makes such highly diverse materials 'speak' is Bloch's sense of their rebellious and liberating dimensions, which reveal the *Vorschein*, or pre-appearance, of a classless society without domination and alienation.

Many scholars are so fixated on Bloch's 'eschatological' goals that they overlook his methodological claim to develop the utopian elements out of the most proximal realities: 'the Here and Now, what is repeatedly beginning in nearness, is a utopian category, in fact the most central one'.[49] Bloch's approach is not 'idealistic', but *materialist* in the sense of a philosophy of praxis that starts, as Enrique Dussel observes, from 'living being [*ser-vivente*] in connection to a possible new future'.[50]

Particularly in his aphorisms on daydreams, Bloch emphasises what at times gets lost in the more general parts of his philosophy of hope – namely, the extent to which everyday wishes are over-determined by class rule and ideology. The wishful image in the mirror often only reflects 'how the ruling class wishes the wishes of the weak to be'.[51] In other words, 'the threatened man looks at himself with the eyes of his master', and when putting himself at an advantage, it is actually 'the advantage which the real masters gain from the

---

45 Bloch 1986, vol. 3, p. 1368.
46 Bloch 1986, vol. 1, p. 1.
47 Marx 1975c, p. 144.
48 Bloch 1985d, p. 621.
49 Bloch 1986, vol. 1, p. 12.
50 Dussel 2013, pp. 335–6.
51 Bloch 1986, vol. 1, p. 13.

little man'.[52] Indeed, many small daydreams 'present life that should just yield a better pay-off'.[53] What qualifies such dreams nevertheless as a possible anchor point of good sense is their anticipatory potential: 'even the most private and unknowing wishful thinking is to be preferred to the unconscious walking in single file; because it can be informed'.[54]

The arc leading from Bloch's notion of daydreams to his Marxist *doctrine of warmth* cannot be explained simply from his early pre-Marxist works nor from a philosophical position 'between' Marx, Hegel and Schelling. It must above all be seen in the light of the strategies he employs when intervening in the contentious force field of contemporary Marxism. Central to this context are the worldwide split of the labour movement into social democracy and Communist International and an atrophy of anticipatory potentials which he perceives on both sides. The labour movement in both its reformist and revolutionary guises understood Marxism above all as a 'science of the laws of history' and a 'doctrine of development'.[55] Both social democracy and Marxism-Leninism tended to invoke (and to rely on) the notion of an 'objective' historical determination, independent of human initiative.[56]

Bloch therefore had good reasons to bend the stick in the opposite direction. In *Heritage of Our Times*, he criticised determinism and one-sided rationalism as contemporary Marxism's main shortcomings which facilitated fascism's ideological appeal and successful 'thefts from the commune'.[57] Here, again, we encounter different temporalities. The Nazis occupied the contemporary communist claims of a Workers' Party, the colour red, the street, the procession, 'the dangerous songs', May Day, the 'forest of flags', the primacy of praxis.[58] 'Thus the enemy is not content with torturing and killing workers. He not only wants to smash the red front but also strips the jewellery off the supposed corpse'.[59] But for Bloch the fascist theft from the commune has a wider meaning: the Nazis also captured the dreams of a golden age, which contained memories of the early commune, ancient myths of a Thousand-Year Reich, the chiliastic hopes and social-revolutionary ideals of Christian heresy.[60] Marxist dismissals of these dreams as backwards and irrational – such

---

52 Bloch 1986, vol. 1, p. 340.
53 Bloch 1975, p. 42.
54 Bloch 1986, vol. 3, p. 1365; translation modified.
55 Cf. Rehmann 2014, pp. 61–3.
56 Ibid.
57 Bloch 1991, p. 64.
58 Bloch 1991, pp. 64–8.
59 Bloch 1991, p. 68.
60 Bloch 1991, pp. 118 and 128–9.

as Karl Kautsky's 'soft arrogance' towards apocalyptic mysticism – had facilitated fascism's hegemony: when 'vulgar Marxism had forgotten the inheritance of the German Peasant Wars and of German philosophy, the Nazis streamed into the vacated, originally Münzerian regions'.[61] Against the advancement of fascism, Bloch proposed a 'Triple Alliance' of proletariat, impoverished peasants and middle classes that is able to 'release those elements even of the non-contemporaneous contradiction which are capable of aversion and transformation, namely those hostile to capitalism, homeless in it, and to remount them for functioning in a different connection'.[62] His proposal revealed a significant prospective insight at the time: the text is from May 1932, three years before the Seventh World Congress of the Comintern of July–August 1935, in which Georgi Dimitrov pronounced the dramatic strategic reversal from the theory of 'social fascism' (which applied the concept of fascism to social democracy) to a concept of fascism as 'the open terrorist dictatorship of the most reactionary ... elements of finance capital'.[63] This definition is of course disputed, because it leaves out the populist class base of fascist movements and their ideological appeal. But, if applied earlier, it could have opened the way to a broad and potentially successful 'popular front' against fascism.

According to Bloch, then, Engels's proclamation of socialism's progress from utopia towards science had led to an 'undernourishment of revolutionary imagination', as a result of which 'the pillar of fire in utopias' was 'liquidated along with the cloud'.[64] His own philosophical project must be understood as an attempt to reconnect the split-off utopian impulse with the analytical toolkit of Marxist critique and to remodel their relationship in a new dialectical combination. The 'determinate negation' of Marxist critique is reframed as a *cold stream* characterised by a concrete 'science of conditions, ... of struggle and opposition' coupled with the 'unmasking of ideologies' and the 'disenchantment of metaphysical illusion' – an indispensable warning against utopian tendencies of 'overhauling, skipping over, flying over'.[65] The concept of a *warm stream* articulates the liberating intentions that are orientated towards a 'utopian totum', in which humans, their world and nature are no longer alienated from each other.[66] As a 'doctrine of warmth', Marxism becomes a 'theory-praxis

---

61 Bloch 1991, pp. 132 and 140.
62 Bloch 1991, p. 113.
63 Dimitrov 1939.
64 Bloch 1986, vol. 2, p. 622.
65 Bloch 1986, vol. 1, p. 208.
66 Bloch 1986, vol. 1, pp. 208–9.

of reaching home'.⁶⁷ Similar to Rosa Luxemburg, who tried to reconnect the far goals of a classless society with the near goals of realistic reform through her famous formula of 'revolutionary Realpolitik', Bloch describes the two sides of progressive politics as both contradiction – acerbity versus faith [*Glauben*] – and complementarity: 'Only coldness and warmth of concrete anticipation together ... ensure that neither the path in itself nor the goal in itself are held apart from one another undialectically and so become reified and isolated'.⁶⁸

By way of this theoretico-practical reformulation, the abstract juxtaposition of *utopia* and *science* is substituted by the opposition between *abstract utopia*, a 'dream lantern [which] shines into an empty space', and *concrete utopia*, which transforms the world through 'disciplined work in and with actual tendencies'.⁶⁹ It is here that Bloch's anthropology segues into his ontology of the not-yet. The work in and with actual tendencies presupposes and requires that reality itself is not 'closed, full of fixed, even perfected facts', but is rather a dynamic process which brings about a 'widely ramified mediation between present, unfinished past and ... possible future'.⁷⁰ All our transcending thinking, imagining and dreaming would not change anything if the real conditions did not come up to meet them, as it were [the phrase Bloch uses is *helfend entgegenkommen*].⁷¹ This is the reason why Bloch characterises hope in a threefold way: as 'the most human of all mental feelings', as a 'directing act of a cognitive kind' which is capable of logical and concrete correction and sharpening, and as a 'place in the world [*Weltstelle*] which is as inhabited as the best civilised land and as unexplored as the Antarctic'.⁷² The concrete-utopian task of connecting the 'not-yet-conscious' of humans with the 'not-yet-become' of the world is possible because both domains contain spaces of possibility that are not fully determined.⁷³

1.3 Can We Read Bloch's Ontology of the Not-Yet in a Praxis-Philosophical Key?

Bloch, who as a student already wanted to design an overall philosophical system 'compared to which Hegel's edifice would look like a doghouse',⁷⁴ inscribes

---

67   Bloch 1986, vol. 1, pp. 209–10.
68   Luxemburg 1970–5, vol. 1.1, p. 373; Bloch 1986, vol. 1, pp. 208–9.
69   Bloch 1986, vol. 2, pp. 579 and 620.
70   Bloch 1986, vol. 1, p. 196.
71   Bloch 1985f., p. 139.
72   Bloch 1986, vol. 1, pp. 75, 12, 112, 6.
73   Bloch 1986, vol. 2, p. 623.
74   Quoted in Zudeick 1987, p. 48.

his Marxist philosophy of praxis in the framework of classical *Systemphilosophie*. Of course, such inscription does not come without speculative risk. But while taking up traditional philosophical concepts – origin, essence, teleology, identity, highest good and so on – Bloch simultaneously severs them from their dependence on pregiven objectives and redefines them from the perspective of an ontology of the not-yet, according to which the 'true genesis is not at the beginning but at the end'.[75]

Whether we consider Bloch's ontology as a non-Marxist 'utopian system' (as Lukács does)[76] or as a materialist anchor of his anthropology depends on whether we read it as a teleology in-built in history and nature *or* in the hermeneutical key of open possibilities. Both readings can be supported by citations from Bloch, at times even by different aspects within one and the same sentence. It seems as if Bloch wrote in both keys at the same time and used this ambiguity as a subversive stylistic means, as though he tried (to use the young Marx's famous formula) to force 'these petrified relations ... to dance by singing their own tune to them'.[77]

Adorno applies one of the hermeneutic keys when he calls Bloch an 'idealist *malgré lui*' whose philosophy is haunted by an 'innermost antinomy': it 'conceives the end of the world as its ground, that which moves what exists, which, as its *telos*, it already inhabits'.[78] On this interpretation, Bloch construes – notwithstanding his emphasis on the genuinely new – a circular relation between telos and origin. Similarly, Jürgen Habermas maintains that Bloch skips over a proper socio-historical analysis of objective possibilities and instead transitions immediately to 'pregnant' matter, which as *natura naturans* has a propensity toward humanity. Bloch – Habermas claims – is therefore really a kind of Marxist Schelling: his philosophy is a Schellingian doctrine of potency in Marxist disguise.[79] In response to such criticisms, Eberhard Braun has argued that Bloch's philosophy retains a practical-humane core. As in Hegel's *Phenomenology of Spirit*, the subject increasingly opens up and assimilates the objective world. Hence, Bloch's *telos* does not possess the status of necessity but belongs to the mode of possibility: its future reality is not yet decided.[80] I will return to this issue later on.

Indeed, the transition from Bloch's anthropology to his ontology of the not-yet takes place in chapters 17 and 18 of the *Principle of Hope*; that is to say, in the

---

75 Bloch 1986, vol. 3, p. 1375.
76 Cited in Bloch 1975, pp. 33–4.
77 Marx 1843, p. 178.
78 Adorno 1991, p. 213.
79 Habermas 1960, pp. 1085–6 and 1090–1.
80 Braun 1983, pp. 124–5, 128, 131.

middle of its anthropological part on *anticipatory consciousness*, which Bloch characterises as 'founding and supporting everything else'.[81] This transition is centred on the concept of *real possibility*, in which utopian imagination finds its 'concrete correlate' in the world.[82] On the side of subjectivity, we find an 'active possibility', a 'capability-of-doing-other', a potency to turn things around; on the side of objectivity, we find a 'passive possibility', a 'capability-of-becoming-other', potentiality, turnability, changeability of the world.[83] Bloch also differentiates the complex of possibilities in terms of the scope of anticipation. There exists a 'reverse side', associated with Aristotle's 'what is *according to possibility* [*kata to dynaton*]', which Bloch characterises as 'measures of what is possible in each given situation [*Maße des jeweils Möglichen*]' and which is to be explored by a cold-stream analysis; and a 'front side', associated with Aristotle's 'what is in possibility [*dynamei on*]', which Bloch recasts in terms of the 'Totum of the *finally* Possible' and which provides the horizon for the warm-stream analysis.[84]

Bloch's formulations of the utopian-far goals are inspired above all by the young Marx's perspective in the *Economic and Philosophic Manuscripts of 1844*, according to which the overcoming of alienation in a classless society does not only apply to human beings, their social relations, their labour and their potential as a species, but also includes a reconciliation with nature, to which they belong. For the societal human being [*gesellschaftlicher Mensch*], nature exists 'as a bond with man', as a '*foundation* of his own *human* existence', so that the communist society is characterised by 'the complete unity of man with nature – the true resurrection of nature – the accomplished naturalism of man and the accomplished humanism of nature'.[85] Bloch reformulates this perspective as the 'well-founded hope' that non-human – and even inorganic – nature and the human world have the tendency to 'become identical'.[86] The Marxian reconciliation between humans, their world and nature thus becomes in Bloch's philosophy the core of *summum bonum*, the highest good. The most diverse *Hoffnungsbilder*, or images of hope, designate a 'peak of the dreams of a better life'.[87] They contain the 'irrefutable feeling that the better cannot be surpassed infinitely', that there must be a fulfilling 'thus far and no fur-

---

81   Bloch 1986, vol. 1, p. 11.
82   Bloch 1986, vol. 1, p. 197.
83   Bloch 1986, vol. 1, pp. 232–3 and 247.
84   Bloch 1986, vol. 2, pp. 206–7; translation modified.
85   Marx 1975b, p. 298.
86   Bloch 1986, vol. 3, p. 1328.
87   Bloch 1986, vol. 1, p. 305.

ther' – a 'stay a while, you are so fair', as Goethe's Faust says.[88] What has been called *God*, the *Kingdom of God* or the *realm of freedom* – 'for the last time in a long time' by Kant – is 'the identity of man who has come to himself with his world successfully achieved for him'.[89] What characterises Bloch's specific conjunction of anthropology and ontology is the proposition that this identity is not only the ideal high point of human hopes, but that it also marks the unresolved 'real problem' of matter and the 'metaphysical latency problem of nature'.[90]

The standard interpretation of Bloch's *ultimum* and *summum bonum* as expressions of a quasi-religious eschatology[91] overlooks the fact that his this-worldly translation of *last things* provides neither a Saviour nor any guarantees. As Johan Siebers emphasises, Bloch expresses the eschatological principle that 'the last hour remains hidden [*ultima latet*]' in a 'tentative image [*Versuchs-gestalt*] of identity' of existence and essence, or *Heimat*.[92] This leads to the paradox that as soon as one interprets such a 'tentative image' in an empirical manner, one is faced with the problem that any completely achieved 'identity' would result in entropic stasis, which is incompatible with the dialectical understanding of history as driven by contradictions.

Bloch is well aware of this methodological problem. The highest good, he says, 'does not encounter the process with its transitorinesses, and consequently is not encountered by them either', because any achieved identity 'would no longer enter ... into any process ... there would no longer be any occasion for process'.[93] Now, if Bloch's ultimate goal were 'exterritorial to the process', as Siebers suggests,[94] then one might argue that it possesses a status similar to Kant's regulative idea. However, this interpretation, which is put forward by, among others, Helmut Fahrenbach, contradicts Bloch's objection that Kant's postulate of a fundamental elusiveness of the highest good reveals an 'abrupt undialectical dualism' which erects an unsurmountable barrier between ideal and reality.[95] For Bloch, the tension between the imagined highest good and the open process of becoming belongs to the 'true materialist *aporias* and *antinomies*'.[96] As he points out in an interview in 1975, his book

---

88   Bloch 1986, vol. 3, p. 1313.
89   Bloch 1986, vol. 3, p. 1321 and Bloch 1986, vol. 1, p. 313.
90   Bloch 1986, vol. 3, p. 1324.
91   For example, Holz 2012, pp. 503 and 507.
92   Siebers 2012b, pp. 582 and 587.
93   Bloch 1986, vol. 3, p. 1179.
94   Siebers 2012b, p. 588.
95   Fahrenbach 2017, pp. 44–5, and Bloch 1986, vol. 3, pp. 1320–1; cf. Bloch 1985b, pp. 446–7.
96   Bloch 1985a, p. 116.

Experimentum Mundi deals with the paradoxical contradiction between the openness of process and the theoretical concept of an 'end as "finis operum" that shines into the future [*vorleuchtet*] ... and operates as a hope content, which was meant all along and was never reached'.[97] The book deals precisely with 'this invariant ... which itself is process – and therefore again a paradox'.[98]

Bloch's 'practical-materialist' approach is apparent from the way he reformulates the young Marx's notion of a reconciliation between humankind and nature in terms of a 'technology of alliance [*Allianztechnik*], which is mediated with the co-productivity of nature'.[99] Whereas 'our technology up to now stands in nature like an army of occupation in enemy territory', without knowing the interior of the country, a 'Marxism of technology' has the task of ending 'the naive application of the standpoint of the exploiter and animal tamer to nature' and to forge a non-exploitative 'nature alliance [*Naturallianz*]' that frees up 'the creations slumbering in the womb of nature'.[100] The objective is an 'unparalleled hook-up [*Verhakung*] ... a real installation of human beings (as soon as they have been socially mediated with themselves) into nature (as soon as technology has been mediated with nature)'.[101]

What is at stake in the *summum bonum* is therefore what we would nowadays call an eco-socialist perspective. Notwithstanding some illusions regarding technological progress – above all his support for the peaceful use of nuclear energy[102] – Bloch's concept of alliance technology represents an alternative to the environmental destruction in the 'Capitalocene'. As Wolfdietrich Schmied-Kowarzik puts it, Bloch was 'one of the first thinkers, who, with recourse to Schelling and Marx and before the general debate about the ecological crisis, raised the problem of an alliance between humans and nature ... and thought it through'.[103] Read in a praxis-philosophical key, Bloch's philosophy of nature also provides a useful counterbalance to the 'sociological' one-sidedness of critical theories that transform Marx's interlocking of humanism and naturalism into some thinned-out, 'nature-free' humanism. Already in 1923, in a generally enthusiastic review of Lukács's *History and Class-Consciousness*, Bloch diagnosed a 'simplistic inclination towards an exclusive sociological homogenisation of the process', which both ignores the 'poly-

---

97 Bloch 1975, p. 264.
98 Ibid.
99 Dietschy 1983, p. 181, and Bloch 1986, vol. 2, p. 690.
100 Bloch 1986, vol. 2, pp. 695–6; cf. Bloch 1985f., p. 251.
101 Bloch 1986, vol. 2, p. 698.
102 Bloch 1986, vol. 2, pp. 660 and 663–4.
103 Schmied-Kowarzik 1986, p. 228.

rhythmic fabric' of history and restricts the focus to a 'purely *social* matter', so that physical nature is not grasped historically.[104]

Bloch's philosophy of nature, as we will see, is not without speculative exaggerations. Yet its basic argument regarding the connection between natural history and human history contains important insights. Similar approaches can today be found in ecological theories that characterise the relationship between human beings and nature as one of co-evolution or as 'double internality' (humanity in nature / nature-in-humanity).[105] Aspects of Bloch's alliance technology have been taken up under the heading of 'converging technology', but within a framework of a 'capitalist-individualistic project of human self-enhancement'.[106] In any case, Marxist concepts of praxis need to be deepened to include our natural roots in the past and the present and to move 'the orientation towards sustainable human-nature relationships into the centre of the humanum'.[107]

1.4 A Weak Teleological Force of Open Possibilities

Bloch's oscillation between *philosophy of praxis* and *Systemphilosophie* can best be explained with reference to his discussion of teleology. The traditional understanding of the concept – according to which the telos is preordained from the beginning and exists there 'according to its "disposition [*Anlage*]" in reduced form, as if *encapsulated*' – is discredited, Bloch says.[108] What remains unsolved is the 'genuine teleology problem itself', according to which the purposes in question 'are only just forming in active process, always arising anew within it and enriching themselves'.[109] Matter itself contains something 'logical' that proceeds primarily 'teleologically', that is 'with a driving tendency, entelechetical latency'.[110] However, since 'entelechy' means for Bloch that 'which contains the goal as one to be realised',[111] one could infer that this containing is to be understood as a disposition that is determined beforehand. Since Bloch uses this term frequently and also talks for example about an 'urge of the material being towards self-reflection', Adorno's objection that he 'conceives the end of the world as its ground' seems to be valid.[112]

---

104 Bloch 1985d, pp. 618–9.
105 Cf. Foster 2010, pp. 230, 239, 247 and 262, as well as Moore 2015, pp. 5, 13, 48 and 77.
106 Cf. Nordmann 2007, pp. 262 and 269.
107 W.F. Haug 2017, p. 187.
108 Bloch 1986, vol. 3, p. 1373.
109 Bloch 1986, vol. 3, p. 1374.
110 Bloch 1985a, p. 474.
111 Bloch 1985a, p. 475.
112 Bloch 1985a, p. 464, and Adorno 1991, p. 213. Terry Eagleton quips that, according to

Yet there are at least as many passages that explicitly deny such an in-built entelechy. Bloch argues, for example, that the humanisation of nature 'has no parental home at the beginning from which it runs away and to which, with a kind of ancestor cult in philosophy, it returns'.[113] When he uses the term 'seed [*Keim*]', he does so in quotation marks and adds that it 'awaits many leaps', while the 'inherent propensity [*Anlage*]', again in quotation marks, 'unfolds itself in the unfolding itself to ever new and more precise beginnings of its potentia-possibilitas'.[114] Bloch thus takes up the traditional notions of *Keim* and *Anlage* and defines them in a way that playfully subverts their traditional meanings.

Indeed, Bloch's teleology is far from being a linear construct. It is already broken off by the fact that the *summum bonum* is only one possibility of what he calls the *ultimum*, which is characterised by the 'changeable alternative between absolute Nothing and absolute All'.[115] As proletariat and bourgeoisie can perish in the same 'barbarism', we might expect what in mythologies was imagined as *hell*: an 'absolute In-Vain of the historical process', the 'sealed frustration of utopia'.[116] Contrary to Günther Anders's assumption that Bloch is 'unable not to hope', so that his faithful optimism tops all progress-philosophies so far,[117] we can see that the main concepts of Bloch's ontology of the not-yet are shot through with alternatives between 'salvation' and 'disaster'.

Let us look at some examples. The concept of *latency*, which represents the not-yet become goal-content within the tendency, is operative 'without any heavenly geography' and without any 'mythologically ready-made' world.[118] Yet at the same time there is a 'latency of Nothing', which designates what was traditionally called *evil* and announces itself as annihilation, disintegration, threatening chaos.[119] The *tendency*, which provides the fundamental support structure for any concrete utopia, is designed as an anti-deterministic concept which is in tension with the concept of *law* prevailing in both contemporary social democracy and Marxism-Leninism.[120] It is true that Bloch at times uses the term *laws* as well, but he does so with the understanding that they are 'solely

---

Bloch's ontology, communism is already 'implicit in the structure of the amoeba' (Eagleton 2015, p. 99).
113 Bloch 1986, vol. 1, p. 204.
114 Bloch 1986, vol. 1, p. 238.
115 Bloch 1986, vol. 1, p. 312.
116 Bloch 1986, vol. 1, pp. 312–13.
117 Anders 1982, pp. 138 and 159–60.
118 Bloch 1985f., pp. 147–8. Cf. Zeilinger 2012a, p. 232.
119 Bloch 1986, vol. 3, p. 1296.
120 Cf. Zeilinger 2012c, pp. 560–1.

tendency-laws', the course of which is 'both determined by present conditions and open at its front side'.[121] Objective preconditions of possible developments are not to be understood in terms of 'law-like causes', but rather of conditions which cannot be realised without an active subject: they only create a 'charged atmosphere, into which the subjective factor ... needs to intervene'.[122] Tendency is by definition 'still undecided' and 'keeps the place open for the Novum'.[123]

The Novum, which Bloch provides with the paradoxical status of a 'specific repetition ... of the still un-become goal-content itself',[124] is nevertheless not necessarily designed 'to be something good', but due to the contingency of the world can 'engender both fear and hope, contain both collapse and ascension'.[125] The positive outcome in the possible is itself not more than a possibility. It is not anchored in the world process as a fixed disposition but can only become a reality when it has 'active hope as an ally'.[126] And *possibility*, which is built on the confluence of a capacity-of-doing-other and a capacity-of-becoming-other, carries with it possible salvation and disaster, both militating against each other. The disaster character is exemplified among others by 'the eruption of fascist hell, a possibility that was and still is concealed in the final stage of capitalism'.[127] The objective factors of potentiality are reliant on the 'capacity, the potency of the actualizing subject' – everything depends on 'setting to work a subjective capacity in order to realise the real-objective possible'.[128]

This openness of Bloch's major concepts helps explain the vehemence with which Bloch criticises the 'automatic progress-optimism' as a 'new opium for the people', to which 'even a dash of pessimism would be preferable', because 'at least pessimism with a realistic perspective is not so helplessly surprised by mistakes and catastrophes, by the horrifying possibilities ... precisely in capitalist progress'.[129] This resembles Gramsci's critique of 'mechanical determinism' as a 'substitute for the Predestination' and a 'religion of the subaltern', which makes that the 'activity of the will' is present 'only implicitly, and in a veiled and, as it were, shamefaced manner'.[130] And when Bloch proposes to combine

---

121   Bloch 1985e, p. 319.
122   Bloch 1985f., p. 129.
123   Bloch 1985f., p. 146.
124   Bloch 1986, vol. 1, p. 202.
125   Bloch 1985f., p. 141.
126   Ibid.
127   Bloch 1986, vol. 1, p. 233.
128   Bloch 1985f., p. 255.
129   Bloch 1986, vol. 1, pp. 198–9.
130   Gramsci 1971, pp. 336–7.

a 'thinking ad pessimum' with a 'militant optimism', he describes a similar attitude of working in and with contradictions as expressed in Gramsci's famous formula 'pessimism of the intelligence, optimism of the will'.[131]

As soon as one reads Bloch's ontology of the not-yet in the hermeneutic key of open possibilities and undecided tendencies, one discovers an approach that is clearly distinguished from the pathos of a 'matter driving forwards' equipped with its own (though only hypothetical) 'nature subject' and 'utopia'.[132] Beneath such indications of a *strong teleology*, there is a much more modest and careful orientation towards the not-yet, which we could characterise, with reference to Walter Benjamin's 'weak messianic force',[133] as a *weak teleological force of open possibilities*. The core of this weak teleology is that 'it is not yet the evening to end all days, every night still has a morning'.[134] When Bloch, after his forced retirement in the GDR and his emigration to West Germany, gave his inaugural address at the University of Tübingen, he reflected on the question of why well-founded hope can be frustrated as well as fulfilled. He argued that hope contains 'eo ipso the precariousness of failure' because it stands in the undecidedness of the world process.[135] We need to be aware that 'foiling as a function of Nothingness goes about in the world, that an in-vain [*Umsonst*] is also latent in the objectively-real possible, which carries salvation as well as disaster': concrete hope, which does not give up when faced with setbacks, presumes that possibilities are still open and that the world remains an 'experimenting laboratory possibilis salutis'.[136]

2 For a Renewal of Bloch's Philosophy: Five Theses

Working and thinking seriously with Bloch's philosophy requires us to confront it critically with the challenges of the twenty-first century and to ask what is still relevant today and what is in need of a correction and renewal. It is obvious that Bloch had long repressed the crimes of Stalinism. It was only from 1956 onwards that he recognised the extent of the deformations of Soviet state

---

131 Bloch 1986, vol. 1, p. 199, and Gramsci 1975, Q 9, § 60, p. 1131.
132 For example, Bloch 1985e, p. 207, and Bloch 1985f., p. 251.
133 Benjamin 2007, p. 254.
134 Bloch 1986, vol. 1, p. 305. Cat Moir comes to a similar conclusion when she argues that Bloch's teleology is one 'without a pre-given *telos*, in which the goal itself, the "essence" of what the world might be, is still being worked out in a complex dialectical process of becoming from which contingency and chance are ... far from absent' (Moir 2019, p. 72).
135 Bloch 1985c, p. 387.
136 Bloch 1985c, pp. 389 and 391.

socialism.[137] Its ultimate downfall, which impacts our 'post-socialist' age was, however, not foreseeable for him. His self-understanding as an organic intellectual of a socialist labour movement which saw capitalist society in decline and itself in the ascendant (in spite of all the setbacks and defeats) certainly set the ground tone of his writings. We need to take this historical distance to our post-1989 era into consideration when evaluating and updating his philosophy today. Against this backdrop, I wish to formulate the following five theses.

2.1 First Thesis: Reformulating the *summum bonum*

Even if we, under the conditions of a neoliberal high-tech capitalism and seemingly without an alternative, agreed with Habermas's diagnosis that there is an 'exhaustion of utopian energies',[138] this would not be a valid argument against a philosophy of the not-yet, which deciphers the utopian impulses in people's daydreams and the big outlines of a better world. This also applies to Bloch's courage to take up and think through the different utopias of a *summum bonum*. Gramsci pointed out that the sober-minded analysis of a 'passive revolution' must not beguile us into adopting its passive world view.[139] In times of neoliberal fragmentation and disillusion, leftist projects and social movements should not be content with living 'hope-lessly and in the present', as Christine Thürmer-Rohr proclaims,[140] but rather need to develop appealing, convincing and powerful counter-images of a 'good life' for all, which is sustainable and in alliance with nature.

However, what we need to leave behind is the way Bloch formulates the overcoming of alienation between humans and their social world and nature in terms of 'identity'. The implied lack of contradictions and differences would result in an end of history, and, as we have seen, Bloch is well aware of this antinomy. In order to avoid the aporia that the *ultimum* is 'extraterritorial' to the historical process so that its hope-content assumes (against Bloch's intention) the function of a Kantian 'regulative idea', we should conceptualise our far goals as contradictory forms of movement as well. The *summum bonum* is accordingly to be re-formulated within the framework of a dynamic process by which antagonistic contradictions are again and again transformed into nonantagonistic and workable contradictions and differences. These transformations are not just long-term goals but take place already in our present: people

---

[137] According to a friend's report, he collapsed when he learned about Khrushchev's secret speech at the 20th Party Congress of the CPSU in 1956; cf. Zudeick 1987, p. 227.
[138] Habermas 1985, pp. 144–5.
[139] Gramsci 1975, Q. 10.I, § 6, pp. 1236–7, and § 9, p. 1242.
[140] Thürmer-Rohr 1991, p. 22.

are actually trying to bring them about in their daily lives, though usually in limited areas like relationships, friendships, neighbourhoods and the workplace, whereas the fundamental structures of class domination, patriarchy and racism remain out of reach.

2.2 *Second Thesis:* Towards a Teleology of Praxis

Since the notion of an immanent force in history pushing towards a communist future has collapsed and gone for good in Marxist theory, we need to ask whether or in what respect we need to de-teleologise Bloch's philosophy, or to pluralise its perspective. It appears that Bloch intended to go in this direction as well. In *Heritage of Our Times*, he tries to uncouple the concept of progress from its traditional linear framework and connect it with the notion of a 'polyrhythmic and multi-spatial' history.[141] He later systematises this insight by way of his concept of a polyphonic spatial-temporal 'multiverse'.[142] The concept of progress is therefore not to be understood in a unilinear way, but needs a 'broad, elastic, completely dynamic multiverse, an upholding and entwined counterpoint of historical voices'.[143]

However, we should not indulge too easily in the anti-teleological *Zeitgeist* of our 'postmodern' times, which is rather to be critiqued as an ideological side-effect of neoliberal capitalism's lack of perspective. For a nuanced assessment, it is important to differentiate between the two versions of Bloch's teleology. What we need to deconstruct is his strong teleology of a matter driving forwards. Bloch is right when he objects to Hegel that nature is no pre-historical 'gigantic corpse',[144] but rather a creative *natura naturans*, which, as an ensemble of efficacious processes, permanently engenders new developments, contents and forms. But when Bloch attributes this productivity to a 'nature subject', even though only a 'hypothetical' one, and to an 'entelechy', though an 'unfinished' one,[145] he brings his ontology into conflict with modern science, which rightly insists that processes in nature, including the mechanisms of selection discovered by Darwin, are non-teleological. Both the development of nature and human history are more adequately conceptualised without the presupposition of a big, intentional and directing subject. The notion that nature by virtue of its specific beauty speaks to us through 'real ciphers' and 'real symbols', in which 'objective-utopian archetypes' are at work, is a beauti-

---

141   Bloch 1991, p. 62.
142   Bloch 1985e, pp. 125 and 128–9.
143   Bloch 1985e, p. 146.
144   Bloch 1985e, p. 235.
145   Bloch 1985a, pp. 461 and 476.

ful poetic image, inspired by Goethe's *West-östlicher Divan*, but it reveals above all the human desire 'to find a mirror in the shapes of anorganic nature'.[146] We do not need a teleology of nature in order to conceptualise a 'nature alliance' by which human labour and technology connect with nature's co-productivity in a sustainable way.

This criticism does not apply to what I described as Bloch's *weak teleological force of open possibilities*. The fact that we humans are equipped with the ability to imagine goals and to anticipate future outcomes means that we are bound to project our thoughts and actions towards objectives. In this sense, we can use Antonio Negri's concept of a 'teleology of praxis' orientated towards the construction of the common.[147] Social movements and political projects need to develop their teleologies (and corresponding genealogies) in order to intervene effectively in the force fields of social purposes. There is no reason to consider this as philosophically objectionable per se, as long as the projects are aware of the projected perspective and lay it open. Viewed from this angle, Bloch's strong teleology can be re-interpreted as a subversive intervention into the domain of philosophy: it operates as a 'grand narrative' that takes up the traditional philosophical categories and changes them over to the utopian magnet of a classless society. It is precisely by recognising the praxis-philosophical rationale of this intervention that we can also discover the limits of Bloch's ideology critique: his futuristic pole reversal to the not-yet is not sufficient for a theoretical critique of the ideological forms of traditional philosophy or of religion, natural law, morality and other ideologies (including fascist ones).[148]

2.3 Third Thesis: De-Essentialising the Concept of Hope

Many of the controversies around Bloch's philosophy touch upon the question of whether his concept of hope is essentialist in the sense that it is conceived as a fundamentally benign and life-affirming force that is only afterwards and secondarily hijacked and manipulated by the powers that be. We can indeed see some symptomatic blank spaces that corroborate such a suspicion. As feminist critics have pointed out, the patriarchal patterns inscribed in everyday wishes usually go unnoticed in Bloch's interpretation.[149] He is fascinated by

---

146   Bloch 1986, vol. 3, p. 1312 ('Let secret ciphers' message / The world's attention claim, / Till every changing passage / Translates into the same'), and Zeilinger 2012b, p. 346.
147   Negri 2013, pp. 8 and 78–9.
148   As Beat Dietschy has argued in his analysis of *Heritage of Our Times*, Bloch's strategy of 'futurisation' is not sufficient to destroy fascism's fascination and does not yet open up an alternative to the right-wing populist myth (Dietschy 2018, p. 37).
149   Cf. F. Haug 1984, pp. 690–3; cf. Thürmer-Rohr 1991, pp. 24–7.

the communist 'basic resonance' of the biblical Exodus story and the utopian splendour of the Promised Land 'flowing with milk and honey', but he disregards the account in the book of Joshua about the mass butchery that followed after the Israelites entered Canaan.[150] When dealing with Christopher Columbus, Bloch focuses on the former's utopian fantasies of an earthly paradise, but he does not consider Columbus's role in the colonial conquests and their genocidal outcomes.[151] His juxtaposition of the 'strength and dignity' of Columbus's intentions and the later conquests of 'criminals like Cortez and Pizarro'[152] does not hold water and reproduces a Eurocentric myth. 'War ships, too, can … carry the figurehead of Speranza', argues Beat Dietschy, who proposes a postcolonial deconstruction of Bloch's approach that starts from the 'absences of the others, who have been rendered invisible'.[153]

These blind spots are symptomatic. Bloch designs the anthropological and ontological foundation of hope on a general philosophical level that threatens to obscure the fundamental ambivalence of hope in class societies. Here, we need to develop what Bloch so convincingly demands in other areas – namely, a stronger *cold stream* that analyses the contradictory manifestations in the domain of hope. In actual life, we do not move around as human species beings in general, but rather as specific social subjects whose *habitus* are formed by different positions in the systems of class, race and gender relations. Since in antagonistic societies the success and good fortune of some goes hand in hand with the failure and misery of others, the hopes of some coincide with the despair of others. What on a general anthropological level can be conceptualised as a creative force for the good life for all is so only according to possibility. Hope itself is in reality an antagonistic force field traversed by multiple contradictions.

2.4 *Fourth Thesis:* Combination with a Critical Ideology Theory

Bloch considers the utopian dimensions as '"excesses" over and above ideology', which do not coincide with it and 'whose day is not yet done when the ideology which bore them disappears'.[154] By focusing on this 'exceeding' dimension, he is contributing to a nuanced Marxist ideology critique. It allows him, for example, to address what was largely overlooked in Marxist critiques of religion at the time – namely, 'the uplift motif [*Auftriebsmotiv*], which so painfully,

---

150   Cf. Bloch 1986, vol. 2, pp. 496, 502 and 759.
151   Bloch 1986, vol. 2, pp. 752 and 776–7.
152   Bloch 1986, vol. 2, p. 777.
153   Dietschy 2017, pp. 236–7.
154   Bloch 1986, vol. 1, p. 14, and Bloch 2009, p. 253.

image-fully and hope-fully fills' the different religions.[155] His project of a 'multi-layered dialectic' that 'remounts' the elements of non-contemporaneous contradictions 'for functioning in a different connection' intersects with Gramsci's notion of a differentiated ideology critique, which intervenes in the 'ensemble of the superstructures' in order to induce a 'process of differentiation and change in the relative weight': 'What was previously secondary ... becomes the nucleus of a new ideological and theoretical complex'.[156]

Of course, Bloch, who died in 1977, could not be cognisant of the ideology-theoretical turn since the late 1970s, initiated by Louis Althusser and modified, among others, by Stuart Hall and the Berlin *Projekt Ideologietheorie*.[157] He therefore did not know the paradigm shift from the critique of inverted consciousness to an analysis of ideological apparatuses, social fields (Bourdieu), practices and interpellation, which shape not only specific ideas but also the ideological *subjects* themselves, their attitudes, desires and ways of feeling. Bloch applies the term ideology primarily to certain socially determined world views, ideals and 'value images'[158] and thus underestimates the intensity with which ideological practices and interpellations also work on formatting the expectant emotions of hope. What does not appear on his radar screen are the multiple ways that the subjects 'hopefully consolidate' their own ideological subjection.[159]

Therefore, Bloch's philosophy needs to be combined with a critical theory of ideological subjection, which would in turn help us de-essentialise his concept of hope. When Bloch argues that hope enables us to 'throw [ourselves] actively into what is becoming',[160] this emphasis needs to be complemented by an analysis of how the given structures and fields into which we 'throw' ourselves and through which we move are impacting and forming our wishing, wanting and hoping. The expectant affects are not just 'there' but are socially construed and habitualised. Hope, no less than religion, can function as an opiate of the people. It can easily be kindled, exploited and betrayed; say, by *yes we can* slogans that are not actually meant to give the people the power that would allow them to do what they are capable of. Every time such popular hopes are torched, they risk turning into their opposite, into anxiety, despair, hopeless-

---

155 Bloch 1986, vol. 3, p. 1294.
156 Bloch 1991, p. 113, and Gramsci 1975, Q 8, § 195, p. 1058; cf. the evaluation of Gramsci's ideology critique in Rehmann 2014, pp. 144–6.
157 Cf. the overview in Rehmann 2014.
158 Bloch 1986, vol. 3, p. 1316.
159 Cf. F. Haug 1984, p. 693.
160 Bloch 1986, vol. 1, p. 1.

ness and resentment. What we need is a dialectical approach to hope that is able to discern between empty hope and founded hope. And here, we are of course again on Bloch's own terrain, his specific combination of cold-stream analysis and warm-stream goals and impulses.

2.5 *Fifth Thesis:* Hegemonic Conditions of Hope and Hopelessness

Bloch's anthropological and ontological foundation helps us to understand why periods of social emancipation both engender mass revivals of hopes and are fuelled by them. Successful movements of liberation depend both on liberative perspectives of a 'good life' and on paths towards these goals that seem feasible and realistic. One of the most difficult challenges of politics is to understand the conditions under which social movements, projects and discourses gain popular appeal and lose it again, set free hopes on a mass scale and disappoint them.

For that, it is imperative to complement Bloch's philosophy of hope with Gramsci's theory of hegemony, which helps to investigate the *conditions* of both hope and hopelessness. The hegemony of neoliberal capitalism manifested itself in a privatisation of hope, by which the dreams of a better world were narrowed down to those for oneself and for one's own family.[161] But this de-socialisation of hope is not the last word either. Since the global economic crisis of 2007/8, we have been experiencing a new cycle of struggles that, in contrast to the struggles of the 1990s, are characterised by various attempts to create broad intersectional alliances between different movements that bring people's common sense to the left. As could be observed in, for example, the Occupy Wall Street movements or in the electoral campaigns of Bernie Sanders, progressive upswings on a mass scale can shift again the force-field for hope.[162]

Such shifts can occur when the movements overcome the neoliberal fragmentations connected to identity politics and politics of recognition. Gramsci has theorised such a dynamic with the concept of *catharsis*. It captures the moment when subaltern classes and groups overcome their egoistical-corporatist restrictions and enable themselves to build alliances with other subaltern classes. For Gramsci, this cathartic moment is so significant that he declares it 'the starting-point for all the philosophy of praxis'.[163] It marks the moment when the subaltern classes transition from 'objective to subject-

---

161 Cf. Thompson 2013, p. 5.
162 For a Gramscian analysis of the Occupy movements and the 2016 Bernie Sanders campaign, see Rehmann 2013 and 2016.
163 Gramsci 1971, pp. 366–67; Gramsci 1975, Q.II, 13, § 6, p. 1244.

ive' and from 'necessity to freedom' – that is, from being a passive 'object' of social conditions to becoming an active historical subject.[164] It is in these cathartic moments that hope – the anthropological and ontological foundations of which Bloch has so beautifully reconstructed – can emerge concretely. In our current constellation, hope manifests itself as a cathartic effect of the confluence and pulling-together of dispersed and fragmented subaltern subjects to a common project of transformation – one that does not negate its inner contradictions, but finds ways to bring them into a productive arrangement.

Bibliography

Adorno, Theodor W. 1991, *Notes to Literature 1*, translated by Shierry Weber Nicholsen, New York: Columbia University Press.

Anders, Günther 1982, *Ketzereien*, Munich: Beck.

Benjamin, Walter 2007 [1940], 'Theses on the Philosophy of History', in *Illuminations: Essays and Reflections*, translated by Harry Zohn, New York: Schocken Books.

Bloch, Ernst 1975, *Gespräche mit Ernst Bloch*, Frankfurt am Main: Suhrkamp.

Bloch, Ernst 1985a, *Das Materialismusproblem, seine Geschichte und Substanz*, Frankfurt am Main: Suhrkamp.

Bloch, Ernst 1985b, *Subjekt-Objekt. Erläuterungen zu Hegel*, slightly enlarged edition, Frankfurt am Main: Suhrkamp.

Bloch, Ernst 1985c, *Literarische Aufsätze*, Frankfurt am Main: Suhrkamp.

Bloch, Ernst 1985d, *Philosophische Aufsätze zur objektiven Phantasie*, Frankfurt am Main: Suhrkamp.

Bloch, Ernst 1985e, *Tübinger Einleitung in die Philosophie*, Frankfurt am Main: Suhrkamp.

Bloch, Ernst 1985f., *Experimentum Mundi. Frage, Kategorien des Herausbringens, Praxis*, Frankfurt am Main: Suhrkamp.

Bloch, Ernst 1985g, *Tendenz – Latenz – Utopie*, Frankfurt am Main: Suhrkamp.

Bloch, Ernst 1986, *The Principle of Hope*, 3 Volumes, translated by Neville Plaice, Stephen Plaice and Paul Knight, Cambridge, Mass.: MIT Press.

Bloch, Ernst 1991, *Heritage of Our Times*, translated by Neville and Stephen Plaice, Berkeley: University of California Press.

Bloch, Ernst 2009, *Atheism in Christianity: The Religion of the Exodus and the Kingdom*, translated by J.T. Swann, London and New York: Verso.

Braun, Eberhard 1983, 'Antizipation des Seins wie Utopie. Zur Grundlegung der Onto-

---

164 Ibid. Cf. Thomas 2009.

logie des Noch-Nicht-Seins im *Prinzip Hoffnung*', in *Seminar zur Philosophie Ernst Blochs*, edited by Burghart Schmidt, Frankfurt am Main: Suhrkamp.

Dietschy, Beat 1983, '*Experimentum Mundi*: Prinzip und System gelingender Praxis', in *Seminar zur Philosophie Ernst Blochs*, edited by Burghart Schmidt, Frankfurt am Main: Suhrkamp.

Dietschy, Beat 1988, *Gebrochene Gegenwart. Ernst Bloch, Ungleichzeitigkeit und das Geschichtsbild der Moderne*, Frankfurt am Main: Vervuert.

Dietschy, Beat 2012, 'Wunschlandschaften, entdeckt und gebildet', in *Bloch-Wörterbuch. Leitbegriffe der Philosophie Ernst Blochs*, edited by Beat Dietschy, Doris Zeilinger and Rainer Zimmermann, Berlin and Boston: de Gruyter.

Dietschy, Beat 2018, 'Im Mischdunkel nationaler Berauschung. Ernst Blochs *Erbschaft dieser Zeit* in Zeiten des Rechtspopulismus gelesen', *Das Argument* 325: 31–44.

Dimitrov, Georgi 1939, *The Fascist Offensive and the Tasks of the Communist International: Main Report Delivered at the Seventh World Congress of the Communist International*, Moscow: Foreign Languages Publishing House.

Dussel, Enrique 2013, *Ethics of Liberation in the Age of Globalization and Exclusion*, Durham, NC: Duke University Press.

Eagleton, Terry 2015, *Hope without Optimism*, Charlottesville: University of Virginia Press.

Engels, Friedrich 1990 [1886], *Ludwig Feuerbach and the End of Classic German Philosophy*, in *Marx and Engels Collected Works*, Volume 26, London: Lawrence & Wishart.

Fahrenbach, Helmut 2017, *Ernst Blochs Philosophie der Hoffnung und Utopie im Kontext und Diskurs*, Mössingen: Thalheimer.

Foster, John Bellamy, Brett Clark and Richard York 2010, *The Ecological Rift: Capitalism's War on the Earth*, New York: NYU Press.

Gekle, Hanna 1986, *Wunsch und Wirklichkeit. Blochs Philosophie des Noch-Nicht-Bewußten und Freuds Theorie des Unbewußten*, Frankfurt am Main: Suhrkamp.

Gramsci, Antonio 1971, *Selections from the Prison Notebooks of Antonio Gramsci*, translated by Quintin Hoare and Geoffrey Nowell Smith, New York: International Publishers.

Gramsci, Antonio 1975, *Quaderni del carcere*, 4 Volumes, Torino: Einaudi.

Gramsci, Antonio 1985, *Die neue Unübersichtlichkeit. Kleine politische Schriften V*, Frankfurt am Main: Suhrkamp.

Habermas, Jürgen 1960, 'Ein marxistischer Schelling. Zu Ernst Blochs spekulativem Materialismus', *Merkur*, 153: 1078–91.

Haug, Frigga 1984, 'Tagträume – Dimensionen weiblichen Widerstands', in: *Das Argument*, 147: 681–98.

Haug, Wolfgang Fritz 2012, 'Marxismus', in *Bloch-Wörterbuch. Leitbegriffe der Philosophie Ernst Blochs*, edited by Beat Dietschy, Doris Zeilinger and Rainer Zimmermann, Berlin and Boston: de Gruyter.

Haug, Wolfgang Fritz 2017, 'In der Höhle des Löwen. Kann man das *Kapital* von den Feuerbach-Thesen her lesen?', *Das Argument*, 322: 178–89.

Haug, Wolfgang Fritz 2018, 'Antonio Labriolas Grundlegung der Philosophie der Praxis', *Das Argument*, 326: 159–81.

Haug, Wolfgang Fritz 2012, 'Spekulativer Materialismus', in *Bloch-Wörterbuch. Leitbegriffe der Philosophie Ernst Blochs*, edited by Beat Dietschy, Doris Zeilinger and Rainer Zimmermann, Berlin and Boston: de Gruyter.

Holz, Hans Heinz 1975, *Logos spermatikos. Ernst Blochs Philosophie der unfertigen Welt*, Darmstadt-Neuwied: Luchterhand.

Holzkamp, Klaus 1985, *Grundlegung der Psychologie*, Frankfurt am Main: Campus.

Jonas, Hans 1984, *Das Prinzip Verantwortung. Versuch einer Ethik für die technologische Zivilisation*, Frankfurt am Main: Suhrkamp.

Jung, Werner 2012, 'Augenblick, Dunkel des gelebten Augenblicks', in *Bloch-Wörterbuch: Leitbegriffe der Philosophie Ernst Blochs*, edited by Beat Dietschy, Doris Zeilinger and Rainer Zimmermann, Berlin and Boston: de Gruyter.

Labriola, Antonio 1966, *Essays on the Materialist Conception of History*, translated by Charles H. Kerr, London: Monthly Review Press.

Luxemburg, Rosa 1970–75, *Gesammelte Werke*, 5 Volumes, edited by the Institut für Marxismus-Leninismus beim ZK der SED, Berlin: Dietz.

Marx, Karl 1975a [1843], 'Contribution to the Critique of Hegel's Philosophy of Right: Introduction', in *Marx and Engels Collected Works*, Volume 3, London: Lawrence and Wishart.

Marx, Karl 1975b [1844], *The Economic and Philosophic Manuscripts of 1844*, in *Marx and Engels Collected Works*, Volume 3, London: Lawrence and Wishart.

Marx, Karl 1975c [1844], 'Letters from the Deutsch-Französische Jahrbücher', in *Marx and Engels Collected Works*, Volume 3, London: Lawrence and Wishart.

Marx, Karl 1976a [1845], 'Theses on Feuerbach', in *Marx and Engels Collected Works*, Volume 5, London: Lawrence and Wishart.

Marx, Karl and Friedrich Engels 1976b [1845], *The German Ideology*, in *Marx and Engels Collected Works*, Volume 5, London: Lawrence and Wishart.

Marx, Karl 1976c [1867], *Capital: A Critique of Political Economy*, Volume 1, translated by Ben Fowkes, London: Penguin Books.

Moir, Cat 2019, *Ernst Bloch's Speculative Materialism: Ontology, Epistemology, Politics*, Leiden and Boston: Brill.

Moore, Jason 2015, *Capitalism in the Web of Life: Ecology and the Accumulation of Capital*, London and New York: Verso.

Müller-Schöll, Ulrich and Francesca Vidal 2017, 'Ernst Blochs "neue Philosophie" des "Neuen"', in *Ernst Bloch: Das Prinzip Hoffnung*, edited by Rainer E. Zimmermann, Berlin and Boston: de Gruyter.

Negri, Antonio 2013, *Spinoza for Our Time: Politics and Postmodernity*, New York: Columbia University Press.

Nordmann, Alfred 2007, 'Renaissance der Allianztechnik? Neue Technologien für alte Utopien', in *Utopie heute 1. Zur aktuellen Bedeutung, Funktion und Kritik des utopischen Denkens und Vorstellens*, edited by Beat Sitter-Liver and T. Hiltbrunner, Fribourg and Stuttgart: Kohlhammer.

Pelletier, Lucien 2017, 'Das Noch-Nicht-Bewusste', in *Ernst Bloch: Das Prinzip Hoffnung*, edited by Rainer E. Zimmermann, Berlin and Boston: de Gruyter.

Queiser, Daniel 2018, 'Vorwärts zu Aristoteles? Ernst Blochs Komposition einer linksaristotelischen Linken', *Das Argument*, 135: 74–88.

Rehmann, Jan 2012, 'Antizipation', in *Bloch-Wörterbuch. Leitbegriffe der Philosophie Ernst Blochs*, edited by Beat Dietschy, Doris Zeilinger and Rainer Zimmermann, Berlin and Boston: de Gruyter.

Rehmann, Jan 2013. 'Occupy Wall Street and the Question of Hegemony – A Gramscian Analysis', *Socialism and Democracy*, 27, 1: 1–18.

Rehmann, Jan 2014, *Theories of Ideology: The Powers of Alienation and Subjection*, Chicago: Haymarket.

Rehmann, Jan 2016, 'Bernie Sanders and the Hegemonic Crisis of Neoliberal Capitalism: What Next?', *Socialism and Democracy*, 30: 1–11.

Rehmann, Jan 2019, 'Power ≠ power: Against the Mix-Up of Nietzsche and Spinoza', *Critical Sociology*, 42, 2: 239–52.

Schiller, Hans-Ernst 2017, *Freud-Kritik von links. Bloch, Fromm, Adorno, Horkheimer, Marcuse*, Hamburg: Zu Klampen.

Schmied-Kowarzik, Wolfdietrich 1986, 'Ernst Bloch – Hoffnung auf eine Allianz von Geschichte und Natur', in *Ernst Bloch – Utopische Ontologie*, Volume 2, edited by Gvozden Flego and Wolfdietrich Schmied-Kowarzik, Bochum: Germinal.

Siebers, Johan 2012a, 'Novum', in *Bloch-Wörterbuch. Leitbegriffe der Philosophie Ernst Blochs*, edited by Beat Dietschy, Doris Zeilinger and Rainer Zimmermann, Berlin and Boston: de Gruyter.

Siebers, Johan 2012b, 'Ultimum', in *Bloch-Wörterbuch. Leitbegriffe der Philosophie Ernst Blochs*, edited by Beat Dietschy, Doris Zeilinger and Rainer Zimmermann, Berlin and Boston: de Gruyter.

Thomas, Peter 2009, *The Gramscian Moment: Philosophy, Hegemony and Marxism*, Leiden: Brill.

Thompson, Peter 2013, 'Introduction: The Privatization of Hope and the Critics of Negation', in *The Privatization of Hope: Ernst Bloch and the Future of Utopia*, edited by Peter Thompson and Slavoj Žižek, Durham and London: Duke University Press.

Thürmer-Rohr, Christine 1991, *Vagabonding: Feminist Thinking Cut Loose*, Boston: Beacon Press.

Zeilinger, Doris 2012a, 'Latenz', in *Bloch-Wörterbuch. Leitbegriffe der Philosophie Ernst Blochs*, edited by Beat Dietschy, Doris Zeilinger and Rainer Zimmermann, Berlin and Boston: de Gruyter.

Zeilinger, Doris 2012b, 'Natur', in *Bloch-Wörterbuch. Leitbegriffe der Philosophie Ernst Blochs*, edited by Beat Dietschy, Doris Zeilinger and Rainer Zimmermann, Berlin and Boston: de Gruyter.

Zeilinger, Doris 2012c, 'Tendenz', in *Bloch-Wörterbuch. Leitbegriffe der Philosophie Ernst Blochs*, edited by Beat Dietschy, Doris Zeilinger and Rainer Zimmermann, Berlin and Boston: de Gruyter.

Zudeick, Peter 1987, *Der Hintern des Teufels. Ernst Bloch – Leben und Werk*, Moss and Baden-Baden: Elster.

CHAPTER 10

The Possibility of Envisioning Utopias

Nina Rismal

Ernst Bloch believes that we are able to envisage utopia: we have been able to do so in the past, and we are able to do so now. He refers to this future society with the term *Heimat*.[1] Other thinkers use different terms. For example, the contemporary French philosopher Quentin Meillassoux, who like Bloch belongs to the tradition of speculative materialism, calls it 'the fourth World'.[2] According to Bloch, we cannot foresee exactly what kind of utopian society might one day arise. *Heimat* cannot be known and articulated comprehensively and systematically, but only vaguely intimated. However, Bloch also argues something else. He maintains that what he calls *concrete utopia* can in fact be *conceptualised*. That is to say, we can *anticipate* it through conceptualisations that do not correspond to its actual future manifestation, but which present its possibilities or potentials. Such prefigurations, the undeveloped or incomplete versions of the actual utopia that might exist in the future, can be articulated correctly – Bloch says – before *Heimat* materialises fully.

Karl Marx had a different understanding of the possibility of envisioning utopia. A sharp critic of what he called *utopian socialists* and their various blueprints of the ideal society, he famously claimed that philosophers should not concern themselves with writing 'recipes' for 'the cookshop of the future'.[3] His reasoning appears somewhat convoluted and is undercut by the fact that *The Communist Manifesto*, *The German Ideology* and *The Economic-Philosophic Manuscripts of 1844* all contain clear hints as to the nature of a future communist society. Yet one critical reason why Marx opposed conceptualising the utopian society of the future is clear: he perceived it as an impossible task.

How is this difference between the two thinkers to be explained? I would argue that for Marx the object of utopian thinking is limited to the actual uto-

---

1 The German word *Heimat* is usually translated as 'home' or 'homeland'. As neither of these translations captures the word's full meaning, I will continue to use the German term. Another term that Bloch appears to use synonymously with that of *Heimat* is *Zuhause* (cf. Koch 2012, p. 178). For a discussion of the difficulties in translating *Das Prinzip Hoffnung*, including the concept of *Heimat*, see Wuilmart 1985, p. 217.
2 This phrase appears in Meillassoux's unpublished manuscript *L'Inexistence divine*; cf. Harman 2011, pp. 99–100.
3 Marx 2010c, p. 17; translation modified.

pian society of the future. For Bloch, by contrast, utopian thinking is something else: it is an attempt to envisage the potential contours of the utopian society. In other words, whereas Marx's argument is that we *cannot* say what the future *will* look like, Bloch maintains that we *can* know what it *might be* like.

Why does Bloch think so? How does he justify the idea that it is possible to envision utopia in ways that do indeed somehow resemble that future society? Why does he not think, as Marx does, that our conceptual articulations of the utopian world cannot but be rearticulations of the present one? The answers to these questions are not straightforward and depend on the perspective – that is to say, on the specific aspect of Bloch's philosophy – from which we attempt to formulate them. In the next two sections, I will address the questions on the basis of Bloch's conceptions of the human mind and of matter. In the final section, I will approach the question of the possibility of utopian thinking negatively by explaining why the actual utopian society *cannot* be known. Here, the keys lie in Bloch's philosophy of history and his notion of processual utopia.

1 The Prefigurations of Utopia in the Not-Yet-Conscious

Bloch has a highly developed conception of utopian consciousness, for which he uses the term *das Noch-Nicht-Bewußte*, or the not-yet-conscious. A marked characteristic of this not-yet-conscious is that it constitutes an *essential* part of the human psyche. Although its content depends to some extent on existing historical conditions, it invariably retains a certain independence from them and produces what truly is its own utopian content. Bloch describes this not-yet-conscious variously as 'the mental representation of what is coming up', 'the actual space of receptivity of the New and production of the New' and 'the preconsciousness of that which is coming up, the birthplace of the New'.[4] Wishing, desiring, hoping and imagining are the cognitive processes that occur within this part of the human psyche, and the contents of these processes – that is, our wishes, desires and hopes – are prefigurations or adumbrations of the utopian society.

Bloch maintains that the not-yet-conscious has so far remained 'disregarded' and 'unnoticed'.[5] This disregard – he says – has resulted in a multi-layered misunderstanding of the meaning, nature and function of the human mind.

---

4 Bloch 1977a, vol. 1, pp. 131 and 157.
5 Bloch 1977a, vol. 1, pp. 150 and 131.

He posits that for a long time in the intellectual history of the human mind it was believed that human beings were generally completely aware of their inner mental life. A breakthrough was achieved when it was discovered that this was not the case and that 'mental life does not coincide with consciousness'.[6] This breakthrough in its turn led to the discovery of the unconscious, which was assumed to consist in mental activities of which humans are not aware. It is this assumption – the idea that the unconscious is entirely subordinated to the conscious – that Bloch considers erroneous. He suggests that rather than viewing the unconscious as something that 'lies beneath consciousness and has dropped out of it', we should understand it as possessing two sides: one that is *subordinated* to the conscious – Bloch calls this side *das Nicht-Mehr-Bewußte*, or the no-longer-conscious – and another one that is *supraordinated* to the conscious.[7] The not-yet-conscious is this second side of the unconscious.

The way Bloch speaks about the misinterpretation of the human psyche is emblematic of his understanding of knowledge more generally. He considers the advancement of knowledge to be progressive, but in a specific way. His notion of progress entails the temporal structure of a continuously delayed development. Put simply, an idea never arrives as a fully formed insight, but always lacks something of that towards which it is advancing. At first, our inner life was conceived of as conscious, then also as unconscious, and now – with Bloch – this unconscious is further differentiated into the no-longer-conscious and the not-yet-conscious. Each of these categories anticipates the one that follows it: consciousness anticipates unconsciousness, and unconsciousness anticipates the no-longer-conscious and the not-yet-conscious. As Wayne Hudson notes, this temporal structure also applies to Bloch's own thought and writing.[8] Indeed, Bloch never fully answers the questions at the point at which he poses them.

Accordingly, it is more accurate to claim not that Bloch argues that the existence of the not-yet-conscious has so far been disregarded – that it has been left out of previous conceptions of the human mind altogether – but rather that it has been misunderstood. In what follows, I will explain what exactly this misunderstanding of the not-yet-conscious consists of. Specifically, I will suggest that there are two aspects to this misunderstanding: the view of the not-yet-conscious as a purely subjective sphere, and the view that it is interconnected only with the past. In fact, Bloch conceives the not-yet-conscious as an object-

---

6 Bloch 1977a, vol. 1, p. 130.
7 Ibid.
8 Hudson 2013, p. 23.

ive as well as a subjective phenomenon, and as interconnected with the future as well as with the past.

Viewing the not-yet-conscious as a purely subjective phenomenon means interpreting it as originating, advancing and terminating in the subject. It means positing the merely subjective relevance of the cognitive material produced by the not-yet-conscious. Yet according to Bloch, this – the idea that our wishes and dreams pertain only to ourselves and have no wider significance for either the people around us or humanity and indeed the world at large – is precisely the mistake. The main intellectual source of this misinterpretation identified by Bloch is Freud's theory of dreams.[9]

According to Bloch, Freud sees the main function of dreaming to be the provision of a space in which the subject both expresses and provisionally gratifies essentially unrealistic wishes or fantasies. The dream that I live by the ocean reveals to me that living by the ocean is my wish *and* it fulfils this wish, since in the dream I am living by the ocean and am, thereby, 'realising' my wish.[10] There is, of course, a difference between realising this wish in my life materially and realising it through dreaming. Bloch therefore talks about this gratification as 'hallucinated wish-fulfilments'.[11] In order for these wishes to be fulfilled, even in this non-material manner, the space in which dreaming takes place – the unconscious – must be completely removed from reality. Only then can our minds feel sufficiently secure to express these wishes, which are deemed incompatible with reality.

Although Bloch does not object to Freud's reading of nocturnal dreaming, he criticises him for not adequately distinguishing nocturnal dreaming from daytime dreaming – that is to say, for seeing the latter merely as a subcategory of the former.[12] Bloch argues instead that daytime dreams are not just a 'stepping

---

9   For an account of the influence of Freud on the genesis of Bloch's philosophy, see Schiller 2017, pp. 27–86.
10 Strictly speaking, Freud does not assume that our dreams represent our wishes in such a straightforward manner. More often than not – he says – dreams are *disguised* wishes. Suppose I have murderous feelings towards my superiors because they frustrate me. According to Freud, I would probably not dream that I kill them, but rather, say, that I kill myself, with everyone grieving over me. In order to understand what the underlying wish is, the dream would need to be analysed. In particular, what would need to be subjected to close scrutiny is what Freud calls the *dream-work*, the process by which the wish is censored and hence distorted, disguised (in my example, that process is one of displacement). See, for example, Freud 1989a.
11 Bloch 1977a, vol. 1, p. 87.
12 Bloch seems to exaggerate the degree to which Freud neglects the category of daydreaming. In some of his writings, Freud clearly distinguishes between daydreams and night dreams. See, for example, Freud 1989b.

stone' to the nocturnal ones, but rather should be analysed separately.[13] The fundamental distinction – he says – is that between the backward orientation of nocturnal dreams (remembering the past) and the forward orientation of daydreams (anticipating the future). Whereas 'night-dreams mostly cannibalise the former life of the drives ... feed on past or even archaic image-material, and nothing new happens under their bare moon', daydreams are 'forerunners and anticipation'.[14] I will return to this distinction below. A further distinction relates to the creative or productive potential of daydreams:

> In contrast to the nocturnal dream, that of the daytime sketches freely chosen and repeatable figures in the air, it can rant and rave, but also brood and plan. It gives free play to its thoughts in an indolent fashion ... [to] political, artistic, scientific thoughts. The daydream can furnish inspirations which do not require interpreting, but working out, it builds castles in the air as blueprints too, and not always just fictitious ones.[15]

Here, Bloch notes that the material engendered by our daydreaming is not merely fictitious or unrealistic. Precisely because daydreaming does not occur in the realm of the unconscious but the conscious, a link with external reality is maintained. Because during daydreaming 'the relationship to the outside world is in no way screened out', as it is in the night-dream, this type of dreaming produces wishes that are relevant to reality, realistic and capable of being fulfilled in the future.[16] In this sense, they are objective. 'What is essential to the daydream ... is the seriousness of the pre-appearance of the possibly real'.[17]

The category of the *possibly real* is one of Bloch's phrases for the objective, or realistic, ideas we have about the future. The reason why the products of daydreams indicate objective possibilities lies not just in the fact that they possess this relationship with external reality in the course of their production, but also in the fact that they are extraverted – orientated towards external reality, towards the reality outside the subject itself. That is to say, while nocturnal dreams are orientated towards themselves in that they can find their fulfilment in themselves, this is different for daytime dreams. The fulfilment of daydreams proceeds via their effects on our actions, which in their turn affect external

---

13 Bloch 1977a, vol. 1, p. 96.
14 Ibid.
15 Ibid.
16 Bloch 1977a, vol. 1, p. 102.
17 Bloch 1977a, vol. 1, p. 109.

reality. 'More than one daydream has, with sufficient vigour and experience, *remodelled* reality to make it consent'.[18] Whereas the night-dream is idle, the daydream contains a self-innervation, a tireless incentive towards the actual attainment of what it envisions.[19] In other words, the daydream is not fulfilled through its mere articulation, but through its actual fulfilment – through the modification of reality in accordance with the content of the dream.

The not-yet-conscious, then, is not merely tied to the past. It cannot be understood simply as a manifestation of what has already happened, of what has always been. This – Bloch contends – is precisely the mistake that his forerunners made, who viewed the not-yet-conscious as some sort of collection device or repository of experiences already undergone and events already completed. He traces this idea back to the early nineteenth century, above all the intellectual-artistic movement of Romanticism. Now, the Romantics – he says, singling out Byron, Shelley and Pushkin, as well as the pre-Romantics of the German 'Sturm und Drang' movement (ca. 1770–85) – were on the whole at least still ambivalent. They appear to be glorifying the past *and* the future, looking backwards *and* forwards, seeing the Golden Age as one already passed *and* still to arrive. It was only the theory of psychoanalysis, which started to emerge around 1900, that cemented the content of the not-yet-conscious as one of the past.[20] Yet Romanticism too – for all its ambiguities and complexities, its progressive character and revolutionary strands – was ultimately rooted in and attached to the past. 'In a manner hard to understand today, the Romantics fell victim to the past ... preferring to build nothing but knights' castles in the magical moonlit night'.[21]

Bloch nonetheless finds in Romanticism images of the good and the new, including even the aforementioned 'knights' castles in the magical moonlit night', and he does not condemn these images per se. In fact, he sees them as constitutive of genuinely utopian material, providing visions of something better. Romanticism possesses its own ideas of what a better world could be. The problem he sees is that 'the Romantics do not understand utopia, not even their own'.[22] Specifically, he argues that they misunderstand the location of the utopias they are envisaging. In Romanticism, utopia is viewed as belonging to the past, as a world that did exist but has passed and is now gone.

---

18 Bloch 1977a, vol. 1, p. 98. The German word that Bloch uses for 'remodelled' is *umgearbeitet*.
19 Ibid.
20 Bloch also identifies a number of genuinely conservative precursors to Freudian and Jungian psychoanalysis, such as the Catholic writer Joseph Görres (1776–1848).
21 Bloch 1977a, vol. 1, p. 152.
22 Bloch 1977a, vol. 1, p. 160.

Bloch makes this point by differentiating between the act of production and the act of reflection. The former corresponds to the creation of an artwork, the latter to the interpretation of the artwork once it has been conceived. He illustrates this difference by commenting on the German Romantic novelist Jean Paul. 'Even Jean Paul, the creator of the most beautiful wishful landscapes shimmering ahead, ultimately sought the light, as soon as he was not creating but reflecting on it, only in the past, not in the future'.[23] In other words, what is at issue is not the artistic substance, not the question of whether that substance is truly utopian, but rather the author's relation to it, or – to be even more precise – the author's relation to the act of its creation. For Jean Paul – Bloch argues – writing entailed representing the past as opposed to creating the future. Jean Paul's landscapes were – and in his mind remained – mere objects of thought, ideas on paper, without any corresponding material counterpart. One might say that the Romantics were too modest with respect to their own artistic potential: where they were in fact producing something new, they thought they were only reproducing the old. They wrongly perceived themselves as epigones, as merely following or imitating past practitioners. This is what Bloch means when he writes: 'All productivity, especially the expectation which paradoxically characterises so much of Romanticism, lost itself here in antiquarian images, in the past, in the immemorial, in myth'.[24] The new ideas that the Romantics created were deprived of their very newness because they were deemed to have been sourced from the past. And because the Romantic creation of the not-yet-conscious part of the human mind was not seen as productivity, but instead as reproduction or epigonism, something valuable was lost.

In brief, Bloch argues that the correct interpretation of the not-yet-conscious is to view it as being tied not only to the past but also to the future, and thus to recognise its productive, creative and dynamic capacities. The not-yet-conscious does not merely collect events and experiences that have already happened, but also points to events that could happen in the future.

One reason why Bloch sees the content of the not-yet-conscious as something that could yet happen, as anticipating the future, is that he does not regard the past as completed, as having occurred entirely or fully, as already having been realised according to its potential. This idea is encapsulated in one of his best-known dictums, 'S is not yet P'.[25] This sentence – which can be seen as the shortest summary of Bloch's philosophy, with S standing for 'subject' and

---

23 Bloch 1977a, vol. 1, p. 154.
24 Bloch 1977a, vol. 1, p. 153.
25 Bloch 1977d, p. 42.

P for 'predicate' – means that the subject has not yet fully become its predicate, that the two have not (yet) become identical. The predicate represents the entirety, or the full extent, of possibilities of an object or event; the subject constitutes those possibilities that were in fact realised, and hence the object or event as it actually existed.

For Bloch, the valuable function of the not-yet-conscious lies precisely in the fact that it does not store these events merely as what the subject already is, but that it can also capture them as what the subject is yet to become. In the latter act resides the productive or creative potential of the not-yet-conscious, which does not *articulate* events as they were but *rearticulates* them as they could have been. Bloch perceives the gap between what they were and what they could have been as their unrealised possibilities, or their future content. One might say that the not-yet-conscious productively *misremembers* past events by endowing them with something more than they actually were.

2   Incompleteness of the World as the Not-Yet-Become

Bloch's revision of Freudian dream theory helps us understand better why, and in what way, he opposes Marx's dismissal of wishes and desires as possible tools for social transformation. Unlike Bloch, Marx does not discuss the value of dreams and dreaming. He does, however, touch on a related cognitive capacity, which he refers to as imagination or fantasy. For example, in the first draft of *The Civil War in France*, Marx criticises the utopian socialists and their followers for trying to 'compensate for the historical conditions of the movement by fantastic pictures and plans of a new society'.[26] In other words, for Marx, fantasising is synonymous with producing ideas of a good society that cannot possibly be realised. The reason he offers to support this contention is that fantasy is not influenced by external, objective reality: it takes place within the subject itself, removed from non-subjective conditions.

In *The German Ideology*, Marx and Engels contrast their view of materialism with that of the Young Hegelians. Their own view is premised on a conception of individuals 'as they really are', by which they mean that this conception is simply the articulation of the material or objective situation of individuals.[27] In contrast, the theories of the Young Hegelians stem from a conception of individuals as they may appear in their own or other people's imagina-

---

26   Marx 1975, p. 499.
27   Marx and Engels 2010d, p. 39.

tion. In the *Poverty of Philosophy*, Marx criticises Proudhon along similar lines (albeit without employing the term 'imagination'), highlighting that Proudhon's ideas are not based on social reality but result instead solely from his mind.[28] In his own late writings, Engels codifies this view of imagination most concisely. Compared to all other existing theories of communism and socialism, his and Marx's theory of communism was not a 'concoction' engendered by means of the 'imagination' but was instead derived from observations of the external world, corresponding directly to 'an insight into the nature, the conditions and the consequent general aims of the struggle waged by the proletariat'.[29]

In fact, Marx's and Engels's view that fantasy is wholly removed from objective conditions is paradoxical: whereas in their general philosophical orientation they consider the whole of reality – including subjects and their consciousness – to be conditioned in the final instance by material circumstances, their comments on fantasising have a heavily idealistic overtone. While residing in consciousness, fantasising is nonetheless assumed to be wholly autonomous and not at all affected by objective material conditions – as if the engendered ideas somehow emerged from themselves.

Marx does not frame the relation between the objective and the subjective, between material circumstances and consciousness, in a deterministic fashion. Yet his understanding of the relationship between these categories appears less dialectical than that of Bloch.[30] Marx all too often appears to maintain some sort of separation between the object and the subject. While consciousness is both conditioned by material reality and works back on it, it nevertheless exists, in Marx's system, as something that is ultimately separate from matter.

This is different for Bloch. As Hans Heinz Holz puts it, for Bloch all 'layers of the living, the spiritual and the psychological' are grasped 'as manifestations of material nature' and, moreover, consciousness itself is 'a kind of material being'.[31] This means that mind and consciousness are themselves part of material reality. Hence, any product of consciousness – including wishes, dreams and imaginary ideas – is not a merely subjective phenomenon, but also an objective one. Bloch's term *objektive Phantasie*, or objective imagination, is a good example of the operation of his dialectical analysis of the relationship between subject and object, consciousness and matter. In this relation-

---

28   See Marx 2010a.
29   Engels 2010, p. 318.
30   Cf., for example, Marx 2010b.
31   Holz 2012, p. 485.

ship, fantasy, hope, dreams and possibility are predicated on what is objectively possible. At the same time, what is objectively possible can be changed by the way in which dreams, hopes, and fantasies are expressed and mobilised.

A helpful term to conceive of Bloch's consciousness-matter relation is *articulation* or *manifestation*: ideas, wishes, hopes and dreams are one possible manifestation of material reality. This relation, however, does not apply just to ideas and the like, but to consciousness as such. In Bloch's ontology, each individual dimension of consciousness should itself be understood as a manifestation of a certain dimension of matter, including the not-yet-conscious. Its corresponding material dimension is *das Noch-Nicht-Gewordene*, the not-yet-become.[32] The not-yet-conscious gives us access to the not-yet-become, which on its own is not directly comprehensible to human beings.

What exactly Bloch means by the not-yet-become is far from obvious. The concept implies that something that is material – in the sense of being tangible, physical and as such already existent – at the same time, by virtue of its belonging to the not-yet, does not exist. But how can this ontological non-existence hold for matter itself? Is not matter defined by its ontological existence or presence? If matter is that which really exists out there, does it not simply have to exist and be present?

The answer can be found in Bloch's distinctive view of matter. In his *Tübinger Einleitung in die Philosophie*, he puts it as follows: 'the world-substance, mundane matter itself, is not yet finished and complete, but persists in a utopian-open state, a state in which its self-identity is not yet manifest'.[33] Bloch's view of materialism is thus more complex than the basic contention that matter is simply 'the stuff that is out there'. He conceives of matter as a process, an essentially dynamic entity, rejecting conceptions of matter as *Klotz*, as a lump or lumps of inert stuff. 'Matter is moving, in that in its open possibility it is also a Being not carried out, and it is not passive like wax, but it moves itself, forming and shaping'.[34]

Bloch's conception of matter as something dynamic and creative builds on an intellectual current he refers to as Left Aristotelianism.[35] Specifically, the not-yet-become can be understood as Bloch's attempt to re-conceptualise the Aristotelian categories *dynamei on* [that which might become possible] and *kata to dynaton* [that which is possible]. These categories are not easy to under-

---

32 See, for example, Bloch 1977a, vol. 1, p. 160.
33 Bloch 1977c, p. 102.
34 Bloch 1977c, p. 234.
35 See, for example, Bloch 1977a, vol. 3, p. 1371; cf. Geoghegan 2013, p. 45.

stand, nor is it entirely transparent how Bloch converts them into his concept of the not-yet-become. The central tenet, however, is clear: matter exists in both actual and potential forms, and both forms are equally essential to what matter 'is'.

3   Processual Utopia

Bloch's position on the possibility of utopian thinking as I have outlined it so far might be summarised as follows: whereas the content of the absolute utopian society – that is to say, the one specific better society that will exist materially in the future – cannot be known in the present, the multiplicity of potential utopian societies *can* be known now. In other words, Bloch maintains that we are able to plan for the unforeseen and to map out what we think this unknown might possibly hold for us. His conceptions of human consciousness and of matter as containing the not-yet serve as justification of this position – in particular of its positive dimension, or the idea that we *can know or anticipate the future*. However, they do not fully account for the other, negative side of Bloch's position – his idea that we *cannot know the one actual utopian society*. Why are we not able to know this society? The answer lies in Bloch's idea that history is an open process, not a predetermined path, and, correspondingly, in his idea that utopia is the outcome of this open process, not the telos of a predetermined path.

According to Bloch, history is open in that each event is the outcome of conditions that could have been different: it is contingent on contingencies. Peter Thompson has therefore characterised Bloch's conception of history as being underpinned by a *metaphysics of contingency*.[36] This emphasis on contingency does not imply that these events are arbitrary, emerging from nowhere. Rather, each event is determined by everything else that preceded it.[37] This means that each event, besides being contingent, is also necessary, in the sense that it is the unique outcome of all events that have happened before it. The following example might serve as illustration. The French Revolution might not have happened, or might not have happened in the way that it did, if events preceding it had not happened. Say, Robespierre might not have been around in 1789; he could have died of a heart attack two years earlier. But precisely because he *was* there and acted in the way he did, as well as because of all the other events

---

[36] See Thompson 2012, 2013 and 2016.
[37] Cf. Thompson 2016, p. 443.

that took place, the revolution *of necessity* took the form it did. The revolution was thus at the same time contingent and necessary.

The actually existing utopian society of the future should be understood in the same manner: as the outcome of everything that happened until its emergence. This idea of utopia is implied in Bloch's most famous lines, the final passage of *The Principle of Hope*:

> [M]an everywhere is living still in prehistory. Indeed all and everything still stands before the creation of a right and proper world. *True genesis is not at the beginning but at the end* and it starts to begin only when society and existence become radical, i.e. grasp their roots. But the root of history is the labouring, creating human being who reshapes and overhauls the given. Once he has grasped himself and established what is his, without expropriation and alienation, based in real democracy, there will arise in the world something which shines into the childhood of all and in which no one has yet been: Home.[38]

The reputation of these lines does not necessarily facilitate our grasp of the passage as a whole, nor of the paradoxical claim at its heart: 'The true genesis is not at the beginning, but at the end'. Bloch changes the meaning of 'genesis', disentangling it from its Biblical meaning. In the Bible, the term designates God's creation of the world and implies merely the fulfilment of God's creativity. In Bloch, however, genesis comes as a result of a process that preceded it, namely of 'prehistory' – a Marxian term to which Bloch gives a deeper meaning: for him, it designates also the arrival of 'Home', the beginning of history. Genesis is thus paradoxically both an end and a beginning. Peter Thompson's analogy between genesis and birth shows nicely how Bloch's repurposing of this concept can make sense: 'birth comes at the end of a pregnancy, not at the beginning, even though from the first day we anticipate what the birth and the life of the new New will be like'.[39] Adopting this comparison, we can see how the true utopian society of the future, 'the new New', can be present both at the beginning and at the end at the same time: as the last phase of pregnancy, it presents the end; as the start of the life of a new human being, or at least the more independent kind of life, it presents the beginning. The essential point here is that even if the essence of the true utopian society lies in its radical difference from the entire history preceding it – the prehistory – the true utopian society cannot

---

38   Bloch 1977a, vol. 3, p. 1628.
39   Thompson 2012, p. 45.

be thought of as independent of it. The true utopian society comes into being only as the outcome of this contingent process of prehistory.

The nature of this *processual utopia* (to use Peter Thompson's phrase) becomes clear when contrasted with what might be called *teleological utopia*.[40] The latter notion implies that utopia simply needs to be realised or implemented in practice, and must therefore somehow already exist, completed and perfected, even if not in material form. In Christian thought, this idea applies to the utopia that is the Kingdom of God: it simply needs to be transferred onto Earth. The coming about of this earthly kingdom will happen by some miracle or apocalypse from outside the material world and without active human intervention. This is not the case with a processual utopia. While this utopia also already exists now, it does so only as potentiality. It is thus not fully but only partially prefigured. It will become fully formed only once it starts to be realised, which requires human action. In other words, unlike the Kingdom of God, it does not exist in some separate domain of reality but is constituent of reality itself.

Bloch's concept of utopia, then, does not have nihilistic epistemological implications: it does not imply that *nothing at all* can be known, said or foreseen about this ensuing outcome. Bloch conceives existing reality as being permeated with possibilities we can access through our not-yet-conscious, hence we do know something about the utopian future. The crucial thing is not to claim that any vision of utopian society that we posit in the present moment is identical to the society of the future. The utopian society that we can conceptualise – the point bears repeating – does *not* coincide perfectly with the society that might in fact be realised in the future. Instead, our conceptualisation of this society might best be thought of as one constitutive step in the realisation of this society, one 'new' on the way to 'the new New'.

Finally, it is worth stressing that this kind of utopian thinking – processual utopianism – is not inherently dangerous or destructive of desirable social change. The idea that positive conceptualisations of a better future are actually harmful has been put forward by, among others, Michel Foucault: 'the idea of a program of proposals is dangerous. As soon as a program is presented, it becomes a law, and there's a prohibition against inventing ... The program must be wide open'.[41] Foucault, then, views utopian thinking as consisting not just of programmes, but of programmes that eventually become or evolve into

---

40 A similar phrase – *prozeßhaft gehende Utopie* – appears in Bloch's own writings, such as his inaugural lecture at the University of Tübingen (Bloch 1977b, p. 388).
41 Foucault 1997, p. 139.

laws.[42] As a set of laws, utopian thinking is destructive because it proscribes any deviation from itself, thereby prohibiting the creation, development and invention of other, potentially even more desirable ideas of the good. But why should utopian thinking need to become law? Why should we recognise its ideas as fixed, absolute or universally valid? Once we substitute a teleological utopia with a processual utopia, utopian thinking no longer amounts to formulating programmes: it becomes something much more fluid and open. In Peter Thompson's phrase, if there is a 'plan', it is one that is 'purely contingent' in that it forever remains responsive to the contingent emergence of new circumstances.[43] This processual notion restores utopian thinking in that it does not go so far as offering a programmatic blueprint with its associated limitations and dangers. In other words, there is no claim to any true, absolute utopia. At the same time, processual utopian thinking goes beyond a mere blueprint: the contingency of its content neither restricts nor inhibits human thought and action. In fact, rather than being restricted to the realisation of absolute utopia, utopian thinking in its processual form is constructive of it. Once we adopt the notion, utopia becomes a world that 'could be there if we could only do something for it. Not simply if we travel there, but *because* we travel there the island of utopia arises out of the sea of the possible'.[44]

Bibliography

Bloch, Ernst 1977a, *Das Prinzip Hoffnung*, 3 Volumes, Frankfurt am Main: Suhrkamp.
Bloch, Ernst 1977b, 'Kann Hoffnung enttäuscht werden? Eröffnungs-Vorlesung Tübingen 1961', in *Literarische Aufsätze*, Frankfurt am Main: Suhrkamp.
Bloch, Ernst 1977c, *Tübinger Einleitung in die Philosophie*, Frankfurt am Main: Suhrkamp.
Bloch, Ernst 1977d, *Experimentum Mundi*, Frankfurt am Main: Suhrkamp.
Bloch, Ernst 1977e, 'Etwas fehlt ... Über die Widersprüche der utopischen Sehnsucht. Ein Rundfunkgespräch mit Theodor W. Adorno, 1964', in *Tendenz – Latenz – Utopie*, Frankfurt am Main: Suhrkamp.

---

42   This citation is not meant as a comprehensive representation of Foucault's stance on utopian thinking generally. In fact, Foucault considers that, especially under the circumstances of the post-war era, a viable alternative to socialism needs to be constructed and that intellectuals have a role to play in this construction (Foucault 2003). In addition, he advances the notion of *heterotopia* as an alternative to singular utopian blueprints, a notion not dissimilar to Bloch's processual utopia (Foucault 1986).
43   Thompson 2016, p. 444.
44   Bloch 1977e, p. 352.

Engels, Friedrich 2010, 'On the History of the Communist League', in *Marx and Engels Collected Works*, Volume 26, London: Lawrence & Wishart.

Foucault, Michael 1986, 'Of Other Spaces', translated by Jay Miskowiec, *Diacritics*, 16, 1: 22–7.

Foucault, Michael 1997, *Ethics: Subjectivity and Truth*, translated by Robert Hurley et al., New York: The New Press.

Foucault, Michael 2003, 'Das Wissen als Verbrechen', in *Schriften*, Volume 3, translated by Daniel Defert et al., Frankfurt am Main: Suhrkamp.

Freud, Sigmund 1989a, 'The Interpretation of Dreams', in *The Freud Reader*, translated by James Strachey et al., New York: W.W. Norton.

Freud, Sigmund 1989b, 'Creative Writing and Day-Dreaming', in *The Freud Reader*, translated by James Strachey et al., New York: W.W. Norton.

Geoghegan, Vincent 2013, 'An Anti-Humanist Utopia?', in *The Privatization of Hope: Ernst Bloch and the Future of Utopia*, edited by Peter Thompson and Slavoj Žižek, Durham: Duke University Press.

Harman, Graham 2011, *Quentin Meillassoux: Philosophy in the Making*, Edinburgh: Edinburgh University Press.

Holz, Hans Heinz 2012, 'Spekulativer Materialismus', in *Bloch-Wörterbuch: Leitbegriffe der Philosophie Ernst Blochs*, edited by Beat Dietschy, Doris Zeilinger and Rainer Zimmermann, Berlin and Boston: de Gruyter.

Koch, Gerd 2012, 'Heimat', in *Bloch-Wörterbuch: Leitbegriffe der Philosophie Ernst Blochs*, edited by Beat Dietschy, Doris Zeilinger and Rainer Zimmermann, Berlin and Boston: de Gruyter.

Marx, Karl 1975, 'The First Draft of the *Civil War in France*', in *Marx and Engels Collected Works*, Volume 22, London: Lawrence & Wishart.

Marx, Karl 2010a, *The Poverty of Philosophy*, in *Marx and Engels Collected Works*, Volume 6, London: Lawrence & Wishart.

Marx, Karl 2010b, 'Wage Labour and Capital', in *Marx and Engels Collected Works*, Volume 9, London: Lawrence & Wishart.

Marx, Karl 2010c, 'Afterward to the Second German Edition [of *Capital*]', in *Marx and Engels Collected Works*, Volume 35, London: Lawrence & Wishart.

Marx, Karl and Friedrich Engels 2010d, *The German Ideology*, in *Marx and Engels Collected Works*, Volume 5, London: Lawrence & Wishart.

Moir, Cat 2016, 'Beyond the Turn: Ernst Bloch and the Future of Speculative Materialism', *Poetics Today*, 37, 2: 327–51.

Schiller, Hans-Ernst 2017, *Freud-Kritik von Links. Bloch, Fromm, Adorno, Horkheimer, Marcuse*, Springe: Klampen Verlag.

Thompson, Peter 2012, 'What Is Concrete about Ernst Bloch's Concrete Utopia?', in *Utopia: Social Theory and the Future*, edited by Michael Hviid Jacobsen and Keith Tester, Farnham and Burlington: Ashgate.

Thompson, Peter 2013, 'Religion, Utopia and the Metaphysics of Contingency', in *The Privatization of Hope: Ernst Bloch and the Future of Utopia*, edited by Peter Thompson and Slavoj Žižek, Durham: Duke University Press.

Thompson, Peter 2016, 'Ernst Bloch and the Spirituality of Utopia', *Rethinking Marxism*, 28, 3–4: 438–52.

Wuilmart, Françoise 1985, 'Problematik beim Übersetzen von Ernst Blochs "Das Prinzip Hoffnung" ins Französische', *Bloch-Almanach*, 5: 204–22.

CHAPTER 11

Hegel, Marx, Bloch: On the Margins of the Spirit

Johan Siebers and Sam Dolbear

1   Aura, Ornament, Materialism[1]

In the Ernst-Bloch-Zentrum's reconstruction of Bloch's last Tübingen office, the room where he collapsed and died of a heart attack in August 1977, there is a copy of Hegel's *Phänomenologie des Geistes* [Phenomenology of Spirit, 1807] from 1952.[2] On a visit to Ludwigshafen in 2013, we opened this volume and discovered a large number of marginal notes. The preface above all contains a dense network of spider-like lines, marked in a spectrum of coloured pens and pencils. Between the pages were pressed pieces of pipe-tobacco, suggesting that the volume had not been opened much since Bloch had used it in 1966.[3] The markings are messy and look as if they were drawn in haste. They accumulate on the page: lines overscore lines, comments in one colour are underlined or circled in another, arrows and lines establish connections and associations with other lines and marks. The margins represent a space of effacement, qualification and clarification, but they also reveal a certain *narcotics* (a term to which we will return) of thought, writing and reading. After seeing the book, our attention was drawn to Bloch's death mask, locked in a box in a room upstairs. A similar atmosphere emanated from both artifacts, monuments to a crystallisation of gesture, of petrified unrest, now lost and solidified, visible only in this moment.

The text's image-like impression persisted for some time. This was partly a negative experience: Bloch's handwriting was notoriously messy, elongated and

---

1 Sam Dolbear first discovered the marginalia and conceived the idea of writing this text. Johan Siebers wrote the first paper on the marginalia, which was published in the *Bloch-Almanach* (Siebers 2017). We collaborated on the present chapter, retaining the mosaic, associative and spontaneous quality of the marginal notes in the fragmented character of our own text.
2 This edition of the *Phänomenologie* is that of Johannes Hoffmeister (Hegel 1952).
3 The marginalia mention a seminar of 6 July 1966, but the layers of pens and pencils on the page suggest that they were written down over a larger period of time, perhaps as early as Bloch's first lectures at Tübingen in 1961/62 and extending to his final seminars some years before his death in 1977. Bloch did not take any books with him when he left the GDR in 1961; cf. Zudeick 1985.

loose, and here even more so, perhaps because he made the notes solely for himself and at a time when his bad eyesight had deteriorated even further. They reflect the rapidity of his thoughts and gestures. At times, the pencil blunts so much the text is barely legible. This made the process of detection, decoding and transcription difficult. A host of academic and palaeographic endeavours was required: first with Frank Degler at the Ernst-Bloch-Zentrum, then with Cat Moir and finally with Klaus Kufeld. Parts of the text retained their image-like character for a long time and could be resolved only after speculation followed by a critical moment of decision. Letters occasionally had to become lines in order to become letters again. From words to letters to marks and then back to words.

The consideration of the page as an image allowed for the appearance of the margin as a space for instrumental clarification and elaboration, but also for the interplay between foreground and background, past and present, closed and open, adding a new dimension to the meaning of the text. The margin forecloses the foreclosing of the text, enlivening Hegel's words with new spirit. This spirit is auratic and sensual. It speaks of certain smells, of places where the book had once been held. The book has returned home, but to a home reconstructed in an institutional setting – an aura of displacement evoked in Walter Benjamin's 'Kleine Geschichte der Photographie' [Little History of Photography, 1931]:

> What is aura, actually? A strange weave of space and time: the unique appearance or semblance of distance, no matter how close it may be. While at rest on a summer's noon, to trace a range of mountains on the horizon, or a branch that throws its shadow on the observer, until the moment or the hour become part of their appearance – this is what it means to breathe the aura of those mountains, that branch.[4]

This copy of the *Phänomenologie* smelt – of tobacco, must, book. It was in Bloch's company that Benjamin first used the word *aura* in a text. In his 'Hauptzüge der zweiten Haschisch-Impression' [Main Features of My Second Impression of Hashish, written in 1928 but not published during his lifetime], he wrote: Bloch wanted to touch my knee gently. I could feel the contact long before it actually reached me. I felt it as a highly repugnant wound to my aura.[5] Under

---

4 Benjamin 2006, vol. 2.2, pp. 518–19. Benjamin refines this definition of aura in 'The Work of Art in the Age of Mechanical Reproducibility' (Benjamin, vol. 4, p. 255).
5 Benjamin 2004, vol. 2.1, p. 87.

the influence of hashish, all movements grow in 'intensity and intentionality',[6] which Benjamin considers impossible to handle. This comes from a particular experience of the narcotic. In his own protocol of the same drug experiment, Bloch captures this experience:

> I can transform the Goethe house into the London opera. Can read from it the whole of world history. I see, in this space, why I collect colportage images. Can see everything in this room – the sons of Richard III and what you will.[7]

Within a colportage experience of time and space, distance and proximity collapse. The mountains enter the interior, the book the archive. Aura is activated. It is unclear whether Bloch actually touched Benjamin's knee, but the violation of aura comes at a time of mutual distrust between them.[8] At certain points in their friendship, there was a porosity of exchange, a communist practice of mutual intellectual endeavour, eventually inscribed under a single authorship, which generated mutual accusations of plagiarism between both of them. When published, these industrial realities are solidified and distributed in the commodity form. But then, the margin can become a means to re-establish a porous relationship, now between absent writer and present reader, even in its commodified, congealed form. This act occurs within the generations – between, say, Bloch and his contemporaries, including Benjamin – but also between the generations, in this case between Bloch and Hegel.

At this point, the marks on the page alongside the shreds of tobacco become *ornamental*, a concept that featured prominently in the first edition of Bloch's *Geist der Utopie* [Spirit of Utopia, 1918], which Benjamin had read before meeting Bloch, a reading that would inform Benjamin's concept of *Eingedenken* [a form of remembrance which breaks through the homogeneity of time], another case of plagiarism or porosity. For Bloch, the ornament is an excess or surplus that has no place in the identity of the object or its environment, showing the object as that which it is not. He argues that the ornament is not an embellishment, but also that it cannot be interpreted as simply an element

---

6 Benjamin 2004, vol. 2.1, p. 88.
7 Cited in Benjamin 1999, p. 31.
8 This was a time of plagiarism between the two of them: after spending time together in Capri in 1924, Benjamin wrote 'Naples' with Asja Lācis, published in the *Frankfurter Zeitung* on 19 August 1925. A year later, in the same newspaper, Bloch's 'Italy and Porosity' appeared, which explored very similar themes. Later, the same happened with Benjamin's aphoristic *Einbahnstraße* [One-Way Street, 1928] and Bloch's *Spuren* [Traces, 1930].

in the self-manifestation of the object. Both views of the ornament – as embellishment and as self-manifestation – reduce it to a mere factor in the fetishised consistency of the thing. Ornament is not-yet, both too much and not enough. It is the margin of the object as it appears in its world. It carries the promises of the object, its communication to other objects, to humans and animals and to the world as a whole. Taken in this way, Bloch's marginal notes in the *Phänomenologie* express an intention with respect to the text on which they comment; they circle around the not-yet of Hegel's philosophy. In other words, they can be understood as the intention to express an aspect of Bloch's materialism that is always present but often only implicitly – and never unambiguously – acknowledged by him: the place of truth is the place unoccupied, and incapable of being occupied, by dialectics. Dialectical materialism embodies that place because it is a materialism and therefore always more than dialectical. Materialism for Bloch is, after all, that mode of thought that affirms some kind of unmediated real residue in whatever relational or ideational framework we might develop. 'Matter' is a name for that which escapes mediation by mind and hence lies outside dialectical relations, for that which is always more than what we can grasp in thought. When we hear the paradox in the term dialectical materialism, we catch a glimpse of the epistemology of the margin.

2   Library as Margin

Bloch first encountered Hegel's writings in the library of his adolescence – the palatial library in Mannheim on the other side of the Rhine from Ludwigshafen, the proletarian river port of his birth. In the library was the 'whole speculative spectrum from Leibniz to Hegel and his school',[9] the distance from school, the family, the smokestacks of the industrial port. Philosophy grounded in homesickness turns material here: the shelter that is the library is a shelter from the outside world. The promise to return home, as with the call to return to a childhood that never was, as evoked in the final pages of *Das Prinzip Hoffnung* [The Principle of Hope, 1954–9], is located in home's negation, when it is left on the other side of the river. Displacement was a permanent feature of Bloch's life: he found refuge along lines connecting Switzerland, Italy, Prague, Paris, the United States (New York and Cambridge, Massachusetts), Leipzig and Tübingen. On his journeys into various forms of exile, his library was lost many times

---

9   Traub and Wieser 1975, p. 29.

– an enduring reminder of destruction and precarity, of a both material and spiritual homelessness. It followed him around everywhere.

When Bloch eventually settles late in life, in Tübingen, he does so with what he described as a *Kutscherbibliothek*, a cabbie's library.[10] He left behind the carefully cultivated scholar's library, built up in sedentary circumstances over a lifetime of study, as much as the bourgeois book collection 'still in glorious binding [*Prachteinband*]'.[11] The cabbie's library, though encrusted with jewels, is marked by the traces of transgression and displacement. It is a migratory and always preliminary collection in which what is missing is perhaps even more present than what is there. The library itself is marked by the marginality of the incidental and accidental. But this *neben-bei*, the 'alongside' of the collection, becomes the moment of illumination, the light shone on a childhood that never was, the discovery of a marginal life as a place of truth. This is a process of discovery *into* the margin. In the end, you do not want it any other way.

And then, when Bloch sits down with this late 1952 edition of the *Phänomenologie*, sometime around 1966, he discovers the margin again, the experience of his generation's life, of his thought, returning in a new moment of displacement. In this sense, the marginal notes can be understood as a late work: in the reading and marking of an early text that shone through childhood, in the home away from home that was Bloch's first library – where he 'misunderstood and yet understood' the text, reading it 'erotically, botanically', as he heard the nightingale singing in its pages.[12] At this point, late in life, he returns to the margins and finds the promise of a cab ride – of momentum, liberation and openness, of what he came to formulate as materialism. Marx understood the materiality of his age. Bloch marks out these moments in his late reading of Hegel (as it appears in the margins we are considering here) the traces of a journey, a stagecoach of the spirit (this time on the margins), both digressive and transgressive. But, for Bloch, in contrast to Hegel, it is a journey whose destination is not yet known, a journey of history, not just of ideas that unfold themselves in a pregiven logical realm. In Bloch, the dialectic jolts and jumps; in Hegel, it proceeds along a path mapped out for all eternity. The margin is the place of the new, of dialectical advance. The materiality of this book, which Bloch held in his hands, is emblematic of his philosophical relation to Hegel, of Bloch's discovery of the openness in the dialectic – always a hotel, never a home.

10	Zudeick 1987, p. 363.
11	Bloch 1965, p. 18.
12	Traub and Wieser 1975, p. 29.

3 Hotel as Residency

On the eleventh page of his edition of the *Phänomenologie*, Bloch wrote 'hotel' in the margin. At least, we think, or hope, this is the word. This notation is underlined twice, but the context gives little indication as to what he might have had in mind. He noted down: 'The specific difference of a thing is rather its limit; it is where the thing stops'. The remark echoes the classical metaphysical notion of the degrees of being. Each finite entity that can be defined by a proximate genus and specific difference is a limitation of being conceived of as a pure act, which itself cannot be contained in a genus, specific difference or category, as it ranges across and over all of them. Every finite being is a stage, a point on the journey to absolute being or, in Hegel, the actualisation of absolute spirit.

But why *hotel*? Hotel, perhaps, as a transient and transgressive space on the journey of the spirit. The place of rest, but the rest of a temporary intermission of travel. A hotel is a place of sojourn. The hotel simulates the home as a lost object and may put us in touch with the awareness that we never actually possessed what now appears to us as lost. The object as such is constituted by its lack, a kind of *surplus enjoyment* – expressed also through the pencil markings themselves, both in their colour and frozen gesture.[13]

The hotel may also take the form of the 'Grand Hotel Abyss', Georg Lukács's metaphor for Schopenhauer's (and later for Adorno's) philosophy as sitting on the edge of groundlessness, an 'off-ground', in the refined comfort of private enjoyment on the edge of catastrophe.[14] The hotel is a refuge from the world, but only as a simulation, like the palatial Mannheim library; it curiously gives with one hand what it takes with the other. A hotel can give us a closer approximation of home than anywhere else, and yet we are always expelled from it. Are not arrival and departure in dialectical relation, both suspended in an uncanny moment of rest in which sounds cease to travel beyond themselves and we are *in* the world but no longer *of* the world? For Bloch, the hotel is a real symbol, like the bridge, the mountain or the correspondence between the deep blue of the sea and the deep blue of the sky, the reflection into each other of deep and high. In the same way, the hotel can provide a mythical retreat, a world away from the world.

---

13 Cf. Muñoz 2019 for the relation between gesture and Bloch's conception of historical anticipation. The 'upright gait' is gestural in its semantics, perhaps flowing and preliminary in its anticipatory character, and certainly not a march into an already given future.

14 Bloch refers to Lukács's 1952 evocation of the 'Grand Hotel Abyss' in Bloch 1985b, vol. 4, p. 390.

During this time, a time of generational displacement, the hotel became the residence of exiled life. Walter Benjamin's address book, used from 1933 until his death, is testament to this: names are crossed out, hotel rooms recorded – rooms which the occupant has probably already vacated.[15] In this instance, the hotel is a simulation of home where the violence of the world is guarded against, if only temporarily.

This was our first understanding of the notation. For the word 'hotel' also seems remarkably out of context. We take our immediate response as itself a marginal note, a thought that occurred in the interstices of the gap between foreground and background that provides the framing of our reading of these marginalia; a thought for which the practice of transcription provided only temporary lodgings.

4   Hegel's Denial of the Margin

Hegel's philosophy is a philosophy without margins.[16] Just think of the dialectical cancellation of the introduction performed in the very text we are here considering. Where there are moments in the development of the spirit that as yet remain unmediated, they will in due course be taken up into the movement of the unfolding of the concept. Indeed, the beginning of the preface to the *Phänomenologie* explicitly reflects on the impossibility of providing an introduction to philosophy, because philosophy as speculative reason has no outside from which we might watch it run its course and decide to jump in or not.[17] The speculative proposition holds together articulation and unity in a permanent, paradoxical buzzing of the living spirit, a 'sharp pizzicato' as Bloch says about the dialectic of being and nothingness at the beginning of Hegel's *Logik*, so that there exists no outside to thought in the end.[18] Indeed, the dialectic between internal and external, spirit and nature, underlies the whole movement of Hegel's thought, ultimately affirming the identity of the

---

15   Cf. Fischer-Defoy 2006.
16   See Derrida's *Margins of Philosophy* for an alternative, poststructuralist, account of the margins of thought (Derrida 1982). Whereas for Derrida the margin is a space of permanent displacement of signification, for Bloch the margin is the space of the not-yet and the new, the pre-figuration of utopia. The new embodies a relation to the ultimate for Bloch, for otherwise novelty would reduce to the sameness of mere variety. On the now largely historical relation between Bloch's philosophy and postmodernism, see Owen and Moyland (eds.) 1997.
17   Cf. Williams 2019.
18   Bloch 1962b, p. 165.

two, of identity and difference. Nothing remains outside of thought as the realisation of the concrete universal. Hegel's philosophy is thus properly speaking without context: it evacuates itself from every contextuality and contextualisation because it is concerned to think this single obliging thought – that the true is the whole.

Bloch was especially sensitive to the problems this created with respect to negation, the negative and also the satanic as the obstructing dimension of reality. For Hegel, negation is either a straightforward element in the dialectical process, albeit with different functions, or something that drops out of the history of the spirit and is mere chaff, mere issueless nothingness. Human tragedies and immense suffering are sometimes rather casually dismissed by Hegel as of no function in the history of the spirit and therefore ultimately meaningless. We might say that if there is room for a margin, a contingency that does not become necessity, it is to be found here. Bloch often refers to Hegel's view of the Thirty Years' War as pure negativity that had no sublated afterlife, that led to nothing.[19] One cannot even use the word *example* here, for of what universal could we say that this event was a mere instance? Pure nothingness is not a concept.[20] We miss something if we think of the singularity of suffering and destruction in this way. The critical reception that began with the Left Hegelians, Feuerbach, Kierkegaard and indeed Marx was continued into the twentieth century along these lines: the concrete, irreducible entity or individual becomes an unmediated and invisible other to this way of thinking.

As Bloch puts it in the first edition of *Geist der Utopie*, we must not forget Kant over Hegel: 'Kant burns through'.[21] It is regrettable that much of the contemporary reception of Hegel in both analytical and Continental schools of thought has little time (or little understanding) of this dynamic and seeks to avoid or suppress it by decapitating Hegel – that is to say, by eliminating the speculative proposition from its interpretation of Hegel. In this way, we achieve the worst of two worlds: the spirit becomes naturalised or socialised as the concrete historical manifestation of reason, while the radical, revolutionary dynamic that results from Hegel's absolute universalism is removed. We end up with a recipe for a stifling, ignorantly gloating conservatism that

---

19 See, for example, Bloch 1975, pp. 230–8.
20 We refer here to the classical view of this matter since Plato: we cannot form a positive conception of pure nothingness, precisely because it is nothing.
21 Bloch uses the verb *durchbrennen* in its double meaning of 'burn through' (Kant's thing-in-itself burns through the logical web of Hegel's dialectic; it cannot be mediated by that web) and 'run away', 'elope' (Kant's regulative idea always transcends the world as it is given). In other words, there is an aspect of Kant that survives after Hegel and in a way remains untouched by Hegel's philosophy.

reminds us of the worst of Hegel's own flirtations with the state. Such a reading of Hegel reverts to a kind of Feuerbachian bourgeois thought in which the human being, while conceptualised in its concrete individuality, is not seen as embodied and engaged in transgressive development, but merely as individual subjective consciousness. The interpretation of Hegel becomes *liberal*, in the sense of seeking to cure the ailments of the state by returning to the bourgeois subject and ascribing a transcendent status to it. To this entire symptomatic complex, the turn to materialism had once been the antidote. For our purposes, we suggest that it is precisely the philosophical relevance of materialism that becomes apparent in the status of the marginalia.

What do Bloch's markings reveal? In their materiality, they reveal the materiality of the text, the words on the page. We skip over them all too easily, seeing the physical copy of the text as precisely that – a copy of an ideal score that has an existence outside space and time even if we can trace its origin to certain historical occurrences (Hegel writing the text and so on). We overlook the fact that it is only because of the blank page that words can be put down at all. The marginalia occupy the margins of the printed text, highlighting the background – the blank page – against which the words of the text can be foregrounded. Marginalia occupy the region between foreground and background, bringing them to our attention as something that cannot go, and has not gone, into the text and yet makes that text possible. A form of 'negativity' becomes palpable, one that is given with the material form of the text and which turns out to be a universal feature of all forms of meaningful utterance; the letter has a material embodiment. Yet the relation between background and foreground is not a dialectical one. There is no resolution of one into the other, and there is no higher synthesis in which they both become moments of a totality. The object, the book here in front of us, is no dialectical totality of background and foreground, but a play of one against the other in which both remain what they are even if they cannot be separated from one another. By inscribing itself into the margin of the text, a note illuminates what must escape all attempts at a conceptual recuperation: the material process itself.

Bloch himself struggles with this dimension. In his version of dialectical materialism, he tries to combine the preponderance of unity and resolution with the irreducibility of interruption in the process. But he is never unambiguous, often suggesting that the interruption of the materially unison, the foundation of spirit, is ultimately at one with the material process. The basic question of what the space is within which matter can be cut or interrupted, torn apart, receives no answer. Yet here, in the marginal notes to Hegel's text, which Bloch had read so often and for so long, the awareness of the intractable that signals truth is visible on the page. The markings appear like drawings and as such they express – as Jean-Luc Nancy suggests – how we are drawn out and sketched out by lines we draw:

> To exist is to sketch oneself [*s'esquisser*]. One would like to write *s'exquisser* – to open oneself to a form which shows itself in the movement of its uprising [*surgissement*]. No one would consent to live if they did not experience this desire – to open oneself to the desire of (letting oneself) being drawn to the outside.[22]

We have here a dialectical materialism of the margin.

Bloch shows his awareness of the materiality of the text in the lectures on Hegel that he held in Leipzig between 1948 and 1956. There, he discusses various editions of Hegel's works, concluding that while modern scholarship is useful and necessary, it is only the 'old edition', published by the Verein der Freunde des Verewigten [Society of Friends of the Immortalised One], that has history and patina and that is marked out by contemporaneity, *viva vox*, the living voice of the professor. With respect to the modern editions, he says that 'too many cooks spoil the broth'.[23] We can add friends and not just cooks to the spoiling. What stands out is the singularity, the localisation of a form of thought that seems itself to accord no truth value to the historical specificity of mere circumstance. Yet, for Bloch, these contextual dimensions are essential if we wish to understand what Hegel's philosophy has to say to us and had to say to others. Bloch's verdict in *Subjekt-Objekt* – 'Hegel repudiated the future, [but] no future will repudiate Hegel'[24] – is here enacted in the discussion of the afterlife of the texts. Even the eternalised subject is determined by the time and space of actuality. It would be wrong to say that the eternalised subject *cannot exist in a vacuum*, for the context or background we spoke of is by metaphorical extension a kind of vacuum within which something can exist as foregrounded. Hence, everything exists in a vacuum to some extent. It would thus be better to say that Hegel's *horror vacui* was so great that he sought to eliminate it completely.

---

22 Nancy 2013, p. xiii.
23 Bloch 1985b, vol. 4, p. 269.
24 Bloch 1962b, p. 12.

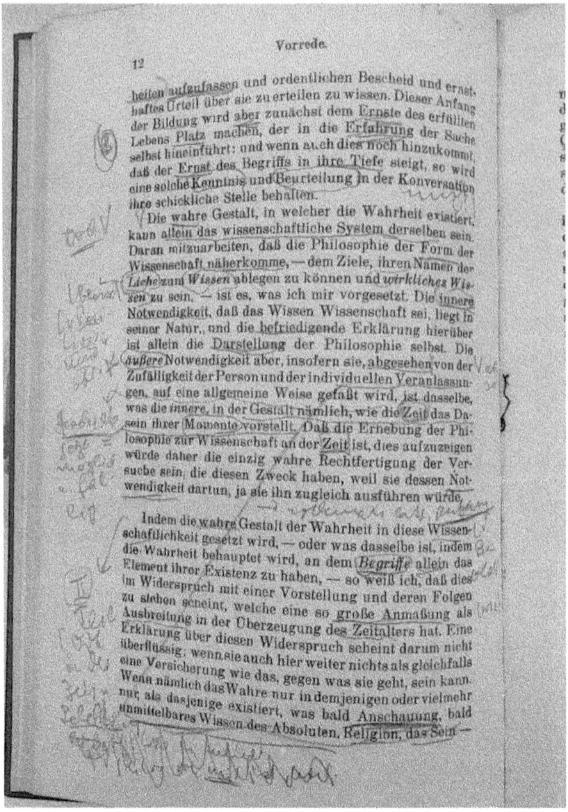

12 Vorrede.

heiten aufzufassen und ordentlichen Bescheid und ernsthaftes Urteil über sie zu erteilen zu wissen. Dieser Anfang der Bildung wird aber zunächst dem Ernste des erfüllten Lebens Platz machen, der in die Erfahrung der Sache selbst hineinführt: und wenn auch dies noch hinzukommt, daß der Ernst des Begriffs in ihre Tiefe steigt, so wird eine solche Kenntnis und Beurteilung in der Konversation ihre schickliche Stelle behalten.

Die wahre Gestalt, in welcher die Wahrheit existiert, kann allein das wissenschaftliche System derselben sein. Daran mitzuarbeiten, daß die Philosophie der Form der Wissenschaft näherkomme, — dem Ziele, ihren Namen der *Liebe* zum *Wissen* ablegen zu können und *wirkliches Wissen* zu sein, — ist es, was ich mir vorgesetzt. Die innere Notwendigkeit, daß das Wissen Wissenschaft sei, liegt in seiner Natur, und die befriedigende Erklärung hierüber ist allein die Darstellung der Philosophie selbst. Die *äußere* Notwendigkeit aber, insofern sie, abgesehen von der Zufälligkeit der Person und der individuellen Veranlassungen, auf eine allgemeine Weise gefaßt wird, ist dasselbe, was die *innere*, in der Gestalt nämlich, wie die Zeit das Dasein ihrer Momente vorstellt. Daß die Erhebung der Philosophie zur Wissenschaft an der Zeit ist, dies aufzuzeigen würde daher die einzig wahre Rechtfertigung der Versuche sein, die diesen Zweck haben, weil sie dessen Notwendigkeit dartun, ja sie ihn zugleich ausführen würde.

Indem die wahre Gestalt der Wahrheit in diese Wissenschaftlichkeit gesetzt wird, — oder was dasselbe ist, indem die Wahrheit behauptet wird, an dem *Begriffe* allein das Element ihrer Existenz zu haben, — so weiß ich, daß dies im Widerspruch mit einer Vorstellung und deren Folgen zu stehen scheint, welche eine so große Anmaßung als Ausbreitung in der Überzeugung des Zeitalters hat. Eine Erklärung über diesen Widerspruch scheint darum nicht überflüssig; wenn sie auch hier weiter nichts als gleichfalls eine Versicherung wie das, gegen was sie geht, sein kann. Wenn nämlich das Wahre nur in demjenigen oder vielmehr nur als dasjenige existiert, was bald Anschauung, bald unmittelbares Wissen des Absoluten, Religion, das Sein —

FIGURE 11.1
Bloch marginalia I

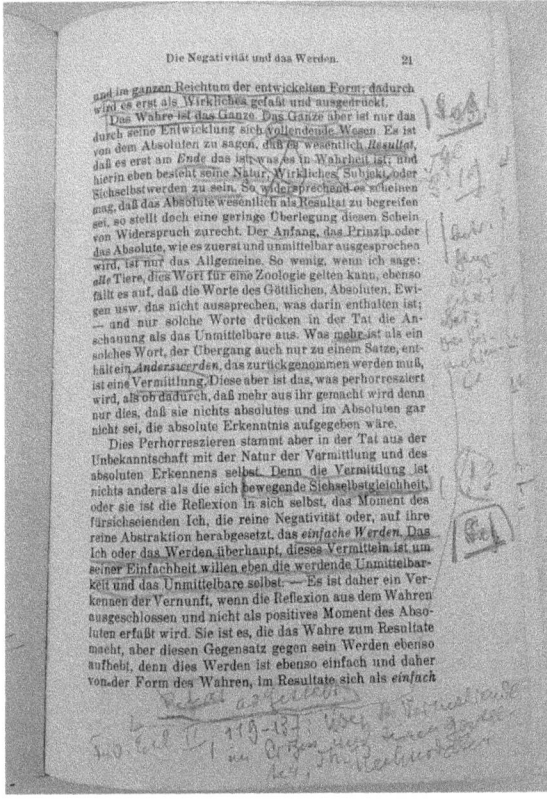

FIGURE 11.2
Bloch marginalia II

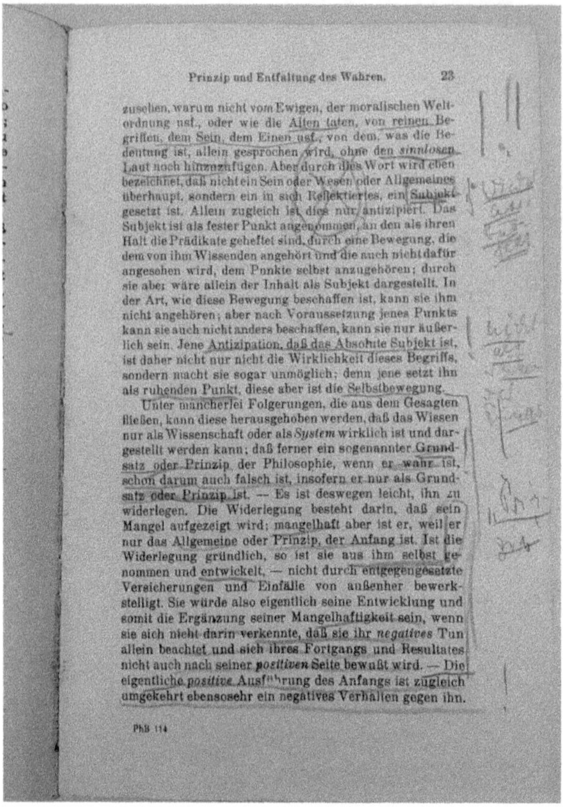

Prinzip und Entfaltung des Wahren. 23

zusehen, warum nicht vom Ewigen, der moralischen Weltordnung usf., oder wie die Alten taten, von reinen Begriffen, dem Sein, dem Einen usf., von dem, was die Bedeutung ist, allein gesprochen wird, ohne den *sinnlosen* Laut noch hinzuzufügen. Aber durch dies Wort wird eben bezeichnet, daß nicht ein Sein oder Wesen oder Allgemeines überhaupt, sondern ein in sich Reflektiertes, ein Subjekt gesetzt ist. Allein zugleich ist dies nur antizipiert. Das Subjekt ist als fester Punkt angenommen, an den als ihren Halt die Prädikate geheftet sind, durch eine Bewegung, die dem von ihm Wissenden angehört und die auch nicht dafür angesehen wird, dem Punkte selbst anzugehören; durch sie aber wäre allein der Inhalt als Subjekt dargestellt. In der Art, wie diese Bewegung beschaffen ist, kann sie ihm nicht angehören; aber nach Voraussetzung jenes Punkts kann sie auch nicht anders beschaffen, kann sie nur äußerlich sein. Jene Antizipation, daß das Absolute Subjekt ist, ist daher nicht nur nicht die Wirklichkeit dieses Begriffs, sondern macht sie sogar unmöglich; denn jene setzt ihn als ruhenden Punkt, diese aber ist die Selbstbewegung.

Unter mancherlei Folgerungen, die aus dem Gesagten fließen, kann diese herausgehoben werden, daß das Wissen nur als Wissenschaft oder als *System* wirklich ist und dargestellt werden kann; daß ferner ein sogenannter Grundsatz oder Prinzip der Philosophie, wenn er wahr ist, schon darum auch falsch ist, insofern er nur als Grundsatz oder Prinzip ist. — Es ist deswegen leicht, ihn zu widerlegen. Die Widerlegung besteht darin, daß sein Mangel aufgezeigt wird; mangelhaft aber ist er, weil er nur das Allgemeine oder Prinzip, der Anfang ist. Ist die Widerlegung gründlich, so ist sie aus ihm selbst genommen und entwickelt, — nicht durch entgegengesetzte Versicherungen und Einfälle von außenher bewerkstelligt. Sie würde also eigentlich seine Entwicklung und somit die Ergänzung seiner Mangelhaftigkeit sein, wenn sie sich nicht darin verkennte, daß sie ihr *negatives* Tun allein beachtet und sich ihres Fortgangs und Resultates nicht auch nach seiner *positiven* Seite bewußt wird. — Die eigentliche *positive* Ausführung des Anfangs ist zugleich umgekehrt ebensosehr ein negatives Verhalten gegen ihn.

PhB 114

FIGURE 11.3
Bloch marginalia III

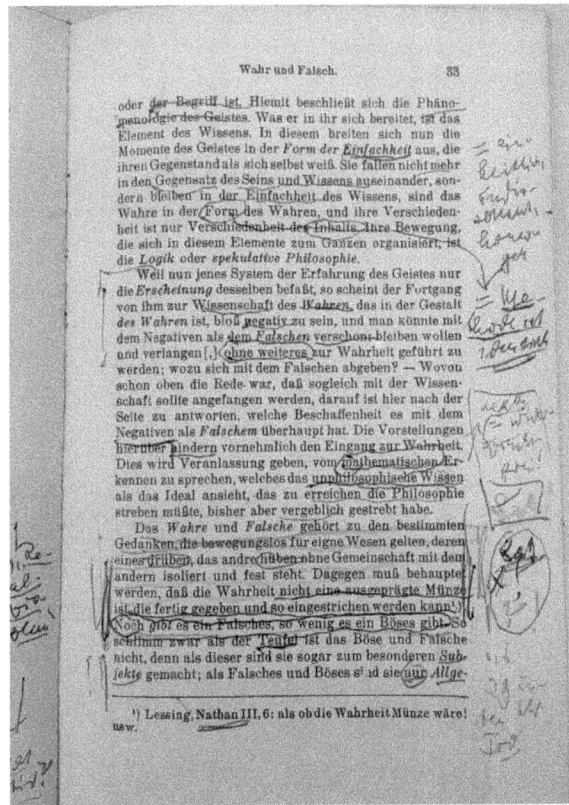

FIGURE 11.4
Bloch marginalia IV

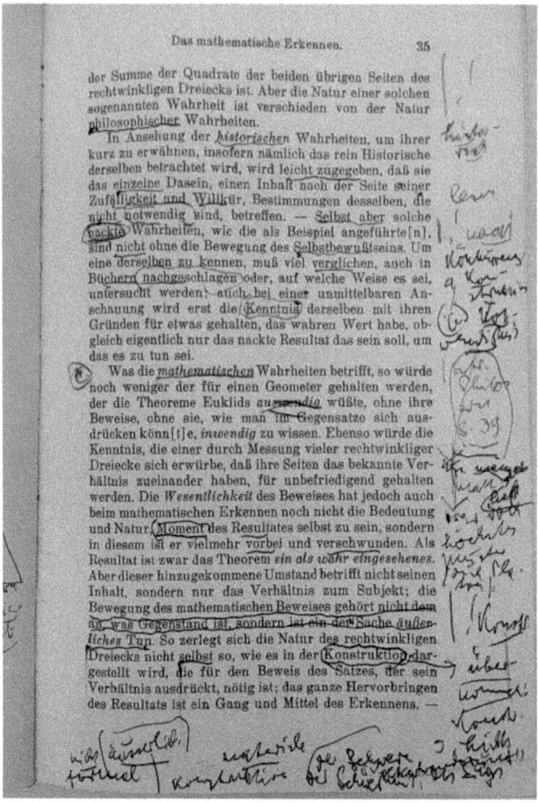

Das mathematische Erkennen. 35

der Summe der Quadrate der beiden übrigen Seiten des rechtwinkligen Dreiecks ist. Aber die Natur einer solchen sogenannten Wahrheit ist verschieden von der Natur philosophischer Wahrheiten.

In Ansehung der *historischen* Wahrheiten, um ihrer kurz zu erwähnen, insofern nämlich das rein Historische derselben betrachtet wird, wird leicht zugegeben, daß sie das einzelne Dasein, einen Inhalt nach der Seite seiner Zufälligkeit und Willkür, Bestimmungen desselben, die nicht notwendig sind, betreffen. — Selbst aber solche nackte Wahrheiten, wie die als Beispiel angeführte[n], sind nicht ohne die Bewegung des Selbstbewußtseins. Um eine derselben zu kennen, muß viel verglichen, auch in Büchern nachgeschlagen oder, auf welche Weise es sei, untersucht werden; auch bei einer unmittelbaren Anschauung wird erst die Kenntnis derselben mit ihren Gründen für etwas gehalten, das wahren Wert habe, obgleich eigentlich nur das nackte Resultat das sein soll, um das es zu tun sei.

Was die *mathematischen* Wahrheiten betrifft, so würde noch weniger der für einen Geometer gehalten werden, der die Theoreme Euklids *auswendig* wüßte, ohne ihre Beweise, ohne sie, wie man im Gegensatze sich ausdrücken könn[t]e, *inwendig* zu wissen. Ebenso würde die Kenntnis, die einer durch Messung vieler rechtwinkliger Dreiecke sich erwürbe, daß ihre Seiten das bekannte Verhältnis zueinander haben, für unbefriedigend gehalten werden. Die *Wesentlichkeit* des Beweises hat jedoch auch beim mathematischen Erkennen noch nicht die Bedeutung und Natur, Moment des Resultates selbst zu sein, sondern in diesem ist er vielmehr vorbei und verschwunden. Als Resultat ist zwar das Theorem *ein als wahr eingesehenes*. Aber dieser hinzugekommene Umstand betrifft nicht seinen Inhalt, sondern nur das Verhältnis zum Subjekt; die Bewegung des mathematischen Beweises gehört nicht dem an, was Gegenstand ist, sondern ist ein der Sache *äußerliches* Tun. So zerlegt sich die Natur des rechtwinkligen Dreiecks nicht selbst so, wie es in der Konstruktion dargestellt wird, die für den Beweis des Satzes, der sein Verhältnis ausdrückt, nötig ist; das ganze Hervorbringen des Resultats ist ein Gang und Mittel des Erkennens. —

FIGURE 11.5
Bloch marginalia v

5 Bloch's Place in Hegel's Margin

After Hegel's *Enzyklopädie* was published in 1817, he ordered a volume with blank pages inserted between the printed sheets.[25] On these blank pages he would write a parallel text that eventually worked itself into the second edition of the *Enzyklopädie*, which appeared in 1827. In this case, the page had become the margin; space intended for elaboration became the text itself. As a stage in the completion of thought, the margin lists what is yet to be incorporated into the movement of thinking itself. In Hegel's attempt to raise the margin to the level of a blank page we find the attempt to eliminate the distinction between printed text and notebook as well as a blindness to the ontological and epistemological status of the margin. How does Bloch occupy the margin of the spirit, the site that for Hegel's self-understanding remains invisible?

Hegel's *Vorrede*, or preface, to the *Phänomenologie* famously opens with the acknowledgement that the traditional form of the preface masks the inability of philosophy to begin to speak [*-rede*] from a predetermined [*Vor-*] standpoint. There can be no didacticism in philosophy because any universally transparent starting point has to emerge from the process of philosophical thinking itself. Though the positivist might be able to summarise arguments, state the aims and conclusions of the work, the outcome can appear as nothing but 'a string of random assertions and assurances'.[26] You cannot place yourself outside it to watch it run its course. Philosophy starts in the place where the 'I' is now. This means that the 'we' constituted by an authorial voice and a readership cannot be presupposed; it must forever remain abstract, distinct from the individual act of reading or writing which affords a beginning act of reflection. Hence, the *Vorrede* acknowledges its ability to not yet speak; Hegel's philosophy, despite its mobilisation of the principle of negation, is from the start a massive, solid, if intellectual, activism without cracks. Truth, Hegel says, does not appear like a ready-minted coin and is not shot out of a pistol like a bullet[27] – but these avowals of thought's processual nature are in tension with the impossibility of occupying anything but centre stage when we begin to think. In other words, there is ultimately no room for marginalia in Hegel's philosophy; yet until the moment of philosophy's completion, marginalia can be understood as entirely necessary. The marginal comments, the sidelong glances, are only ciphers of what remains to be incorporated into the march of the concept. After all, a completed system has no room for marginalia. Until you get to that

---

25   See Brinkmann and Dahlstrom 2010, p. ix.
26   Hegel 1952, p. 9.
27   Hegel 1952, pp. 26 and 33.

point, the marginalia are necessary sites where the work of producing the system can be carried out. As the work of philosophy proceeds, the margins are being eliminated. They slowly reduce until there is nothing left to incorporate into the system. The insertion of blank pages becomes the deferral of philosophy's beginning, the acknowledgement that the subject matter itself is not yet immediately comprehensible to either the writer or the reader.[28]

The blank page is the moment in which deferral is further grounded as a new starting point, or, in Bloch's terms, as the opening up of a new world. This would be a reading of Hegel's empty pages on Hegelian terms. The typography of philosophy parallels the unfolding of *its* logic. A defining feature of Bloch's materialist rethinking of Hegel's logic involves the recognition that the empty page, the margin, that which is not or not yet part of the system – the sphere of contingency as such – is a necessary condition for the process of actualisation or, in Bloch's terminology, for 'the actualisation of the actualising [*die Realisierung des Realisierenden*]'.[29] Only in the interplay between blank page and printed letter can the text materialise. The margin as a writeable plane refers to the background-foreground structure of experience. An experienced content always stands out against a background that remains implicit but without which explicit thematic experience could not take place. This dimension of experience is missing from Hegel's philosophy. Focusing our attention on the margins of this philosophy, on its hidden and ignored background, renders palpable that which remains resistant to inclusion in the system. This allows Bloch to 'rescue' the dialectic in his dialectical materialism, for the background promise of the dialectic is much more even than what Hegel held the explicit content of the dialect of the concept to be. The utopian redemption of the world appears in the backlight of the explicit, ignorant, absolute idealist dialectical movement – its condition of possibility – and shows this movement as a sleepwalker through history, unaware of the sign it carries on its forehead even as it dreams of absolute truth. This sign is the trace of the utopian; we find it in a number of instances in the margins of the *Phänomenologie*. The margin as the text's unconscious remains unthought and yet constitutes a utopian trace. Hegel's obliviousness to the background is, *ex negativo*, his truth moment as a trace, the child-like expectation that all can be said, that the whole can be embraced, as an image of utopia.

Bloch, then, takes a very different approach than does Marx with his inversion of Hegel's dialectic. Bloch offers the possibility of saving something that

---

28 Cf. Hegel 1952, p. 26.
29 Bloch 1975, p. 241.

cannot be incorporated into the dialectic. That is to say, whereas Marx tries to put something straight, Bloch – in a more complex move – seeks to rescue an insight that remains implicit in Hegel but that is necessary both for the correct interpretation of Hegel's and for Bloch's own philosophy.

At this point, the margin again becomes an auratic space. Here lurks danger. A halo of untouchability and uniqueness surrounds the material object and denies it its reproducibility. One should not overlook the playfulness in the marginalia – nor the playfulness in our text, which seeks to add more marginalia onto these margins. If Benjamin, when taking hashish with Bloch, had seen better that the aura is a margin – and hence a marker of contextuality and a cognitive, perhaps even an aesthetic, principle – he might have experienced his friend's closeness in a different way – namely, as forever assigned to its own space on the margins of his own writing. There would have been no threat. By the same token, our reading of the marginalia is not meant to issue in an auratic elevation of the margin. We should be happy to remain in the wings.

Bloch uses the margins of the *Phänomenologie* to insert his own anticipatory philosophy as a comment on Hegel's philosophy while also transcending that philosophy. There are a large number of references to anticipation, to modelling, to the 'real models' of his *Tübinger Einleitung in die Philosophie* and specifically to his lecture 'Über das Vermehrende im Prozeß und seinen Gestalten' [On Augmenting in Process and Its Shapes].[30] Indeed, Bloch often emphasised that the utopian kernel in the world tends to be found in the accidental, the sideline. His *Spuren* is full of such intimations of the incidental:

> More and more appears among us to the side. One should observe precisely the little things, go after them. What is slight and odd often leads the furthest.[31]

There, Bloch argues that certain things can only be thought about in the form of a story. They are too delicate and indirect, or too concrete and embodied, to survive the attempt at conceptualisation and theorisation. This idea can be extended to the note in the margin. The core of the utopian process – which Bloch variously called the darkness of the lived moment, the inconstruable question, the invariant of direction and latency – resists conceptualisation. Yet it can flash up in the non-dialectical space between background and foreground.

---

30 Cf. Bloch 1970.
31 Bloch 2006, p. 5.

6   Graphic Margins

When preparing the manuscript of *Die deutsche Ideologie* [The German Ideology, written 1845–6, but only published in 1932], Marx and Engels developed a formal technique of collaboration. They folded large sheets so that each sheet of manuscript could hold four pages of writing.[32] As Terrell Carver observes, the process of construction was fairly elaborate:

> These sheets were actually offcuts, notes to be used later in other versions: Hence Marx's numbering was most probably an ordering device to keep track of loose pages. These pages had been set aside for copy/paste usage at the time of extraction, because Marx and Engels were rewriting the critiques of Bauer and Stirner as 'fair copy'. Possibly, they were saving these offcuts for further re-use piecemeal in future polemical critiques as circumstances arose – always at this time a complex web of political ambitions, publisher prospects, and financial backing. Their marginal notes from somewhat later on in 1846 suggest that they had any number of interests and subjects on their minds as they – for reasons we cannot adequately determine – looked over their previous thoughts. Feuerbach is mentioned there, but he is not the only subject of interest.[33]

The book that is now *The German Ideology* was once the margins of something else. Marx and Engels wrote in the other's margins. In Terrell Carver's and Daniel Blank's words, the manuscript of *The German Ideology* reveals 'what can be learned about the thinking of Marx and Engels as they worked' rather than answering 'doctrinal' questions concerning their 'final ... thought'.[34] As for Bloch, the margins become a demonstrative space of incompletion. Displaying the construction of the manuscript renders visible the collaboration as a process of construction within the margins. As Terrell Carver argues, the publication of the manuscript of *The German Ideology* leads to the identification of two separate authorial hands effaced by the single 'typography of the ... volume'.[35] *Text-Schichten*, or layers of text, accumulate on the page, page upon page, margin upon margin. As with Bloch's marginalia, writing is crossed out, negated, emphasised, augmented. One sees the *process* of writing, its enjoyment, frus-

---

32   See Carver and Blank 2014, p. 2.
33   Carver 2019, p. 146.
34   Carver and Blank 2014, p. 1.
35   Carver 2019, p. 146.

FIGURE 11.6
Engels's sketch of Max Stirner

FIGURE 11.7
Second sketch of Max Stirner

trations, openness and truncations. The process of reading and writing creates *Spielraum* in the double sense of that word – room for manoeuvre and play space. On one page, in the chapter on Feuerbach, a large number of doodles appear on the right-hand column of the page. There are faces of people, lambs, dogs and masks. There are shapes and words. There are people upon people, so much so that faces and eyes become blurred. On another page, there is what looks like an archer, upside down, transcribed like a constellation in the night's sky. On another, one finds an orchid-like flower in a geometric form. There are half-moons and squares and circles. The doodle presents the movement of the blank page: it is a mark of the inadequacies of the blank page, the necessity to overcome it. To doodle is to work into boredom and beyond. Engels is the likely author of these sketches, perhaps practicing for his caricatures of Max Stirner, 'Saint Max' as he is called in *The German Ideology*.[36]

7   History's Place

The defacement or destruction of the book is referred to in a remark from the first edition of *Geist der Utopie*. In the section entitled 'On the Metaphysics of Inwardness', expanded and retitled 'On the Metaphysics of Our Darkness' in the

---

36   Cf. Derrida 1994.

1923 edition, Bloch follows Schelling: human existence, he contends, begins in the blind spot of the moment, which remains invisible because it is 'too near', 'lived in' [*gelebt*] but not experienced [*erlebt*].[37] The reader is grounded in the darkness of the lived moment, its distance from itself. The book, like its writer, refuses to make peace with the world.[38] '[*D*]*as innere Buch* [*ist*] *letzthin weder Welt noch überhaupt ein Buch* [the inner book is ultimately neither the world nor a book at all]'.[39] The openness of the world – the possibility of the elimination of suffering and exploitation, or the hope that the world could become home, a dwelling place for all that exists – is contained in the margins: in that which cannot yet be read, detected, deciphered, understood. There, we find a free space, away from the annexation of things by the relations in which they are caught up. By denying the completeness of the book, Bloch simultaneously affirms the incompleteness of the world – and this very incompleteness is our only ground for hope. Hegel, 'the gravedigger', wrenches everything inward to the outside, which is the 'regrettable achievement of an explicitly concluded system'.[40] In the 1923 edition of *Geist der Utopie*, Bloch states:

> ... the solution at least can sediment itself essentially in no book and just as little in an earthly church as in any kind of philosophy which would remain to be studied, if we finally constitute the correctly understood question as absolutely serious, which, when once it has occurred to us, signifies nothing less than the ineluctable end of this world, with all its books, churches, systems.[41]

As the margins and the traces of reading deface the book, they point beyond the text to an outside that remains incommensurable with the act of writing as well as with the act of reading what has already been written.

In her essay 'Benjamin's Endgame', Rebecca Comay has analysed the relation between the blank and history. For Comay, the blank represents the interruption of catastrophic and homogeneous time:

> Hegel, observing the 'slaughter-bench' of Spirit's progress, comments that, in the chronicle of history, periods of happiness are like 'blank pages [*leere Blätter*]', blank in the sense of an utter absence of determination

---

37 Cf. Hudson 1982, p. 26.
38 Bloch 1962a, p. 247.
39 Bloch 1985a, p. 289.
40 Bloch 1985a, p. 179.
41 Bloch 1962a, p. 249.

– historicity – of the past. He calls these blanks holidays in that the interval or spacing of the blank, the condition of the possibility of the blank, the gap or fissure – *Sprung* – which ruptures the catastrophic continuity of tradition, exposing this as the merely factual continuity of hereditary power lines, thus revealing a jagged foothold for a new beginning.[42]

Just like storytelling, historical materialism explodes the 'cosmic clock' of progressive history. The blank page or the margin is the 'dispersing by endlessly rewriting what can be told'.[43] Just like history, the manuscript is told and retold, the past exploding into actuality. This is the sustaining hope of the palimpsest philosopher. In Bloch's marginalia, the philosophy of anticipatory consciousness and anticipatory history inscribes itself into the blanks of Hegel's philosophy, where – to revert to Bloch's youthful botanical reading of the *Phänomenologie* – it found the soil from which to spring. On page 32 of the marginalia, Bloch writes: '"Conclusion" of – Phän. d. Geistes, as a book. And then? Not contemplative?'. And again, on page 58, with words taken from the Gettysburg Address: 'Tolling bell of the philosophies = something thus far not emphasised in this way comes forward, at its hour, as principle and will – in its concept as in its praxis – no longer perish from the world!'. The margins are the moment of enjoyment, the excess of reading, when reading is no longer the end – but history is.

Bibliography

Benjamin, Walter 1999, *On Hashish*, translated by Howard Eiland et al., Cambridge, Mass. and London: The Belknapp Press.
Benjamin, Walter 2006, *Selected Writings*, 4 Volumes, translated by Edmund Jephcott et al., Cambridge, Mass. and London: The Belknapp Press.
Bloch, Ernst 1962a [1921], *Geist der Utopie*, Frankfurt am Main: Suhrkamp.
Bloch, Ernst 1962b [1951], *Subjekt-Objekt. Erläuterungen zu Hegel*, slightly enlarged ed. Frankfurt am Main: Suhrkamp.
Bloch, Ernst 1965, *Literarische Aufsätze*, Frankfurt am Main: Suhrkamp.
Bloch, Ernst 1970, *Tübinger Einleitung in die Philosophie*, Frankfurt am Main: Suhrkamp.
Bloch, Ernst 1975, *Experimentum Mundi. Frage, Kategorien des Herausbringens, Praxis*, Frankfurt am Main: Suhrkamp.

---

42 Comay 1994, pp. 268–9.
43 Comay 1994, p. 269.

Bloch, Ernst 1985a, *Geist der Utopie. Erste Fassung: Faksimile der Ausgabe von 1918*, Frankfurt am Main: Suhrkamp.

Bloch, Ernst 1985b, *Leipziger Vorlesungen zur Geschichte der Philosophie 1950–1956*, 4 Volumes, Frankfurt am Main: Suhrkamp.

Bloch, Ernst 2006 [1930], *Traces*, translated by Anthony Nassar, Stanford: Stanford University Press.

Brinkmann, Klaus and Daniel Dahlstrom 2010, 'Introduction', in Georg Wilhelm Friedrich Hegel, *Encyclopedia of the Philosophical Sciences in Basic Outline*, translated by Klaus Brinkmann and Daniel Dahlstrom, Cambridge: Cambridge University Press.

Carver, Terrell 2019, 'Whose Hand is the Last Hand? The New MEGA Edition of *The German Ideology*', *New Political Science*, 41, 1: 140–8.

Carver, Terrell and Daniel Blank 2104, *Marx and Engels's German Ideology Manuscripts*, London: Palgrave Macmillan.

Comay, Rebecca 1994, 'Benjamin's Endgame', in *Walter Benjamin's Philosophy: Destruction and Experience*, edited by Andrew Benjamin and Peter Osborne, London: Routledge.

Derrida, Jacques 1982 [1972], *Margins of Philosophy*, translated by Alan Bass, Chicago: University of Chicago Press.

Derrida, Jacques 1994 [1993], *Spectres of Marx: The State of the Debt, the Work of Mourning, and the New International*, translated by Peggy Kamuf, London and New York: Routledge.

Fischer-Defoy, Christine 2006, *Das Adressbuch des Exils, 1933–1940*, Leipzig: Koehler & Amelang.

Hegel, Georg Wilhelm Friedrich 1952 [1807], *Phänomenologie des Geistes*, Hamburg: Meiner.

Hudson, Wayne 1982, *The Marxist Philosophy of Ernst Bloch*, London: Palgrave.

Muñoz, José Esteban 2019 [2009], *Cruising Utopia: The Then and There of Queer Futurity*, 2nd ed., New York: NYU Press.

Nancy, Jean-Luc 2013, *The Pleasure in Drawing*, translated by Philip Armstrong, New York: Fordham University Press.

Owen, Jamie and Tom Moyland (eds.) 1997, *Not-Yet: Reconsidering Ernst Bloch*, London: Verso.

Siebers, Johann 2017, 'Das "Merke" des Lesens: Blochs Randbemerkungen zur Vorrede der *Phänomenologie des Geistes*', *Bloch-Almanach*, 34: 263–74.

Traub, Werner and Harald Wieser (eds.) 1975, *Gespräche mit Ernst Bloch*, Frankfurt am Main: Suhrkamp.

Williams, Seán 2019, *Pretexts for Writing: German Romantic Prefaces, Literature, and Philosophy*, New Brunswick, NJ: Rutgers University Press.

Zudeick, Peter 1987, *Der Hintern des Teufels. Ernst Bloch – Leben und Werk*, Moos: Elster.

CHAPTER 12

Something's Missing: Bloch's Unfinished Project of Humanity

Peter Thompson

1   Introduction

If ideology is part of zoology, as Destutt de Tracy had it, then the ideology of utopia is quite clearly part of the human project.[1] Is it possible to imagine humanity without the drive, the ideological impetus and the desire for utopia as part of the move towards a new horizon? It is in that sense that this chapter deals with what Jürgen Habermas has called *the unfinished project of modernity*: by addressing it in the context of Ernst Bloch's contention that the human animal itself is an unfinished essence. It asks, with Eric Santner, whether the 'subject-matter' that makes the human being more than the sum of its parts is in any way as complete as its biological evolution would seem to be.[2] Indeed, perhaps even humanity's biological journey is unfinished. Trotsky, for example, famously saw communism as the force that would create a higher socio-biological type, while Günther Anders's influential *Die Antiquiertheit des Menschen* [The Obsolescence of Man] posited the antiquated nature of homo sapiens in an increasingly mechanised and automated world.[3] Today's discussions surrounding transhumanism, as well as the emergence of various types of cybernetic brain-machine interface, raise the issue with even greater urgency. The nature of humanity appears to be such that it continuously produces (the search for) a utopian surplus. This chapter is an attempt to discern the philosophical, social and psychological underpinnings of Bloch's view of this unfinished project that is the human species.

---

1 'L'idéologie est une partie de la zoologie' (Destutt de Tracy 1804, p. xiii).
2 Cf. Santner 2016, p. 23.
3 See Trotsky 2005, especially pp. 262–3, and Anders 1956; cf. Gray 2011 and Groys and Hagemeister (eds.) 2005.

2   The Human Becoming

Bloch transforms Kant's question 'what is the human being?' into 'what is the human becoming?'.[4] This new question does not start with the assumption of a fixed human essence, but posits the historically variable nature of the human animal. What Bloch calls the *not-yet* includes not only that which is external to human consciousness with its supposedly unchanging categories, but also human consciousness itself. It therefore stretches beyond any project that human beings set themselves in any given epoch. According to this particular adaptation of Hegel, any attempts to understand human behaviour must take its autopoietic nature into account. Modernity is thus not simply a project that has to be 'finished', not simply a pregiven endpoint that now has to be reached fully, but merely one of the branch lines that human development has taken.

Bloch's concept of *Ungleichzeitigkeit* [non-synchronicity], which I will discuss in detail further below, can likewise be used to show that no period is ever truly finished, over and done with. Any given point in human history contains within it both retrospective appeals to previous periods and anticipations of that which may lie ahead. Given that we are never able fully to comprehend the moment in which we are living, the present is really only ever comprised of past and future elements. Indeed, one might go further and argue that the present as such does not even exist.

The question is how we implement these past and future elements in an ideological sense. One only has to look at political movements to see the ways in which past and future continue to have decisive power over concerns of the present. In order to 'Make America Great Again', for example, it is necessary to possess an image of how it used to be. Factually, of course, both the image of the past and that of the future are as opaque and open to interpretation as is the present. People are therefore tempted to take what (they believe) has empirically emerged from the process and make an inevitability out of it. Hence the view that America should 'remain', or 'become again', a white Christian nation. For dogmatists everywhere, humanity's evolution will always tend towards necessity and inevitability, as with Stalinism's iron wheel of history, fascism's racial superiority or theologies of divine predestination. Each of these dogmatic approaches claims some sort of Gnostic awareness, of which the 'unawake' must forever remain oblivious.

In Bloch, by contrast, there is nothing but the contingency of the process. The process has no outside, no external determining force. It is the process itself

---

4   Bloch 1977, p. 173.

that moves in mysterious ways. Hegel uses the image of the mole in this context: 'Spirit often seems to have forgotten and lost itself, but, inwardly opposed to itself, it is inwardly working ever forward (as when Hamlet says of the ghost of his father, "Well done, old mole!") until, grown strong in itself, it bursts asunder the crust of earth which divided it from the sun, its concept [*Begriff*], so that the earth crumbles away'.[5] Slavoj Žižek, for his part, turns Hegel's mole into a Kraken, slumbering in the deeps, ready to awaken at any point, but occupying an undetermined, quasi-rhizomatic non-space.[6] Bloch himself famously applies this idea – the multi-layered movement of history with its slow tectonic shifts which can lead to seismic changes – in his analysis of fascism, notably in *Heritage of Our Times*.

This raises the question of how we are able to stand outside any given moment in history and to make a judgement about how we have arrived at that point and how we understand it in ideological terms. As we saw earlier, Bloch uses Hegel against Kant to argue that it is not a question of human beings' ability to stand outside their own nature in order to make a judgement about that nature, but that human beings are an integral part of that which is being judged. The not-yet in Bloch is thus not simply a description of external conditions that are not yet ready for a fully human society. Rather, it implies that the human itself is not yet ready either to comprehend or to become what it is. As the Automobile Association puts it in more prosaic terms, 'you are not stuck in traffic, you are traffic'. What this means is that we must be aware of the radical contingency of our own position and of the thoughts emanating from it. To see history as an unfinished and under-determined process enables us both to recognise our own position within it and to stand at least at its margins, if not outside it.

The not-yet is the seemingly simple and yet highly complex centre of Bloch's philosophy. What is often overlooked is that Bloch also believes that evolution itself, or at least the evolution of the human capacity to implement utopia, is *not yet* fully developed. For him, the development of the human species is intrinsically bound up with the search for utopia. Here, it is important to realise – the point bears repeating – that for Bloch both the evolutionary development of human beings and their concept of utopia are not characterised by a teleological dimension. There is no more a fixed and pre-existing endpoint to how human beings will develop through the process of social and biological evolution than there is a fixed and pre-existing endpoint to the sort of soci-

---

5 Hegel 1995, vol. 3., pp. 546–7; translation modified. The allusion is to *Hamlet*, 1.5.170.
6 Cf. Žižek 2016.

ety human beings will eventually reach. The outcome of any development in human society is a complex mixture of tendency, latency and anticipation.[7] Surplus human consciousness – what Bloch calls the *principle of hope*[8] – has continued to develop beyond our merely biological needs. It is out of this surplus that utopian thinking is created.

The problem is that modernity – based as it is on an essentially republican secularism – has abolished, or at least defamed, the very idea of metaphysical transcendence. Where once gods and kings ruled as worldly and transcendent surpluses, society after the French Revolution was increasingly left to its own human devices. Yet the demand for these transcendent surpluses remained even after the irrational base for them had been cut away. Hyper-rationalism and other forms of reductionist thinking do not provide us access to this surplus. The question that Bloch poses is: how is it possible to maintain the belief in a transcendence of that which exists (an immanent transcendence) without postulating the transcendent (a religious or otherwise supernatural transcendence)?

The unfinished project of modernity, then, is at the same time the unfinished project of humanity. This will be the case until modernity gives way to the full realisation of human potential. To put it differently, modernity is not just about liberal humanism and rationalist discourse; rather, it has to be completed by a social revolution that puts humanity and human concerns at the centre. Modernity and humanity cannot be completed as long as they are not allowed to go beyond the confines of liberal capitalism. This means that in order to complete the project of modernity we have to develop an anticipatory consciousness of that which might be possible, regardless of how impossible things seem. (We should not forget that Bloch was a Jewish communist writing under and fleeing fascism). Bloch calls such future possibilities 'utopia', and the drive towards it the 'spirit of utopia'. Utopian thinking offers the possibility of maintaining a sense of enchantment in the face of universal disenchantment.

Within the human species, there is – Bloch says – an 'invariant of direction' underpinned by a latent desire to move beyond hunger towards 'freedom' and by a tendency to search constantly for ways to achieve it, be it in the form of private and limited ontic utopian futures or in the form of a conscious and collective ontological utopia. For Bloch, such a utopia is *concrete*. His use of this term is often misunderstood. He takes the term from Hegel, who used its Latin basis to distinguish it from its opposite, the abstract.[9] Con-

---

7 Cf. Bloch 1977.
8 See, for example, Bloch 1975, p. 30, and Traub and Wieser (eds.) 1975, p. 263.
9 Cf. Hegel 1966.

crete in this sense is a *con crescere*, a growing together of disparate elements in a gradual sense. Accordingly, concrete utopia is the gradual and processual emergence of the utopian out of the given in ways which are unpredictable and yet shaped by the process itself. As Bloch puts it, 'processus cum figuris, figurae in processu [the process is made by those who are made in the process]'.[10] By the same token, *abstract* becomes the opposite of what we usually mean by this term. Abstraction, or *abstrahieren*, means to abstract an individual example from the ontological process and to see it as a reified object. In this way, and not for the first time, language itself is turned on its head by Hegel and Bloch in order to emphasise the unfinished and ongoing nature of modernity.

In many ways, not least his reliance on Hegel and Marx, Ernst Bloch is one of the preeminent philosophers of modernity. Yet, paradoxically, his modern way of philosophising is underpinned by a commitment to what we would normally see as pre-modern and metaphysical thought. Bloch reaches back to Greek philosophy (Aristotle), early Islam (Avicenna) and pre-modern expressions of communism (Münzer), all of which emerge out of a metaphysical world view underpinned by essentially materialist viewpoints. He does not do so out of an unconscious dependence on the philosophical tradition nor out of mere convenience. Rather, he is consciously seeking to learn from, exploit, update and recast the future-orientated insights of past times. In his view, these essentially metaphysical expressions of materialist needs (the ideology in zoology) driving us towards utopia emerged out of the essentially *ungleichzeitig* nature of historical development and the limitations placed upon it by material conditions. A utopia cannot be constructed out of conditions that are not yet possible, yet the desire for it remains a relatively constant invariant of direction throughout human history – and for us today, the historical expressions of that desire are both an inspiration and a source of knowledge.

Bloch's use of these various sources makes it clear that he is convinced that religion, or at least metaphysical belief, has played and continues to play an in many ways positive role in the development of humanity. Metaphysical belief is not some kind of 'junk DNA' that needs to be jettisoned for modernity to be fully realised, but rather a self-misunderstood apprehension of what is necessary in order to be able to complete the unfinished project of humanity. Hence, Bloch searches within the works of thinkers such as Aristotle, Avicenna and Münzer not simply for that which can be rescued for the onward journey, but also for those elements that can be seen to contain as yet unrealisable outcomes. Just

---

10   Bloch 1977, p. 171.

as history can only set itself tasks for which there are already solutions, so it produces thinkers who – however obscure their ideas may be – have begun to think about those very solutions.

It is here that we can see the crucial importance of Hegel for Bloch. Both thinkers seek to create a totalising system of thought in which, at the same time, there can be no limitations on totality. Totality itself is an unfinished project. Bloch views himself as taking up Hegel's historical analysis by transforming it into an open processual dynamic in which the idea of 'the end of history' has to be rejected in favour of an essential historical openness. Indeed, Žižek argues that already the traditional interpretation of Hegel as a thinker of a pre-given totality is a misunderstanding of that thinker's project. Hegel – he says – developed an open dynamic: when Hegel speaks of 'the end of history', he merely speaks of the point at which history has come to an end in the present. It is an endpoint but not an ending. In *Disparities*, Žižek maintains that Hegel's dialectics is a theory of modernity and that the Kraken awakes precisely at the tipping point between tradition and modernity.[11]

On this reading, the only major difference between Hegel and Bloch is that the latter is prepared to think history further, even if only in terms of his not-yet. This is why Žižek states in the preface to *The Privatization of Hope: Ernst Bloch and the Future of Utopia*: '[Bloch] remains our contemporary, and maybe he belongs even more to our time than to his own'.[12] Similarly, in the introduction to *Absolute Recoil*, which seeks to develop a new foundation of dialectical materialism, Žižek reminds us of Lenin's point that, in order to understand a materialist conception of the world, it is necessary for materialism itself to become part of its own project and therefore to become malleable. This, too, is an essentially Blochian approach: Bloch also claims that Marxism demands a constant revision of its own natural-philosophical base in order to be generally applicable.

According to Žižek, Hegel reaches this point with his concept of 'absolute recoil', whereby a thing emerges out of its own loss.[13] More specifically, the loss of a concept is the precondition for its re-emergence in reality, but in a reified, fetishistic and metaphysical form. In Žižek's own Lacanian terminology, what emerges from this process is the 'objet petit a' that both *stands in for* and *is* the non-existent big A. By contrast, the standard view of Hegel follows a much more reductive model, which is referred to in the *Stanford Encyclopaedia of*

---

11   Cf. Žižek 2016, p. 3.
12   Žižek 2013, p. xx.
13   Žižek 2014, p. 27. The German phrase is *absoluter Gegenstoß*; di Giovanni's translation has 'absolute counter-repelling' (Hegel 2015, p. 348).

Philosophy: '[Hegel] is perhaps most well-known for his teleological account of history, an account that was later taken over by Marx and "inverted" into a materialist theory of an historical development culminating in communism'.[14] Bloch and Žižek challenge this still widely accepted view of Hegel as a teleological thinker, while also showing how this misunderstanding of Hegel leads to a misunderstanding by those thinkers who came after him and adapted his ideas. This has affected particularly the development of Marxism and the Marxist movement. Many of Bloch's best-known concepts – say, the principle of hope, non-synchronicity, concrete utopia and *Heimat* – are directed precisely against such reductionism: they contain within them a processual dimension which amounts to what he calls an *open system*. With this open system, we discover a series of dialectical paradoxes, such as non-finitude without infinity, transcendence without the transcendent, and the noumenal without a noumenon. Bloch's transcendental realm exists purely as an ontology of not-yet-being, of an integral incompleteness in being itself, in which becoming becomes the central operator.

Bloch considers Hegel to be the philosopher for whom becoming was of central importance. Thus, he states in *Subjekt-Objekt*, his extended study of Hegelian philosophy: 'From the very beginning, Becoming was the password that Hegel used'.[15] At the same time, the study is critical of Hegel's essentially idealist framework, which – Bloch says – needs to be corrected by a Marxist inversion. That is to say, it needs to be sublated into materialism. Yet Bloch is equally critical of this 'sublation' within the dominant Marxist tradition from the late nineteenth century onwards. In his view, Marxism had developed into what he calls *Klotzmaterialismus*, or vulgar and mechanistic materialism, in which the 'cold stream' of socio-economic analysis had driven out the 'warm stream' of the human desire for freedom from material and intellectual need. This vulgar materialist conception of economic determinism went hand in hand with an equally vulgar historical determinism in which communism was seen as the natural and inevitable outcome of history. In Stalinism, this became the 'iron wheel' which simply had to grind on, regardless of the short-term costs. As the Party was considered to be the only social organ that understood this inevitability, it 'was always right', as in the SED's *Die Partei hat immer Recht*.[16]

14 Redding 2020.
15 Bloch 1971, p. 226.
16 The SED's official party song ('*Sie hat uns alles gegeben* ... / *Was wir sind, sind wir durch sie* [The Party has given us everything ... / What we are, we are because of the Party]' and so on) was and is best known for the first line of the chorus, '*Die Partei, die Partei, die hat immer Recht*'. Žižek quotes this line – ironically, of course – in the dedication in *Less Than Nothing* (Žižek 2012).

3 The Dialectics of Contingency: From Chance to Necessity and Beyond

Bloch – as we have seen – effects a double negation, a negation both of the original Hegelian metaphysical conception of *becoming* and of its vulgar materialist adaptation in Marxism.[17] On this view, there is no iron necessity to historical development. But neither is history a series of pure coincidences. What appears to be the arbitrary emergence of a particular event or set of conditions always has a back story. This is Bloch's dialectics of contingency. History is a non-synchronous and non-teleological – and in this sense 'open' – process in which that which actually occurs is prompted by and reflects events from both the past and future. It is therefore simplistic to believe that any historical phenomenon can simply be dismissed as a thing of the past, as if all that is needed were negation, not sublation. Hence Bloch's approach to religion, which I touched upon earlier: rather than denigrating the role of religion in society, he seeks to understand how religion became one of the means by which human beings attempt to find answers to unanswerable questions. Moreover, the way in which we try to understand historical phenomena is itself non-synchronous. We constantly search backwards and forwards in time both to remembered past events – even to the extent that we invent past events in order to provide us with answers – and to anticipated future events, lending our thoughts a utopian or messianic edge. I would contend that the twentieth century, in particular, was centrally concerned with such proleptic and analeptic utopian and messianic messages, as humanity moved firmly into the realm of an (at least in the Western world) increasingly secular modernity.

It follows from all this that there is a retrospective dimension to meaning. As Žižek puts it in his Lacanian terminology, in the process of sublation the vanished mediator returns in such a way that 'there is a moment of contingency in every emergence of meaning'.[18] That is so say, it is not the case that a specific contingent event is carried into the future on a fully conscious layer of meaning. Rather, when a contingent event emerges, its meaning has to be reconstituted from a historical process of which it is itself largely unaware. What looks like mere chance – 'it came out of nowhere' – is actually the result of specific conditions that are forgotten or ignored. All too often, religious (mis-)understanding then steps in: meaning is fully handed over to the process, and the process

---

[17] It is this that leads Bloch to describe himself as 'not a non-Marxist', just as Marx, after reading the economic theories of some French Marxists, famously declared that if that kind of thinking was Marxism, he was not a Marxist.

[18] Žižek 2014, p. 21.

becomes a religious one. This is the idea behind the belief that 'God moves in mysterious ways'. In this view of history, there is no human meaning to be adduced. Indeed, in the more orthodox versions of Christianity the search for any underlying or causative meaning is blasphemous in that it questions God's actions.[19]

The challenge we are faced with, then, is not that we are constantly dealing with the arbitrary nature of an emergent reality, but rather that the process of emergence itself is not conscious and therefore needs, in order to be able to emerge properly, to develop a self-conscious narrative of its own necessity. The dialectic of contingency is thus the interplay of chance and necessity, with necessity being only redeemed at a later juncture. In order for me to have been born, it was necessary for all previous generations of my family to have come together in the way that they did. However, there is no substantive necessity for all those previous generations to have come about in the first place. This means that the dialectic of contingency is one in which we find unnecessary necessity working together with necessary un-necessity (another term for contingency and process).

Expanding this principle out into human evolution as a whole may make this paradox slightly clearer. The interaction within and between species emergence forms the basis of an unnecessary evolutionary dynamic. Any species that emerges from evolution does so in a way determined by the process itself. As Marx puts it in the introduction to the *Grundrisse*: 'Human anatomy contains a key to the anatomy of the ape. The intimations of higher development among the subordinate animal species, however, can be understood only after the higher development is already known'.[20] In other words, the development of any species can only be known retrospectively. There is no point in looking into the anatomy of 'lower' species for what might come next. However, evolution is not necessarily a smooth transition and development of one form into another, but proceeds by what we might call *dialectical disruption*. Traditionally, this has been seen as the transformation [*Umschlagen*] of quantity into quality.

This tipping point is the juncture where subject and substance come briefly into alignment. Of course, as Hegel, Bloch and Žižek all point out, there is no distinct difference between subject and substance, the one being entirely enmeshed with the other within the dialectic. This enmeshing only becomes visible at particular – usually revolutionary – moments. This is why revolutions

---

19 Hence Job's explicit refusal to blame God for his misery: 'the Lord gave, and the Lord hath taken away, blessed be the name of the Lord' (Job 1:21).
20 Marx 1973, p. 105.

form such an important background to the works of Hegel (1789), Bloch (1917) and Žižek (1989 and ?). Revolutions are the point at which contingency produces a disruptive rather than a stabilising narrative. Only revolution and love can have such disruptive and productive effects. As Wordsworth famously put it, and as Hegel undoubtedly felt: 'Bliss was it in that dawn to be alive / but to be young was very heaven! – Oh! Times / in which the meagre, stale, the forbidding ways / of custom, law and statute, took at once / the attraction of a country in romance!'[21]

Wordsworth's 'times' are precisely the point at which contingent events emerge out of, and put a new complexion on, that which already exists, as it were. It is the point at which Aristotle's *kata to dynaton* [that which is possible] changes over qualitatively into *dynamei on* [that which may become possible]. In other words, subject becomes substance, if only for a fleeting moment, inevitably to be disappointed and re-sundered. The impossibility of taking hold of and maintaining the surplus created by revolutionary *élan* means that, given that real transformation is not yet possible, the spirit of utopia becomes transmuted into its own spectre. Each revolution is dominated and ultimately haunted and undermined by this *spectre of utopia*, so that all that is left behind is fidelity – not to the greater utopian ideal, but to the pragmatic accommodation with that which has emerged (in either its Stalinist or liberal forms). What has haunted Europe since 1848 is precisely this spectre of utopia – an unfulfilled and yet continuing desire for something that is missing.

However, as Žižek reminds us: 'the subject does not come first – it emerges through the self-alienation of the substance. In other words, while we have no direct access to the substantial pre-subjective Real, we also cannot get rid of it'.[22] Revolution is the moment in which the 'meagre, stale, the forbidding ways' take on 'the attraction of a country in romance'. In modernity, revolution transforms what would have been a religious phenomenon – the belief in God's mysterious ways – into romantic love. Yet revolutionary developments still retain a quasi-religious dimension, which is then reified into the worship of revolutionary iconography in which the subject is transformed back into substance, as the Real of revolutionary transformation refuses to emerge fully.

Bloch has a quasi-mathematical formula for this revolutionary and emotional transformation: 'S is not yet P; the Subject is not yet Predicate'.[23] In couching the matter in these terms, he is re-inscribing the transitional and processual dynamic into the relationship between subject and substance (or subject and

---

21   Wordsworth 1970, p. 196.
22   Žižek 2014, p. 29.
23   Bloch 1970, p. 219.

object, as he puts in his book on Hegel). What prevents S from becoming P is only a question of time and appropriate conditions. Yet what emerges out of these pre-existing real conditions – the dialectics of contingency tell us – is a *contingent* reality. This contingent reality then works back on the real conditions, creating historical movement. Hence, the not-yet between the S and the P is more important than either the S or the P, both of which will themselves be transformed, either retrospectively in the case of the subject or proleptically in the case of the predicate. The very invisibility of the not-yet, its motivating negativity, becomes the force that will take us from an unfixed S to an unfixed P. Žižek arrives at a remarkably similar conclusion when he states that 'the subject ... is a predicate-becoming-subject, the passive screen asserting itself as a first principle, i.e., something posited which retroactively posits its presuppositions'.[24]

Viewed from this perspective, contingency – the active yet unconscious process of emergence of the predicate-becoming-subject – is both a foreshadowing of Aristotle's *dynamei on* [that which may become possible] and a retrospective view of his *kata to dynaton* [that which is possible]. Bloch is so important in this context because he foregrounds this blind spot between the two forms of possibility, calling it the *Dunkel des gelebten Augenblicks*, or the darkness of the lived moment. Indeed, the last book he published during his lifetime – *Experimentum Mundi* – is a full-length treatment of this inaccessible gap between S and P.[25]

This darkness becomes the motivating force behind change because it contains within it an anticipatory consciousness that separates us from all other species. To be human is to anticipate a different future. At the same time, it means to carry false memories of the past, memories that are bent and shaped into the form that is required. As Nietzsche famously said, in the battle between memory and pride, pride tends to be the winner.[26] The German word for 'remember', *sich erinnern*, can be broken down as *sich er-innern*, the internalisation and hypostatisation of a process into an image. Memory construction is thus part of the construction of history and – together with the anticipation of the future – aids the metaphysical dimension of human past and human future. The resulting metaphysics is, as I will show below, a *materialist metaphysics*.

It is at this point that Bloch warns us against the danger of Platonic anamnesis, of looking backwards in order to recover ideas from the past so as to

---

24 Žižek 2014, p. 29.
25 See Bloch 1977.
26 Cf. Nietzsche 1966, p. 80.

mobilise them in an unquestioning fashion for the future. Anamnesis has the appearance of being forward looking but is in fact dogmatically wedded to the supposed certainties of the past. Plato asks how we are to know what it is that we do not know. His answer is that we can rely on past experience in order to project ourselves into the future. Bloch, by contrast, asks us to trust our anticipatory unconscious, which knows that something has to be better than that which exists, but does not yet know what that thing might be. We might have an inkling of this from our past, but it is not a past that is correctly and accurately remembered. It is, paradoxically, a past that only exists in the future. The most important formulation of this anti-anamnetic position comes at the end of *The Principle of Hope*:

> Man everywhere is still living in prehistory, indeed all and everything still stands before the creation of the world, of a right world. *True genesis is not at the beginning but at the end*, and it starts to begin only when society and existence become radical, i.e. grasp their roots. But the root of history is the working, creating human being who reshapes and overhauls the given facts. Once he has grasped himself and established what is his, without expropriation and alienation, in real democracy, there arises in the world something which shines into the childhood of all and in which no one has yet been: homeland.[27]

As Bloch explains in *Subjekt-Objekt*, an idea that is transmitted simply from the past without being transformed by its own transmission becomes old as soon as it is thought.[28] This is the fate that awaits the owl of Minerva, who can only take flight when it is already dark. For Bloch, this Hegelian motif is the prime example of the problem of anamnesis.

Contingency, then, has not only a contemporary function, but also an anticipatory one. Our contingent existence and the way in which we interact with past contingencies inform the way we anticipate the future. We know that it is impossible to leap over contingent events, but we also know that we are able to shape the future on the basis of contingencies which arise at all points, though in ways not predicted by some dogmatic theory. By contrast, the dialectic of contingency contains within it an anticipatory moment that enables us both to plan for the unforeseen and to map out what we think this 'unknown known' (to use Žižek's Rumsfeldian category) might possibly hold for us.

---

27 Bloch 1996, vol. 3, p. 1376.
28 Bloch 1971, p. 474.

4 Materialist Metaphysics

Having established that the non-substantial difference between subject and predicate produces the gap into which the not-yet rushes, we must now examine what form this not-yet-ness takes. At this point, it might be objected that what we are dealing with is merely a continuation of Plekhanov's famous contention that Hegel is the point at which philosophical idealism shades over into a materialism that was simply waiting to emerge (although Plekhanov does not demonstrate quite how this happens).[29] However, rather than looking back to Plekhanov and the various other philosophers whose metaphysics remained determinedly mechanistic, Bloch attempts to liberate matter from the given and to put it in the service of the what-might-be. In his 1968 book *Atheism in Christianity*, he argues that religion [*re-ligio*] meant a tying down or tying back to a preordained message;[30] and by returning to an Aristotelian conception of *potentia* within matter, he seeks to show that a religious understanding of the universe was one that was merely constrained by the times that produced it. By the same token, *materialism* found and finds it difficult to liberate itself from its deterministic and vulgar origins. It became stuck in its own time, unable to go beyond its given parameters. It is for this reason that Bloch develops a close interest in quantum theory and the ways in which it promised liberation from the *Klotzmaterialismus* of previous scientific models. Once again, then, Bloch effects a double negation, a negation both of religion and of the materialism that views reality as some fixed quantity against which religious forces are pitted (the view of nineteenth-century positivism as well as of today's New Atheists). A frontal war with religion would therefore be counterproductive. Instead, as the title *Atheism in Christianity* suggests, atheism can only be developed from within a specific religious tradition. For Bloch, coming from a Jewish background within a family that converted to Christianity, the latter faith provides the springboard from which it is possible to understand and implement an open atheism.

Žižek similarly argues that he is a Christian atheist, not merely because he has been socialised in a post-Christian environment, but because the Hegelian concept of the social development of humanity sees Christianity as the final – and effectively secular – form of religious belief. Only through Christianity is it possible to move forward to atheism, all other religions still being tied back to a

---

29 For a discussion, see Pavlov 2016.
30 Cf. Bloch 2009.

more or less dogmatic ideological fidelity to certain traditions and ideas. Christianity, on the other hand, requires nothing but a commitment to an absent God. Indeed, it is based on the idea that God is not to be found in any metaphysical realm, but is represented as the 'son of man', rather than the 'son of God'. That, after all, is the purpose of the crucifixion. The point at which Christ asks 'why hast thou forsaken me?' is the point at which he himself becomes aware of the non-existence of God, the absent father.

On Bloch's and Žižek's view, then, religion must be sublated into atheism, and materialism into the complexity of the 'multiversal'. Metaphysical materialism thus becomes the necessary correlate to the dialectics of contingency, as it describes the space into which anticipatory consciousness, liberated from both religion and reductionist materialism, can be projected.

5 The Metaphysics of Contingency

Hegel speaks of an intermediary *objektiver Geist* located somewhere between subjectivity and the absolute. It is in the workings of objective spirit that we find the emergence of practical arrangements for civil society. Objective spirit also provides a conceptual framework for the interaction between contingency and necessity. In the *Philosophy of Right* as well as in the *Encyclopaedia*, Hegel points out that in order to break out of the immediate subject of circumstances and move towards the absolute, it is necessary to develop a narrative of transition and change. Viewed from a dialectical perspective, the narrative adopted to explain transition and change becomes itself the motivating force behind transition and change. Confronted with the reality of his age, which was one of revolution in both society and science, Hegel – no less a product of his time than any other philosopher at any other time – played no other role than to help construct this narrative. He remains important today precisely because his overarching narrative is one of transition from one historical state to another. The objective spirit that emerges, he contends, fills the gap between what is and what might be. It is this transitional role of the objective spirit that Marx turns on its head, arguing that it is the material conditions of production, not simply people's ideas, that revolutionise society. In order to be able to take conscious control of the transition, it is necessary to wrest that control from metaphysical gods and put it in the hands of humanity.

For Hegel, this change in social being is brought about by changes in self-consciousness. For Marx, it is being that determines consciousness. Somewhere between these two positions – the idealist and the materialist – there exists an indeterminate and unknowable realm in which the interplay of ideas and reality produces what I have called the 'metaphysics of contingency'.[31] Objective spirit is the 'jellied' product of contingent reality, but to the extent that we find ourselves faced with it at a *decisive moment* in time (and here we should bear in mind the paradoxical insight discussed above: namely, that the decisive nature of the moment might well be the retroactive result of our own actions subsequent to the moment), it possesses a certain openness towards the future. It is this openness that enables us to construct both a retrospective narrative and an anticipatory consciousness. Yet this *Augenblick* (and this we also saw further above) invariably remains obscure and distorted; seeing it therefore requires a kind of oblique look.[32]

The theoretical and ideological development that is at issue remains an open one in which any attempts to tie thought back to dogmatic certainties can only be negative. The key operator is once again the not-yet. However, it would be a mistake to think that Bloch uses the not-yet as some sort of anticipatory stand-in for the Lacanian Real or the Hegelian Absolute. That which is not-yet is also that which *is*. Employing a classical Hegelian reversal, we can say that the not-yet is the true confluence of subject and substance. If we take it as defining something that is present through its absence, then it becomes akin to Hegel's concept of the spirit as the self-healing wound of nature. Hegel – as Žižek argues in *Absolute Recoil* – posits that the wound itself is not inflicted on the subject by the substance, but present in the subject from the start. Indeed, the subject is nothing without the substance of its own wound. In order to be able to overcome this wound, it is necessary to see it as a central part of its own existence rather than as something external to and imposed upon it. This point is crucial to my reading of Bloch (and indeed my argument as a whole), but it is not easy to understand. Let me therefore cite Žižek at length:

> ... the Spirit is itself the wound it tries to heal, that is, the wound is self-inflicted. 'Spirit' at its most elementary is the 'wound' of nature. The subject is the immense – absolute – power of negativity, the power of introducing a gap or cut into the given-immediate substantial unity ... The paradox is thus that there is no Self that precedes the Spirit's 'self-alienation': the very process of alienation generates the 'Self' from which Spirit is alienated and to which it then returns ... Spirit's self-alienation is the same as, fully coincides with, its alienation from its Other (nature), because it constitutes itself through its 'return-to-itself' from its immer-

---

31   Cf. Thompson 2013.
32   Bloch discusses this oblique look in *Experimentum Mundi* (1977); cf. the reflections on the 'parallax view' in Žižek 2006.

> sion in natural Otherness. Spirit's return-to-itself creates the very dimension to which it returns ... Spirit heals its wound not directly, but by getting rid of the full and sane Body into which the wound was cut. It is in this precise sense that, according to Hegel, 'the wounds of the Spirit heal, and leave no scars behind'. His point is not that Spirit heals its wounds so perfectly that, in a magical gesture of retroactive sublation, even the scars disappear; the point is rather that, in the course of the dialectical process, a shift of perspective occurs which makes the wound itself appear as its opposite – the wound itself is its own healing when seen from another standpoint.[33]

The not-yet-ness in Bloch and the self-healing nature of the wound in Hegel have clear parallels in Christian theology, according to which original sin is not some external substance corrupting an otherwise pristine natural subject to which we are always attempting to return, but rather an essential part of the subject's desire and movement towards its sublation into the Absolute. The Fall is not something inflicted on us through the sinfulness of the individual subject (Eve, in the patriarchal tradition); it is an essential part of what it is to wish to rise. But rise from what and to what? What is the self-liberating dynamic that human beings have conceived for themselves?

In Bloch's reading of Hegel, we find the idea that an entity arises out of its own loss. *Etwas fehlt* [something is missing] is the phrase that Bloch borrows from Brecht's 1930 play *Mahagonny* in order to illuminate this point. The thing of the *some*thing is only constituted by the fact that it is missing. Negativity – the absence of something – is the very means by which that something is constituted. Not-yetness is the space in which this gradual constitution takes place. At the same time, appearance is the only way that essence can be discerned. Bloch and Žižek systematically shy away from Nietzsche, but this point can be best explained with the latter's famous dictum (later disavowed as a youthful dialectical mistake) that Apollo and Dionysus speak in contradictory and complementary unity through each other.

6   *Ungleichzeitigkeit* and the Post-Political World

According to Bloch, any historical moment is not merely that moment itself, as it were, but carries within it multiple layers of history (leftover elements

---

33   Žižek 2014, pp. 140–1. The citation of Hegel comes from Hegel 1997, p. 406.

from the past) and of futurity (anticipatory elements). We exist in and look to these various strands both for explanations of where we have arrived and for programmes underpinning future activities. For Bloch, the dialectic does not move along one main road, but along many different roads, byways and even what seem like cul-de-sacs. Its pattern is protean, its journey a long process in which the original impetus or agent of change becomes invisible. Because of this invisibility of past and future elements in the present, we live in perpetual darkness about what is happening historically. The mediator between subject and predicate keeps disappearing – but only to reappear in another form. To put it differently, it never entirely vanishes but merely goes underground to complete its work, like Hegel's mole and Žižek's Kraken, discussed earlier. This means that there is general surprise when a historical trend that appears to be a thing of the past suddenly reappears on the (political) agenda. The fascist, or proto-fascist, tropes in Donald Trump's political campaign and subsequent presidency are a clear – and particularly worrying – example of the way in which seemingly discredited ideas can resurface in a new historical context. Fascism, or even just extremist right-wing populism, continues to haunt us in different guises as historical conditions give rise to its rebirth – the first time as tragedy, the second time as Farage. It is, of course, never the exact same thing twice, and any new-fangled fascism does not necessarily appear wearing jackboots and carrying swastikas. Yet given the 'correct' historical circumstances – such as we are now experiencing – the reappearance of more extreme forms of fascism can by no means be excluded.

This example may also serve to illustrate what I mean by *dialectical contingency*. The contingent emergence of a phenomenon such as fascism is not simply due to a sudden complete breakdown of society, but rather carries within it trends that have long been present, if invisible. In *Heritage of Our Times*, Bloch uses this idea to argue that fascism is *both* the continuation of an old, pre-modern trend *and* a modern reflection of the kind of social tensions that arise within modern capitalist societies. The incomplete process of modernisation gives rise to a high degree of dissatisfaction and a longing for some – non-existent – pristine world in which *Heimat* represents a safe and untouched idyll. This is, precisely, one of the reasons why Bloch sought to imbue the concept of *Heimat* with a forward-looking – positive and anticipatory – function. The *Heimat* that has never yet existed and that nevertheless we are all aware of from childhood is not an imaginary retrotopia but a concrete utopia, to be brought about by the transformation from quantity into quality and by purposeful human activity towards that goal.

The modern thinkers that emerged out of the French Revolution and its secular tradition tended (and tend) to view modernity as the end of non-synchronous thinking. Science – they believed – had replaced, or at any rate was about to replace, the belief in a metaphysical realm with a rational understanding of the way the universe works, situating the human being's role within it. Yet the stubborn persistence of pre-modern forms of thinking and 'non-rational' theories should come as no surprise. Metaphysical speculation will always capture the minds of a species that, uniquely, casts its attention both backwards and forwards in order to find explanations while possessing relatively little insight into the here and now. Bloch is part and parcel of this metaphysical tradition. Yet his metaphysics is and remains a materialist one, working through the autopoietic process that turns the subject into its predicate. This materialist metaphysics is non-teleological, and the predicate to be arrived at is not one that pre-exists in some Platonic realm of forms or indeed any other form. The process is everything; its developmental logic is that of a dynamic ontology of not-yet-being. It can to some extent be shaped and guided by labouring, creating human beings, but its outcome is not predetermined and cannot be predicted.

The question is whether this autopoiesis requires some kind of historical kenosis. In order for history to restart, is it not necessary for it first to recognise its self-alienation? Is that what we are witnessing? Do Brexit, Donald Trump's presidency and the Trumpification of the Republican Party show that history has been – and still is – going through a process of self-alienation? Of course, these things too shall pass. But what will the pile of Benjaminian rubble we are left with look like?

True genesis arrives not at the beginning, but at the end. Our job in this time of crisis is to determine whether we are at the end of the beginning or the beginning of the end.

Bibliography

Bloch, Ernst 1970, *Tübinger Einleitung in die Philosophie*, Frankfurt am Main: Suhrkamp.
Bloch, Ernst 1971 [1951], *Subjekt-Objekt. Erläuterungen zu Hegel*, Frankfurt am Main: Suhrkamp.
Bloch, Ernst 1977, *Experimentum Mundi*, Frankfurt am Main: Suhrkamp.
Bloch, Ernst 1985, *Tendenz – Latenz – Utopie*, Frankfurt am Main: Suhrkamp.
Bloch, Ernst 1996 [1954–9], *The Principle of Hope*, 3 Volumes, translated by Neville Plaice, Stephen Plaice and Paul Knight, Cambridge, Mass.: MIT Press.
Bloch, Ernst 2009 [1968], *Atheism in Christianity: The Religion of the Exodus and the Kingdom*, translated by J.T. Swann, London and New York: Verso.
Destutt de Tracy, Antoine-Louis-Claude 1804 [1801], *Élemens d'idéologie. Première partie: Idéologie proprement dite*, Paris: Courcier.

Gladwell, Malcolm 2000, *The Tipping Point: How Little Things Can Make a Big Difference*: Boston, Mass.: Little, Brown and Company.

Gray, John 2011, *The Immortalization Commission: Science and the Strange Quest to Cheat Death*, London: Allen Lane.

Groys, Boris and Michael Hagemeister (eds.) 2005, *Die Neue Menschheit. Biopolitische Utopien in Russland zu Beginn des 20. Jahrhunderts*, Frankfurt am Main: Suhrkamp.

Hegel, Georg Wilhelm Friedrich 1966, 'Who Thinks Abstractly?', translated by Walter Kaufmann, in Walter Kaufmann, *Hegel: Reinterpretation, Texts, and Commentary*, London: Weidenfeld and Nicolson, 460–5.

Hegel, Georg Wilhelm Friedrich 1977, *Phenomenology of Spirit*, translated by A.V. Miller, Oxford: Oxford University Press.

Hegel, Georg Wilhelm Friedrich 1995, *Lectures on the History of Philosophy*, 3 Volumes, translated by E.S. Haldane and Frances H. Simson, Lincoln and London: University of Nebraska Press.

Hegel, Georg Wilhelm Friedrich 2015, *The Science of Logic*, translated by George di Giovanni, Cambridge: Cambridge University Press.

Jameson, Fredric 2003, 'Future City', *New Left Review*, available at: https://newleftreview.org/II/21/fredric-jameson-future-city.

Marx, Karl 1973 [1857–8; first published 1939–41], *Grundrisse*, translated by Martin Nicolaus, Harmondsworth: Penguin.

Nietzsche, Friedrich 1966 [1886], *Beyond Good and Evil: Prelude to a Philosophy of the Future*, translated by Walter Kaufmann, New York: Vintage.

Pavlov, Evgeny V. 2016, 'Comrade Hegel: Absolute Spirit Goes East', *Crisis and Critique*, 3, 1: 157–89.

Redding, Paul 2020, 'Georg Wilhelm Friedrich Hegel', *The Stanford Encyclopedia of Philosophy*, available at: https://plato.stanford.edu/archives/win2020/entries/hegel/.

Santner, Eric 2016, *The Weight of All Flesh*, Oxford New York: Oxford University Press.

Thompson, Peter, 'Religion, Utopia, and the Metaphysics of Contingency', in *The Privatization of Hope: Ernst Bloch and the Future of Utopia*, edited by Peter Thompson and Slavoj Žižek, Durham and London: Duke University Press.

Traub, Rainer and Harald Wieser (eds.) 1975, *Gespräche mit Ernst Bloch*, Frankfurt am Main: Suhrkamp.

Williams, Evan Calder 2010, *Combined and Uneven Apocalypse: Luciferian Marxism*, Winchester and Washington: Zero Books.

Wordsworth, William 1970 [1850], *The Prelude*, Oxford: Oxford University Press.

Žižek, Slavoj 2006, *The Parallax View*, Cambridge, Mass.: MIT Press.

Žižek, Slavoj 2012, *Less Than Nothing: Hegel and the Shadow of Dialectical Materialism*, London and New York: Verso.

Žižek, Slavoj 2013, 'Preface: Bloch's Ontology of Not-Yet-Being', in *The Privatization of Hope: Ernst Bloch and the Future of Utopia*, edited by Peter Thompson and Slavoj Žižek, Durham and London: Duke University Press.

Žižek, Slavoj 2014, Absolute Recoil: Towards a New Foundation of Dialectical Materialism, London and New York: Verso.

Žižek, Slavoj 2016, *Disparities*, London: Bloomsbury.

Index

Abeles, Frida   18
Abeles-Josephson, Mirjam   18
Absolute Recoil (Žižek)   296, 305–306
Adler, Alfred   216–217, 226
Adorno, Theodor W. *passim*
Agamben, Giorgio   42, 54n38, 56n41, 63n55, 65, 66
Agar, Jolyon   3
Althusius (Johannes Althaus)   158, 173n69
Althusser, Louis   153, 245
amor mundi (in Arendt)   39
anagogical exegesis   119
Anarchie des Helldunkels [anarchy of light and dark] (in Lukács)   118n108
Anders, Günther   20, 238, 291
Anderson, Perry   207
Aquinas *See* Thomas Aquinas
archetypes   215, 242
Archimedes   148
Archiv für Sozialwissenschaft und Sozialpolitik   13
Arendt, Hannah   39
Aristotle, Aristotelianism *passim*
Aufbau (journal)   25
Aufbau Verlag   24, 25, 27–28, 33
Augustine (Saint Augustine of Hippo)   46, 112
aura (in Benjamin)   127n137, 268–270, 285
Aurora Verlag   22
Averroes (Ibn Rushd)   54–62, 97, 117, 196–197
Avicebron (Solomon ibn Gabirol)   54–62, 196
Avicenna (Ibn Sina)   54–62, 97n37, 117, 157, 196–198, 295

Babeuf, François-Noël   161
Bach, Johann Sebastian   142
Bachofen, Johann Jakob   173n69
Bacon, Francis   143–144, 189
Badiou, Alain   152–153
Bahr, Erhard   28
Bahro, Rudolf   28
Balibar, Etienne   152
Ball, Hugo   13
Barth, Karl   39

Bauer, Bruno   136, 188, 286
Beckett, Samuel   39
Beethoven, Ludwig van   195n96
Behrens, Fritz   24
Being and Time (Heidegger)   23
Benhabib, Seyla   175
'Benjamin's Endgame' (Comay)   288–289
Benjamin, Walter *passim*
Benn, Gottfried   20, 217
Bergson, Henri   217
Bernstein, Eduard   159–162
Blake, William   63
Blank, Daniel   286
Bloch (*née* Feitel), Berta   11
Bloch (*née* von Stritzky), Else   10, 12, 14, 15
Bloch, Ernst *passim*
Bloch, Jan-Robert   18, 22
Bloch (*née* Piotrkowska), Karola   17–18, 21–22, 28, 32, 211
Bloch (*née* Oppenheimer), Linda   14
Bloch, Max   11
Bloch-Wörterbuch (eds. Dietschy et al.)   4
Blumenberg, Hans   5, 38–70, 176
Böhme, Jacob   43–44, 48, 121n116, 189
Boldyrev, Ivan   3, 5
Book of Sentences (Peter Lombard)   135
Börne, Ludwig   164
Bourdieu, Pierre   245
Braun, Eberhard   227, 233
Braun, Volker   28
Brecht, Bertolt   14, 22, 24, 29, 100, 306
Bruckner, Anton   142
Bruckner, Ferdinand   22
Buhr, Manfred   28, 157–158
Bush, George W.   219
Byron (George Gordon, Lord Byron)   257

Camellone, Mauro Farnesi   5
Carver, Terrell   286
Cervantes, Miguel de   113n80
Cézanne, Paul   75
Chesterton, G.K.   92
Chvostismus und Dialektik (Lukács)   86n8
Clara (Schelling)   185n22
Colletti, Lucio   6, 160

colonialism 244
Columbus, Christopher 244
Comay, Rebecca 288–289
Concept of Utopia, The (Levitas) 2
Copernicus, Nicolaus 96
Cortez (Hernán Cortés de Monroy y Pizarro Altamirano) 244
Critical Theory of Creativity, A (Howells) 3
Cruising Utopia (Muñoz) 1–2
Cunico, Gerado 5

Damus, Renate 165
Das Argument (journal) 4
Das Wort (journal) 20
David of Dinant 197
Degler, Frank 269
De l'esprit des lois (Montesquieu) 171
Deleuze, Gilles 58n45, 214
Democritus 139, 181, 188–189
De musica (Augustine) 112n80
Der Ausflug der toten Mädchen (Seghers) 22
Der Einzige und sein Eigentum (Stirner) 162
Der geschlossene Handelsstaat (Fichte) 6–7, 156
Der Rabbi von Bacherach (Heine) 19–20
Derrida, an Egyptian (Sloterdijk) 71–72
Derrida, Jacques 5, 43, 67, 71–83, 153, 274n16
Der Turm von Babel (Mayer) 23
Descartes, René 91, 182
Destruction of Reason, The (Lukács) 218
Destutt de Tracy, Antoine-Louis-Claude 291
Deutsche Zeitschrift für Philosophie (journal) 25–26, 28
Deutsch-Französische Jahrbücher 112n79, 229
Die Antiquiertheit des Menschen (Anders) 291
Die Legitimität der Neuzeit (Blumenberg) 5, 38–39, 56n41
Dietschy, Beat 4, 222–23, 243n148, 244
Dieu est mort (Garaudy) 91n26
Die Vorläufer des neueren Sozialismus (Kautsky) 16
di Giovanni, George 296n13
Dimitrov, Georgi 231
Disparities (Žižek) 296
Dostoevsky, Fyodor 49n29, 175n81
Duns Scotus, John 135

Dürer, Albrecht 46
Dussel, Enrique 229
Dutschke-Klotz, Gretchen 31, 33
Dutschke, Rudi 10, 30–31, 33

Eagleton, Terry 122–123, 124, 125, 152, 222, 237–238n112
East German workers' revolt 26
Ebert, Friedrich 16
Eckhart (Meister Eckhart) 48
ecology 4, 7, 181, 182, 198–201, 236–237 and *passim*
Edschmid, Kasimir 89n21, 90n22
Edwards, Caroline 3, 7
Egyptian art 5, 71–83
Eingedenken (in Benjamin) 270
Eisler, Hanns 14, 24
Emilia Galotti (Lessing) 56–57
Engels, Friedrich *passim*
Enneads (Plotinus) 62
Epicurus 173n69, 181, 188–189
Erbeproblem 89n20, 222
Ernst Bloch (Geoghegan) 1
Ernst Bloch (Zipes) 1
Ernst Bloch and His Contemporaries (Boldyrev) 3
Ernst Bloch Archive 32
Ernst Bloch Assoziation 32
Ernst Bloch Gesellschaft 32
Ernst Blochs Revision des Marxismus (ed. Horn) 27
Ernst Bloch's Speculative Materialism (Moir) 3
Ernst-Bloch-Tage 32
Ernst Bloch zu ehren (ed. Unseld) 31
Ernst Bloch zum 70. Geburtstag (ed. Gropp) 26
Ethics (Spinoza) 227
Expressionism 12, 13, 20–21, 73, 75–76, 88–90, 122, 209
Expressionism-Realism debate 20–21, 88–90, 122

Fahrenbach, Helmut 235
'Faith' (Miłosz) 38n1
Faust (Goethe) 94n32, 210, 235
Fetscher, Iring 163–164
Feuchtwanger, Lion 22
Feuerbach, Ludwig *passim*

INDEX

Fichte, Johann Gottlieb   6–7, 102*n*53, 103–104, 144, 156, 162–163, 166, 167, 170–173, 184, 186
Fidelio (Beethoven)   195*n*96
Fons Vitae (Avicebron)   196–197
Foucault, Michel   153, 264–265
Fra Angelico (Guido di Pietro)   217
Frankfurter Zeitung   17, 18, 270*n*8
Frankfurt School   10, 21, 214 *See also* Western Marxism 10
Frederick III 15
Freudo-Marxism   214
Freud, Sigmund   22, 71–72, 121–122*n*120, 214–217, 226, 227, 254–255, 257*n*20, 259
fringes of consciousness (in James)   225

Garaudy, Roger   91*n*26
Gastl, Julie   28
Geoghegan, Vincent   1
Geschichte des antiken Kommunismus und Sozialismus (Pöhlmann)   160*n*19
Gettysburg Address   289
Geworfenheit [thrownness] (in Heidegger)   40, 227
Giotto (Giotto di Bondone)   142
Gneisenau, August Neidhardt von   95*n*32
Gnosis und spätantiker Geist (Jonas)   39
Gnosticism   5, 38–70
Goethe, Johann Wolfgang   7, 88, 94*n*32, 206, 210, 225, 235, 243
Goldman, Loren   3–4, 57*n*43, 194*n*83
good sense [*buon senso*] (in Gramsci)   228–229
Görres, Joseph   257
Gospel of Truth, The (Valentinus)   41
Gould, Glenn   56*n*41, 63*n*55
Graf, Oskar Maria   22
Gramsci, Antonio   7–8, 222–251
Gropp, Rugard Otto   26–27
Grotius, Hugo (Hugo de Groot)   158, 173*n*69
Groys, Boris   152
Grünewald, Matthias   142, 200
Guattari, Félix   214
Günther, Hans   19
Gutzkow, Karl   164

Habermas, Jürgen   29, 32, 66, 166*n*46, 175, 181, 199, 233, 241, 291
Hager, Kurt   27

Haller, Karl Ludwig von   111
Hall, Stuart   245
Hamlet (Shakespeare)   121–122*n*120, 293
Harich, Wolfgang   26–28
Harnack, Adolf von   39
Hartmann, Eduard von   4
Havemann, Robert   28
Haym, Rudolf   163
Hegel, Georg Wilhelm Friedrich, Hegelianism *passim*
Heidegger, Martin   23, 39, 40–45, 66, 118, 124, 127, 128, 129, 210, 217, 227
Heine, Heinrich   19–20, 164
Herzfelde, Wieland   22
Hesse, Hermann   13, 20
Heß, Moses   188
heterotopia (in Foucault)   265*n*42
History and Class Consciousness (Lukács)   86, 208, 229, 236–237
History of Western Philosophy (Russell)   86–87
Hitler, Adolf   17, 21
Hobbes, Thomas   139, 158, 163, 166, 169, 173*n*69, 174, 182–183
Hoffmeister, Johannes   268*n*2
Hölderlin, Friedrich   103, 157
Holz, Hans Heinz   30, 64*n*57, 65, 222, 260
Holzkamp, Klaus   226
Holzkamp-Osterkamp, Ute   226
Horkheimer, Marx   20, 21
Horster, Detlef   7
hotel   272–274
Howells, Richard   3, 7
Hudson, Wayne   1, 10, 209*n*7, 254
Human Condition, The (Arendt)   39*n*5
Humiliated and Insulted (Dostoevsky)   175*n*81
Hungarian uprising   24, 27, 207, 222
Hyppolite, Jean   6

'I Looked at Zero through Dark Glass' (Weisskopf)   200–201*n*117
Inquiry into the Principles of Political Economy, An (Steuart)   101*n*52
Institutiones iuris naturae et gentium (Wolff)   163*n*31
Internatsionalnaya Literatura   19
Isenheim Altarpiece (Grünewald)   200

Jameson, Fredric   7
James, William   145, 181, 225
Janka, Walter   27
Jay, Martin   7, 11
Jean Paul (Johann Paul Friedrich Richter)   258
Jens, Walter   29
Johnson, Uwe   24n66
Jonas, Hans   39, 40–41, 222
Joyce, James   88
Jung, Carl Gustav   215–218, 226, 257n20

Kant, Immanuel *passim*
Karl Marx (Korsch)   208–209
Kautsky, Karl   16, 231
Kehre [turn] (in Heidegger)   41–42
Khrushchev, Nikita   26, 241n137
Kierkegaard, Søren   85, 152, 209, 275
Klages, Ludwig   217–218
Klemperer, Otto   15
Kojève, Alexandre   6
Kołakowski, Leszek   26
Korngiebel, Wilfried   158
Korsch, Karl   207–209
Korstvedt, Benjamin   2, 73n7
Krauss, Werner   24
Kufeld, Klaus   269
Kuhlmann, Georg   147
Külpe, Oswald   2
Kurella, Alfred   20, 88
Kurras, Karl-Heinz   30

Labriola, Antonio   7, 223
Lacan, Jacques   153, 296, 298, 305
Lācis, Asja   270n8
Lafargue, Paul   98n41
Lamprecht, Karl   4
Lask, Emil   4, 159
Latour, Bruno   182n7
Laube, Heinrich   164
Lawrence, D.H.   217–218
Lederer, Emil   13
Leibniz, Gottfried Wilhelm   45, 271
Lenin, Vladimir I.   13, 21, 102n48, 146n71, 148, 151, 296
Lessing, Gotthold Ephraim   56–57
Lévinas, Emmanuel   82n45
Levitas, Ruth   2
liberation theology   2

L'Inexistence divine (Meillassoux)   252n2
Listening for Utopia (Korstvedt)   2
Locke, John   166, 189
logical positivism   86
Lowe, Adolf   22
Lukács, Georg   1, 3, 6, 12, 13, 14, 19, 20, 24, 27, 76n24, 78n34, 84, 86, 88–90, 97, 118n108, 122, 124, 151, 207–208, 210, 218, 224, 229, 233, 236, 273
Luporini, Cesare   162
Luria, Isaac   39, 51–52
Luther, Martin   15–16
Luxemburg, Rosa   232
Lyotard, Jean-François   214

Magee, Glenn Alexander   87
Malevich, Kazimir   63n55
Mann, Klaus   20
Mann, Thomas   71
Man Who Was Thursday, The (Chesterton)   92
March Revolution (of 1848)   15, 94n31
Marcion, Marcionism   38–70
Marcuse, Herbert   6, 31, 207, 210
Marcuse, Ludwig   29
Maréchal, Sylvain   161
Margins of Philosophy (Derrida)   77n27, 274n16
Marxism and Philosophy (Korsch)   208
Marxist Philosophy of Ernst Bloch, The (Hudson)   1
Marx, Karl *passim*
Mass Psychology of Fascism, The (Reich)   214
Materialism and Empirio-Criticism (Lenin)   21
Maximilian II   11
Mayer, Hans   23, 24
Meillassoux, Quentin   252
Melsheimer, Ernst   27
Melville, Herman   65n61
Mende, Georg   25
Meno (Plato)   149n86
Menzel, Wolfgang   164
Merleau-Ponty, Maurice   207n3
Metaphysics (Aristotle)   54
Metzger, Arnold   22
Metz, Johann Baptist   30

INDEX 315

Mill, John Stuart   182
Miłosz, Czesław   38n1
Moir, Cat *passim*
mole of history (in Hegel)   293, 307
Moltmann, Jürgen   2, 30
Monet, Claude   10–11
Montesquieu (Charles Louis de Secondat, Baron de la Brède et de Montesquieu)   171
Morelly, Étienne-Gabriel   161
Morgenröte (anthology)   22
Morgner, Irmtraud   28
Moses and Monotheism (Freud)   71–72
Müller, Heiner   28
Muñoz, José Esteban   1
Münster, Arno   4, 9
Münzer, Thomas   15–16, 97n37, 153, 231, 295
music   2, 63n55, 72, 81, 110, 119, 126, 195n96, 213, 229
Mutmaßungen über Jakob (Johnson)   24n66

Nacht der Welt [night of the world]   118, 172
Nancy, Jean-Luc   277
National Socialism   9–10, 14, 16–21, 89, 90, 119, 144, 146, 214, 217, 228, 230–231, 243n148, 293, 307
natural law   6–7, 155–179 and *passim*
Negri, Antonio   243
neo-Kantianism   5, 11–12, 159, 225
neo-Platonism   44–45, 57, 62n53, 66, 97, 185, 196–197
Neues Deutschland   27, 122n124, 222
New Atheism   303
Ní Dhúill, Catríona   1–2
Nietzsche, Friedrich   4, 12, 56n41, 144, 151, 182, 216–217, 301, 306
Nineteen Eighty-Four (Orwell)   87n18
Noske, Gustav   16
Novalis (Friedrich von Hardenberg)   185n26
November Revolution (of 1918)   16, 164, 208

Obama, Barack   218
Occupy Wall Street   218n30, 246
Ockham (William of Ockham)   56n41
Of Grammatology (Derrida)   82n45
Ohnesorg, Benno   30
Open Society and Its Enemies, The (Popper)   86
original sin   306

Orwell, George   87n18
Owen, Robert   140

parallax view (in Žižek)   305n32
Parmenides (Plato)   42–43n13
patriarchy   242, 243
Paul (Saint Paul)   51, 84n2, 129, 196
Peasant War   15–16, 231
Pelletier, Lucien   4–5
Peter Lombard (Petrus Lombardus)   135
Petrović, Gajo   31
Pinkard, Terry   111n76
Pit and the Pendulum, The (Poe)   77n27
'Pit and the Pyramid, The' (Derrida)   77
Pizarro, Francisco   244
Plato, Platonism   32, 41, 42–43n13, 45, 55, 144n51, 148–149, 224n12, 275n20, 301–302, 308
Plekhanov, Georgi   303
Plotinus   62
Poe, Edgar Allan   77n27
Pöhlmann, Robert von   160n19
Popper, Karl R.   86, 111
positivism   12, 92, 121, 283, 303
post-secularism   3
Post-Secularism, Realism, and Utopia (Agar)   3
pragmatism (as philosophical movement)   145–146
Pragmatism (James)   145
Praxis (journal)   31
Privatization of Hope, The (eds. Thompson and Žižek)   4, 296
Projekt Ideologietheorie   245
Proudhon, Pierre-Joseph   260
Pushkin, Alexander S.   257

Quodlibeta (Ockham)   56n41

Reagan, Ronald   219
Reed, T.J.   87, 106
Reich, Wilhelm   214
rescuing critique (in Benjamin)   222
Restauration der Staatswissenschaft (Haller)   111
Revolutionäre Kämpfe und revolutionäre Kämpfer 1919 (Zetkin)   16
revolutionary Realpolitik (in Luxemburg)   232

Revue internationale de philosophie (journal) 4
Rickert, Heinrich 11
Riedel, Manfred 3, 23
Rise and Fall of the City of Mahagonny (Brecht) 100, 306
Robespierre, Maximilien de 103, 262
Roces, Wenceslao 25
Rochhausen, Rudolf 198
Rorty, Richard 152
Rosenzweig, Franz 39
Rousseau, Jean-Jacques 173n69, 174
Ruge, Arnold 112
Russell, Bertrand 86–87, 111
Russian Revolution 10, 13, 207, 209

Sanders, Bernie 218, 246
Santner, Eric 291
Savigny, Friedrich Carl von 173n69
Scharnhorst, Gerhard von 95n32
Scheidemann, Philipp 16
Schelauske, Hans Dieter 158
Schelling, Friedrich Wilhelm Joseph *passim*
Schiller, Hans-Ernst 222
Schmidt, Alfred 29, 181, 189, 199
Schmied-Kowarzik, Wolfdietrich 236
Scholem, Gershom 39, 48–54, 66–67
Schopenhauer, Arthur 98, 144, 151, 216–217, 273
Schumacher, Joachim 22
SED (Socialist Unity Party) 26, 297 and *passim*
Seghers, Anna 22
Sex in Imagined Spaces (Ní Dhúill) 1–2
Sexual Revolution, The (Reich) 214
Shelley, Percy Bysshe 257
show trials (in Moscow) 21, 26
Siebers, Johan 4, 48, 60n50, 235
Simmel, Georg 12, 13
Sloterdijk, Peter 71–73, 80, 82, 83
Socrates 109, 149
Soul and Form (Lukács) 207
Sozialistisches Büro 32
Speusippos 45
Spiegelberg, Herbert 174
Spinoza, Baruch de 54, 59, 60–61, 117, 121n116, 227
Stalin, Joseph 21, 24, 25, 157
Stalinism 1, 24, 26, 29, 31, 32n88, 121, 207, 208, 240–241, 292, 297, 300

Star of Redemption, The (Rosenzweig) 39
Steigerwald, Robert 86n7
Stern, Günther *See* Anders, Günther
Steuart, James 102n52
Stirner, Max (Johann Caspar Schmidt) 136, 147, 162, 188, 286–287
Strauß, David Friedrich 188
Strauss, Leo 39
Switzerland 12–13, 18, 271 and *passim*

Taubes, Jacob 40n8
Teller, Jürgen 32
Thälmann, Ernst 16
Theologico-Political Fragment (Benjamin) 40n8
Theory of the Novel, The (Lukács) 76n24, 207
Theses on the Concept of History (Benjamin) 18
Thirty Years' War 275
Thomas Aquinas 56, 135, 173n69
Thomasius, Christian 97n37, 157n6
Thompson, Peter 1, 2, 3–4, 57n43, 101n49, 194n83, 262, 263, 264, 265
Thürmer-Rohr, Christine 241
Three Sources and Three Components of Marxism (Lenin) 146n71
Timaeus (Plato) 55
Tradition und Utopie (Riedel) 3
transhumanism 291
Trotsky, Leon 291
'true socialism' 120
Trump, Donald 219, 307–08

'Über den dichterischen Expressionismus' (Edschmid) 89n21, 90n22
Ulbricht, Walter 26–27, 122n124, 222
Unseld, Siegfried 24, 31
Uses of Bodies, The (Agamben) 42
Utopia and the Contemporary British Novel (Edwards) 3
utopian socialism 23, 161, 252–253, 259

Valentinus, Valentinianism 41, 47, 49n28, 58
van Gogh, Vincent 75
via affirmativa (in Jonas) 39
Viertel, Berthold 22

Waldinger, Ernst 22
Waldmann, Elisabeth 18

INDEX   317

'Wanderer's Storm-Song' (Goethe)   88
Warnke, Camilla   25
'Was wir wollen und was wir nicht wollen' (Ulbricht)   27, 122*n*124, 222
Weber, Max   12
Weil, Simone   40*n*8
Weiskopf, F.C.   22
Weisskopf, Victor   200–201*n*117
Weltbühne (magazine)   17
Western Marxism,   7, 21, 84, 206–207 *See also* Frankfurt School
West-östlicher Divan (Goethe)   242–243
What Is Metaphysics? (Heidegger)   42
What Is to Be Done? (Lenin)   101*n*48
White on White (Malevich)   63*n*55
Wienbarg, Ludolf   164
William (of) Ockham, *See* Ockham
Wilson, Woodrow   13

Winstanley, Gerrard   161
'Winter Journey in the Harz' (Goethe)   88
Wolf, Christa   28
Wolff, Christian   163
workers' council republic (in Bavaria)   17

Young Germany   164
Young Hegelians *passim*
Young Hegel, The (Lukács)   97

Zeilinger, Doris   4
Zetkin, Clara   16
Ziegler, Bernhard *See* Kurella, Alfred
Zimmermann, Rainer E.   4
Zipes, Jack   1
Žižek, Slavoj   4, 9, 118*n*108, 293, 296–307
Zudeick, Peter   9

www.ingramcontent.com/pod-product-compliance
Lightning Source LLC
Chambersburg PA
CBHW070610030426
42337CB00020B/3745